THE ANGLO-DUTCH F

# POLITICS AND CULTURE IN NORTH-WEST EUROPE 1650–1720

Series Editors

Dr Tony Claydon, University of Wales, Bangor, UK
Dr Hugh Dunthorne, University of Wales Swansea, UK
Dr Charles-Edouard Levillain, Université de Lille 2, France
Dr Esther Mijers, University of Reading, UK
Dr David Onnekink, Universiteit Utrecht, The Netherlands

Focusing on the years between the end of the Thirty Years' War and the end of the War of Spanish Succession, this new monograph series seeks to broaden scholarly knowledge of this crucial period that witnessed the solidification of Europe into centralised nation states and created a recognisably modern political map. Bridging the gap between the early modern period of the Reformation and the eighteenth century of colonial expansion and industrial revolution these years provide a fascinating era of study in which nationalism, political dogma, economic advantage, scientific development, cultural interests and strategic concerns began to overtake religion as the driving force of European relations and national foreign policies.

The period under investigation, c.1650–1720 corresponds to the decline of Spanish power and the rise of French hegemony that was only to be finally broken following the defeat of Napoleon in 1815. This shifting political powerbase presented opportunities and dangers for many countries, resulting in numerous alliances between formerly hostile nations attempting to consolidate or increase their international influence, or restrain that of a rival. Three of the most influential nations at this time, France, Great Britain and The Netherlands, were all at some stage during this period either at war or in alliance with one another.

Despite this being a formative period in the formation of the European landscape, there has been remarkably little joined-up research that studies events from an international, rather than national perspective. By providing a forum that encourages scholars to engage with the subject of politics, diplomacy, war and international relations on a broad European basis, it is hoped that a greater understanding of this pivotal era will be forthcoming.

The Anglo-Dutch Favourite

The Career of Hans Willem Bentinck, 1st Earl of Portland
(1649–1709)

DAVID ONNEKINK
Universiteit Utrecht, The Netherlands

LONDON AND NEW YORK

First published 2007 by Ashgate Publishing

2 Park Square, Milton Park, Abingdon, Oxon OX14 4RN
711 Third Avenue, New York, NY 10017, USA

Routledge is an imprint of the Taylor & Francis Group, an informa business

First issued in paperback 2016

Copyright © David Onnekink 2007

David Onnekink has asserted his moral right under the Copyright, Designs and Patents Act, 1988, to be identified as the author of this work.

All rights reserved. No part of this book may be reprinted or reproduced or utilised in any form or by any electronic, mechanical, or other means, now known or hereafter invented, including photocopying and recording, or in any information storage or retrieval system, without permission in writing from the publishers.

Notice:
Product or corporate names may be trademarks or registered trademarks, and are used only for identification and explanation without intent to infringe.

British Library Cataloguing in Publication Data
Onnekink, David
　The Anglo-Dutch favourite : the career of Hans Willem Bentinck, 1st Earl of Portland (1649–1709)
　1. Portland, William Bentinck, Earl of, 1649–1709 2. Statesmen – Great Britain – Biography 3. Statesmen – Netherlands – Biography 4. Great Britain – History – William and Mary, 1689–1702 5. Great Britain – Politics and government – 1689–1702
　6. Netherlands – History – 1648–1714 7. Netherlands – Politics and government – 1648–1714
　I. Title
　941'.068'092

Library of Congress Cataloging-in-Publication Data
Onnekink, David.
　The Anglo-Dutch favourite : the career of Hans Willem Bentinck, 1st Earl of Portland (1649–1709) / by David Onnekink.
　　　p. cm.
　Includes bibliographical references and index.
　ISBN 978-0-7546-5545-9 (alk. paper)
　1. Portland, William Bentinck, Earl of, 1649–1709. 2. William III, King of England, 1650–1702. 3. Great Britain – Court and courtiers – Biography. 4. Great Britain – History – William and Mary, 1689–1702. 5. Great Britain – Foreign relations – 1689–1702. I. Title.

　DA462.P7O66 2006
　941.06'8092—dc22

　　　　　　　　　　　　　　　　　　　　　　　　　　　　　　2006005529

ISBN-13: 978-0-7546-5545-9 (hbk)
ISBN-13: 978-1-138-25931-7 (pbk)

This book is dedicated to my parents

Contents

List of Illustrations — ix
Acknowledgments — xi
List of Abbreviations — xiii
Notes on Style and Dates — xv

Introduction — 1

1 The Making of a Favourite (1649–85) — 7

2 For Religion and Liberty? The Crises of 1688 — 37

3 The Consolidation of the Williamite Settlement (1689–91) — 63

4 'Lord Portland takes all': The Re-emergence of the Favourite — 85

5 'The Spirit of Contention': Politics and Parties — 123

6 'The Great Affair': War on the Continent — 147

7 Ganymede: The Image of the Favourite — 175

8 *Arcana Imperii*: War and Peace (1697–1700) — 197

9 The Vestiges of Power (1697–1709) — 229

Conclusion — 261

Bibliography — 267
Index — 289

List of Illustrations

1 William III and Hans Willem Bentinck. 100 x 140 cm. Painting. By permission of Iconografisch Bureau/RKD, The Hague.
2 Anne Villiers. Oil on canvas. By permission of Iconografisch Bureau/RKD, The Hague.
3 Jane Martha Temple. Oil on canvas. By Simon Dubois. 36 x 31 cm, Middachten, De Steeg. By permission of Iconografisch Bureau/RKD, The Hague.
4 Hans Willem Bentinck. Oil on canvas. By Simon Dubois. 36 x 31 cm, Middachten, De Steeg. By permission of Iconografisch Bureau/RKD, The Hague.
5 Plan of the Dutch invasion fleet, 1688. By Hans Willem Bentinck. By permission of Manuscripts and Special Collections, The University of Nottingham (Ref. Pw A 2197/2).
6 'Hollands hollende koe', 1690. By permission of Atlas van Stolk (Ref. 2827).

Acknowledgments

This book is based upon my MA thesis (University of York) and PhD thesis, started at University College London in 1999 and completed at Utrecht University in 2003. During the course of the years I have worked on this subject, I have inevitably accumulated many debts to colleagues, supervisors and friends, who through their criticism, ideas, and suggestions have all helped me get a clearer idea of my work (needless to say any shortcomings are entirely my own). I would like to thank Johan Aalbers, Sonia Anderson, John Childs, John O'Connor, Hugh Dunthorne, Ophelia Field, Conrad Gietman, Beatrice de Graaf, Andrew Hanham, John Hattendorf, Karen Hearn, Siegfried Jansen, Kevin Jones, Sue Kinder, Caroline Knight, Harriet Knight, Karl de Leeuw, Nigel Little, Esther Mijers, Olaf van Nimwegen, Gijs Rommelse, John Rule, Henry Snyder, John Stapleton, Guus Veenendaal, Freya Wolf, my colleagues at Utrecht University and the members of the Low Countries Seminar at the Institute of Historical Research. I would like to thank Loic Bienassis, Jorge Giovannetti, Stephane Jettot, Sonja Kmec, Julia Kuehn and Alexandra Veyrie for advice on translations, Kate Delaney for proofreading and editing the manuscript, Tom Gray of Ashgate Publishing, my examiners Simon Groenveld, John Miller, Wijnand Mijnhardt, Henk van Nierop and Maarten Prak, and my supervisors Dwyred Jones and Ronald Clayton (York), Jonathan Israel, Julian Hoppit and Nicholas Tyacke (UCL) and Duco Hellema (Utrecht). I would particularly like to thank my supervisors in Utrecht, Guido de Bruin and Jeroen Duindam, as well as Charles-Edouard Levillain and James R. Jones, for showing an enduring interest in the project and commenting on drafts in various stages, and staffs of the following institutions for their valuable assistance: the British Library, the National Archive, University of Nottingham (in particular Lynda Crawford), Surrey County Record Office, Lambeth Palace Library, the House of Lords archives, Buckinghamshire County Records, Bodleian Library Oxford, National Archives of Scotland, National Library of Scotland, Nationaal Archief The Hague, Gemeentearchief Amsterdam, Rijksarchief Utrecht, Iconografisch Bureau, Utrecht University Library, Bibliothèque National, the Huntington Library and the Andrew W. Clark Memorial Library. My research could not have been undertaken without generous scholarships from the British Council in Amsterdam and Utrecht University, and financial assistance for research trips from NWO (Netherlands Organisation for Scientific Research). Lastly, I would like to thank my friends and family, and especially my parents for their support.

David Onnekink
Utrecht

List of Abbreviations

AAE, CPA: Archives du Ministère des Affaires Etrangères (Paris), Cahiers Politiques Angleterre.
AAE, CPH: Archives du Ministère des Affaires Etrangères (Paris), Cahiers Politiques Hollande.
Bath Mss: *Manuscripts of the Marquis of Bath etc.* (3 vols, Hereford, 1908).
Buccleugh Mss: *Manuscripts of the Duke of Buccleugh and Queensberry* (2 vols, London, 1903).
BL, Add Mss: British Library (London), Additional Manuscripts.
BL, Eg Mss: British Library (London), Egerton Manuscripts.
CSPD: *Calendar of State Papers, Domestic Series, in the Reign of William and Mary*, ed. W.J. Hardy and E. Bateson (11 vols, London, 1969).
CTB: *Calendar of Treasury Books 1689–1702*, ed. William A. Shaw (7 vols, London, 1931–34).
Downshire Mss: *Manuscripts of the Marquess of Downshire preserved at Easthampstead Park Berkshire, Papers of Sir William Trumbull* (2 vols, London, 1924).
Finch Mss: *Manuscripts of the late Allan George Finch, Esq., Of Burley-on-the-Hill Rutland* (5 vols, London, 1913–2004).
GA: Gemeentearchief Amsterdam.
HMC: Historical Manuscripts Commission.
Huygens, *Journaal*, I-i, I-ii: *Journaal van Constantijn Huygens, den Zoon, van 21 Oct. 1688 tot 2 Sept.1696* (2 vols, Utrecht, 1876).
Huygens, *Journaal*, II: *Journaal van Constantijn Huygens, den Zoon, gedurende de Veldtochten der Jaren 1673, 1675, 1676, 1677 en 1678* (Utrecht, 1881).
Huygens, *Journaal*, III: *Journalen van Constantijn Huygens, den Zoon* (Utrecht, 1888).
Japikse, *Correspondentie*: *Correspondentie van Willem III en van Hans Willem Bentinck, Eersten Graaf van Portland*, ed. N. Japikse (5 vols, Rijksgeschiedkundige Publicatiën 'Kleine Reeks', XXIII, XXIV, XXVI, XXVII, XXVIII, The Hague, 1927–37).
NA: Nationaal Archief, The Hague.
NAS: National Archives of Scotland, Edinburgh.
NLS: National Library of Scotland, Edinburgh.
NUL, PwA: Nottingham University Library, Portland of Welbeck Archive.
Portland Mss: *Manuscripts of His Grace the Duke of Portland Preserved at Welbeck Abbey* (10 vols, London, 1891–1931).
TNA: PRO, SP: The National Archives (London) State Papers.
RU, HA: Rijksarchief Utrecht (Utrecht), Huisarchief Amerongen.
SHC: Surrey History Centre (Woking).
Somers, *Collection*: *A Collection of Scarce and Valuable Tracts etc.*, ed. J. Somers (16 vols. in 4 parts, London, 1748–52).

Notes on Style and Dates

Throughout the text New Style dates have been adopted, with regard to both British and continental events. Dates of letters have been printed as they appear in the letter; OS or NS has been printed when there is cause for confusion. Where possible, the place where letters by Portland were written is indicated between brackets.

Quotations from manuscripts follow the original spelling as closely as possible and have not been modernised. Portland almost never wrote in English. His correspondence with non-Dutchmen or Dutch nobles was in French and has been translated, as has been his correspondence in Dutch, which he normally maintained with non-noble Dutch officials. All quotations in foreign languages have been translations (by the author when indicated in the footnote, with help from those mentioned in the acknowledgements).

Names of foreigners have been spelled in the original language, unless the person is well known, hence William III but Willem van Schuylenburg, Fürstenberg rather than Furstenberg. Titles are introduced when chronologically appropriate, hence Hans Willem is used as a name during his youth, followed by Bentinck in adulthood and Portland as from the spring of 1689 when the title was bestowed upon him. 'Anglo-Dutch' refers to British (rather than English) and Dutch throughout this book for stylistic reasons only. The 'Anglo-Dutch favourite', however, refers both to Portland's position as favourite on the British Isles and the United Provinces as well as his double English and Dutch nationalities.

Explanatory remarks between square brackets in quotations are the author's.

We live in an age where the spirit of contention reigns, but we have to live in this age.

Hans Willem Bentinck, 1st Earl of Portland, to the Duke of Shrewsbury,
3/13 January 1698, Kensington Palace

Introduction

The late seventeenth century has not attracted much interest from either Dutch historians, for whom the 'Golden Age' came to an end around the middle of the century, or British historians, who have tended to focus primarily on the Civil War.[1] The 1690s in particular have rather suffered from historiographical neglect.[2] The history of Dutch politics after 1688 remains as yet unwritten. Arguably, however, the last decade of the century was pivotal in the political history of both countries. England's rise to greatness resulted primarily from the developments following the Glorious Revolution, whereas the wars against France marked the demise of the Dutch Republic. The unique character of this decade partly stems from the union between the two countries during the reign of the King-Stadholder, although Anglo-Dutch political relations during this period have been almost completely ignored.[3] The decade signified a unique period in Anglo-Dutch history, because a 'composite state' emerged comprising Britain and the United Provinces. The King-Stadholder

---

1   Although currently there seems to be an historiographical reappraisal by British historians of the period of the Restoration and by Dutch historians of the early eighteenth century.

2   In fact, Craig Rose's 1999 monograph on British politics in the 1690s marked the first synthesis on this period since the studies of Henry Horwitz on the English parliament and Patrick Riley on Scotland. C. Rose, *England in the 1690s: Revolution, Religion and War* (Oxford, 1999); H. Horwitz, *Parliament, Policy and Politics in the Reign of William III* (Manchester 1977); P.W.J. Riley, *King William and the Scottish Politicians* (Edinburgh, 1979).

3   But see G. van Alphen, *De Stemming van de Engelschen tegen de Hollanders in Engeland tijdens de Regeering van den Koning-Stadhouder Willem III 1688–1702* (Assen, 1938) and G.N. Clark, *The Dutch Alliance and the War against French Trade 1688–1697* (New York, 1923). The tercentenary commemoration of the Glorious Revolution witnessed an outburst of bilateral research, see for instance K.H.D. Haley, 'The Dutch Invasion and the Alliance of 1689' in: L.G. Schwoerer (ed.), *The Revolution of 1688 – Changing Perspectives* (Cambridge, 1992), J.I. Israel, 'The Dutch Role in the Glorious Revolution' in: J.I. Israel (ed.), *The Anglo-Dutch Moment. Essays on the Glorious Revolution and its World Impact* (Cambridge, 1991) and S. Groenveld, '"J'equippe une Flotte très Considerable": the Dutch Side of the Glorious Revolution' in: R. Beddard (ed.), *The Revolutions of 1688* (Oxford, 1988). Few historians, however, have considered Anglo-Dutch relations in the aftermath of the 1688/1689 events. Moreover, after a brief upsurge of historiographical interest in William's reign in 1988, the past decade has remained relatively barren in this respect, but see A.M. Claydon, *William III and the Godly Revolution* (Cambridge, 1996) and two new biographies of William: W. Troost, *William III, the Stadholder-King: A Political Biography* (Aldershot, 2005), and A.M. Claydon, *William III* (London, 2002). See also E. Mijers and D. Onnekink (eds), *Redefining William III: The Impact of the King-Stadholder in International Context* (Aldershot, 2007).

headed a 'personal union', of which the separate parts co-operated on various levels.[4] An Anglo-Dutch army operated in the Low Countries under William's command, and a joint fleet protected the shores and merchant ships of the Allies. British and Dutch diplomats worked together, and counter-espionage networks exchanged intelligence. However, despite a certain degree of integration within the personal union, the three kingdoms and the republic also developed independently, each experiencing distinct domestic political and economic changes. To rule the independent parts of these realms and at the same time to co-ordinate their war efforts was a complex task.

This personal union was conjoined only at the highest level by the King-Stadholder, who was well served by a small circle of confidants.[5] Most literature refers to them as 'Dutch favourites',[6] but they constituted an international rather than a specifically Dutch entourage. This circle of foreign confidants assisting William III has been one of the blind spots in the historiography of the 1690s. Consequently, little is known about the influence of the so-called 'Dutch counsels' and of foreign advisers such as Everard van Weede van Dijkveld, the Duke of Schomberg and the Earls of Galway, Albemarle and Portland.[7]

In 1924 Marion Grew wrote a biography of the Hans Willem Bentinck, 1st Earl of Portland (1649–1709), undoubtedly the most prominent of these, but recently Mark Kishlansky, in his synthesis on Stuart politics, acknowledged the need for a modern study of his career.[8] Both vilified and praised during his long career, the Earl played a prominent role in the political history of both the British Isles and the United Provinces. As the closest confidant of William III, his career was inextricably connected to that of the man who helped shape the political history of Western Europe during the last quarter of the seventeenth century, dominated by the foreign policy of Louis XIV. As a result of the Anglo-French struggle, the reign of William III witnessed profound domestic political changes in England as well as prolonged warfare.

It is within this configuration that Portland played an important role. It has not been my intention to write his biography as such, but rather a case study in Williamite policy, which will investigate the role of the favourite within the Anglo-Dutch union. Past historiography has often regarded Portland as no more than an

---

4   To what extent Britain and the United Provinces did in fact form a personal union is open to debate, as the Stadholder was formally a servant to the sovereign provincial assemblies. Given William's *de facto* influence in the United Provinces, such a view has been accepted by several historians. E.g. S.B. Baxter, *William III* (London, 1966).

5   Cf. Baxter, *William III*, 280; N. Japikse, *Prins Willem III, de Stadhouder-Koning* (2 vols, Amsterdam, 1933), II. 292.

6   E.g. M. Kishlansky, *A Monarchy Transformed. Britain 1603–1714* (London, 1996), 291; T. Harris, *Politics under the late Stuarts. Party Conflict in a Divided Society 1660–1715* (New York, 1993), 165.

7   But see Van Alphen, *Stemming van de Engelschen* and D. Onnekink, '"Dutch Councils": the Foreign Entourage of William III', *Dutch Crossing*, 29 (2005), 5–20.

8   M.E. Grew, *William Bentinck and William III (Prince of Orange). The Life of Bentinck, Earl of Portland, from the Welbeck Correspondence* (London, 1924); S.B. Baxter, 'Recent Writings on William III', *Journal of Modern History*, 38 (1966), 256–67, 260; Kishlansky, *A Monarchy Transformed*, 359.

executive servant of William III. Although analysing their relationship has proved essential for understanding his position, an attempt has been made to study his career on its own merits. The central concern of this book will be to establish the nature and significance of Portland's role and position as William's favourite, and aims to connect three recent historiographical debates.

Firstly, Portland's role will be situated within an Anglo-Dutch and European context.[9] From the 1960s, revisionist historians largely demolished traditional, often nationalist, perspectives, and applied international interpretative models. By now, historians have become aware of the necessity to write British history, encompassing the Scottish and Irish as well as the English contexts.[10] Jonathan Israel has rightly pointed out the need to expand on this tendency, to place British history within a wider European framework, or more specifically, to study the 'Anglo-Dutch moment' of 1688/1689 and its aftermath.[11] In his biography of William III, Stephen Baxter as well stressed the significance of the supranational nature of the 'Dual Monarchy' of the British Isles and the Dutch Republic.[12] Only within this British–Dutch – indeed European – context can William's reign be properly understood. His Dutch background was essential to understanding his policy after 1688, a view endorsed in recent works, including the two latest biographies of William III. To Tony Claydon, William was as much an Orange as a Stuart. Wout Troost paid attention to the United Provinces and England as well as Ireland and Scotland.[13] Nevertheless, until now little research has been conducted into the actual co-operation between the Dutch and British on military, naval, and political matters during the 1690s.

---

9   Such an international perspective has not always been taken, as Dutch and British historians are not always familiar with each other's historiography or source material. Whig historians have traditionally applied national models, e.g. G.M. Trevelyan, *England under the Stuarts* (edn London, 1997); T.B. Macaulay, *History of England from the Accession of James II* (6 vols, London, 1914). Japikse's solid biography of the King-Stadholder (mentioned in footnote 5) is entrenched in traditional Orangism and is Dutch-centred. Primary sources that have been published also bear the mark of national interpretations. While Japikse's publication of the letters of William and Portland favoured Dutch correspondence, the *Calendars of State Papers Domestic* for the reign of William and Mary, for instance, have downplayed references to Dutch politics. *Calendar of State Papers, Domestic Series, in the Reign of William and Mary*, ed. W.J. Hardy and E. Bateson (11 vols, London, 1969); *Correspondentie van Willem III en van Hans Willem Bentinck, Eersten Graaf van Portland*, ed. N. Japikse (5 vols, Rijksgeschiedkundige Publicatiën 'Kleine Reeks', XXIII, XXIV, XXVI, XXVII, XXVIII, The Hague, 1927–37).

10   Following the proposal of J.G.A. Pocock, 'British History: A Plea for a New Subject', *Journal of Modern History*, 47 (1975), 601–21, some historians now advocate this 'New British History' approach.

11   Israel, *Anglo-Dutch Moment*, 11.

12   Baxter, *William III*, 280.

13   Jonathan Scott's recent study on Stuart history emphasised the lasting and structural influence of the Dutch on English institutions in the 1690s, *England's Troubles. Seventeenth-Century English Political Instability in European Context* (Cambridge, 2000), 474 ff. Cf. M. 't Hart, 'The Devil or the Dutch: Holland's Impact on the Financial Revolution in England 1643–1694', *Parliaments, Estates and Representations*, 11 (1991), 39–52; Claydon, *William III and the Godly Revolution*; Troost, *William III*.

Secondly, this book will also explain the role of Portland against the background of the changes that occurred after the Glorious Revolution. The emergence of the favourite coincided with the Nine Years War and the profound political changes on the British Isles. Revisionist historians have argued that there was a connection between the Revolution and these changes, triggered by William's quest for funds to finance the war on the continent. William's reign saw the emergence of a 'standing Parliament' which provided the King with the financial means to conduct the war and made it necessary for him to develop a means of managing Parliament. Portland's role in this process will be studied.

Lastly, this study will build upon the findings of a recent volume of essays which sought a model for the favourite as a European phenomenon. At the same time it will engage the editors' conclusion that the favourite disappeared after 1660, and explain its re-emergence in England between 1689 and 1710.[14] Literature dealing with the phenomenon of the favourite has moved away from 'superficial psychological explanations' and concentrates on the 'growing complexity of the early modern state' as a way of understanding the significance of the favourite.[15] Indeed, recent literature on the 1690s suggests that Portland's activities as favourite should be rather explained in light of the profound changes that occurred during this decade. John Carswell has drawn attention to Portland's pivotal role during the Glorious Revolution. Patrick Riley, Wout Troost and John Simms have pointed to Portland's involvement in the government of Scotland and Ireland. John Kenyon has analysed his connection with the Earl of Sunderland and their involvement in ministerial and parliamentary management in England. Rather than emphasising Portland's personal relationship with William, therefore, this study will focus on the political and military developments of the 1690s and will provide a new overall interpretation and evaluation of Portland's role as favourite.[16]

It is the purpose of this book to show how these factors were intimately connected and thereby to define the role of the Anglo-Dutch favourite in Williamite politics. The career of Portland will be narrated and analysed in nine chapters in a more or less chronological order. Chapter 1 presents 'the making' of the favourite and covers his years in the United Provinces until 1685. It will analyse his responsibilities as

---

14   L.W.B. Brockliss and J.H. Elliott (eds), *The World of the Favourite* (New Haven/London, 1999). Cf. M. Kaiser and A. Pečar (eds), *Der Zweite Mann im Staat: Oberste Amtsträger und Favoriten im Umkreis der Reichsfürsten in der Frühen Neizeit* (Berlin, 2003).

15   J.H. Elliott, 'Introduction' in: Brockliss and Elliott, *The World of the Favourite*, 1–10, 4. Elliott specifically refers to the work of Jean Bérenger.

16   W. Troost, 'William III and the Treaty of Limerick 1691–1697' (Unpublished PhD thesis, University of Leiden, 1983); J.G. Simms, 'Williamite Peace Tactics 1690–1691' in: J.G. Simms, *War and Politics in Ireland 1649–1730*, eds D.W. Hayton and G. O'Brien (London, 1986), 181–201; J. Carswell, *The Descent on England* (London, 1973); J.I. Israel, 'Propaganda in the Making of the Glorious Revolution' in: S. Roach (ed.), *Across the Narrow Seas. Studies in the History and Bibliography of Britain and the Low Countries* (London, 1991), 167–78; L.G. Schwoerer, 'Propaganda in the Revolution of 1688–1689', *American Historical Review*, 132 (1977), 843–74; Riley, *Scottish Politicians*; J.P. Kenyon, *Robert Spencer, Earl of Sunderland 1621–1702* (London, 1958).

a politician, diplomat and military officer. The next chapter is essentially a case study, analysing Portland's activities preceding and during the Glorious Revolution. It will also pay attention to the wider international context in which the invasion took place. Chapters 3 to 7 are organised thematically rather than chronologically. Occasionally there may be some overlap or gaps, and chapter 3 sometimes refers to events explained in subsequent chapters. Nevertheless it is hoped that such a thematic and structural approach will provide a better insight into Portland's career. The five chapters form the core of this book and study the zenith of Portland's career between 1689 and 1697. They concentrate on the power, policy and perception of the Anglo-Dutch favourite. Rather than providing an exhaustive chronological account, they will focus on core issues which illuminate the nature of his activities and influence, as well as his role in the formulation of William's policy. Chapter 3 tracks Portland's role in stabilising the Revolution settlement, whereas the next chapter seeks to analyse his position as Anglo-Dutch favourite. Chapter 5 looks at his political activities and ideas, whereas the next chapter studies his military and diplomatic activities during the Nine Years War. Chapter 7 discusses Portland's role in the development of Williamite ideology and the emergence of an anti-favourite rhetoric. Chapter 8 will discuss his diplomatic activities towards the end and after the Nine Years War, most notably during the peace negotiations at Ryswick and the talks on the Spanish Partition Treaties. The final chapter analyses the reasons behind his retirement, initially in 1697 and finally in 1699, and covers his last years until his death in 1709.

The most important source on which this study has been based is Portland's archive from Welbeck Abbey, which has now been transferred to Nottingham University Library.[17] Although Nicolaas Japikse has published the most material part of the correspondence, much remains unpublished.[18] While Portland's vast archive has proved a solid basis for this study, its several limitations have posed methodological problems. Firstly, part of the archive has been lost, and it is not always clear to what extent it is actually representative and as such relevant in the reconstruction of his activities and network of correspondents. Secondly, there are few minutes of outgoing correspondence in the archive, and often analyses had to be based on indirect evidence. This is particularly disappointing as his important letters to, for instance, the Earl of Sunderland, have gone missing. Lastly, Portland preferred to discuss behind closed doors what was not essential to write down on paper, and often conjecture must be employed to reconstruct his role. The very essence of his powerful position as favourite was that it was based on his informal confidential relationship with William III. As a result, the exact dimensions of Portland's role and the extent of his influence cannot always be fully reconstructed.

These shortcomings can only be partly overcome by using his scarce and often curt outgoing letters in other archives. The Historical Manuscripts Commission has

---

17   A small section has ended up in the Egerton Manuscripts in the British Library, see footnote 18.

18   Nottingham University Library, Portland Welbeck Archive PwA 1–2870, Pw2A 1–29; British Library Egerton Manuscripts 1704–09, 1717, 1754B; Japikse, *Correspondentie*. His excellent introduction provides an analysis of the archive and its history.

published his correspondence with several politicians.[19] The most important letters are those written to William III and are fully printed in Japikse's edition and in the Calendars of State Papers Domestic. The State Papers Foreign in the National Archive in London – a vast source much neglected by historians – have correspondence with English diplomats. As an international approach has been adopted in this book, much material has been used from non-English archives. The Nationaal Archief in The Hague and the printed Heinsius-correspondence shed light on Portland's activities in the United Provinces and his involvement in foreign policy.[20] The National Archives of Scotland and the National Library of Scotland contain a considerable quantity of letters to and from Portland that have often been overlooked. Additional material has been found in the published correspondences of George Melville and William Carstares.[21] Lastly, the Archives du Ministère des Affaires Etrangères in Paris contain numerous letters of Portland which have been previously overlooked. They provide an outward perspective of Dutch and British affairs. In addition, a wide range of contemporary correspondence, journals and diaries has been consulted to provide an insight into Portland's socio-political context – the Court, the army and Parliament. Pamphlet material has been analysed to reconstruct political discourse on the Anglo-Dutch favourite. Lastly, remnants of his material heritage – his estates, gardens and art collection – illustrate the representative aspects of the position of the Anglo-Dutch favourite.

---

19   E.g. correspondence with the Earl of Nottingham: HMC, *Finch Mss*, with the Duke of Shrewsbury: *Buccleugh Mss*, and with Matthew Prior: *Bath Mss*. The Surrey History Centre has the important correspondence with John Somers.

20   *De Briefwisseling van Anthonie Heinsius 1702–1720*, ed. A.J. Veenendaal (20 vols., The Hague, 1976–2001).

21   *Leven and Melville Papers. Letters and State Papers chiefly Addressed to George Earl of Melville, Secretary of State for Scotland, 1689–1691*, ed. W.L. Melville (Edinburgh, 1843); *State Papers and Letters Addressed to William Carstares*, ed. J. McCormick (Edinburgh, 1774).

Chapter 1

The Making of a Favourite (1649–85)

Reflecting upon his long career as the favourite of William III, Hans Willem Bentinck impressed upon his son Henry in 1692 the importance of his duty to be loyal to and serve the King faithfully.[1] Such loyalty was due to the man who was both a prince of Orange and a Stuart king, but also to his cause, which was perceived to be the defence of Protestantism and liberty. That Bentinck's career would be epitomised by warfare in the service of William III was far from obvious when he was born in 1649, during a prolonged period of peace for the United Provinces after the Westphalia settlement, and on the eve of the demise of the Orange family.

Born the third son of a landed nobleman in the eastern periphery of the United Provinces, Hans Willem Bentinck could not have anticipated a distinguished career when appointed page to the Court of the Prince of Orange in 1664. In 1672, with his fortunes inextricably connected to those of his master, he emerged as William's favourite, a position he maintained and strengthened largely thanks to his qualities as a military organiser. When the Dutch War ended in 1678, other qualities were required, and Bentinck again managed to adapt to changing circumstances and the emerging demands. His several embassies to London in 1677, 1683 and 1685 offer windows on key moments in Anglo-Dutch relations during these years.

The stadholderly system in the seventeenth century has attracted surprisingly little attention from historians, let alone the phenomenon of favouritism in the Dutch Republic which reached a peak during the age of William III.[2] The rise of Hans Willem Bentinck and the small circle of confidants around the Orange court were indicative of the quasi-monarchical nature of William III's court.[3] This chapter traces Bentinck's social background and considers how his education, capacities and character contributed to his career, as he developed considerably as a politician, diplomat and military organiser. It also analyses his position at the Orange court and assesses the nature and limitations of his influence, placing him within the framework of William's entourage.

---

1   Japikse, *Correspondentie*, XXIV. 711.
2   But see A.J.C.M. Gabriëls, who studied this for the eighteenth century in *De Heren als Dienaren en de Dienaar als Heer: het Stadhouderlijk Stelsel in de Tweede Helft van de Achttiende Eeuw* (The Hague, 1990). Cf. footnote 87. Few favourites stood out and to date no study of Dutch favouritism has been published.
3   On this circle, see D.J. Roorda, 'Le Secret du Prince. Monarchale Tendenties in de Republiek 1672–1702' in: S. Groenveld, et al. (eds), *Rond Prins en Patriciaat: Verspreide Opstellen door D.J. Roorda* (Weesp, 1984), 172–92.

I

The Bentincks were predominantly a Protestant and Orangist family. In 1618, Hans Willem's grandfather Hendrik Bentinck had supported the Contra-Remonstrant[4] policy of Stadholder Maurice, but with the demise of the House of Orange with the death of William II in 1650 the family lost influence, although Hans Willem's father remained *Proost* (deacon) of Deventer. The Bentincks could trace their noble family tree back well into the thirteenth century and had played a significant role in the history of the provinces of Gelderland and Overijssel.[5] During the fifteenth century two generations had been *drosten* (stewards) of the Veluwe quarter of Gelderland. Overijssel, responsible for about three and a half percent of the revenue of the Generality (making it the least significant of the seven provinces) was governed jointly by the cities of Kampen, Zwolle and Deventer and the three noble quarters of Salland, Twente and Vollenhoven. This parity between the cities and the nobility tilted towards the latter, whose *drosten*, the nobility's spokesmen, also chaired the annual provincial assembly. The *drosten* played a significant role in local government, supervised the appointment of magistrates and were responsible for jurisdiction.[6]

Hans Willem's great-grandfather Eusebius had been *Drost* of IJsselmuiden and was succeeded as such by his son Hendrik. The latter was appointed *Drost* of Salland, the foremost office in Overijssel, in 1611. Around 1637 Hendrik had acquired three estates which were to be divided at his death amongst his sons Wolf, Eusebius Borchard and Berend. Hence Berend inherited the estate of Diepenheim in 1639 and was accordingly admitted into the *Ridderschap* (knighthood) of Overijssel, the noble elite of that province.[7] The *Ridderschap* consisted of a selection of a few dozen noble families holding a seat in the provincial assembly. They were required to be of noble and ancient lineage, and had to be in possession of a certain fortune and a qualified *havezate* (country house).[8] The self-conscious and vigorous Overijssel nobility still regarded itself as a distinct, superior estate, and was remarkably successful in checking the influx of burghers into its ranks.[9] The Bentincks were among the four most influential families in Overijssel, and consolidated their dynastic position by intermarrying with the foremost families in Gelderland and Overijssel, such as the Van Haersoltes and the Sloets.[10]

---

4   The Contra-Remonstrants were the orthodox Calvinists who emerged victoriously after the Synod of Dordt in 1618/1619.
5   M.E. Grew, *William Bentinck and William III (Prince of Orange). The Life of Bentinck, Earl of Portland, from the Welbeck Correspondence* (London, 1924), 2.
6   A.J. Gevers and A.J. Mensema, *De Havezaten in Twente en hun Bewoners* (Zwolle, 1995), 14.
7   Gevers and Mensema, *Havezaten*, 16–19, 176–7.
8   Ibid., 12–26.
9   Ibid., 39–42 and *passim*.
10   J.C. Streng, 'Le Métier du Noble: De Overijsselse Ridderschap tussen 1622 en 1795' in: A.J. Mensema, J. Mooijweer and J.C. Streng (eds), *De Ridderschap van Overijssel. Le Métier du Noble* (Zwolle, 2000), 49–109, 61.

Hans Willem Bentinck was born on 20 July 1649 at Diepenheim, the *havezate* of Berend Bentinck (1597–1668) and his wife Anna van Bloemendaal (1622–1685).[11] Little is known about his early years, which must have been spent in relative tranquillity. Berend Bentinck was *Proost* of Deventer and did well for himself. He had Diepenheim rebuilt, Hans Willem being the first to be born in the new house in 1649. The house was situated in a rural setting close to the village of Diepenheim. It must have been a lively, pleasant and uncomplicated atmosphere with eight children growing up in this relatively small but also luxurious house.[12] Hans Willem's youth was quite different from that of William, who grew up an orphan and a sole child in a hostile environment. The fifth of nine children and the third son, Hans Willem could not expect to inherit the estate and would be required to pursue an alternative career.[13] A second son, Wolf Willem, died in infancy, and Hans Willem's elder brothers Hendrik (1640–1691) and Eusebius (1643–1670) inherited the two estates of their father and uncle after their deaths. Hans Willem must have been close to his elder sister, Eleonora Sophie, as she would take care of his children after the death of his wife Anne Villiers. There were four younger sisters, Isabella, Anna Adriana, Agnes and Johanna Elizabeth.[14]

Unlike William, Hans Willem was a healthy boy with a strong constitution. As a young man he once took the field as officer immediately after having recovered from near-fatal smallpox.[15] According to the anonymous chronicler 'Monsieur de B.', describing him as a grown-up, Hans Willem 'was quite tall, a bit stiff, blond-haired tending to red ... the face, though not irregular, had nothing attractive'.[16] He had little inclination for intellectual pursuits; Gilbert Burnet later spoke of the 'defects of his education'.[17] As a younger son, Hans Willem was probably trained and prepared for service in the army.[18] Overijssel was particularly vulnerable to invasion; Hans Willem's family experienced an attack from Munster in 1665 during the Second Anglo-Dutch War. Hence the province's nobility had acquired a strong sense of responsibility with regard to military service. Overijssel had suffered heavily from the invasion, but Hans Willem was already residing in The Hague by then.

---

11   A *havezate* was a country house or manor in Overijssel with feudal rights attached to it, making the owner eligible for a seat in the *Ridderschap* (knighthood).

12   Gevers and Mensema, *Havezaten*, 176 ff.

13   Berend's brother appeared to have remained childless, so Hans Willem's second brother inherited the Schoonheten estate.

14   Based on D. Schwennicke (ed.), *Europäische Stammtafeln*, IV. *Standesherrliche Häuser* (Marburg, 1981), I. table 12. See also the table on page 97.

15   W. Temple, 'Memoirs 1672–1679' in: *The Works of Sir William Temple* (4 vols, Edinburgh, 1754), I. 223.

16   'Monsieur de B.', 'Mêmoires ... ou Anecdotes, tant de la Cour du Prince d'Orange Guillaume III, que des Principaux Seigneurs de la République de ce Temps', ed. F.J.L. Krämer, B[ijdragen en] M[ededelingen betreffende de] G[eschiedenis der] N[ederlanden], 19 (1898), 62–124, 90, transl. from French. The author served in a regiment under Bentinck.

17   *A Supplement to Burnet's History of my Own Time etc.*, ed. H.C. Foxcroft (Oxford, 1902), 196.

18   Cf. Gevers and Mensema, *Havezaten*, 43; Cf. Streng, 'Le Métier du Noble', 52.

In 1651 the abolition of the stadholderate in five of the seven provinces was confirmed at the Grand Assembly, the Frisian Nassaus remaining in office in the North. Three years later Oliver Cromwell forced Grand Pensionary Johan de Witt to accept the secret clause of seclusion, preventing the Oranges (suspected of being in league with the Stuarts because of the marriage of William II and Mary) from regaining the stadholderate.[19] Factional rifts between William's mother, Mary Stuart, and his grandmother, Amalia van Solms, deepened the misfortunes of the Orange family. Throughout the 1650s the low tide in the fortunes of the Oranges and Stuarts darkened the spirits of those two women. In 1660, months after the return of her brother, Charles II, to England, Mary died, leaving the young prince an orphan. The Court remained a hotbed of intrigue. Despite the political insignificance of the Orange court, a rudimentary court structure was maintained, and the first and foremost noble family in the United Provinces functioned as a centre of Dutch noble society. Traditionally the connection between the nobility and the Orange family was strongest in the eastern provinces of Gelderland and Overijssel, where the nobility was strong in the States Assemblies and had sympathised with the continental strategy of the stadholders Maurice, Frederick Henry and William II.[20] Hence it was not surprising that Hans Willem, the son of an Orangist squire from one of the eastern provinces, was accepted as page to the Prince of Orange at the Court in The Hague in 1664.

Two years after Hans Willem's arrival a major change took place at the Orange court which swept a number of influential courtiers out of office. The Second Anglo-Dutch War (1665–67) had prompted De Witt to purge the princely household of a number of sympathisers of the Stuarts. Boreel and the dashing nobleman and governor of the Prince, Frederik van Nassau-Zuylestein, of whom William was particularly fond, were forced to leave Court despite the latter's appeal to the Grand Pensionary. It is difficult to estimate the impact of these measures. Although the *Kamerheer* (Chamberlain), the *Hofmeester* (Steward) and the *Stalmeester* (Master of the Horse) were replaced by Holland noblemen, the ramifications of this purge may not have reached down to the lower echelons at Court.[21] One of the newcomers at Court was *Stalmeester* Hendrik van Nassau-Ouwerkerk, who like Bentinck would remain an esteemed courtier; William rewarded loyalty of the members of his entourage, most of who would continue to play an important role in his reign.

Of Hans Willem's early years at Court only fragments are known. As page – of which there would be two or three – he became a member of the entourage of the Prince and accompanied him on various occasions. One of the first appearances of *Jonker* Bentinck was at the funeral of the Frisian Stadholder Willem Frederik in 1664

---

19   See P. Geyl, *Orange and Stuart 1641–1672* (London, 1969).

20   On the continuing importance of the Orange court during this period and its connection with the nobility in the eastern provinces, see O. Mörke, 'William III's Stadholderly Court in the Dutch Republic' in: E. Mijers and D. Onnekink (eds), *Redefining William III: The Impact of the King-Stadholder in International Context* (Aldershot, 2007), 227–40.

21   N. Japikse, *Prins Willem III – De Stadhouder-Koning* (2 vols, Amsterdam, 1933), I. 131.

on behalf of the Prince of Orange, with two other pages and Nassau-Zuylestein.[22] In 1668 he accompanied William at a reception celebrating the wedding of the *Greffier*'s daughter.[23] It is difficult to estimate what impact the change of environment, both geographical and social, had on Hans Willem. Coming from the east to The Hague, the page entered an unfamiliar socio-political environment.[24] The relative alienation must have encouraged a confidential relationship with William, intensified by the surrounding atmosphere of intrigue, distrust and political frustration that characterised the Orange court. There is an anecdote that Hans Willem had gained the trust of William when he 'had shown' his friend the daughter of a local landlord.[25] One year his junior, William often drew strength from the less complicated Hans Willem, but they were also both taciturn and steady characters. As an orphan, William was drawn to Hans Willem's stable family background, his brothers and sisters and their children. In 1668 William visited the parents of Hans Willem and made a pledge to take care of their son's future.[26] The Prince's oldest preserved letter to his friend dates from August of that year, conveying his condolences over the death of Hans Willem's father. The expressions William uses about his loyalty to his page and the fortunes of his family are quite extraordinary:

> I can assure you in truth that there is no one who is more touched than me by the affliction your house has suffered, and you most of all, as I will always be among your friends who will consider everything that happens to you as if it happened to myself.[27]

In 1668 the isolated princely court was drawn into the vortex of resurgent Orangism. In the aftermath of the Second Anglo-Dutch War and the wake of the War of Devolution a debate developed over the Prince's taking political office, a move endorsed by the majority of provinces. To restrain the tide of mounting Orangism, the States of Holland had issued the Perpetual Edict in 1667 abolishing the stadholderate. The 'Harmony', stipulating the separation between the stadholderate and the captain-generalship in the other provinces, was made a precondition for William's entry into the *Raad van State* (Council of State), an executive body dealing mainly with military matters. It was not until 1670 that William took his seat. The Edict had been devised by the Haarlem Pensionary Gaspar Fagel and the Amsterdam regent Gilles Valckenier. Its ambiguous nature, aimed at satisfying both Orangists and 'True Freedom' regents, failed on both accounts as De Witt only grudgingly accepted it, and William's

---

22   *Hollandsche Mercurius, behelsende het Gedenckweerdigste in Christenrijck voor-gevallen, binnen 't gansche Jaar 1664* (Haarlem, 1665), 195. A *jonker* was a nobleman without a title.
23   Japikse, *Willem III*, I. 114, 132–4. The *Greffier* was the Clerk of the States-General, an influential office.
24   Cf. O. Mörke, *Stadtholder oder Staetholder? Die Funktion des Hauses Oranien und seines Hofes in der Politischen Kultur der Republik der Vereinigten Niederlande im 17. Jahrhundert* (Munster, 1997), 113.
25   10 April 1678, Huygens, *Journaal*, II. 243, transl. from Dutch.
26   Japikse, *Prins Willem III*, I. 114; Japikse, *Correspondentie*, XXIV. 710–11.
27   William to Bentinck 13 August 1668, Japikse, *Correspondentie*, XXIII. 3, transl. from French.

grandmother Amalia van Solms lukewarmly received the news.[28] From 1668 the Orangist advance gained momentum. Amalia, in conjunction with Nassau-Odijk and the Zeeland pensionary Pieter de Huybert, had prepared a plan for William, now of age, to demand his position as First Noble of the province of Zeeland. William, with Bentinck in his train, travelled to Middelburg in September, where he took his seat in the States of Zeeland.[29] Bentinck made his first journey abroad in the autumn of 1670, when William travelled to England to meet his uncle Charles II. The company (also including Nassau-Ouwerkerk, Nassau-Odijk and Nassau-Zuylestein) travelled around, and visited Oxford and Cambridge universities, where some, among whom Bentinck, were awarded honorary degrees.[30] In London William lodged in Whitehall Palace, and Bentinck gained his first impression of the English court.

II

The political significance of the mission was limited, and the Prince was oblivious to the secret Anglo-French dealings earlier that year to the prejudice of the Dutch state. The increasing threat from France had prompted Gelderland to propose the appointment of the Prince as Captain-General in May 1671 in defiance of the Harmony. In December William urged Godard Adriaan Reede van Amerongen, an influential Utrecht nobleman, to have that province concur. Under pressure, Holland decided to appoint William Captain-General for one season with restrictions in January 1672. But the surprise of the combined Anglo-French attack in the spring of 1672 dramatically altered the situation, and in July William was appointed Stadholder as well. The task facing him was daunting. Although Admiral Michiel de Ruyter managed to fend off the English fleet, French invasion forces crushed Dutch defences and crossed the rivers Rhine and IJssel in June. The demise of William's political opponent De Witt – who was lynched by a frenzied crowd – also deprived him of a political mentor.[31] According to Bentinck, William had been shocked upon receiving the news of his death.[32] The invasion of 1672 had cast a shadow over the fate of the Republic, and it was mainly because of the success of the *Waterlinie* (a defensive string of waterways and inundated land at the eastern border of Holland) that the Dutch army was not completely destroyed. The military predicament was the main concern of the new Captain-General.

A loyal and assiduous servant, Bentinck managed to keep his position during the major changes of 1672. Continuous access to the Prince was assured by his appointment as Chamberlain in April 1672. The post had hitherto been of moderate

---

28 It could also be argued that it succeeded on both accounts, as the compromise paved the way for William to take office, but also satisfied the Republicans who hailed the measure as the apotheosis of 'True Freedom'. W. Troost, *William III, the Stadholder-King: A Political Biography* (Aldershot, 2005), 58–9.

29 Japikse, *Willem III*, I. 146–7.

30 Grew, *Bentinck*, 18–24, has an account of this visit.

31 Cf. J.I. Israel, *The Dutch Republic. Its Rise, Greatness and Fall 1477–1806* (Oxford, 1998), 796–806.

32 Japikse, *Willem III*, I. 250.

importance, but was now visibly ranking higher amongst courtiers as Bentinck was recognised as William's confidant.[33] Although he was, in his new capacity, required to perform a number of menial tasks, proximity to the Prince provided plentiful opportunities to converse about matters of importance which would otherwise have required an audience. His rivals soon complained that Bentinck had 'very much the ear' of the Prince.[34] The ambitious young man was not contented with the mere exercise of routine business and the easy life of a courtier. The anonymous 'Monsieur de B.', wrote that

> He has preserved the affection of his master by an assiduity which bordered on slavery, having no liberty apart from those hours in which he was occupied with giving audiences. Such a favour would have been an example for all sovereigns.[35]

'Monsieur de B.' was sceptical, however, of Bentinck's qualities and observed:

> The great attachment he had had to the Prince since his tender youth, had deprived him of the means to acquire skills other than a certain routine in affairs, which his master communicated to him; ignorant of everything else ... .[36]

In matters of diplomacy and policy, his was a backstage role. Whereas William's older bastard cousin, Nassau-Ouwerkerk, for instance, had been sent to England in 1669 on a diplomatic mission, Bentinck had no part in the negotiations between the English ambassadors and William in June 1672.[37] Bentinck had had no diplomatic or political training, and William was now well served by seasoned advisers and diplomats to guide him through the most difficult year of his life. At 23 Bentinck was the youngest in William's entourage, men like Solms, Nassau-Odijk, Nassau-Ouwerkerk and Waldeck being between ten and thirty years his senior. The young prince, faced with enormous responsibility and challenges, tended to rely on older and more experienced men.[38] Unlike most members of the stadholderly entourage Bentinck was entirely William's creature and did not possess an independent position. While friendship and continuous close proximity were precious advantages in the pursuit of influence, it was insufficient as a basis for the young chamberlain to attain real power.

One avenue for achieving more influence was Bentinck's serving William as a sort of secretary for military affairs. It is not surprising that he started his career as a soldier. He had received his first commission in the army in July 1668, being appointed Cornet in the battalion of Lord 's Gravenmoer.[39] He attended the Prince

---

33   NUL, PwA 2865; Mörke, *Stadtholder oder Staetholder?*, 107n, 117.
34   Quoted in Japikse, *Willem III*, I. 359, transl. from Dutch. Cf. *Négociations de Monsieur le Comte d'Avaux en Hollande depuis 1679 jusqu'en 1688* (6 vols, Paris, 1752–53), IV. 240.
35   'Monsieur de B.', 'Mêmoires', 91, transl. from French.
36   Ibid., 90, transl. from French.
37   TNA: PRO, SP 84/189, f° 143–52, 157–60.
38   Cf. S.B. Baxter, *William III* (London, 1966), 249.
39   NUL, PwA 2866.

at the latter's meeting with De Ruyter in August 1672 in Den Helder.[40] Bentinck soon immersed himself in military affairs, and rapidly climbed through the military ranks. By 1672 he was Captain of the infantry. In April of that year he was appointed Cavalry Captain, and in July 1674 he was promoted to Colonel of a regiment of horse.[41] But it was as staff officer rather than on the battlefield that his talent shone forth. He became engaged in military organisation, although his exact responsibilities are unclear due to scant sources. The first evidence dates from 1673, when he systematically ordered battle plans and military reports on such subjects as estimations of the strength of armies and their positions.[42] Possibly before, but certainly from 1675 he was responsible for some logistic aspects of the campaigns, having daily marching orders for the troops drafted by his aides.[43] An annotated memorial from 1676 shows Bentinck active in military planning, discussing not only the supply of troops and weapons but also various tactical options with regard to an attack on Wijck.[44]

Indicative of his growing influence, Bentinck's increasing interference in military matters naturally incited the animosity of army commanders. When he tried to arrange a promotion for one of his cousins who was serving under the command of the Rhinegrave, he was summoned by the latter and given to understand that as chamberlain he should restrict his activities to 'fetching the slippers' of the Prince.[45] The young officer had been intimidated and retreated, but in 1675 he had allied himself with a faction at Court, powerful enough to turn against the Prince of Waldeck, the intimate confidant of the Captain-General, situated at the apex of the military establishment.[46]

It was not uncommon for courtiers and members of the stadholderly entourage to wield both political and military power. Some men who were essentially courtiers were given a military rank. Olaf Mörke has aptly observed that men such as Waldeck and Bentinck were 'political officers', superseding their military tasks and also employable as politicians. This military entourage of William proved particularly stable, and would continue to serve him in England as well.[47]

It was therefore not surprising that Bentinck soon also immersed himself in diplomatic and political correspondence. Under William III the stadholderly secretary lost political influence due to the separation of routine and confidential correspondence. Constantijn Huygens's secretaryship still wielded some political significance, but his son Constantijn jr. acted merely as a clerk of routine business. William himself handled confidential correspondence and was assisted by Bentinck

---

40   Japikse, *Willem III*, I. 301.
41   NUL, PwA 2865–6.
42   NUL, PwA 2039–59, PwA 2085.
43   BL, Eg Mss 1704.
44   NUL, PwA 2048.
45   J.H. Hora Siccama, 'Mevrouw van Zoutelande en hare Gedenkschriften', *Bijdragen voor Vaderlandsche Geschiedenis en Oudheidkunde*, 4th series (1903), IV. 123–221, 173–4, transl. from Dutch.
46   TNA: PRO, SP 84/198, f° 290r°. Cf. page 18.
47   Mörke, *Stadtholder oder Staetholder?*, 122.

rather than Huygens.[48] A 1675 letter from the Prince to the Earl of Arlington, for example, is clearly in Bentinck's handwriting.[49] This personal secretaryship proved a stepping stone to a more politically significant position in ensuing years. Confidential correspondence of highly placed statesmen, foreign and native, passed through Bentinck's hands. He was responsible for conveying orders to the supreme commanders, but also discussed foreign affairs. He had a good relationship with the English ambassador Gabriel Sylvius. He learned a great deal about English politics, the relationship between Charles II and Parliament and the configuration of court factions. In the anxious years between 1672 and 1674 these matters must have been continuously discussed.[50] He thus gained some experience in foreign affairs, although his diplomatic career would not take off until 1677.[51] Although the extent of political influence attached to the secretaryship should not be overestimated, due to its evolution Bentinck developed a thorough knowledge of foreign and domestic policy.[52]

In 1675 Bentinck consolidated his position as the Prince's most loyal servant when the latter fell ill with smallpox in 1675 and his life was in danger. Sir William Temple recorded the event, commenting:

> I cannot here forbear to give Monsieur Bentinck the character due to him, of the best servant I have ever known in Prince's or private family. He tended his master, during the whole course of his disease, both night and day; nothing he took was given him, nor he ever removed in his bed, by any other hand; and the Prince told me, that whether he slept or not he could not tell, but, in sixteen days and nights, he never called once that he was not answered by Monsieur Bentinck, as if he had been awake. The first time the Prince was well enough to have his head opened and combed, Monsieur Bentinck, as soon as it was done, begged of his master to give him leave to go home, for he was able to hold up no longer: he did so, and fell immediately sick of the same disease and in great extremity; but recovered just soon enough to attend his master into the field, where he was ever next his person.[53]

It must have been his youth and physical strength that pulled Bentinck through the disease himself. There is a tradition that he shared William's bed, as it was believed the taking over of the disease could cure the infected. There is, however, no contemporary evidence to support the story. Be that as it may, the event represented a powerful testimony of Bentinck's willingness to serve his master with his life. It would become one of the milestones in his life as well as a key ingredient in panegyric literature.[54]

---

48   Ibid., 140. Cf. 7 June 1677, Huygens, *Journaal*, II. 175.
49   Letter to Arlington, 3 Feb. 1675, TNA: PRO, SP 8/1, f° 10–11. Cf. Japikse, *Willem III*, I. 360.
50   NUL, PwA 2041.
51   Dona to Bentinck 28 December 1676, NUL, PwA 363.
52   E.g. NUL, PwA 2046.
53   Temple, 'Memoirs 1672–1679', I. 223.
54   E.g. *An Elegy, Occasioned by the much Lamented Death of ... Portland* (s.l., 1709), NUL, PwA 2864.

Although William would remain grateful to his favourite, Bentinck's sacrifice was not the main cause of the acceleration of his political career. Already in 1674 William had appointed him *Drost*, Bailiff and Deputy-Stadholder in Breda, and one year later *Drost* in Lingen. As he assumed his new position he reached an equal footing with his brothers in Overijssel. It was a position he had fiercely pursued. One of his competitors complained that Bentinck had 'bitten out of favour' Lord Wotton who had retained the post in Breda for several years.[55] More significantly, in September 1676 William granted him the estate of Drimmelen. Its value was relatively small – an estimated ƒ4,000 only – but due to the feudal rights accompanying the estate Bentinck was eligible to take a seat in the *Ridderschap* of Holland.[56] There were about a hundred noblemen in Holland, but only some ten of the most prominent would take a seat in the *Ridderschap*.

The order had adopted the system of co-optation, and unanimous support was required to incorporate a non-Holland nobleman such as Bentinck.[57] Its pensionary was Gaspar Fagel, who also presided over the States of Holland. An exceptionally skilled politician and orator, well versed in constitutional and legal affairs, Fagel was able to facilitate William's policy in the States institutions as due to his office he held seats in both the States General and the States of Holland.[58] Until his death in 1688, Fagel was undoubtedly William's mainstay in political affairs. This was surprising, as the office of grand pensionary formed a natural counterbalance to that of the stadholder. During the Twelve Years Truce, Prince Maurice and Grand Pensionary Johan van Oldenbarnevelt had become two fierce opponents, leading the Orangist and Republican parties in what amounted almost to civil war. The precise nature of the relationship between William and Fagel therefore leaves room for speculation, but it largely depended on mutual trust and shared opinions on the direction of policy. Fagel could manage affairs in the States when William's direct interference would perhaps cause friction.[59] Whereas William had ostensibly not pressed Bentinck's admission into the *Ridderschap*, Fagel had arranged for its members to accept his inclusion. Bentinck himself recognised that his 'care and good direction much

---

55   Japikse, *Willem III*, I. 359, transl. from Dutch.
56   The Dutch guilder was about one eleventh the value of the English pound sterling. Drimmelen was only granted to Bentinck as a device to have him in the Order. When in 1703 William's heir Johan Willem Friso reclaimed the estate, Bentinck admitted that the grant 'had only been made with that intention, and no other'. BL, Eg Mss 1708, f° 100–103. Grant of Drimmelen Manor 1676, BL, Egerton Charter 103.
57   Cf. H.M. Brokken and A.W.M. Koolen (eds), *Inventaris van het Archief van de Ridderschap en Edelen van Holland en West-Friesland 1572–1795* (The Hague, 1992), i–xvi; H.F.K. van Nierop, *Van Ridders tot Regenten. De Hollandse Adel in de Zestiende en de Eerste Helft van de Zeventiende Eeuw* (s.l., 1984), 220 ff.
58   Cf. G. de Bruin, *Geheimhouding en Verraad. De Geheimhouding van Staatszaken ten tijde van de Republiek (1600–1750)* (The Hague, 1991), 251 ff. *passim*.
59   Cf. E. Edwards, 'An Unknown Statesman: Gaspar Fagel in the Service of William III and the Dutch Republic', *History*, 87 (2002), 353–71.

contributed to that end'.[60] Hence, from 1676 he assumed his life-long seat in the States of Holland, the locus of political influence in the United Provinces.

By the middle of the 1670s Bentinck had assembled a number of important offices, and the Chamberlain had become one of the most prominent noblemen in Holland. In 1674 he had bought the country house of Sorgvliet near The Hague, which would continue to be his main residence. Nine years later he would purchase the lordships of Rhoon and Pendrecht for the sizeable sum of f154,000.[61] He was recognised as William's foremost confidant. He was consistently part of his inner entourage and frequently observed having confidential conversations with the Prince and one or two other confidants.[62] An anonymous English agent in The Hague commented in 1675: 'Monsr. Benthem, they consider as ye man ye Prince most confides in, & to who he unbosomes his private thoughts, his feares & his pleasures, and as on y^t will never contradict him in any thing.'[63] Thus Bentinck managed to remain William's closest aide throughout turbulent changes during his reign and despite the proliferation of a number of advisers and favourites at Court. Perhaps the most interesting observation is from Burnet:

> Mr. Bentinck was bred about the prince, and he observed in him that application to business and those virtues that made him think fit to take him into his particular confidence, and to employ him in the secretest of all his concerns as well as the looking to all his private affairs. He is a man of great probity and sincerity, and is as close as his master is. ... He has all the passion of a friend for the prince's person, as well as the fidelity of a minister in his affairs, and makes up the defects of his education in a great application to business; and as he has a true and clear judgement, so the probity of his temper appears in all his counsels, which are just and moderate ... .[64]

Understandably, William's favouring of Bentinck was deeply disliked by other courtiers. Nassau-Ouwerkerk, one of William's most intimate advisers, particularly resented the position of the young upstart.[65] Complaints were made that Bentinck antagonised and outrivaled other courtiers, but accounts about his behaviour and attitude at Court are invariably contradictory and not easy to interpret.[66]

Perhaps Bentinck's perceived haughtiness was prompted by an urge to compensate for feelings of social inferiority towards William's other confidants and his fellow

---

60   William to Fagel 12 June 1676, Bentinck to Fagel 3 July 1676, Japikse, *Correspondentie*, XXVII. 107–9, 118, transl. from Dutch.

61   Japikse, *Prins Willem III*, II. 127. Rhoon was valued in 1709 at f198,584: 8, BL, Eg Mss 1708, f° 279. According to Tessin and Harris this was a gift from William. J.D. Hunt and E. de Jong (eds), *The Anglo-Dutch Garden in the Age of William and Mary. De Gouden Eeuw van de Hollandse Tuinkunst* (London/Amsterdam, 1988), 168.

62   Cf. 27 May 1675, 22 July 1675, Huygens, *Journaal*, II. 29, 46, and *passim*.

63   TNA: PRO, SP 84/198, f° 289.

64   Burnet continued: '... though I naturally hate favourites, because all those whom I have known hitherto have made a very ill use of their greatness, yet by all I could ever discern, the prince has shewed a very true judgement of persons in placing so much of his confidence on him.' Foxcroft, *Supplement*, 196–7.

65   E.g. 11 May 1677, Huygens, *Journaal*, II. 164.

66   Japikse, *Willem III*, I. 359.

noblemen in the *Ridderschap*. Although he could boast an ancient noble family tree, his was obviously inferior to the princely Nassau, Waldeck, or even the noble Van Noordwijks and the Van Wassenaars pedigrees.[67] It was not until Bentinck had made his fortune as Earl of Portland that the Wassenaar-Duyvenvoordes, for instance, were eager to become attached to his family.[68] Bentinck must have been regarded as an intruder as well, a relative outsider from Overijssel conspicuously ushered into the *Ridderschap*, though he had spent some years in The Hague at the Orange court and had become part of Holland society.

Bentinck's position was never unchallenged, and faction struggle within William's circle was perennial, although evidence is scarce. According to the anonymous agent mentioned above:

> All these men, y^t are most in his favour wth ye Prince, are divided into factions amongst themselves. Fagels [sic] relyes only upon the ye Princes [sic], C. de Waldeck & ye Pentioner cannot agree. The Rhinegrave, Mons. Odijke, & Monsr. Benthem are united & cannot abide Waldeck who I am assured lost much ground by his absence.[69]

In the summer of 1686 the French ambassador Count d'Avaux witnessed a 'frost' in the relation between Fagel and Bentinck which lasted for months, as a result of which Fagel's favour with the Prince, D'Avaux stated, diminished.[70] As Bentinck became increasingly influential, the bulk of antagonism was aimed at him. In 1680 Willem van Nassau-Zuylestein and Nassau-Ouwerkerk were enraged with William 'out of hatred that he does good to Mr. Bentinck'.[71]

It is doubtful whether such factionalism constituted anything more than mere competition for favour, and it cannot not be seen as a reflection of any significant differences in opinion with regard to policy. William demanded that his aides endorse his views, and would not allow one of his aides to overrule him. In later years in England William would sometimes hold the major offices of state in commission. 'His chief characteristic', one commentator would later observe, 'is great distrust, so that very few people, even amongst those who are in office, are acquainted with his secrets'.[72] A few of William's closest confidants were employable in more than one way, holding military rank as well as political office. They also tended to maintain a regional clientele and were active in domestic as well as international affairs.[73] But essentially Japikse was correct in arguing that William compartmentalised various aspects of his government, entrusting military, diplomatic and political issues to different men.[74] In military matters he relied on the experienced Prince of Waldeck. Grand Pensionary Fagel was his mainstay in the complicated world of Holland factional politics, whereas

---

67   Ibid., I. 357–9.
68   His daughter Anna Margaretha would marry Arend van Wassenaar-Duyvenvoorde.
69   TNA: PRO, SP 84/198, f° 289–90.
70   D'Avaux to Louis 23 January 1687, AAE, CPH 150, f° 82v°, transl. from French. Unfortunately D'Avaux did not give a reason.
71   4 October 1680, Huygens, *Journaal*, III. 25, transl. from Dutch.
72   Quoted in W.L. Sachse, *Lord Somers, a Political Portrait* (Manchester, 1975), 146.
73   Mörke, *Stadtholder oder Staetholder?*, 194.
74   Japikse, *Prins Willem III*, I. 357–9.

the veteran diplomat Everard Weede van Dijkveld was an important adviser in matters of diplomacy and foreign policy. The anonymous English report of 1675 confirmed this view:

> ... the Prince only consults Waldeck on affairs of moment abroad and at home. But someone else said that his influence has been much impaired since his absence, and he consults with the Pensioner only about affairs both abroad and home. I wanted to know in whom he relies in connection with English affairs, that is mainly Fagel, and some of the ministers who contact the presbyterians in Scotland and England, Odijke is only involved when things have to be communicated to the English court.[75]

Within this compartmentalised system, however, Bentinck's star was clearly rising. Mörke has argued that within this configuration Bentinck held a special position, as he 'constantly emerged as the closest companion to the Stadholder in many political contexts'.[76] As from about the late 1670s he was engaged in every aspect of William's policy and became the Prince's closest confidant.

III

Although Bentinck thus held some military and political offices, his power base was at the stadholderly court, which had gained in significance under William III. Under the Habsburgs, the stadholders, as representatives of the sovereigns of the provinces, had held a vice-royal-like court. After the break with Spain in 1581, the stadholders attempted to establish a quasi-monarchical dynasty, using the Court to enhance their prestige. The Oranges and Nassaus were the only family of high nobility in the United Provinces, making them a natural magnet for members of the lower nobility. The noble entourage of William III formed the nucleus of a supraprovincial network connecting the Orangist regional aristocracy and one with international ramifications. William's closest associates were often recruited from the eastern provinces where they held key political positions in town councils and provincial assemblies.[77] William's relatives, the brothers Nassau-Ouwerkerk and Nassau-Odijk, were members of the Utrecht and Zeeland nobility respectively. The Amerongen family held strong positions in Utrecht, whereas Johan van Arnhem was a prominent supporter of William in the province of Gelderland. Bentinck's brothers and cousin held the prestigious offices of *hoogschout* (sheriff) and *drost* in the States of Overijssel.[78] The decision to put Bentinck and Van Reede in the *Ridderschap* was a conscious attempt by William to have his associates in key political positions in Holland and Utrecht.[79] In 1674 William had already put three clients in the *Ridderschap*, Wolfert van Brederode, Maurits Lodewijk van Nassau-Beverweert and

---

75 TNA: PRO, SP 84/198, f° 289–90.
76 Mörke, *Stadtholder oder Staetholder?*, 111, transl. from German.
77 Ibid., 112.
78 Mensema, Mooijweer and Streng, *De Ridderschap van Overijssel*, 87.
79 S. Groenveld, *Evidente Factien in den Staet. Sociaal-Politieke Verhoudingen in de 17ᵉ eeuwse Republiek der Verenigde Nederlanden* (Hilversum, 1990), 62.

Frederik van Reede, making it a reliable Orangist body in the States of Holland.[80] In this manner an Orangist noble network covered the United Provinces. In Mörke's view Bentinck 'formed in this constellation the pinnacle of a hierarchy of influential persons, whose political and social influence went beyond the confines of the Court and into the Republic'.[81]

Most stadholders were influential in the eastern provinces: Gelderland, Overijssel and Utrecht. They were strong in Zeeland but never quite controlled the province that mattered most, Holland, although the *Ridderschap* there normally functioned as his mouth-piece in the Assembly. The northern provinces, Friesland, Groningen and Drenthe, were governed by the Frisian Nassaus for the larger part of the seventeenth and eighteenth centuries.[82]

In the early seventeenth century a courtly society flourished in The Hague. After the Battle at the White Mountain in 1620 the exiled Frederick I of the Palatinate held court in The Hague. One of the ladies-in-waiting to his wife Elizabeth Stuart, Amalia van Solms, would marry Frederick Henry of Orange, indicating the close ties between the Palatinate and Orange courts in The Hague. The latter had become more important after Stadholder Maurice sidelined the Remonstrant party in 1618. It was the second son of William the Silent, however, Frederick Henry, who after 1625 managed to systematically transform the stadholderly court, its splendour attaining quasi-monarchical features. The stadholderly court could compete with that of any of the lesser German princes, the number of courtiers fluctuating between a hundred and fifty during Maurice's early years in the 1580s and about 220 at the end of his stadholderate.[83] An emphatic builder of palaces, he was also the patron of artists such as Gerard Honthorst and Rembrandt van Rijn. His dynastic ambitions culminated in his marrying his son William to Mary Stuart in 1641, linking the Oranges to the foremost Protestant dynasty in Europe.[84]

The stadholders wielded much power, but theoretically they remained subservient to the States-General. Much depended on their personalities and ability to exert influence without upsetting the neatly balanced power relations in the Dutch Republic. Their influence was based as much upon their formal competences as the informal exercise of power and their affirming their authority. William the Silent and his second son Frederick Henry had been conciliatory characters, but Maurice and especially William II had sought confrontation with the regent elites. Whereas Maurice had succeeded in achieving his goals in 1618, the conflict of William II with Amsterdam ended in political disaster in 1650, and his son William III must have been acutely aware of the limits of

---

80 Japikse, *Willem III*, I. 352; Mörke, *Stadtholder oder Staetholder?*, 113.

81 Mörke, *Stadtholder oder Staetholder?*, 170–71, transl. from German.

82 William III was Stadholder of Drenthe between 1696 and 1702.

83 C.J. Zandvliet, 'Het Hof van een Dienaar met Vorstelijke Allure' in: C.J. Zandvliet (ed.), *Maurits Prins van Oranje* (Amsterdam, 2000), 36–63, 43.

84 Israel, *The Dutch Republic*, 306, 480–81, 493; S. Groenveld, 'Frederick Henry and his Entourage: a Brief Political Biography' in: P. van der Ploeg and C. Vermeeren (eds), *Princely Patrons. The Collection of Frederick Henry of Orange and Amalia of Solms in The Hague*. (The Hague/Zwolle, 1997), 18–33.

stadholderly power. These formal limits could be transcended by the employment of an informal clientele of favourites, who maintained relations with political bodies on local, provincial and national levels. In the cities, confidants were entrusted with taking care of his interest in the city councils, advising him on nominations and providing the 'good party' with leadership. Since cities could vote on matters of national interest, the links between the stadholder and such local favourites were not unimportant. First among the stadholder's favourites were the provincial managers, who normally held a pivotal position in the States Assemblies.

Faction struggles among the stadholders' favourites were not uncommon, but were more often connected to personal rivalry and local and provincial interests than to diverging views on political issues.[85] Most of the stadholders' favourites were noblemen rather than regents, not bound to the interest of a specific city. The continuity of the clientele of the stadholders was remarkable.[86] Several families continued to be bound to the Oranges throughout the seventeenth century. Constantijn Huygens, for instance, was in the service of three Princes of Orange and was succeeded by his son Constantijn jr.; the Bentincks can be classified among the staunchly Orangist noble families in the east.

Without this clientele the stadholderly system could not work, since it depended on a mixture of informal and formal power, authority and relations. The municipal and provincial confidants were delegated informal power from the stadholder. This stadholderly system would reach a zenith in Maurice's later years and under Frederick Henry.[87] In Jonathan Israel's words, 'The Republic's political system, under Frederik Hendrik, was shaped by clientage, favours, courtly connections, and noble status, and characterized by a minimum of open debate'.[88] After the disastrous stadholdership of Frederick Henry's son, William II, from 1647–50, the stadholderate was abolished, but reappeared even stronger with the latter's son William III in 1672. Between 1672 and 1674 the Prince assembled arguably more powers than any of his ancestors, particularly in the eastern provinces, where the

---

85   E.g Israel, *Dutch Republic*, 480.
86   Ibid. 525.
87   There has been no study on the stadholderate as such in the seventeenth century (cf. footnote 2). For recent studies on individual stadholders, see K.W. Swart, *William of Orange and the Revolt of the Netherlands, 1572–84*, eds A. Duke et al. (Aldershot, 2003), A. Th. Van Deursen, *Maurits van Nassau, 1567–1625: de Winnaar die Faalde* (Amsterdam, 2000), S. Groenveld, 'Willem II en de Stuarts 1647–1650', *Bijdragen en Mededelingen betreffende de Geschiedenis der Nederlanden*, 103/2 (1988), 157–81, S. Groenveld, 'William III as Stadholder: Prince or Minister?' in: Mijers and Onnekink, *Redefining William III*, 17–38, and W. Troost, *William III*. On the much neglected Frisian stadholders see S. Groenveld et al. (eds), *Nassau uit de Schaduw van Oranje* (Franeker, 2000), G.H. Janssen, *Creaturen van de Macht: Patronage bij Willem Frederik van Nassau (1613–1664)* (Amsterdam, 2005) and Luuc Kooijmans, *Liefde in Opdracht: het Hofleven van Willem Frederik van Nassau* (Amsterdam, 2000). Little has been written on the later stadholders.
88   Israel, *Dutch Republic*, 526.

so-called *regeringsreglementen* (governmental regulations) were introduced. These gave the stadholder extraordinary powers in local and provincial government.[89]

Indicative of this, William's associates in Gelderland managed to have the assembly offer him sovereignty in 1675, which he however felt obliged to decline after Holland protested.[90] No stadholder had ever come closer to obtaining sovereignty in the Dutch Republic, and despite the rebuff the actual concentration of power in the hands of William III and his provincial managers and favourites was unprecedented. William's favourites have almost invariably received a bad press; they have been described as excessively corrupt. Corruption proliferated during stadholderly periods as an essential ingredient in the maintenance of client networks.[91] William did little to combat this as long as his aides remained effective.[92] On a local level, William's favourites sometimes were notoriously corrupt and acted as petty despots, which became an issue of public concern. In Gorcum, the son of Constantijn Huygens, Lodewijk, and in Hoorn François van Bredehoff, were vastly unpopular, as was Willem Adriaan van Nassau-Odijk, William's bastard brother who acted on his behalf in Zeeland.[93] Jacob van Zuylen van Nijvelt, Baillif in Rotterdam, attracted particularly vocal public criticism. A rather vile pamphlet, *De Balliuw van Rotterdam in zijn Hemt*, compared him with Nero, calling him a plague, a monster and a Pharisee.[94]

Bentinck attracted relatively little criticism, and few charges of corruption have been recorded – even though it should be noted that his offices were particularly lucrative.[95] This is surprising, as he stood out as William's favourite and was a natural target for anti-Orangist critiques. Burnet thought that 'He bears his favour with great modesty, and has nothing of that haughtiness that seems to belong to all favourites'.[96] But Bentinck was not among William's governing local or provincial favourites, and perhaps Burnet's observation is more indicative of Bentinck's relative minor, or less visible, role on the political scene. Indeed, critical pamphlets directed against Bentinck first started to appear in Holland in 1690 during his conflict with Amsterdam.[97] Burnet may also have overestimated the political importance of the Orange court, which despite its ambitions could never obtain that centrality of a monarchical court like that of England.

Although due to the lack of relevant source material it is not feasible to get a clear picture of Bentinck's client network, evidence suggests that his power was mainly concentrated at Court. He managed to allot significant posts to his relatives and

---

89 Cf. D.J. Roorda, 'William III and the Utrecht "Government-Regulation": Backgrounds, Events and Problems', *Acta Historiae Neerlandicae*, 12 (1979), 85–109.
90 M.W Hartog, 'Prins Willem III en de Hertogshoed van Gelderland 1673–1675', *Bijdragen en Mededelingen der Vereniging 'Gelre'*, 69 (1976–77), 125–55.
91 De Bruin, *Geheimhouding*, 377–8.
92 Cf. Israel, *The Dutch Republic*, 827.
93 Ibid., 811–27 *passim*.
94 *De Balliuw van Rotterdam in zijn Hemt* (s.l., s.d.).
95 Japikse, *Willem III*, II. 118.
96 Foxcroft, *Supplement*, 196.
97 Cf. Ch. 7.

dependants. In 1680 for instance, he had his cousin Van Voorst appointed steward.[98] Bentinck's position at Court was strengthened through his wife Anne Villiers, who was lady-in-waiting to Princess Mary and a great confidante of hers. The double relationship between the Bentinck and Orange couples was, on balance, certainly beneficial to him. The birth of his eldest daughter and son in 1679 and 1681, named after Mary and William, only strengthened this. More problematic was the role of Elizabeth Villiers, the sister of Bentinck's wife and William's mistress. Though not known for her beauty, she was intelligent, cunning and witty and clearly appealed to William more than did Mary. Bentinck often secretly ushered Elizabeth through his own apartments to those of William.[99] However, a strong dislike of his sister-in-law and a sense of loyalty to Mary – who clearly suffered emotionally from the liaison – led him into perhaps the only outright conflict with his master. When Mary confronted her husband with her knowledge of his amorous affair, both Bentinck and his wife Anne sided with the Princess. William was furious and temporarily banished his confidant from Court.[100] Such a conflict was exceptional, and Bentinck's position at Court remained secure. Adriaan van Borssele described him in 1681 as 'the all-powerful favourite at our Court'.[101]

IV

Towards the end of the Dutch War Bentinck had established himself at Court, and developed a political as well as a military career, although neither very distinguished. In October 1683 he was made one of the five major-generals of the Dutch army, the highest rank under the three lieutenants-general and the commander-in-chief.[102] As military officer he also built up a clientele in the army. Although he yielded when Ginckel passed over his brother Hendrik for promotion in April 1684, he must have been pushing for such an advancement as only nine months later Hendrik received the rank of colonel.[103]

The end of the war in 1678, however, had rendered his duties as military staff officer less important, but Bentinck managed to redirect his career as diplomat. It was only now that the favourite became a more prominent figure on the political scene. In June 1677 the Prince decided to send Bentinck to sound out Charles II about his willingness to mediate in the conflict with France. In order to remove the distrust of his predominantly Protestant parliament, the Lord Treasurer, the Earl of Danby, considered joining an anti-French alliance. Such considerations gained in

---

98 Japikse, *Willem III*, II. 127.
99 M.F. Sandars, *Princess and Queen of England, Life of Mary II* (London, 1913), 142.
100 Ibid., 134; H.W. Chapman, *Mary II, Queen of England* (London, 1953), 123–4.
101 'Gedenkschriften van Adriaan van Borssele van der Hooghe, Heer van Geldermalsen', ed. K. Heeringa, in: *Archief. Vroegere en latere Mededeelingen voornamelijk in Betrekking tot Zeeland* (Middelburg, 1916), 67–136, 81, transl. from French.
102 F.J.G. ten Raa, *Het Staatsche Leger 1568–1795* (The Hague, 1940), VI. 78.
103 Bentinck to Ginckel 27 April 1684 (The Hague), Japikse, *Correspondentie*, XXVII. 637.

importance as Parliament grew increasingly uneasy about the Spanish Netherlands, and pressed the King to counter French territorial ambitions in exchange for generous grants, perhaps even to fund a war. The Dutch ambassador in London, Coenraad van Beuningen, was convinced that Charles II would not support the Dutch, and therefore considered a peace settlement expedient.[104] Frequently reprimanded by the States General on this matter, Van Beuningen had undermined Bentinck's bargaining position by already signalling Dutch eagerness for peace and willingness to make concessions.[105] However, William as well increasingly realised that a peace settlement might be necessary, as can be gleaned from Bentinck's instructions, preserved in a memorandum in his own hand. The apprentice's orders were strict and left little scope for manoeuvring. He was not to make any proposals, but merely to ask the King for his opinion with regard to the state of affairs on the continent. He was to make clear that although William desired to prolong the war, he realised that Charles preferred a peace settlement, and that William was seeking advice on how to conduct himself in that case. Should the King insist on peace, William requested his full diplomatic weight in favour of advantageous terms, whilst being prepared to satisfy the King with territorial gains. Should he still have any 'bad suspicions', Bentinck was to propose that William come over to England.[106]

Bentinck was of course required to sound out those who desired a 'good understanding' between the Oranges and Stuarts. It had really been the influential and ingenious Lord Treasurer who was mainly responsible for the rapprochement evolving during the course of the summer. An exceptionally skilled parliamentary manager, Danby had piloted royal policy through the troubled waters of parliamentary distrust. He was now responsible for steering a cautious pro-Dutch course, labouring to reconcile the war-mongering Commons with their monarch.[107] Unwilling to give Charles the benefit of the doubt, they refused funds and the session was consequently adjourned. William thought, however, that Charles might be more flexible now that the pressure from Parliament was gone, and it was in this conjuncture that Bentinck arrived in London on the 14 June 1677.[108] Ignoring the Dutch ambassador, he went directly to see the King and his brother James, the Duke of York, where he received a warm reception, such that he thought William 'would have reason to be entirely satisfied'.[109] The apprentice's somewhat premature optimism quickly vanished when he found the situation 'on a completely different footing' with Parliament now

---

104 M.A.M. Franken, *Coenraad van Beuningens Politieke en Diplomatieke Activiteiten in de Jaren 1667–1684* (Groningen, 1966), 152.

105 Cf. ibid., 154.

106 Japikse, *Correspondentie*, XXIII. 4–6, transl. from French.

107 A.B. Browning, *Thomas Osborne, Earl of Danby and Duke of Leeds 1632–1712* (3 vols, Glasgow, 1951), I. 225–7. Cf. K.H.D. Haley, 'The Anglo-Dutch Rapprochement of 1677', *English Historical Review*, 73 (1958), 614–48.

108 Browning erroneously suggested that William sent Bentinck *because* Parliament was prorogued. His letter to Bentinck of 11 June 1677 shows that the prorogation took him by surprise. Browning, *Danby*, I. 232; Japikse, *Correspondentie*, XXIII. 6.

109 Bentinck to William 15 June 1677 (Whitehall Palace), Japikse, *Correspondentie*, XXIII. 7, transl. from French; dispatch Courtin 17 June 1677, AAE, CPA 123b, f° 139v°–40r°.

adjourned.[110] Though the Commons tended to favour a Dutch alliance, Bentinck entirely agreed with William that the adjournment was not necessarily detrimental to his interest, for the MPs had shown 'much thoughtless zeal, which has done the more harm to us when we should have expected good for our cause'.[111] But Charles, angered with the conduct of his Parliament, refused to enter into Bentinck's first point as to how the Prince should conduct himself with regard to a possible peace settlement. Bentinck had been irritated with Van Beuningen's untimely concessions to Charles.[112] These must have undermined his somewhat disingenuous reasons which he presumably presented to the King for continuing the war: 'that in case the peace is not advantageous, there are quarrels to be feared' in the United Provinces.[113] However, since he was instructed not to make any proposals so as not to impair the success of his precarious embassy, he refrained from doing so.[114]

Bentinck's mission was brief and yielded few concrete results, but observers credited him for his tact in creating some sort of understanding between Charles and William.[115] If the mission had seemed a failure, it gave Danby the backing he needed to convince Charles of the wisdom of a pro-Dutch foreign policy.[116] All depended, however, on Danby's credit with the King and the latter's willingness to dispatch an emissary to William to discuss the points Bentinck had presented.[117] Bentinck urged the Treasurer 'that you press matters such that the King sends someone as soon as possible to instruct the Prince of his sentiments, so that the good understanding which you yourself have seen beginning to establish itself' could hold.[118] Danby satisfied Bentinck with his assurance that Sir William Temple, a pro-Dutch diplomat, was about to be dispatched.[119] The naiveté of Bentinck's optimism soon became apparent when it appeared that Laurence Hyde, a relative and close confidant of the King, would be dispatched. With regard to Charles's proposals for peace, Bentinck complained, 'the sentiments of the King are very different from what they appeared to me in England'.[120]

However, Hyde was able to offer assurances that William was welcome in England. One of the points in Bentinck's instruction had been to obtain the King's permission for the Prince to come and visit. The issue of a possible marriage between William and Princess Mary, daughter of James, Duke of York, had not been explicitly

---

110   Bentinck to William 18 June 1677 (Whitehall Palace), Japikse, *Correspondentie*, XXIII. 8, transl. from French.

111   William to Bentinck 11 June 1677, Bentinck to William 18 June 1677 (Whitehall Palace), Japikse, *Correspondentie*, XXIII. 6, 8, transl. from French.

112   Bentinck to William 18 June 1677, (Whitehall Palace), ibid., 8.

113   Bentinck's memorandum June 1677, ibid., 5n, transl. from French.

114   Bentinck to William 18 June 1677 (Whitehall Palace), ibid., 8.

115   Haley, 'The Anglo-Dutch Rapprochement', 633.

116   Cf. Browning, *Danby*, I. 233.

117   Bentinck to Danby 25 June 1677 (Lokeren), Browning, *Danby*, II. 390.

118   Bentinck to Danby 25 June 1677 (Lokeren), ibid., 390, transl. from French.

119   Bentinck to Danby 16 July 1677 ('Quartier de Calken'), Danby to Bentinck 29 June 1677, ibid., 391, 392.

120   Bentinck to Danby 18 September 1677 ('A Babin'), ibid., 398, transl. from French.

broached by Bentinck, but preparing the grounds for such a liaison had been one of the main purposes of his mission. The Duke of Ormond, in a letter to Bentinck, had referred to such a connection between the Houses of Orange and Stuart.[121] It had been tentatively discussed as early as 1676 but never formally proposed.[122] The French ambassador Courtin's initial alarm was soon allayed when the Duke of York assured him that a marriage would not be considered at this stage.[123] William had his reservations, as a liaison with Stuart, no matter how desirable, might damage his reputation in Parliament and tie him too closely to the King. But despite James's objections to the marriage between his daughter and a Protestant zealot, Charles gave in to the arguments of the connection's greatest promoter, Danby. In October the Prince, with Bentinck in his entourage, crossed the North Sea to ask for Mary's hand. The marriage took place a few weeks later. Bentinck followed his master's example, and married himself to Anne Villiers, of a distinguished noble family and serving as a lady-in-waiting to the Princess.[124]

The embassy, Bentinck's first diplomatic mission abroad, signified a new stage in his career. Although his responsibilities were restricted, and he only functioned as a personal messenger of the Prince without powers to negotiate, it laid the basis for his increasing involvement in English affairs. His contacts with Ormond and Danby in particular would become fruitful in future years. He also gained experience and became familiarised with the intricacies of the Stuart court. In 1675 the English ambassador had identified Fagel and Nassau-Odijk as William's closest confidants with regard to English affairs, after 1677 Bentinck would increasingly be involved.[125] He was not an exceptionally good diplomat. Men like Nassau-Zuylestein, and Dijkveld in particular, would frequently undertake highly delicate missions with more success. Bentinck showed himself somewhat naive and impressionable during the 1677 mission, which was partly due to his lack of experience. More importantly, however, the quick shifts of court factions and the cynical and volatile nature of Stuart policy required a certain amount of cunning from an ambassador, something Bentinck clearly lacked. William, himself more ingenious, recognised this failure, as, indeed, did Bentinck himself.

And yet William had ample reason to send a confidant to the Court at Whitehall. Referring to his favourite, William wrote to Ossory 'that I esteem him most of all my people'.[126] The French ambassador recognised him as 'the principal confidant of the Prince of Orange'.[127] Equally important, Bentinck had now internationally established his reputation as William's personal emissary. Over the years William would employ Bentinck mainly on missions with regard to his own interest. Bentinck's

---

121 Ormond to Bentinck 12 June 1677 OS, Japikse, *Correspondentie*, XXIV. 3.
122 Browning, *Danby*, I. 248. It was a delicate matter and Danby was hesitant, as a marriage proposal might alienate the Duke of York and force Charles into the Protestant camp.
123 Dispatch Courtin 17 June 1677, AAE, CPA 123b, f° 142r°.
124 Cf. Ch. 4.
125 Cf. page 19.
126 William to Ossory 8 June 1677, Japikse, *Correspondentie*, XXVII. 176, transl. from French.
127 Dispatch Courtin 17 June 1677, AAE, CPA 123b, f° 139v°, transl. from French.

value lay precisely in his role as William's mouthpiece, which provided the Prince with an instrument to voice his personal opinion alongside formal Dutch diplomacy. As such Bentinck held a pivotal position within the Prince's informal network of agents that had proliferated alongside the official Dutch diplomatic service.[128] Often, this parallel service had a different agenda, and the States General's envoys were frequently oblivious as to the underlying purpose of these Williamite missions. With regard to Bentinck's mission in 1677, Van Beuningen informed the States General that Charles II had 'expressed particular confidence in a gentleman who enjoys the intimate favour of His Highness'.[129] His report was certainly tainted with sarcasm, as he must have felt bypassed by the Prince's confidant.

Hence Bentinck was continuously employed by William with regard to the situation in England, to which he was now bound with double dynastic ties. The Exclusion Crisis of 1679–81 was dealt with clumsily by William and his aides.[130] The Stuart court was plagued again in 1683 by the Rye House plot, a conspiracy to assassinate the two royal brothers. Upon its discovery, William again despatched his confidant, ostensibly to congratulate his uncles upon their good fortune, but really to disassociate himself from the conspirators and fathom the King's thoughts concerning foreign affairs. It was a pointless mission and Bentinck did not handle the situation well, nor was his conduct constructive as he frequently lost his temper. But his long private audiences with the King and the Duke of York must have somewhat disconcerted the French ambassador Paul Barillon. Bentinck was under the impression that his attempts to reassure the King that William would do his utmost to pursue suspects of the plot, who were now seeking refuge in the United Provinces, were successful. William was more astute: 'I fear that you slightly flatter yourself'.[131] Bentinck's extreme agitation at Charles's rebuff only worsened matters, and the emissary left dissatisfied with his failed mission.[132]

Obviously, as the French ambassador had noted, 'it is thought that Bentinck is charged for something else than to convey compliments'.[133] Bentinck's chagrin had much to do with his inability to wrest support from Charles in the light of the international crisis arising from Louis's post-war policy. The Peace of Nijmegen had not been unfavourable to the French monarch, but left unsatisfied the need for secure borders. What had not been obtained by the use of force was now sought through legal means by the establishment of the *Chambres des Reunions*. Using ancient charters, these judicial institutions claimed strategic border territories. In the absence of a coherent anti-French alliance, this territorial expansion, supported by the threat of force, met with little resistance. Louis's main opponent, the Emperor,

---

128 Roorda, 'Le secret du Prince'.
129 Van Beuningen to States General 15 June 1677, BL, Add Mss 17677 DD, f° 85v°, transl. from Dutch. Cf. William to Danby 9 June 1677, Browning, *Danby*, II. 388–9.
130 W. Troost, 'Willem III en de "Exclusion Crisis" 1679–1681', *BMGN*, 107 (1992), 28–46.
131 William to Bentinck 2 August 1683, Japikse, *Correspondentie*, XXIII. 4, transl. from French.
132 Barillon to Louis 12 August 1683, AAE, CPA 150, f° 224v°.
133 Barillon to Louis 26 July 1683, ibid., f° 112, transl. from French.

was caught in a desperate defence of the Austrian heartland when a Turkish army besieged Vienna itself in 1683.

During his mission in London, Bentinck had shown himself extremely concerned about what would be the crown on the *reunions*-policy: the capture of Luxembourg. As early as February 1682 he had approached the English envoy Thomas Chudleigh in The Hague to press him to get his master to give assurances with regard to that city.[134] During his embassy, Bentinck had warned Charles 'in much heat ... that the cession of Luxemburg would mean the loss of the Low Countries and that one would better risk everything than to consent to it'.[135] But Charles was unwilling to become embroiled in a conflict with Louis XIV. Bentinck was unable to support the pro-Dutch faction in the Cabinet Council, which had battled in vain for intervention.[136] Nor did Bentinck's exhortations carry much weight, as the Spanish and Dutch ambassadors Pedro Ronquillo and Arnout van Citters did not support him.[137]

The latter was of some concern to William. Ever since the middle of the 1670s the Stadholder and Holland, particularly Amsterdam, had drifted apart in matters pertaining to the general course of foreign policy. Amsterdam was not unwilling to use force under certain circumstances, but someone like Van Beuningen, now burgomaster, thought that firm resistance against French aggression was expedient only if the Dutch were supported by a resolute international alliance. With the Emperor embroiled with the Turks, Charles II unwilling to intervene and the Spaniards lethargic, the only option for the Amsterdammers was not to antagonise the French.[138]

The siege of Luxembourg triggered a domestic crisis when the Captain-General urged the States to send 16,000 troops to the rescue as obliged under a treaty with Spain. Bentinck condemned 'the stubbornness of the gentlemen of Amsterdam, or rather that of Mr Van Beuningen'.[139] He was part of William's train when the latter visited Amsterdam in November 1683 in order to put pressure on the city.[140] A compromise seemed unlikely, as William regarded the integrity of the Barrier against France as the cornerstone of his lifelong strategy. A constitutional crisis occurred when the Captain-General tried to push a resolution through the States General for the recruitment of troops despite fierce resistance from the deputies from Groningen

---

134 Chudleigh to Conway 27 February 1682 NS, *The Dispatches of Th. Plott (1681–1682) and Th. Chudleigh (1682–1685): English Envoys at the Hague*, ed. F.A. Middlebush (Rijksgeschiedkundige Publicatiën 'Kleine Reeks', XXII, The Hague, 1926), 52.

135 Barillon to Louis 2 August 1683, AAE, CPA 150, f° 146v°, transl. from French.

136 Citters to William 6 August 1683 NS, Japikse, *Correspondentie*, XXVII. 585.

137 Barillon to Louis 2 August 1683, AAE, CPA 150, f° 146.

138 Van Beuningen to William 12 November 1683, Japikse, *Correspondentie*, XXVII. 614–16. On Dutch foreign policy in this period, see also M.A.M. Franken, 'The General Tendencies and Structural Aspects of Foreign Policy and Diplomacy of the Dutch Republic in the latter Half of the Seventeenth Century', *Acta Historiae Neerlandica*, 3 (1968), 1–42.

139 Bentinck to Ginckel 13 November 1683 (The Hague), Japikse, *Correspondentie*, XXVII. 616, transl. from French.

140 *Négociations de Monsieur le Comte d'Avaux*, II. 1 ff.; Israel, *The Dutch Republic*, 831–2.

and Friesland.[141] Meanwhile Bentinck had expressed sharp criticism of a meeting between the English ambassador and Amsterdam regents to discuss a French offer for an international truce, accusing them of forming a party against the Prince.

> They [the French] reject the conditions of the proposed cease fire in order to force us to accept conditions more shameful and ruinous, our affairs seem to be in a desperate state if England does not support us, but take guard that we, falling into despair, do not talk like Samson, when he tore down the pillar which maintained the house, may Samson perish with the Philistines.[142]

As a high-ranking officer he was involved in the logistics of the preparations for the campaign to Luxembourg, giving instructions to Ginckel for provisions and marching orders.[143] He was involved in negotiating with provisioners for forage.[144] To Ginckel he complained: 'We are grieved to learn that they defend themselves well in Luxemburg, while we cannot rescue them, although the whole of Germany marches. But I fear that it will be mustard after the meal.'[145] He proved right, as Luxembourg fell in July 1684. Relations between the Prince and Amsterdam reached a low point. Despite casual interventions, there are few indications that Bentinck played a significant role in the political arm-wrestling during the 1683–84 crisis.

V

The death of Charles in February 1685 was a shock to Bentinck, as James II, who succeeded his brother, was a known Catholic.[146] William became immediately embroiled in English affairs as he hosted the Duke of Monmouth, Charles's bastard son. When the Duke had arrived in Holland, William dispatched Bentinck to fetch him to The Hague, and he organised balls in his honour. Bentinck was much concerned with Monmouth, and seems to have held some sway over the impressionable young man.[147] Refuting criticism of their conduct, the favourite let it be known that nothing was done in this matter that did not please Charles.[148]

The situation changed with Charles's death, as James disapproved of the presence of Monmouth, a dynastic rival and magnet of English Protestant discontent, in The

---

141 Troost, *William III*, 166–71.

142 Bentinck to Sidney 4 February 1684, 17 March 1684 (The Hague), BL, Add Mss 32681, f° 263–4, 267v°, transl. from French.

143 Bentinck to Ginckel 28 March 1684 (The Hague), Japikse, *Correspondentie*, XXIV. 632.

144 Bentinck to Ginckel 31 March 1684 (The Hague), 27 April 1684 (The Hague), Japikse, *Correspondentie*, XXIV. 633–4, 637; Bentinck to Sidney 22 February 1684 (The Hague), *Diary of the Times of Charles the Second, by the Honourable Henry Sidney, afterwards Earl of Romney*, ed. R.W. Blencowe (2 vols, London, 1843), II. 238.

145 Bentinck to Ginckel 2 June 1684 (The Hague), Japikse, *Correspondentie*, XXVII. 640, transl. from French.

146 Bentinck to Sidney 21 Feb. 1685 (The Hague), BL, Add Mss 32681, f° 274r°.

147 *Négociations de Monsieur le Comte d'Avaux*, IV. 225 ff.

148 Ibid., 217.

Hague. When the news of Charles's death reached The Hague, Bentinck declared that Monmouth had been sent away from Court – at James's request – but in fact he had sent for the Duke immediately and closeted with him for some time.[149] Monmouth left the following day, but D'Avaux noted that a page of Monmouth's arrived in The Hague at night, spoke to Bentinck only, gave him a letter and returned the following evening to receive an answer. They remained in contact during the ensuing weeks.[150] Meanwhile English and Scottish refugees were planning a descent and managed to draw the Duke into their plot. It is unlikely that Bentinck was wholly unaware of the proceedings, as he remained in contact with Monmouth throughout the spring, but there is no evidence that he was in any way involved.[151] There was a certain cunning to this tactic. William ostensibly complied with James's demand but through Bentinck continued to monitor the Duke's movements. Throughout the spring William went to great lengths to present himself as a dependable ally to the new sovereign, ostensibly detaching himself from Monmouth who appeared to have some support in Amsterdam.

Bentinck's expertise with regard to English affairs enabled him to play a more prominent role in the Holland States Assembly. He created a spectacle during a discussion on the possibility of sending the Anglo-Dutch regiments to James's aid, by ceremoniously drawing from his pocket a paper containing a personal request from the King. The delegates were shocked that such a weighty request was communicated 'through such an unnatural channel'.[152] Bentinck had increasingly become a conduit between English and Dutch politicians, and after the incident he communicated to Lord Treasurer Rochester that he had been instrumental in serving the King's interest in spite of opposition.[153] Meanwhile Nassau-Ouwerkerk, even though he had recently been seen toasting the destruction of the Duke of York, was audaciously dispatched to assure the new king of William's good will.[154] Bentinck assured Rochester that they were doing all they could to inform the new ministry of the movements of Scottish and English refugees, telling the Lord Treasurer that Argyle's three ships that had left for Scotland had completely escaped their attention. The Prince wrote to James that he was also 'exceedingly troubled' at Monmouth's escape, and assured the English ambassador Bevil Skelton that such a thing would not happen again.[155] The disingenuous efforts of William and Bentinck to reassure the English were only partially successful. Rochester was suspicious, and Skelton increasingly hostile to Bentinck who had clearly overplayed his hand in this matter as his connection with

---

149   D'Avaux to Louis 22 Feb. 1685, AAE, CPH 141, f° 190r°. Cf. *Négociations de Monsieur le Comte d'Avaux*, IV. 270–71.

150   E.g. *Négociations de Monsieur le Comte d'Avaux,* IV. 316.

151   Ibid., 347.

152   *Négociations de Monsieur le Comte d'Avaux*, V. 48, transl. from French.

153   William to Rochester 9 June 1685, *The Correspondence of H.H. Earl of Clarendon and of his Brother, Laurence Hyde, Earl of Rochester; with the Diary of Lord Clarendon from 1687 to 1690 ... and the Diary of Lord Rochester during his Embassy to Poland in 1676*, ed. S.W. Singer (2 vols, London, 1828), I. 128.

154   *Négociations de Monsieur le Comte d'Avaux*, IV. 281.

155   Bentinck to Rochester 25 May 1685 (Honselaarsdijk), Singer, *Diary of Clarendon*, I. 125–6; dispatch Skelton 8/18 May 1685, BL, Add Mss 41812, f° 57–60.

Monmouth had been too obvious.[156] Bentinck tried hard to appease the English, frequently feeding Skelton scraps of intelligence which were dismissed as 'canting impudent stuff'. In his despatches, however, Skelton put the blame for Monmouth's escape to England mainly on the Amsterdam authorities.[157] Thus Monmouth's rebellion was also exploited in a domestic dispute between William and Amsterdam over the course of foreign policy and the size of the standing army.[158]

That spring William launched a diplomatic offensive of three missions to London, all dominated by his confidants. At Charles's death William had sent Nassau-Ouwerkerk to congratulate the new king, assuring him that William was willing to admit his past mistakes and follow James's lead.[159] A formal embassy had already been dispatched to London consisting of Wassenaar-Duyvenvoorde, Citters and Dijkveld, all, as Bentinck wrote to Sidney, 'well-intentioned to the interests of His Highness'.[160] James had demanded from William that he abandon Monmouth, appoint new officers to the Anglo-Dutch brigades in the Republic and support his policies. In the new constellation William had to regain the confidence of the new monarch, and promptly complied with the first two conditions, whilst temporising on the latter.[161] 'His Highness will certainly do all that the King will expect of him', Bentinck assured Sidney, 'apart from the religion, I believe you know him well enough that he does not do things half.'[162]

When the news arrived that Monmouth and his rebels were actually sailing to England and Scotland, William realised he must act swiftly. His decision to despatch Bentinck was a calculated risk. D'Avaux, perhaps influenced by Skelton, thought that

> The British king is persuaded that Bentinck is his personal enemy, that he has continuously had commerce with Monmouth and such without any encouragement from the side of the King of England, he is not a proper and agreeable man to be sent.[163]

But William must have been confident that his ambassador would be able to remove James's suspicions as to his conduct in the Monmouth affair. William and Bentinck thought that Skelton had been sending critical reports about their conduct to London, and the Prince demanded his recall, hoping perhaps this would ease

---

156 Bentinck to Rochester 10 April 1685 (The Hague), William to Rochester 10 April 1685, Rochester to William n.d. no. 91, Singer, *Diary of Clarendon*, I. 119–23; dispatch Skelton 15/25 May 1685, BL, Add Mss 41812, f° 76 ff.

157 Dispatch Skelton 15/25 May 1685, BL, Add Mss 41812, f° 76 ff., and *passim*; D'Avaux to Louis 19 April 1685, AAE, CPH 141, f° 395v°.

158 Cf. W.R. Emerson, *Monmouth's Rebellion* (New Haven/London, 1951), ch. 3.

159 Barillon to Louis 1 March 1685, C.J. Fox, *History of the Early Part of the Reign of James the Second* (London, 1808), Appendix, xxxvii ff.

160 Bentinck to Sidney 30 March 1685 (The Hague), BL, Add Mss 32681, f° 278r°, transl. from French.

161 *Négociations de Monsieur le Comte d'Avaux*, IV. 305 ff.

162 Bentinck to Sidney 11 March 1685 (Dieren), BL, Add Mss 32681, f° 276–7, transl. from French.

163 D'Avaux to Louis 5 July 1685, AAE, CPH 142, f° 188v°–r°, transl. from French.

Bentinck's mission.[164] The gamble paid off, and the Prince managed to gain credit with James and discredit his opponents in Amsterdam at the same time. Two Amsterdam representatives were reprimanded by James in the presence of the full Cabinet Council for their failure to stop Monmouth, and the embassy, dominated by William's aides, did little to alleviate the city's plight.[165]

Bentinck was well informed regarding James's sentiments because of Nassau-Ouwerkerk's dispatches. Moreover, he had sent Abel Tassin D'Alonne, his confidant and Mary's secretary, to accompany the Ambassador and to contact a number of allies in England. To Sidney he wrote that he could speak freely with the secretary.[166] Bentinck's instructions make clear the twofold purpose of his mission. In the short term, he needed to assure James of William's sincerity and his willingness to dispatch the Anglo-Dutch regiments should there be a need for them. The eagerness William displayed to come over in person to command the troops and suppress the rebellion shows to what extent he desired a reconciliation with James. It might weaken his appeal to the English opposition, but it was a cunning move, for James would have to acknowledge the offer, even if he was disinclined to accept it. Second, Bentinck was to sound out James about the course of his foreign policy, whether he would rely on the King of France or on the States General.[167] Bentinck arrived in London and immersed himself in a struggle with the French envoy Barillon for James's favour. He found out that Skelton had given the new king a negative impression of him, as a result of which Bentinck was rebuffed on his first audience with James when asking permission for William to come over to command the troops personally.[168] Nevertheless, Bentinck was able to offer James the services of the three regiments, who arrived in Gravesend the day after. On 6 July William was able to inform his ambassador that the three Anglo-Dutch regiments would be sailing to England as well.[169] The Ambassador was working hard to gain James's confidence and remove any bad impressions he might have had of him as well as to dissolve James's scepticism towards his own nephew.[170]

Despite rumours to the contrary, William arduously desired that the rebellion be suppressed.[171] Bentinck's main purpose of course was to draw James into an Anglo-

---

164 William to James 25 June 1685, Blencowe, *Diary*, 251–3. Cf. Grew, *Bentinck*, 92–4.

165 *Verbaal van de Buitengewone Ambassade van Jacob van Wassenaar-Duivenvoorde, Arnout van Citters en Everard van Weede van Dijkveld naar Engeland in 1685* (Utrecht, 1863), 29. Cf. dispatch Skelton 31 March 1685, 5/15 June 1685, BL, Add Mss 41812, f° 7–8, 119; D'Avaux to Louis 6 July 1685, AAE, CPH 142, f° 204r°.

166 Bentinck to Sidney 21 February 1685 (The Hague), BL, Add Mss 32681, f° 274–5.

167 Instruction Bentinck 4 July 1685, Japikse, *Correspondentie*, XXIII. 20–21.

168 D'Avaux to Louis 5 July 1685, AAE, CPH 142, f° 188v°; A. Boyer, *The History of King William III the Third* (3 vols, London, 1702–03), I. 27.

169 William to Bentinck 6 July 1685, Japikse, *Correspondentie*, XXIII. 21.

170 James to William 30 June 1685, J. Dalrymple (ed.), *Memoirs of Great Britain and Ireland etc.* (2 vols, London, 1790), II. 131–2.

171 William to Bentinck 10 July 1685, Japikse, *Correspondentie*, XXIII. 22; Bentinck to Fagel 24 July 1685 (London), Japikse, *Correspondentie*, XXVII. 703.

Dutch alliance, or at least to pull him out of the French sphere of influence. Bentinck was not unsuccessful in this respect.[172] He suggested to James that it could clearly be seen that the rebellion was supported by the French. He seemed to have been convinced, by 'the manner in which the King conducts himself', that James believed him.[173] Obviously he was overly optimistic, and both Barillon and Skelton were convinced that James distrusted him. But the French faction at Court was losing ground rapidly – if only temporarily – when the Ambassador could ensure Dutch military support to suppress the rebellion, whilst Louis snubbed the new king by refusing more French subsidies. Barillon's position at Court was weak; according to Bentinck he 'is not as active at Court as before, the King speaks to him but little'.[174] The lengthy discussions Bentinck held with Rochester caused concern among the pro-French faction at Court, although the exact contents remain unclear and the Lord Treasurer was sceptical.[175] In his letter to William he referred to Bentinck personally rather than elaborating at length about their discussions.[176]

On 20 July, the rebellion having been suppressed, William ordered his ambassador to return to The Hague. He must have talked to the King about the Anglo-Dutch regiments that were to be returned and his inadvisable intention to appoint Catholic officers. Before Bentinck left, James had summoned him to speak to him personally. The contents of the conversation are not recorded, but immediately afterwards Dijkveld was able to re-initiate the deadlocked talks on the renewal of the Anglo-Dutch treaties.[177] Although on 14 July William had written to Bentinck that he feared that the three Dutch ambassadors – Dijkveld, Wasssenaar and Citters – would return without having achieved anything, contrary to the expectations they now made progress in renewing the alliance.[178] In fact, throughout the summer James seemed to be trying to wrest himself free from French interference, and both domestically and internationally William's position strengthened considerably. All existing treaties were renewed in August and the English ambassador in Paris, William Trumbull, was ordered to appeal to the French king on behalf of William with regard to the principality of Orange.[179] In Madrid William's aide Coenraad van Heemskerck was negotiating with the Spanish to renew their treaties with the Republic.[180] Moreover, the Brandenburg envoy Paul Fuchs was ordered to conclude a treaty with the States General as well, and French diplomacy suffered serious setbacks throughout the summer.[181]

---

172   Cf. D'Avaux to Louis 19 July 1685, AAE, CPH 142, f° 219v°.
173   Bentinck to William n.d. July 1685, Japikse, *Correspondentie*, XXIII. 23, transl. from French.
174   Bentinck to William n.d. July 1685, ibid., 23, transl. from French.
175   J.P. Kenyon, *Robert Spencer, Earl of Sunderland 1621–1702* (London, 1958), 118.
176   Rochester to William 20 July 1685, Japikse, *Correspondentie*, XXVII. 705.
177   *Négociations de Monsieur le Comte d'Avaux*, V. 99.
178   William to Bentinck 14 July 1685, Japikse, *Correspondentie*, XXIII. 24.
179   J. Rule, 'France Caught between Two Balances: the Dilemma of 1688' in: L.G. Schwoerer (ed.), *The Revolution of 1688–1689: Changing Perspectives* (Cambridge, 1992), 35–52, 41–2.
180   Heemskerck to William 30 August 1685, Japikse, *Correspondentie*, XXVII. 710.
181   Rule, 'France Caught between Two Balances', 35–51 and *passim*.

If Bentinck's responsibilities during his missions of 1677 and 1683 were restricted and his success limited, his embassy in 1685 was of some significance as the apprentice had matured and developed his diplomatic skills. He had assumed more responsibility now as he also acted as conduit between William and the other ambassadors in London.[182] The Prince had left his ambassador an unusually free hand compared to his first mission, and trusted him to judge the situation on the spot and take measures accordingly. Bentinck's sense of independence as an ambassador clearly resonates in the correspondence, particularly when he twice flatly ignored a direct order to return to The Hague immediately.[183] Bentinck, being intimately informed about William's ideas, was clearly confident that his conduct would be tolerated.

If Bentinck's diplomatic career had taken off, his activities in the States Assembly remained inconspicuous. D'Avaux seldom mentions him with regard to political affairs before 1685. Nassau-Odijk, Dijkveld and Fagel figured as William's most useful aides with regard to the management of the States of Zeeland, Utrecht and Holland respectively, and Bentinck seems to have played a supporting role to the Grand Pensionary. In November 1684, for instance, Fagel could not be present at an important session of the States of Holland, and advised William to be there instead. Unable to attend himself, the Prince asked Bentinck, not so much to take care of affairs, but to have the item postponed for a few days.[184] Although Bentinck sometimes spoke in the States of Holland, unlike Fagel he did not act as a political manager.

This started to change during the course of 1685. The Dutch could still entertain some hopes for an understanding with James II, but their mutual relationship rapidly deteriorated over the ensuing years.[185] Bentinck undertook several informal missions to muster domestic support for William's policy, particularly as the changing configuration abroad affected domestic relations. In the spring of 1685 William and Amsterdam still clashed over an augmentation of the army. During a heated debate in the Holland States Assembly, Fagel had threatened the Amsterdam delegates that if they did not comply other means would be used. Upon the inquiry of the Amsterdammers whether the Grand Pensionary was threatening to use violence, Bentinck flatly answered that they could interpret the Grand Pensionary's words in any way they liked.[186] But despite such quarrels, relations between the Prince and Amsterdam improved as the apparent upsurge of aggressive Catholicism in England and France caused many changes of heart in the city councils as well. While the nucleus of the Orangist provincial faction in Holland gained in significance, the Republican faction led by Amsterdam was losing strength.[187] In Amsterdam Van

---

182 William to Bentinck 14 July 1685, Japikse, *Correspondentie*, XXIII. 24.
183 William to Bentinck 17 July 1685, 20 July 1685, ibid., 25, 28.
184 William to Bentinck 7 November 1684, ibid., 20.
185 J. Miller, *James II – A Study in Kingship* (London, 1989), 158.
186 *Négociations de Monsieur le Comte d'Avaux*, IV. 322–5.
187 Groenveld, *Evidente Factien,* 67.

Beuningen now wheeled into the Prince's interest.[188] In December 1684 Bentinck had been dispatched on a seemingly hopeless mission to detach the Frisian Stadholder Hendrik Casimir II from the 'peace party'. The latter had arrived in Amsterdam to confirm his support for that party and repudiate rumours of a reconciliation with William. Bentinck visited the Stadholder but was slighted and achieved little in several meetings.[189] Now the Leeuwarden theologian Van der Waayen managed a reconciliation between Hendrik Casimir and William.[190]

From about 1685 Bentinck started to play a more prominent role in the States Assembly of Holland. He would attend when matters vital to the interest of the Stadholder and Captain-General were debated, in particular in efforts to persuade the cities to prepare for French aggression. In 1686 Bentinck was dispatched by William to take part in the deliberations on the augmentation of ground and naval forces.[191] Some notes have been preserved as minutes of the meeting of the States of Holland in July deliberating this matter. During 1686 and 1687, despite the rapprochement between Amsterdam and William, his confidants frequently quarrelled with the Amsterdam representatives in the States of Holland. In July 1686 a motion was put forward to prorogue the ineffective session. Bentinck clashed with the Amsterdam Pensionary Jacob Hop in a furious attempt to prolong the session.[192] He lingered on in The Hague until late September without reaching an agreement on the ways and means. In December he was involved in a continuous dispute between William and Dordrecht.[193] March 1687 saw Bentinck in The Hague witnessing debates on the ways and means.[194] Still, these fragmentary insights into Bentinck's activities in the Assembly do not suggest that he played a prominent role, but rather that he acted in tandem with the Grand Pensionary, William's other confidant, who must be identified as his real political manager in the States.

VI

The basis for Bentinck's success as William's favourite had been a close, solid friendship, forged during their teenage years by similar temperaments and interests. But the real key to his success was his ability to emerge from the turbulent changes in 1672 as William's closest adviser. Competing with rivals who were in many ways his superiors in ability and experience, he managed to retain the confidence and favour of the Prince through loyalty and ambition. The years between 1672 and 1676 were

---

188 *Négociations de Monsieur le Comte d'Avaux*, IV. 360–61. The Prince refused to be reconciled with Van Beuningen.

189 Ibid, 183. Cf. G.H. Kurtz, *Willem III en Amsterdam 1683–1685* (Utrecht, 1928), 160–61.

190 *Négociations de Monsieur le Comte d'Avaux*, IV. 294–5.

191 Again evidence is scarce, only two letters of William from 1686 are preserved. William to Bentinck 21 July 1686, Japikse, *Correspondentie*, XXIII. 30.

192 BL, Eg Mss 1754B, f° 34r°; D'Avaux to Louis 1 August 1686, AAE, CPH 147, f° 102.

193 Cf. BL, Eg Mss 1754B, f° 53–4.

194 William to Fagel 27 March 1687, Japikse, *Correspondentie*, XXVII. 747.

the true formative years, during which Bentinck became a staff officer and gained some political experience. His career reached a relative zenith in 1676, epitomised by his acquiring an estate and subsequent entrance into the Holland *Ridderschap*. By that time he had attained high military rank and a significant position in the Holland States Assembly and had emerged as William's favourite at Court, a position he maintain throughout the 1680s. The end of the war necessitated a shift in his career, as his military duties became less important. He developed as a diplomat during his missions to London in 1677, 1683 and 1685.

Undoubtedly Bentinck was the foremost in William's confidence, and he managed to remain in his favour for two decades. Nevertheless, it is not at all clear that he was particularly influential. He held a seat in the Holland States Assembly, in which body he played a rather inconspicuous role, however, aiding the Grand Pensionary. As such he cannot be classified amongst William's provincial managers, such as Dijkveld and Nassau-Odijk who exerted rather more influence in the States Assemblies in Utrecht and Zeeland. As a result, Bentinck was never as odious to William's opponents as were the provincial and local Orangist managers. Bentinck did play an active role in William's diplomatic service, being entrusted with important missions. His diplomatic career had been forged between 1677 and 1685, by which time he had reached an equal footing with men like Nassau-Zuylestein and Dijkveld, although his abilities and experience were clearly inferior. He did seem very capable as a staff officer and military secretary, and he managed to work his way up through the ranks. By the end of 1683 he was one of the highest-ranking officers in the Dutch army. His organisational skills were evident, but as a strategist or commander he appears to have been average. It was only at the stadholderly court that Bentinck became a dominant figure.

Bentinck's role in Williamite politics throughout the 1670s and early 1680s may not have been a dominant one, by the late 1680s he had emerged as the undisputed – although by no means all-powerful – *primus inter pares* among William's favourites, influential in political, diplomatic and military affairs. He was probably the only one of William's favourites who was involved in all aspects of government. He was primarily the Prince's mouthpiece, conveying his opinion in the States of Holland and on diplomatic missions. It was precisely the combination of his experience as soldier, diplomatist, manager and politician that would contribute to his grandest moment in preparing the invasion for the Glorious Revolution. The following chapter, then, will look at the events of 1688 in which Bentinck played a pivotal role.

Chapter 2

For Religion and Liberty? The Crises of 1688

During the course of 1688 a sequence of seemingly unrelated succession crises escalated into grand-scale warfare. In May 1685 the Elector Palatinate, Karl von Simmern, had died, and was succeeded by the anti-French Philip Wilhelm von Pfaltz-Neuburg. Louis XIV disputed the succession on behalf of his sister-in-law, the Duchess of Orleans, and in 1688 threatened to invade under pretence of defending her claim to part of the Palatinate.[1] A similar threat loomed over Cologne, ruled by the sickly archbishop Maximilian Henry of Wittelsbach. In January 1688, with French support, Wilhelm von Fürstenberg had been elected coadjutor, a position in which he was in effective control of the actual administration. Due to his dispute with Louis over the Gallican articles, however, the Pope was unwilling to confirm Fürstenberg's coadjutorship and, after the death of the ecclesiastical prince, unlikely to support his candidacy for the see.[2] A third crisis emerged in England, where James II antagonised the political nation with his controversial religious policies, reaching a climax in June 1688 with the imprisonment of the seven bishops and the controversy around the birth of the Prince of Wales. The vulnerable Dutch state found itself in the middle of these alarming developments. As in 1672 there was an increasing feeling of being prey to the rising powers of absolutism and Catholicism, as France turned its gaze to the Rhine principalities, and England was felt to threaten the United Provinces.

To date, no satisfactory analysis of Dutch strategic considerations in 1688 has appeared. Historians studying the Glorious Revolution, however, have become increasingly aware of the significance of the Dutch intervention in England. To Jonathan Israel, William III and the Dutch army played a decisive role in bringing about the revolution, as part of a strategic masterstroke to win over Britain as an ally against France. Israel's insistence on placing events in a wider, international context, has done much to explain events. Yet taking the consequences of this argument even further, it should be pointed out that in the summer of 1688 the situation in England was not the only priority for the Dutch. Kenneth Haley has already noted that developments in the Holy Roman Empire have often been neglected when

---

1 G. Symcox, 'Louis XIV and the Outbreak of the Nine Years War' in: R. Hatton (ed.), *Louis XIV and Europe* (London, 1976), 179–212.

2 J.B. Wolf, *Louis XIV* (London, 1968), 435–9; for Fürstenberg's career, see J.T. O'Connor, *Negotiator out of Season: the Career of Wilhelm Egon von Fürstenberg 1629 to 1704* (Athens, 1978).

the events of 1688 are studied.[3] The preponderance of an interpretation of Dutch policy as focused mainly on events in England has been reinforced by some of the main contemporary chroniclers, most notably Gilbert Burnet and Count d'Avaux. Their accounts of events (Burnet's *History of My Own Time* and the Ambassador's memoirs) constitute rich sources and are often referred to by historians. Both authors emphasised that William was only using his involvement in the Cologne affair to camouflage his intentions towards England. Most historians seem to accept this view.[4] But these two chroniclers interpreted the events from their own, foreign, perspectives, and were writing with hindsight. Dutch contemporary sources, such as the *Hollandsche Mercurius* but later also Wagenaar's *Vaderlandsche Historie*, pay far more attention to the Cologne affair.[5] To fully understand the Dutch position in 1688, attention must be paid to the international force field, in particular the Franco-German tensions along the Rhine.

This chapter aims to at least partially fill this gap by analysing Bentinck's diplomatic missions to Germany during the summer of 1688, and will situate the decision to invade England within a sequence of interlocking international and domestic events that can provide some explanation for Dutch policy. Bentinck's correspondence and activities during the early months of 1688 strongly suggest that the Dutch were primarily concerned with the crisis in Germany as a possible trigger for war – which indeed it became – rather than with English domestic troubles. It is therefore worth studying Bentinck's diplomatic mission to Berlin, following the death of the Great Elector of Brandenburg in May. The chapter is essentially a case study, and will analyse Bentinck's involvement in the preparations for the invasion of England and his role during the revolution itself. Drawing from Dutch source material illustrating the role of William's Dutch advisers during the dramatic changes in England, it will offer an analysis complementary to the findings of existing English literature. The events in the spring and summer of 1688 also provide a window for the historian on the concentration of power in the hands of the Stadholder and his

---

3   K.H.D. Haley, 'The Dutch Invasion and the Alliance of 1689' in: L.G. Schwoerer (ed.), *The Revolution of 1688, Changing Perspectives* (Cambridge, 1992), 21–35, 24n.

4   Most analyses have paid little attention to the German context: Israel, 'Dutch Role'; S. Groenveld, '"J'equippe une Flotte très Considerable": the Dutch Side of the Glorious Revolution' in: R. Beddard (ed.), *The Revolutions of 1688* (Oxford 1988), 213–46, 240–2. In support of my view, cf. Haley, 'The Dutch Invasion', 24n. Louis was therefore right in his assumption that the most likely course of action the Dutch would take was to intervene in the Rhineland, rather than in England.

5   G. Burnet, *History of His Own Time* (6 vols, London, 1725); *Négociations de Monsieur le Comte d'Avaux en Hollande depuis 1679 jusqu'en 1688* (6 vols. Paris, 1752–53); J. Wagenaar, *Vaderlandsche Historie, vervattende de Geschiedenissen der nu Vereenigde Nederlanden, Inzonderheid die van Holland, van de Vroegste Tyden af* (21 vols, Amsterdam, 1752), XV.

advisers.[6] Although the importance of William's advisers has been recognised, little research has been undertaken which would illuminate their influence and impact.[7]

I

During the late 1680s there seemed to be a gradual shift in the balance of power within the essentially bi-polar system, dominated by Habsburg and Bourbon. In 1683 the Imperial army recovered from the disastrous state of affairs and managed to force the Turkish troops into retreat. This tilted the balance in Eastern Europe to the advantage of Vienna and added to the prestige and quality of the Emperor's forces. The successful military campaigns, gaining impetus after 1683 and culminating in the recovery of Hungary in 1687, enabled the Emperor to turn westward and focus on the Rhine, now once more the epicentre of European politics due to the Habsburg-Bourbon antagonism. At the same time French influence in a number of principalities in the Holy Roman Empire declined. The formation of the League of Augsburg in 1686 and the defection of Brandenburg and Bavaria to the Austrian camp induced Louis XIV to adopt a less aggressive, or even defensive, strategy.[8]

A parallel development saw the re-emergence of aggressive, state-dominated Catholicism.[9] 'Our loss is great enough to occupy all our thoughts, and to fill our minds with fear for the Protestant religion', Bentinck had worriedly written to his friend Henry Sidney upon the death of Charles II and the subsequent coming to the throne of his brother James, the Duke of York, in early 1685.[10] The reasons for his anxiety were by no means unfounded. On various occasions Bentinck had been sent to London to improve relations with the new king. The inherently unstable Stuart monarchy and its capricious foreign policy caused concern abroad, the more so since it soon seemed that Protestant England was now ruled by a popish zealot. The catholicising process appeared to go hand in hand with absolutist tendencies, and was the more sinister for its coinciding with the aggressive and absolutist policies of Louis XIV, culminating in the Edict of Fontainebleau and leading to the persecution

---

6   Cf. G. de Bruin, *Geheimhouding en Verraad. De Geheimhouding van Staatszaken ten tijde van de Republiek (1600–1750)* (The Hague, 1991), 347.

7   N. Japikse, *Prins Willem III – De Stadhouder-Koning* (2 vols, Amsterdam, 1933), I. 357–9; S.B. Baxter, *William III* (London, 1966), 274; J.R. Jones, *The Revolution of 1688 in England* (London, 1984), 222–3; 'Bentink, Dykvelt, Herbert and Van Hulst, were for two months constantly at the Hague, giving all necessary orders, with so little noise that nothing broke out all that while. Even in lesser matters favourable circumstances concurred to cover his design.' Burnet, *History*, III. 1311.

8   J. Rule, 'France Caught between Two Balances: the Dilemma of 1688' in: Schwoerer, *The Revolution of 1688–1689*, 35–52, 35–42. Rule actually distinguishes three power blocs.

9   P.J.A.N. Rietbergen, 'William of Orange (1650–1702) between European Politics and European Protestantism: the Case of the Huguenots' in: J.A.H. Bots and G.H.M. Posthumus Meyjes (eds), *La Révocation de l'Édit de Nantes et les Provinces-Unies* (Amsterdam, 1986), 35–51. See also R. Hatton, 'Louis XIV and his Fellow Monarchs' in: Hatton, *Louis XIV and Europe*, 16–59, 43.

10   Bentinck to Sidney 21 February 1685 (The Hague), BL, Add Mss 32681, f° 274–5, transl. from French.

and (unintended) expulsion of the Huguenots. The shockwaves of indignation from Protestants were shared by Catholics – including the Pope himself, implying that the events did not necessarily lead to renewed religious antagonism. The intertwining, however, of aggressive Catholicism and absolutist tendencies within the framework of the existing balance of power was the main contributor to the forming of new alliances between 1685 and 1688.

During the first two years James had sought various domestic allies to support his policies, but the autumn of 1687 witnessed a noted change in his tactics; the unexpected pregnancy of Mary of Modena opened the possibility of a Catholic heir, and the King now embarked on a steady course to restructure the corporations and pack Parliament. This radicalisation revived the fear of popery and James's supposed secret understanding with Louis.[11] If William had any hopes of drawing James into an anti-French coalition, they were now abandoned. He resolutely distanced himself from his uncle's policy in public and crippled James's attempt to abolish both the Test Act and Penalty Laws. Relations deteriorated and appeared tense beyond reconciliation. The King regarded William's propaganda campaign as a direct attack upon himself. The fact that William maintained relations and harboured on Dutch territory English and Scottish exiles such as Gilbert Burnet infuriated the King. William was obliged to publicly distance himself from them. During the course of 1687 relations between the Dutch and the English gradually deteriorated, and there was a growing need to stay informed about developments across the North Sea. The English diplomatic representation in The Hague was far from satisfactory to the Dutch. After his mission in 1685, Bentinck had suggested to the Secretary of State, the Earl of Rochester, that an envoy be sent to The Hague to continue the 'good understanding' between the King and the Prince. It is likely that he had asked for the recall of Bevil Skelton, who had hindered his mission so much – as is suggested by his draft notes.[12] When Bentinck arrived back at Honselaarsdijk on 3 August 1685, he was accompanied by his friend and confidant Henry Sidney – a bitter enemy of Skelton.[13] Ignoring Skelton, Bentinck stayed in The Hague for a few days and then set out with Sidney for William's hunting lodge in Dieren. Sidney, Bentinck and Abel Tassin D'Alonne held a number of conversations after their return.[14] Bentinck made no secret of his deep antipathy towards Skelton, and William's attitude towards the envoy changed considerably. Because of the presence of Sidney – who maintained a correspondence with the Secretary of State, the Earl of Sunderland – Skelton's position weakened.[15] Bentinck and Sidney ultimately discredited the envoy and had

---

11 'The enforcement of freedom for Catholics by prerogative means revived the old belief that Popery and absolutism were necessarily connected, and the friendship which was known to exist between James and Louis convinced many that the developments of 1686 were only a prelude to an attempt to convert the nation by forcible means.' Jones, *The Revolution of 1688*, 73–4.

12 Japikse, *Correspondentie*, XXIII. 27; transl. from French.

13 D'Avaux to Louis 26 July 1685, AAE, CPH 142, f° 251r°–v°; dispatch Skelton 24 July/4 August 1685, BL, Add Ms 41812, f° 148r°.

14 *Négociations de Monsieur le Comte d'Avaux*, V. 105.

15 D'Avaux to Louis 9 Aug. 1685, AAE, CPH 142, f° 261r°–4r°.

him removed.[16] However, his successor, Ignatius White, Marquis of Albeville, a Catholic, was also deeply distrusted by the Dutch.

During the missions in England several confidants of William had established useful contacts; Bentinck, Everard van Weede van Dijkveld and D'Alonne had freely conversed with Sidney and others during their embassies in 1685.[17] Bentinck's secretary Christoffel Tromer had also been to England that summer.[18] As James's policies became more radical, such infrequent contacts were solidified during the mission of Dijkveld in the spring of 1687. Dijkveld was instructed to attempt a reconciliation with James and convince him of the soundness of William's foreign policy, as well as to make contact with the opposition in England.[19] These contacts were strengthened later that year during the mission of Willem van Nassau-Zuylestein. Ostensibly despatched to congratulate James on the pregnancy of his wife, Mary of Modena, Nassau-Zuylestein's task was to consolidate and encourage the network of supporters established by Dijkveld that spring.

It seems that from the autumn of 1687, it was Bentinck who, building on such contacts, maintained and expanded a network of informers, mainly through the mediation of Sidney, who was politically sidelined during James's reign but retained some influence through his being related to Sunderland. Sidney and Bentinck set up what became effectively a secret intelligence network in England, complementing Dijkveld's contacts that were essentially of a political nature. D'Avaux even suspected Sunderland of having a secret liaison with William, which he though was maintained by Bentinck's underground network.[20] Political correspondence was hazardous, and Bentinck and his correspondents were keenly aware that their contacts might very well be monitored. For example, the Countess of Sunderland's correspondence with Bentinck was studiously superficial and touched upon such matters as garden design, with the explicit purpose to mislead the English authorities should they intercept these letters.[21] One of Bentinck's correspondents, Charles Mordaunt, had jested that he did not dare to speak freely: 'if, gardeners as we are', he wrote to Bentinck, 'we

---

16 D'Avaux to Louis 23 August 1685, ibid., f° 286r°–7r°; D'Avaux was right, as Mordaunt reminded Bentinck later about Skelton 'our discourse is only about the aversion you have had towards him, and the great liaison which there is between Mr Bentinck and Mylord Mordaunt to discredit him. Mr Sidney has his part in it. He is correct to lump us all together, because I think we all have the same opinion about him', Mordaunt to Bentinck 22 October 1687 OS, Japikse, *Correspondentie*, XXIV. 11–12, transl. from French.

17 Bentinck to Sidney 21 February 1685 (The Hague), 11 March 1685 (Dieren), BL, Add Ms 32681, f° 274–7.

18 Anonymous letter 5 August 1685, TNA: PRO, SP 84/220, f° 9.

19 D'Avaux to Louis 6 February 1687, AAE, CPH 150, f° 124; J. Muilenberg, 'The Embassy of Everaard van Weede, Lord of Dykvelt, to England in 1687', *University Studies of University of Nebraska*, 20 (1920), 125.

20 D'Avaux to Louis 6 May 1688, AAE, CPH 155, f° 19–21.

21 Countess of Sunderland to William 7 March 1687, *Diary of the Times of Charles the Second, by the Honourable Henry Sidney, afterwards Earl of Romney*, ed. R.W. Blencowe (2 vols, London, 1843), II. 260.

should speak of plants and flowers, those who are perceptive would find a mystery in it.'[22]

Beginning in December 1687 Bentinck received a steady flow of letters from the Scot James Johnston and initiated what outwardly looked like a prolonged business correspondence.[23] Sidney forwarded relevant correspondence and papers to Bentinck or his aides.[24] Secret correspondence from England was addressed to Abel Tassin D'Alonne, Christoffel Tromer, John Hutton (William's secretary and physician) or John Blancard, most of whom were or would later become personal aides to Bentinck.[25] The letters, partly written in invisible ink, encrypted and sent to undercover addresses both in London and The Hague, ensured the Prince of Orange of a continuous supply of information concerning developments in England.[26] Most historians have regarded these dispatches as mere newsletters, but the contents rather suggest a genuine correspondence, although Bentinck's replies seem to have been lost.[27] Moreover, those involved in the correspondence would be rewarded after the Revolution with prominent posts in the ministry. Sidney would become Secretary of State and Lord Chancellor of Ireland, and Johnston Secretary of State in Scotland under Bentinck's tutelage.[28] Such men were hardly simple reporters. The timing of the establishment of this network, only weeks after the news of the Queen's pregnancy came out, leaves little doubt as to its initial purpose. Increasingly this secret correspondence became the line of communication William and Bentinck relied on when making policy, rather than the dispatches of the Dutch ambassador Arnout van Citters, which were opened and checked, whereas the envoy's movements were closely observed.[29] This is in line with William's tendency to bypass the official envoys and create his own intelligence network.[30]

---

22 Mordaunt to Bentinck 11 March 1687 OS, Japikse, *Correspondentie*, XXIV. 9, transl. from French.

23 Rivers to Sidney 17 November 1687 OS, Bentinck to Sidney 5 December 1687 OS (Antwerp), NUL, PwA 2098, 2105.

24 William to Bentinck 19 September 1687, Japikse, *Correspondentie*, XXIII. 33.

25 D'Avaux to Louis 5? August 1688, AAE, CPH 155, f° 262. Cf. Trumbull to Portland 28 May 1695, HMC, *Downshire Mss*, I-ii. 471–2.

26 Most letters were either anonymous or pseudonymous, but there are clear indications that, in addition to Johnston, a number of correspondents were involved. At least three others are mentioned in NUL, PwA 2110, to 'Honoured Sir' 18 December 1687 OS. Although not all letters are addressed to Bentinck, they all have ended up into his private archive, and on several occasions it is clearly implied that he is managing the operation. NUL, PwA 2087–178.

27 J. Carswell, *The Descent on England* (London, 1973), 132; Jones, *The Revolution of 1688*, 226; anonymous letter 2 July 1688 OS, NUL, PwA 2175.

28 Cf. B.P. Lenman, 'The Poverty of Political Theory in the Scottish Revolution of 1688–1690' in: Schwoerer, *The Revolution of 1688*, 244–60, 249.

29 'Rapport van Jacob van Leeuwen', September 1688, Japikse, *Correspondentie*, XXIV. 607–10. According to Carswell, Citters was fully in touch with William, but the envoy was never in the Prince's inner circle. Carswell, *Descent on England*, 150.

30 D.J. Roorda, 'Le Secret du Prince. Monarchale Tendenties in de Republiek 1672–1702' in: S. Groenveld, H. Mout et al. (eds), *Rond Prins en Patriciaat: Verspreide Opstellen door D.J. Roorda* (Weesp, 1984), 172–92.

Bentinck also functioned as a liaison between William and political and religious exiles. Having served in and commanded Dutch regiments filled with Huguenots, such contacts also had a military dimension. When the Huguenot refugee Isaac Dumont de Bostaquet arrived in The Hague in the summer of 1687, he was received by Bentinck and later accepted a post in the army embarking to England.[31] Bentinck maintained relations with Huguenots as they sent requests to him.[32] A list of grievances to be forwarded to the Prince from English Protestants was delivered into his hands in the autumn of 1688.[33] After Burnet had been banished from the Orange court on James's demand, Bentinck was frequently seen to meet with him.[34] William Carstares, a Scottish exile, was introduced to Gaspar Fagel and subsequently to William and Bentinck.[35] In 1687 Carstares would maintain the famous correspondence with James Steward, in which Fagel and Bentinck would become involved.[36] Burnet was let in on the plan managed by Carstares to print the Fagel-Steward correspondence. It is almost certain that Bentinck was directly involved in the correspondence.[37]

The summer of 1687 saw the Orange court buzzing with visitors from England such as the Earl of Shrewsbury and Charles Mordaunt. In April George Melville arrived from Scotland, another exile to work closely together with Bentinck in the post-revolutionary settlement. Bentinck became a conduit between such exiles and William, who could not receive them in public without antagonising his uncle. Presumably at Het Loo, William sent Bentinck to nearby Hoog Soeren to meet and interview Melville.[38] Such meetings could never remain a complete secret. A certain Forter, a known anti-papist, was spotted travelling with Bentinck to meet William.[39] But the advantage of this scheme was considerable, as William could show the outside world that he did not publicly receive exiles of whom James disapproved. That the actual meeting with Bentinck took place follows from a letter from Patrick Hume, another Scottish exile in Utrecht, written later that month, which shows that Bentinck had had conversations with George Melville and James Dalrymple.[40] The common religious background and sense of political purpose of these exiles

---

31   M. Glozier, *The Huguenot Soldiers of William of Orange and the Glorious Revolution of 1688. The Lions of Judah.* (Brighton, 2002), 58; *Mémoires d'Isaac Dumont de Bostaquet ... sur les Temps qui ont Précédé et Suivi la Révocation de l'Édit de Nantes* (Paris, 1968), 152.

32   Rietbergen, 'William of Orange', 46.

33   BL, Add Mss 32095, f° 283–96.

34   *Négociations de Monsieur le Comte d'Avaux*, VI, 48–51. On Bentinck's pre-revolutionary relationship with Carstares, see G. Gardner, *The Scottish Exile Community in the Netherlands, 1660–1690* (East Linton, 2004), 158, 166, 168 and *passim*.

35   R.H. Story, *William Carstares. A Character and Career of the Revolutionary Epoch 1649–1715* (Edinburgh, 1895).

36   Carstares to Bentinck 1 August 1687, 2 August 1687, Japikse, *Correspondentie*, XXVII. 757–61; Fagel's draft letters are in Bentinck's archive, NUL, PwA 2071–2.

37   TNA: PRO, SP 8/2, f° 29; William to Bentinck 21 September 1687, Japikse, *Correspondentie*, XXIII. 33–4.

38   William to Fagel 13 April 1687, Japikse, *Correspondentie*, XXVII. 750.

39   *Négociations de Monsieur le Comte d'Avaux*, VI. 51.

40   Hume to William 22 April 1687 OS, Japikse, *Correspondentie*, XXIV. 13.

facilitated Bentinck's task to forge those talented individuals into a team.[41] He recognised their qualities and recommended them to William for their discretion, discernment, moderation and contacts.[42] In future years he would continue to work with them.

With regard to England William had three major concerns: domestic troubles as a result of James's policy, rising tensions between the Dutch and the English, and dynastic considerations as a result of the Queen's pregnancy. These issues were inextricably connected, as one of Bentinck's correspondents explained in the autumn of 1687:

> They add y^t they believe things near their crisis, & y^t if ye Greate Belly should any way fail, (of which people have different sorts of jealousies) ye Court will pursue much warmer measures, and y^t a stricter Alliance being lately made, between us and France; 't is believed ye Dutch may next summer find ye effects of it.[43]

Hence Bentinck needed to learn from his English correspondents whether James would actually be able to obtain a loyal parliament, whether there was a secret understanding between Louis and James – the potential military threat of which caused more concern at the Orange court than domestic turmoil – and whether the Queen was pregnant. Although there was concern about James's domestic policy, one of Bentinck's correspondents informed him that most of James's ministers, as well as the Marquis of Halifax (whose opinion William greatly valued), were sceptical about his attempt to create a loyal parliament.[44] Moreover, the Court itself was heavily divided which crippled effective decision-making. 'There are great factions among the Catholics', Bentinck was informed, 'nothing will be concluded at present in their Assemblies, divisions being rife'.[45] By late January 1688 Bentinck was told that the ministry was in crisis, and would not succeed in giving the King the Parliament he wanted; but they might take stronger measures.[46] The disputes assumed a military dimension when the States refused to return the Anglo-Dutch brigades to English soil. It was feared that James would back up his domestic policies by force, and it was also the first sign of a military build-up on both sides of the Channel. The Dutch envoy Arnout Van Citters reported that James now had a fleet of 38 men-of-war; in February 1688, in the face of mounting international tensions Gaspar Fagel persuaded the secret committee for naval affairs to have 21 ships built, in addition to the 21 already existing vessels.[47] But despite the increased threat Bentinck, advised

---

41   Cf. Carswell, *Descent on England*, 26–30.
42   E.g. Melville's correspondence to William in Portland's papers, NUL, PwA 2335.
43   Letter to 'Honoured Sir' 8 December 1687 OS, NUL, PwA 2110, f° 2.
44   Anonymous letter 8 December 1687 OS, La Montagne's letter of 21 December 1687, anonymous letter 27 February 1688 OS, NUL, PwA 2112, PwA 2120, 2147. Cf. Carswell, *Descent on England*, 112.
45   Anonymous letter to Howel 12 January 1688 OS, NUL, PwA 2126, f° 9v°, transl. from French.
46   Jones to Hutton 29 January 1688 OS, NUL, PwA 2137.
47   M. Ashley, *The Glorious Revolution of 1688* (London, 1966), 129, 156; A. van der Kuijl, *De Glorieuze Overtocht. De Expeditie van Willem III naar Engeland in 1688*

both by Citters and Johnston that James was not in a condition to wage war, was not alarmed.[48] The situation thus hardly signified a prelude to open conflict, which neither James nor William considered a viable option.

Despite diplomatic manoeuvring between James and William during the autumn of 1687 there was no hint of any Dutch military design. 'The plan', which Bentinck and Mordaunt had discussed throughout the summer, was to send a fleet to the West Indies and as late as April 1688 Bentinck seemed preoccupied with 'reports from the West Indies'.[49] The situation dramatically changed with James's clash with the seven bishops, who refused to read the controversial Declaration of Indulgence from the pulpit. They were tried for seditious libel and imprisoned in the Tower in June. 'This affair of the Bishops can bring affairs rapidly to a head', William wrote to Bentinck.[50] The King, moreover, was reassured by the birth of the Prince of Wales on 20 June, a male Catholic heir ensuring him of a continuation of his policies. Bentinck was asked to officially congratulate the King, but due to his wife's illness the mission was entrusted to Nassau-Zuylestein.[51] Soon rumours were spread that the child was 'supposititious' and swapped for a stillborn prince. Such talk heated public trepidation to fever pitch, but was hardly taken seriously at the Orange court until Johnston suggested to Bentinck that it should be exploited. He did not believe the rumours himself and ridiculed Hutton being 'really so foolish as to give ear to idle stories, and doubt of the P^{rs} birth'.[52] But still many people did: 'Be it true Child or not, the People will never believe it'.[53]

It may have been at this stage that Bentinck believed it opportune to take political advantage of the situation. One can only speculate as to the precise sequence of events, but the astute D'Avaux noticed William hurriedly convening a meeting with Fagel, Dijkveld and Bentinck, after having received an express message from England. Whether it was the anonymous letter from London written five days earlier, criticising Nassau-Zuylestein's mission, cannot be known, but the French ambassador seems to indicate that after this meeting the public prayers for the new prince were suspended, which is in line with the contents of the secret dispatch.[54] Bentinck himself refused to lend trumpeters to the English ambassador who had organised a fete to celebrate the princely birth, and Nassau-Ouwerkerk and Nassau-

---

(Amsterdam, 1988), 23; Jones, *The Revolution of 1688*, 180.

48   Anonymous letter 4 April 1688 OS, NUL, PwA 2159; Citters to States General 9 April 1688, BL, Add Mss 17677 UUU, f° 539v°.

49   Mordaunt to Bentinck 11 March 1687 OS, Japikse, *Correspondentie*, XXIV. 8–9; De Wildt to Bentinck 17 November 1687, Japikse, *Correspondentie*, XXVII. 768–9; Bentinck to Sidney (Het Loo), 8 April 1688, BL, Add Mss 32681, f° 306r°, transl. from French.

50   William to Bentinck 4 June 1688, Japikse, *Correspondentie*, XXIII. 40–41, transl. from French.

51   Ham to Bentinck 4 July 1688 OS, NUL, PwA 521; Petit to Middleton 29 June 1688, BL, Add Mss 41816, f° 82v°–3r°.

52   Johnston to Hutton 3 August 1688 OS, NUL, PwA 2177.

53   Letter from Rivers 18 June 1688 OS, NUL, PwA 2171.

54   *Négociations de Monsieur le Comte d'Avaux*, VI. 172–4; anonymous letter 2 July 1688 OS, NUL, PwA 2175.

Odijk declared that William would take it ill if anyone were to attend the event.[55] Meanwhile apprehension regarding James's plans was rising. By the late spring both Citters and Johnston reported that Barillon had offered naval and military assistance to James.[56] Historians have often described James's attempts to pack Parliament as unrealistic, but J.R. Jones has shown that by recreating the corporations he might still achieve his objectives.[57] Bentinck probably believed so, having been informed by one of his correspondents in the summer that by the winter of 1688 everything would be changed; the King will have a strong army and a loyal Parliament. William must intervene.[58] If you do not come over, Johnston warned in early August, 'it would be like showing teeth without biting'.[59]

II

The alarming letters from England coincided with the death of the Wittelsbach archbishop of Cologne, Maximilian Henry, in early June 1688.[60] Both William and Louis were quick to grasp the significance of the event; the archbishopric comprised not only Cologne, but also Munster, Liège and Hildesheim, extending along the Rhine frontier, and was therefore of crucial strategic importance. The French Secretary of State, the Marquis of Louvois, realised that the situation was to the advantage of his master, the Emperor being engaged in the Hungarian campaign and Fürstenberg being still in actual control of the territories. He also noted that William was likely to intervene, and in the meantime 4,000 French cavalry were directed towards Cologne to support the coadjutor.[61] The Duke of Schomberg, the Huguenot marshal in Brandenburg service, marched towards Wesel, Brandenburg territory some 50 miles from Cologne. Meanwhile French troops were also converging on the Palatinate to settle by force the succession there, which had been disputed since 1685.

---

55   Dispatch 26 July 1688, BL, Add Mss 41816, f° 124v°.
56   Anonymous letter 9 June 1688 OS, NUL, PwA 2165; dispatch Citters 15 June 1688, BL, Add Mss 17677 UUU, f° 569.
57   Jones, *The Revolution of 1688*, 129.
58   Anonymous letter 23 May 1688 OS, La Riviere to Hutton 27 May 1688 OS, letter from Rivers 18 June 1688 OS, NUL, PwA 2161, PwA 2163, PwA 2173. It was thought much more likely that the King would eventually succeed than that a republic would be established. This is confirmed by the Secret Resolution which the States of Holland took on 29 September 1688. *Secreete Resolutien van de Ed. Groot Mog. Heeren Staaten van Hollandt. Beginnende met den Jaare 1679 en Eyndigende met den Jaare 1696 incluis* (17 vols., The Hague, 1653–1795), V. 229–35.
59   Johnston to Hutton 3 August 1688 OS, NUL, PwA 2173, transl. from French. Cf. letter from Rivers 18 June 1688 OS, NUL, PwA 2177; Jones, *The Revolution of 1688*, 129 ff.
60   O'Connor, *Negotiator out of Season*, 157.
61   A. Richardt, *Louvois* (Paris, 1990), 221; Symcox, 'Louis XIV and the Outbreak of the Nine Years War', 193.

The Dutch were alarmed.[62] Events now seemed to be evolving in a way similar to those of the Year of Disaster, sixteen years earlier, when Munster invaded the United Provinces from the east and France invaded from the south, supported by an English naval assault. These events triggered William's decision; war seemed inevitable now.[63] On 7 June he wrote to Bentinck:

> This will undoubtedly cause a grand change in the affairs, because it is certain that France at all costs will cause Cardinal Fürstenberg to be elected, and to that end send troops into the Archbishopric of Cologne. If the Emperor and the Princes of the Empire will permit the chapters to be forced there as in Munster, Hildesheim and Liège, they must no longer hope for their German liberty, but how can it be prevented? [64]

The Prince decided to despatch his confidant on a mission to the German principalities. Bentinck was to contact Eberhard von Danckelmann, the Brandenburg first minister, to sound out the Elector, and Saxony, Brunswick-Lunenberg, Hesse-Cassel and the Palatinate were to be drawn into a defensive alliance.[65]

The importance of the mission was not lost on interested observers. The Polish ambassador Antoine Moreau wrote that 'The choice the Prince of Orange has made for that person for that mission will indeed be the talk of the town'.[66] By sending his 'Chamberlain and favourite' William clearly attached great importance to the mission.[67] Eager to speculate on its purpose, some supposed it to be a rapprochement and a warning signal to Versailles.[68] Moreau reported, correctly, that one of the reasons for Bentinck's mission was to arrange a meeting between William and the new elector.[69] The English ambassador Marquis d'Albeville suggested that Bentinck would be instrumental in swinging the aloof Brandenburgers definitely into the Allied camp by giving 'advise in modeling the new court and in takeing measurs as to affairs'.[70] It was precisely for that reason that William had despatched Bentinck as his personal emissary, lending weight to the mission. There may have been some truth in D'Avaux's acid comment, that William must have been well assured 'to succeed in that affair because otherwise he would not have entrusted this negotiation

---

62 Albeville to Middleton 18 June 1688, BL, Add Mss 41816, f° 61 and *passim*. But see Albeville to Middleton 22 June 1688, BL, Add Mss 41816, f° 68r°. The reports sent by the Dutch envoy Van Wassenaar-Sterrenburg from Paris concerning French movements of troops towards Cologne were alarming. Carswell, *Descent on England*, 161.

63 Haley, 'The Dutch invasion', 25; Symcox, 'Louis XIV and the Outbreak of the Nine Years War', 195.

64 William to Bentinck 7 June 1688, Japikse, *Correspondentie*, XXIII. 41; transl. from French.

65 William to Bentinck 7 June 1688, ibid., 41–2.

66 BL, Add Mss 38494, Moreau's dispatch, 18 May 1688, f° 68v°, transl. from French.

67 Ibid., transl. from French.

68 Dispatches Moreau 18 May 1688, 22 June 1688, BL, Add Mss 38494, f° 68v°, 77v°.

69 Dispatch Moreau 15 June 1688, BL, Add Mss 38494, f° 75r°.

70 Albeville to Middleton 18 May 1688, BL, Add Mss 41816, f° 24v°. Cf. *Négociations de Monsieur le Comte d'Avaux*, VI. 156.

to Bentinck, who has very mediocre capacities, and he will not want to expose his favourite'.[71] On the other hand, the new Elector, Frederick III, seems to have held Bentinck in high esteem, which to William may have been reason enough to choose his favourite for the mission.[72] Moreover, Bentinck had clearly matured as a diplomat.

The support of Frederick, though himself a zealous Calvinist and averse to allying with France, could not be taken for granted, and there were strong differences in opinion as to how to handle the escalating crisis in Cologne.[73] At the Brandenburg court, pro- and anti-French factions emerged around Franz von Meinderts and Paul Fuchs respectively. The lukewarm commitment of the powerful first minister, Danckelmann, to counter French ambitions, caused William and Bentinck a considerable amount of anxiety.[74] But Bentinck's mission coincided with a definite swing towards a more pro-Dutch policy under Frederick, as Meinderts's influence was rapidly declining and the diplomatic advantages of the French were evaporating. The States General's envoy, Johan Ham, informed Bentinck that Danckelmann and Fuchs were acting in tandem.[75] 'Undoubtedly the Prince of Orange and Mr Bentinck support Fuchs and try to make him have the entire direction of affairs'.[76] Bentinck had managed to persuade the Elector to maintain the pro-Dutch Brandenburg envoy, Ezechiel Spanheim, at his post in Paris. He established good relations with the influential Duke of Schomberg, who had recently left France and was now Commander-in-Chief of the Brandenburg army. During his mission they had talked 'freely on all matters'.[77] According to Schomberg, Bentinck's presence at the Berlin court had had a favourable and inspiring effect on the Elector and his first minister.[78] Due to his wife's illness, Bentinck was urged by William to return to The Hague immediately, where he arrived on 19 June.[79] A few days later D'Avaux worriedly wrote to his king that Brandenburg was now in William's interest.[80]

Bentinck's mission was pivotal in a wider Dutch diplomatic offensive to mobilise German princes. The Utrecht nobleman Godard Adriaan van Reede van Amerongen had been despatched to Aachen to arrange an encounter with the Elector of Saxony who was taking the waters there. On 28 May he had informed Bentinck that the Elector was willing to make a defensive alliance with the States General; in his opinion the new Brandenburg ruler might be inclined likewise. Amerongen kept Bentinck informed about the negotiations.[81] The Prince of Waldeck, Commander-

---

71 D'Avaux to Louis 25 July 1688, AAE, CPH 155, f° 230r°, transl. from French.
72 Ham to Bentinck 4 July 1688 OS, 10 September 1688 OS, NUL, PwA 521, PwA 534; William to Frederick III 17 May 1688, Japikse, *Correspondentie*, XXVIII. 14.
73 W. Troost, 'William III, Brandenburg, and the Construction of the anti-French Coalition, 1672–1688' in: Israel, *The Anglo-Dutch Moment*, 299–333, esp. 332.
74 Ham to Bentinck 11 August 1688, NUL, PwA 527.
75 Ham to Bentinck 23 June 1688, NUL, PwA 518.
76 D'Avaux to Louis 17 May 1688, AAE, CPH 155, f° 42, transl. from French.
77 Schomberg to Bentinck 23 June 1688, Japikse, *Correspondentie*, XXIV. 152, transl. from French.
78 Schomberg to Bentinck 27 June 1688, ibid., 153–4.
79 Albeville to Middleton 22 June 1688, BL, Add Mss 41816, f° 68.
80 D'Avaux to Louis 24 June 1688, AAE, CPH, f° 160–61.
81 Amerongen to Bentinck, 28 May 1688, 1 June 1688, RU, HA 1001/3128.

in-Chief of the Dutch forces and William's old military mentor, was in Arolsen, and corresponded with Bentinck on German affairs.[82] After his mission to Berlin, Bentinck instructed Johan Ham to write regular despatches to him personally. The correspondence is particularly useful as it provides a contrast to the published Danckelmann letters. On his return Bentinck informed Danckelmann that he 'left His Highness in better spirit with regard to all our affairs'.[83] Danckelmann likewise wrote to Bentinck in reassuring terms, but according to Ham the councillors of the Elector were divided, and support was not to be taken for granted.[84] Regarding the Cologne see, William and the Elector held different opinions. Danckelmann was averse to supporting the Emperor's candidate for the see, and in fact preferred Fürstenberg to the Bavarian pretender, Max Emanuel, because it may have been 'useful to be allied with the House of Austria, but not to be surrounded and enclosed by it and its allies'.[85] Bentinck suggested to Danckelmann that they should co-ordinate diplomatic efforts in Munster, and William's envoy had been instructed to support the desired candidate.[86] On 20 June Danckelmann informed Bentinck about discussions with the Brunswick-Lunenberger envoy whose master leaned towards France.[87] Bentinck's labours throughout June to choreograph Brandenburg and Dutch diplomacy were not unsuccessful. Moreover, Fürstenberg's schemes were crippled; the Cardinal did not succeed in keeping all the territories in one hand, and his candidacy for Cologne was deadlocked on 19 July due to his failure to achieve a two-thirds majority.[88]

It is difficult to establish when exactly a sound commitment from the Germans to support the Dutch in their English enterprise materialised. Correspondence with Danckelmann and Waldeck was rather preoccupied with affairs regarding the Empire until late June. It is almost certain that Bentinck and the Elector had discussed the possibility of an intervention in English affairs during his mission. Bentinck had mainly 'prepared matters' for further negotiations, as William suggested.[89] He had also arranged a meeting between the Elector and William which ultimately took place in September in Minden.[90] The decision to intervene militarily in England was possibly made after Bentinck's mission to Berlin. It was now that Bentinck instructed Ham to write directly with every post.[91]

---

82   Waldeck's letters in Japikse, *Correspondentie*, XXIV. 142 ff.
83   Bentinck to Danckelmann 22 June 1688 (The Hague), Japikse, *Correspondentie*, XXIV. 124, transl. from French.
84   Ham to Bentinck 30 June 1688, NUL, PwA 520.
85   Ham to Bentinck 30 June 1688, NUL, PwA 519, transl. from Dutch.
86   Bentinck to Danckelmann 22 June 1688 (The Hague), Japikse, *Correspondentie*, XXIV. 124–5.
87   Danckelmann to Bentinck 20 June 1689, ibid., 123.
88   O'Connor, *Negotiator out of Season*, 160 ff.
89   William to Bentinck 4 June 1688, Japikse, *Correspondentie*, XXIII. 40, transl. from French. This letter, however, contains the first reference to the 'affairs of England' with relation to Brandenburg troop hires.
90   Ham to Bentinck 30 June 1688, NUL, PwA 519.
91   Ham to Bentinck 30 June 1688, ibid.

On 20 July Arthur Herbert arrived in The Hague from England and was closeted the next day at the palace of Honselaarsdijk with William, Dijkveld and Bentinck.[92] Herbert brought with him the 'Invitation', signed by seven leading English politicians, which could serve as a pretext for invasion. That same day Bentinck wrote to Ham: 'The Elector of Brandenburg has shown much fervour and sincerity about that affair [i.e. of England], and has told me at my departure that he wanted to establish "tout pour le tout" in this affair with His Highness; now it is surely time for him to stick to that'.[93] It is interesting to note that Bentinck suggested here that William would intervene: he hoped for an alliance with Brandenburg because the Dutch 'State would intervene in English affairs with all its might'. Bentinck furthermore suggested that unless Brandenburg provided troops for backup and defence against a possible French attack on the Dutch state, 'everything will be lost'.[94] Ham was strictly instructed not to correspond about this with anyone apart from William and himself. To Danckelmann he likewise explained: 'the affairs of England continue to be extremely pressing, and they are currently in such a crisis that His Highness dares to wait no longer to prepare himself, so that he will not be surprised by anything unforeseen'.[95]

On 25 July Bentinck again left for Berlin to arrange a secret meeting with Paul Fuchs, leaving the foreign diplomats the impression that the sole aim of his mission was to confer with the German princes to counter Fürstenberg's ambitions.[96] He passed through Hesse-Cassel, Hanover, Celle and Wolfenbüttel and seemed optimistic about the success of his mission.[97] The Landgrave of Hesse-Cassel promised troops and free passage for the Dutch army.[98] Bentinck had also requested a joint Brandenburg-Dutch diplomatic effort in Hanover and asked for the presence of Danckelmann's brother there. But the Hanoverian Elector was unwilling to risk a rupture with France.[99] Bentinck and Fuchs met in utter secrecy in Celle on 6 August to discuss the critical international situation.[100] The most remarkable aspect of their conversation was that even at this stage the particulars of the expedition were still being discussed, which is in line with the absence of any specific references in correspondence or documents prior to late July. It was only now that the connection was made between the hiring of troops and the expedition to England, whereas formerly troops were directed to the Rhineland. Bentinck's mission was successful. Both Fuchs and the Celle minister Andreas von Bernstorff offered troops, as did the negotiators of

---

92   *Négociations de Monsieur le Comte d'Avaux*, VI. 72–3.
93   Bentinck to Ham 20 July 1688, Japikse, *Correspondentie*, XXIV. 132–3, transl. from Dutch.
94   Bentinck to Ham 20 July 1688, ibid., 133, transl. from Dutch.
95   Bentinck to Danckelmann 20 July 1688, ibid., 132, transl. from French.
96   Albeville to Middleton 26 July 1688, BL, Add Mss 41816, f° 124v°.
97   *Négociations de Monsieur le Comte d'Avaux*, VI. 174.
98   Ibid., 178; Waldeck to Bentinck 16 Aug. 1688, NUL, PwA 1520; F.J.G. ten Raa, *Het Staatsche Leger 1568–1795. VI* (The Hague 1940), 270–71.
99   Ernst August of Brunswick-Lunenburg to William 24 July 1688 OS, Japikse, *Correspondentie*, XXVIII. 35–6.
100   Cf. Bentinck to Danckelmann 20 July 1688, Bentinck to Ham 20 July 1688, Japikse, *Correspondentie*, XXIV. 132.

Württemberg and Brunswick-Wolfenbüttel. The two major dissenting princes of Saxony and Hanover, John George III and Ernst August did, however, participate in the Magdenburger Concert to defend the Empire against French aggression.[101] Bentinck arrived at Honselaarsdijk on 10 August, having secured a sizeable army of German troops to defend the Rhine and Dutch borders against impending French aggression.[102]

III

Meanwhile Bentinck was involved in mustering support domestically. In June Dijkveld and Bentinck had already contacted several Amsterdam burgomasters to acquaint them with the Prince's plans to intervene in England.[103] Upon his return from his German mission in early August, Bentinck was instructed by William to handle the negotiations with Amsterdam. He arranged a secret meeting with Johannes Hudde and Nicolaas Witsen, hoping that his diplomatic successes in Germany would induce the burgomasters to co-operate. They were, however, not convinced. In fact, as late as September the burgomasters's council chamber remained in confusion.[104] Nevertheless, William and his aides had been making preparations all summer. For instance Bentinck had contacted William's agent in Madrid, Francisco Schonenberg, in order to find additional funding for the operation.[105]

While Fagel and Dijkveld were labouring to establish consensus among the regents and to obtain funds, according to Burnet, 'Bentink used to be constantly with the Prince, being the person that was most entirely trusted and constantly employed by him'.[106] Upon his return from Celle in early August, Bentinck devoted himself to the logistic preparations for the expedition. His reports, which were sent daily from The Hague to Het Loo, have unfortunately not survived, but it is still possible to reconstruct his activities, which consisted of the procurement of supplies, the equipage of the fleet and the embarkation of the troops.[107] The provisioning was handled in close co-operation with Job de Wildt, Secretary of the Amsterdam Admiralty.[108] Bentinck and De Wildt also supervised the equipage of the fleet, which was taken care of by the five *Admiraliteitscollegs* (admiralties).[109] On 6 September Bentinck and Captain Gerard Callenburg discussed the issue of the fleet of transport

---

101 W. Troost, *William III, the Stadholder–King: A Political Biography* (Aldershot, 2005), 197–8.
102 Albeville to Middleton 10 August 1688, BL, Add Mss 41816, f° 142v°.
103 J.F. Gebhard, *Het Leven van Mr. Nicolaas Cornelisz. Witsen (1641–1717)* (2 vols, Utrecht, 1882), I. 320–27; Israel, 'Dutch role', 116.
104 Gebhard, *Witsen*, II. 173; G.H. Kurtz, *Willem III en Amsterdam 1683–1685* (Utrecht, 1928), 187.
105 William to Bentinck 4 September 1688, Japikse, *Correspondentie*, XXIII. 56.
106 Burnet, *History*, III. 1311.
107 E.g. William to Bentinck 27 August 1688, Japikse, *Correspondentie*, XXIII. 47.
108 Japikse, *Correspondentie*, XXIV. 604.
109 Van der Kuijl, *De Glorieuze Overtocht*, 31–3. Cf. William to Bentinck 25 August 1688, Japikse, *Correspondentie*, XXIII. 44–5.

ships needed to cross the North Sea.[110] Details were worked out during a meeting on 19 September, attended by Admiral Willem Bastiaansen, Callenburg, Herbert, De Wildt and Bentinck.[111] With the autumn approaching, time was running out now, and the next meeting was planned for 22 September, by which time the fleet had to be ready; meanwhile the States were still formally unaware of the proceedings.[112] Bentinck was directly responsible for the actual embarkation of the troops, which had been encamped on the Mookerheide near Nijmegen since August.

On 7 September 1688, Ambassador d'Avaux presented two memorials to the States, warning the Dutch to intervene neither in the troubles in Germany nor in England. The emphasis here is clearly on the Rhine, which becomes apparent from the Secret Resolution that was actually taken – clear evidence that even then both France and the States were still primarily focused on Germany.[113] It was not clear whether the intentions of the French marshal, the Duke d'Humières, who had built up a defence line along the borders of the Spanish Netherlands, were hostile, and William admitted to Bentinck 'that this makes me feel troubled and restless, fearing that our plan will be aborted and that we will find ourselves engaged in a great war'. But when intelligence had reached 'him that the marshal d'Humières has received order to maintain the cardinal', the direct threat on the border seemed to have been removed as the French armies marched towards Cologne.[114] The final details about troop movements must have been discussed during the meeting of Waldeck, William and Bentinck on 21 September.[115] The last week of September saw the release of tension when Schomberg occupied Cologne and French troops flooded the Palatinate on the 25th, meaning the direct threat on the Dutch borders was removed. The following day William wrote to Bentinck that the troops camped at Nijmegen would be given marching orders for the port of Hellevoetsluis for embarkation.[116]

Naval strategy was discussed by Bentinck and the admirals of the fleet. On 20 September Bentinck had received the Dutch admirals Philips van Almonde and Cornelis Evertsen at his residence, where it was decided that Arthur Herbert would be in command.[117] It was probably after consultation with the admirals that Bentinck drew a diagram representing the sailing order of the fleet, showing the 196 vessels in nine units, each protected by one man-of-war, and one unit of ten ships including Herbert's ship the *Leyden*. Thirty-nine men-of-war surrounded the fleet.[118] This defensive configuration implied that the choice was made not to engage the English

---

110   Japikse, *Correspondentie*, XXIV. 605–6.
111   Carswell, *Descent on England*, 168–9.
112   Albeville to Middleton 24 September 1688, BL, Add Mss 41816, f° 191–4; Japikse, *Correspondentie*, XXIV. 606.
113   Resolution of 18 September 1688, *Secreete Resolutien*, V. 224–6.
114   William to Bentinck 4 September 1688, Japikse, *Correspondentie*, XXIII. 55, transl. from French.
115   Albeville to Middleton 24 September 1688, BL, Add Mss 41816, f° 191v°.
116   William to Bentinck 26 September 1688, 29 September 1688, Japikse, *Correspondentie*, XXIII. 57–9. It is not clear whether William had already received news of the French invasion.
117   Van der Kuijl, *De Glorieuze Overtocht*, 36.
118   Japikse, *Correspondentie*, XXIV. 622; NUL, PwA 2197. Illus. 5.

fleet if that could be avoided. The enormous transport fleet, although shielded by a superior force of men of war, was extremely vulnerable, and Bentinck implored Herbert to shun battle at all costs.[119] Bentinck personally supervised the embarkation of the troops in early October.[120] Around the middle of the month, the expeditionary force was ready to set sail, and Bentinck, Fagel and the admirals were in continuous consultation in The Hague.[121] Astonishingly, the preparations for what may have been the most complicated and extensive naval operation in the seventeenth century were essentially managed by half a dozen men within two months in the utmost secrecy.

With the preparation of the *Declaration of Reasons*, in which William explained his motivation for invading England, the propaganda campaign was approaching its apotheosis. Several draft versions of the *Declaration* had been sent to William in August. According to Wagenaar, these were compiled by Fagel and translated back into English by Burnet, but evidence suggests that the text was debated at length between Fagel, Dijkveld and Bentinck in The Hague.[122] A few hitherto unstudied drafts of the *Declaration* in Bentinck's archive containing (minor) marginal notes in his handwriting provide definite proof of his direct involvement in drafting the text.[123] But his main responsibility was the distribution of the manifesto. He kept copies of the printed *Declaration* safely in his quarters and co-ordinated the ensuing propaganda campaign.[124] His network in England was instrumental in the distribution of the pamphlet in unprecedented numbers and evaluated its impact. The *Declaration* for the English sailors was sent 'to some trusty parson in London, who is usually intrusted with the receiving and dispersing of such secrett papers as ar frequently sent thither from Holland'.[125] Johnston had notified Bentinck that he had no printing facilities available, so that they were dependent on copies printed in the United Provinces.[126] Earlier, the distribution of another pamphlet in England had confronted Bentinck with logistical problems, since according to his agent it was very difficult to obtain even when distributed in large numbers.[127] An effective

---

119 William to Bentinck 26 September 1688, Japikse, *Correspondentie*, XXIII. 58.

120 Van der Kuijl, *De Glorieuze Overtocht*, 43; Albeville to Middleton 10 October 1688, BL, Add Mss 41816, f° 228v°.

121 Albeville to Middleton 15 October 1688, BL, Add Mss 41816, f° 239v°.

122 William to Bentinck 29 August 1688, Japikse, *Correspondentie*, XXIII. 50. Burnet and Wildman were also involved: Albeville to Middleton 1 October 1688, BL, Add Mss 41816, f° 209v°. Cf. J.I. Israel, 'Propaganda in the Making of the Glorious Revolution' in: S. Roach (ed.), *Across the Narrow Seas. Studies in the History and Bibliography of Britain and the Low Countries* (London, 1991), 167–78, 169, 172 and L.G. Schwoerer, *The Declaration of Rights 1689* (Baltimore, 1981), 107.

123 NUL, PwA 2246–52. Cf. NUL, PwA 2288.

124 Albeville to Middleton 24 October 1688, BL, Add Mss 41816, f° 251r°; Albeville to Middleton 15 October 1688, ibid., f° 238v°: 'The manifest or declaration can not be yett had at any rate, for i have offer'd considerably for it'. Cf. Israel, 'Propaganda', 169.

125 Japikse, *Correspondentie*, XXIV. 618–19.

126 Anonymous letter 8 December 1687 OS, NUL, PwA 2112.

127 Anonymous letter 16 February 1688 OS, NUL, PwA 2141.

propaganda campaign was necessarily a sustained one, requiring permanent and reliable lines of communication.

The virtual breakdown of these lines between April and July (apparently because Bentinck had not followed directions properly and his letters miscarried) was affecting the 'Williamites' in England, who complained about the lack of intelligence.[128] Bentinck and William likewise were confronted with an acute shortage of intelligence when it was most needed. Bentinck's intelligence network in England had become less useful with the crossing the North Sea of his foremost agents, Sidney and Johnston, the former arriving at Het Loo in the last week of August.[129] With Citters in The Hague for consultation, it was necessary to send some agent, a task which William naturally delegated to Bentinck. It was difficult to dispatch either Dijkveld or Nassau-Zuylestein, the latter having just returned and no obvious pretext being available.[130]

Bentinck decided to send Jacob van Leeuwen, his personal secretary, to London in secret, where he arrived on 11 September.[131] Armed with credentials and instructions from Bentinck to contact several key Williamites, he arranged to meet Edward Russell and Richard Lumley, both signatories of the 'Invitation'. The former expressed his relief as lines of communication between William and the English opposition had been disrupted for several weeks. They provided Van Leeuwen with detailed information on English fortifications, troop mobilisation and fleet movements. Lumley gave Van Leeuwen the impression that James had refused offers of military support from the French ambassador Bonrepaus. Russell and Danby supplied the secretary with crucial strategic intelligence but urged him to return to the United Provinces immediately, as they were afraid their secret dealings would be discovered. They also advised William to land in the West. Lastly, they claimed that James would concentrate all his forces in London. From another source Bentinck received exhaustive intelligence with regard to the garrison strengths in ports.[132] Van Leeuwen's intelligence report, received by Bentinck probably in late September, was important for its estimation of James's military strength, but no less for the fact that lines of communication had been re-established.[133]

---

128 Anonymous letter 2 July 1688 OS, NUL, PwA 2175.

129 William to Bentinck 27 August 1688, Japikse, *Correspondentie*, XXIII. 47. Johnston had sent a coded message in early August saying that his activities would cease: 3 August 1688 OS, NUL, PwA 2177.

130 Citters had been recalled for consultation to The Hague in July. Probably he was only then briefed about the impending invasion, which may explain his particularly odd behaviour during his first audience with James on his return. See his dispatch of 22 September 1688, BL, Add Mss 17677 UUU, f° 581v°; Japikse, *Correspondentie*, XXIII. 46–7.

131 This must have been Bentinck's personal decision, as William suggested Citters would do, Japikse, *Correspondentie*, XXIII. 47.

132 NUL, PwA 2181.

133 Jacob van Leeuwen's report of September 1688, Japikse, *Correspondentie*, XXIV. 607–10.

Meanwhile William had not waited for the consent of the States of Holland to launch his expedition. On 18 September he had informed the *Edel Groot Mogenden*[134] of his proceedings with regard to the hiring of German troops, a necessity considering the dangerous situation in Cologne and James's understanding with Louis. The apparently lukewarm Amsterdam deputies reached an agreement with the Orangist *Ridderschap* and supported the desired secret resolution.[135] More crucial was the decision taken by the four Amsterdam burgomasters on 26 September. They admitted that their domestic position had become increasingly isolated and recognised that their policy of appeasement was now resulting into an insoluble dilemma ('which considerations brought [Hudde] into a very great perplexity'). Therefore, they decided to support the Stadholder's expedition to England.[136] Burgomaster Hudde emphasised the absolute necessity of having England as an ally in case of war; this was, in fact, the main purpose of the invasion, on which Amsterdam and William now agreed.[137] The provincial states followed suit between 29 September and early October, outraged by the news of Louis's orders to lay a general arrest on all Dutch merchant vessels.

IV

Around the middle of October the States General granted their support and the fleet lay ready, waiting for the turn of the southwesterly wind which prevented the ships from Texel reaching the port of Hellevoetsluis. Bentinck arrived there on 26 October and was engaged with the final preparations, all the while anxious about the declining health of his wife, to whom he daily wrote. On the 29th Bentinck sailed in William's entourage to Maassluis, writing optimistically to his wife: 'The wind is strong enough under God's holy protection'.[138] But the wind suddenly changed and the fleet was driven back into the harbour. Bentinck though laconically remarked: 'it seems that the good God did not want it yet'.[139] He was obliged to labour to restore the disarrayed fleet and was unable to attend to his wife. On 9 November he briefly visited her in The Hague, only to return after two days to hold a meeting on the *Leyden* with the admirals.[140] The decision whether to land in the West or North of England was possibly made then and there. Earlier Bentinck had drafted a memorial listing all places along the coast suitable for landing, thus keeping the options still

---

134 The Honourable High Mighties: the official designation of the delegates in the States of Holland Assembly.

135 Deputy's dispatch 18 September 1688, GA, 5029/89; Israel, 'Dutch Role', 118–19.

136 Gebhard, *Witsen*, II. 173, transl. from Dutch.

137 See also Israel, 'Dutch role', 120.

138 J. Whittle, *An Exact Diary of the late Expedition of his Illustrious Highness the Prince of Orange into England etc.* (London, 1689), 16; Bentinck to his wife 30 October 1688, Japikse, *Correspondentie*, XXIII. 361, transl. from French.

139 Bentinck to his wife 31 October 1688 (Hellevoetsluis), Japikse, *Correspondentie*, XXIII. 361, transl. from French.

140 Bentinck to his wife 8 November 1688, ibid., 365; 9 November 1688, Huygens, *Journaal*, I-i, 111; Japikse, *Correspondentie*, XXVIII. 628–9.

open.¹⁴¹ The council decided what Herbert had already suggested: that the decision should be based on the direction of the wind. On 12 November Bentinck once more suggested to William that 'if this wind continues, we feel that Exmouth or the river of Exeter would be much better to securely land'.¹⁴² So the 'Protestant wind' directed the invasion force westward, evading the English fleet, which was held back by the same wind. Presumably Bentinck paid a last visit to his wife, since on 12 November William strongly urged his adviser to join the fleet which had already put out to sea.¹⁴³ On 14 November Bentinck advised William to set a course for Torbay, which, he had argued, 'can hardly be defended by the King'.¹⁴⁴

The fleet reached Torbay the next day, unscathed by the English fleet. From a high cliff near Brixham, Bentinck and William witnessed the swift disembarkation of the troops.¹⁴⁵ Torrential rain hampered the subsequent march to nearby Paignton, and from there to Exeter, the nearest city, as carts and canons frequently got stuck in the mud. Notwithstanding a festive reception by the citizens of Exeter, William may have been dismayed by the initial lack of support by the local gentry; the mayor of Exeter was even 'playing the beast', according to the Prince's secretary Constantijn Huygens, in proclaiming to Bentinck his loyalty to the King.¹⁴⁶ Bentinck attributed the reservation mainly to the dismal memories of Monmouth's recent failed attempt. To Herbert he suggested:

> The people seem all extremely well inclined here. Only the gentry and the clergy are a bit more reluctant and have not entered into our interests. I am surprised about the latter. It seems to me that the fear of the scaffold has more effect on their spirits than the zeal for religion.¹⁴⁷

Was William lingering in Exeter because he was disappointed with the lack of English support? Bentinck supposed that within a few days gentry from outside Devon would come flocking in – which indeed they did.¹⁴⁸ He seemed to imply

---

141 Bentinck's memorial Oct. 1688, Japikse, *Correspondentie*, XXIV. 617–18.

142 Bentinck to William 12 November 1688 (warship the *Leyden*), Japikse, *Correspondentie*, XXIV. 624, transl from Dutch.

143 William to Bentinck 12 November 1688, Japikse, *Correspondentie*, XVIII. 53.

144 Marginal note in memorial NUL, PwA 2188/8, transl. from Dutch. Cf. Japikse, *Correspondentie*, XXIV. 624. Another document in Bentinck's papers clearly shows that Torbay was not a preconceived landing place, and was decided on because of circumstances, NUL, PwA 2238; J.I. Israel and G. Parker, 'Of Providence and Protestant Winds: The Spanish Armada of 1588 and the Dutch Armada of 1688' in: Israel, *The Anglo-Dutch Moment*, 335–63, 339–41. Cf. Van der Kuijl, *De Glorieuze Overtocht*, 58–66; Japikse, *Correspondentie*, XXIV. 625.

145 'a great tribute to Bentinck's gift as a staff officer', Carswell, *Descent on England*, 184.

146 25 November 1688, Huygens, *Journaal*, I-i. 21, literal transl. from Dutch.

147 Bentinck to Herbert 22 November 1688 (Exeter), Japikse, *Correspondentie*, XXVIII. 58, transl. from French; *Mémoires d'Isaac Dumont de Bostaquet*, 196.

148 This is confirmed by contemporary journals: 'Seker ende omstandigh verhael van het gepasseerde, zedert het overgaen van Syne Hoogheydt naer Engelandt', 'Advysen uyt Engelandt', 'Journael gehouden by Johan Adolphi, Secretaris van Syne Excellentie den

that the break in Exeter was a useful and necessary intermezzo. The twelve days in Exeter were, thus, not spent in anxious passivity, but used to regroup battalions, set up a council comprised of influential gentry and create a revenue system.[149]

Beginning on 15 November, the day of the landing, Bentinck kept a concise journal of events in the form of several letters to Princess Mary.[150] It is one of the few lengthy reports and reflections in his hand and provides a perspective on the invasion of one of William's senior staff. Bentinck seldom wrote anything particularly personal. During the march to London, Citters had brought to him the news of his wife's death. There is hardly a trace in his correspondence reflecting on his loss, just one line to Herbert in which he referred to 'my great sorrow over the death of my wife'.[151] In the journal the events are described in a dry, factual but concise manner, in fact it constitutes a prose version of the marching orders for the troops that Bentinck meticulously drafted. It shows the mindset of a man preoccupied with operational difficulties: the condition of the roads, the marching of the troops and the provisioning of supplies. It is apparently devoid of any sense of excitement. One reason for the journal's lack of enthusiasm may be its purpose; as it basically witnessed a conflict between Mary's husband and father, Bentinck may have attempted to make the account devoid of any drama. But the account is not very different in style from that which Bentinck would write after the Battle of the Boyne in 1690.[152] It also lacks a sense of religious fervour, unlike the diaries and journals of the Huguenot soldiers accompanying William. Isaac Dumont du Bostaquet, for example, felt himself part of a glorious enterprise, and, in his exhilaration, claimed 'that one has never seen such a small army march with such gaiety and with so much confidence in such a troublesome season and in a land so subject to change'.[153] Despite the apparent lack of zeal, Bentinck radiated a clear sense of confidence and purpose: 'I doubt not that God blesses the cause.'[154]

Although James had marched his army to the Salisbury plain and a military encounter seemed imminent, he ultimately decided to negotiate with his nephew. On 17 December his commissioners, the Marquis of Halifax, the Earl of Nottingham and Sidney Godolphin were dispatched to Hungerford to meet William. After having presented their credentials, they conveyed the message that James was prepared now to convene a free Parliament. The commissioners then withdrew into another

---

Luytenant Generael Admirael Herberts etc.' in: *Political Tracts* (s.l., 1688), f° 67–8. Johan Adolphi was secretary of Admiral Herbert, the journal was sent to Schuylenburg.

149   Japikse, *Correspondentie*, XXIV. 627; 27 November 1688, Huygens, *Journaal*, I-i. 22–3; Herbert to William 8 December 1688, William to Herbert 20 December 1688, Japikse, *Correspondentie*, XXVIII. 73, 79.

150   Japikse, *Correspondentie*, XXIV. 626–34.

151   Bentinck to Herbert 20 December 1688 (Newbury), transl. from French; Tromer to Bentinck 22 November 1688, Japikse, *Correspondentie*, XXVIII. 58–60, 80.

152   *Leven and Melville Papers. Letters and State Papers chiefly Addressed to George Earl of Melville, Secretary of State for Scotland, 1689–1691*, ed. W.L. Melville (Edinburgh, 1843), 459–61n.

153   *Mémoires d'Isaac Dumont de Bostaquet*, 199, transl. from French.

154   Bentinck to Herbert 22 November 1688 (Exeter), Japikse, *Correspondentie*, XXVIII. 58, transl. from French.

room with a Williamite delegation, consisting of English peers only, not including Bentinck, as some historians have supposed.[155] In doing so, William clearly signalled his intention not to be an interested party, but rather an arbiter.[156] But the atmosphere is best typified, perhaps, by Nassau-Zuylestein's triumphant exclamation 'that the King sought to capitulate'.[157] William virtually ignored the commissioners' proposals and presented a list of demands, which were not unreasonable, but hardly negotiable.[158] Although William was aware of his position in control of the situation, the demands appeared to be in line with his declaration and aimed at having a free parliament.[159]

There was thus a stalemate, but William did not have to force his hand. In the night of 22 to 23 December Bentinck received a letter from the commissioners informing him that James had decided to leave the country, arguably the most crucial event in the Glorious Revolution. The rationale behind his decision was probably more sound than he has been given credit for. Although William's demands had been moderate, with a military and political disadvantage the King was no longer a free agent and his policies were now doomed to fail.[160] It was clear that William aimed at least to be in a position where he could influence foreign policy and the dispensation of offices. Both Bentinck and Nassau-Zuylestein implied that a power struggle with James was occurring in which William was now in an advantageous position.[161] The possibility of having William as a regent was hardly attractive, and so the King decided to at least retain a free hand. The Prince, for one, was quite pleased with his flight, since it opened a possibility hitherto not seriously considered. It is impossible to know whether William had entertained any hopes for the crown, but ostensibly all his actions until then had been exactly what he claimed them to be: to fulfil his declaration. However, Louis having declared war on the Dutch in November, and William, having noticed the indecision and division among politicians, decided to take full advantage of the possibility James himself had created.

The news of James's arrest in Faversham was brought to Bentinck in the early morning of 25 December.[162] William then despatched Nassau-Zuylestein to

---

155 Ashley, *The Glorious Revolution*, 230; R. Beddard (ed.), *A Kingdom Without a King. The Journal of the Provisional Government in the Revolution of 1688* (Oxford, 1988), 28; Huygens only notes that the commissioners withdrew to 'Bentinck's room'. 18 December 1688, 20 December 1688, Huygens, *Journaal*, I-i. 38, 41. Cf. 8 December 1688, *The Correspondence of H.H. Earl of Clarendon and of his Brother, Laurence Hyde, Earl of Rochester; with the Diary of Lord Clarendon from 1687 to 1690 ... and the Diary of Lord Rochester during his Embassy to Poland in 1676*, ed. S.W. Singer (2 vols, London, 1828), I. 210.
156 Cf. Bentinck to Frederick III 19 Dec. 1688, Japikse, *Correspondentie*, XXVIII. 77.
157 11 December 1688, Huygens, *Journaal*, I-i. 33, transl. from Dutch.
158 Japikse, *Correspondentie*, XXIV. 24–5.
159 Beddard, *Kingdom without a King*, 27.
160 Jones, *The Revolution of 1688*, 309–10; 22 December 1688, Huygens, *Journaal*, I-i. 43.
161 5 December 1688, Singer, *Diary of Clarendon*, II. 216–17; 11 December 1688, 18 December 1688, Huygens, *Journaal*, I-i. 33, 39. Cf. Blencowe, *Diary*, II. 281–91.
162 Japikse, *Correspondentie*, XXIV. 632–3.

safeguard the King, but meanwhile the peers, having assembled in the Guildhall to temporarily take over the administration, had taken the initiative to have James safely accompanied to Rochester. Nassau-Zuylestein thus missed James, who had by then returned to London and settled in St James's Palace, much to William's displeasure. Pressure was now exerted to induce James to repeat his flight. Lieutenant-General Count Solms was sent to forcibly remove James from his quarters in St James's Palace and to escort the King to Ham House for his safety. Quite likely Bentinck sensed it opportune to grant James's request to withdraw instead to Rochester, seeing that he might wish to escape again: 'That it was initially thought that signals the plan he has had to withdraw himself.'[163] Once in Rochester, James found it easy to leave the country for France, facilitated by the Dutch Guards turning a blind eye. The King being out of the country, William was now effectively in control, the peers having requested the Prince to temporarily take over the administration until a Convention could meet.

V

Central to the propaganda campaign was the slogan for the expedition: *pro religione et libertate*, a powerful phrase, since it not only assured the Prince of the ardent support of English Protestants, but also played into the hands of Dutch Calvinist preachers and foreign Protestants, such as the Huguenots. William had several reasons for intervening in England. Firstly, he wanted to protect his dynastic interest. Secondly, it was a strategic attempt to neutralise England or win her over as an ally. Jonathan Israel has added the argument that French economic warfare played a vital role in the decision of the Dutch to undertake the daring expedition. A fourth factor, religion, was in Israel's view not a significant motivation for the invasion. Neither could it be presented as such, for fear of antagonising the Spanish and the Austrians.[164] It could be argued that religion was rather exploited in a sustained propaganda campaign by the Prince to legitimise the intervention. By presenting himself as a hero of Protestantism and liberty, William could appeal to the English to accept him as leader of their cause.

However, downplaying religion as a factor in William's decision may not help to clarify his true intention, nor explain the causes for the intervention and German support. First of all, the correspondence and memoirs of the policymakers in 1688 show a deep concern for the position of the Protestant religion in England, but indirectly also in the United Provinces. There was a sense that the rising forces of absolutism and Catholicism were threatening the Protestant world. Nor was it just William to whom these motivations were crucial. Jonathan Israel has stressed the preponderance of economic and strategic motivations in the decision of the Amsterdam burgomasters to ultimately embrace an anti-French policy, but this is not quite what the draft notes of a crucial meeting in late September suggest. The deputies in the *Gecommiteerde Raden* (the daily governing council of the States of

---

163 Ibid., 634n, transl. from French.
164 Israel, 'Dutch Role', 111–12, 123.

Holland) had conveyed the argument that French economic measures had harmed Dutch trade, but also pointed to the 'scheme of the kings of France and England to ruin us, both with a great zeal for the Catholic religion'.[165]

Such considerations were even more prevalent among many in William's entourage. It has been suggested that William was a lukewarm Protestant, but it is worth noting that he assembled a number of key advisers, such as Schomberg and Bentinck, to whom 'religion and liberty' was hardly an empty phrase.[166] There were, moreover, a large number of clergymen who had been actively involved in the preparation of the invasion, many of whom were contacts of Bentinck. Pierre Jurieu, a Huguenot minister and propagandist would become involved in setting up an intelligence service.[167] Daniel Desmarets, a Huguenot minister, was actively labouring on William's behalf, and the Utrecht minister Vicius had accompanied Dijkveld to England to establish connections with the clergy there.[168] Gilbert Burnet and the reverend William Carstares came to play important roles before and after the Revolution.

Evidently, Bentinck, who devised William's banner with the motto, was aware of the propaganda value of the pretext of William's invasion.[169] But to Bentinck the phrase 'religion and liberty' was not a cynical piece of propaganda; it continuously recurs in his correspondence. In an unusually personal and sincere retrospective letter to William – obviously devoid of propaganda – Bentinck would later reflect on the enterprise of 1688, arguing that it had only been for the 'the service of God, the defence of the laws of England and the liberty of that state and the interest of the whole of Europe'.[170] In mobilising support among German Protestant princes during the summer, William had shown a deep concern for the 'German liberty'.[171] So did Bentinck when he met Paul Fuchs in Celle on 6 August. Although the Brandenburg envoy was well disposed to the Dutch, Bentinck dramatised the supposed designs of Louis and James.[172] He argued that the English nobility urged William to intervene. But Bentinck made it very clear that the main reason for the intended invasion

---

165 Hudde's minutes of a meeting of the Amsterdam *Groot Besoigne*, Gebhard, *Witsen*, II. 169, transl. from Dutch. The notes leave unclear whether the burgomasters themselves agreed with this point of view.

166 William as lukewarm argued by J.I. Israel, 'William III and Toleration' in: O.P. Grell, N. Tyacke and J.I. Israel (eds), *From Persecution to Toleration, the Glorious Revolution and Religion in England* (Oxford, 1991), 129–70.

167 On Jurieu, see F.R.J. Knetsch, *Pierre Jurieu, Theoloog en Politikus der Refuge* (Kampen, 1967). On Jurieu's intelligence network, see for instance the newsletters in TNA: PRO, SP 84/220.

168 E.g. *Négociations de Monsieur le Comte d'Avaux*, IV. 279, 303, 304.

169 Van der Kuijl, *De Glorieuze Overtocht*, 37.

170 Bentinck to William 22 March 1690 (The Hague), Japikse, *Correspondentie*, XXIII. 153, transl. from French.

171 William to Bentinck 7 June 1688, Japikse, *Correspondentie*, XXIII. 41. Transl. from French.

172 The particulars of this meeting are based on a report by Fuchs. In this paragraph I have made use of summaries made by Klopp and Grew: O. Klopp, *Der Fall des Hauses Stuart und die Succession des Hauses Hannover in Grosz-Britannien und Irland im Zusammenhange*

was that James could expect a favourable parliament in the autumn, after which Protestantism would be overturned. Due to a renewed treaty of Dover, James and Louis would invade the United Provinces,[173] and eventually even Germany. Liberty and religion, Ham had argued, depended on the positive commitment of the German princes.[174] Indeed, on several occasions Bentinck explicitly connected the security of the Protestant religion to the integrity of the Dutch Republic. To Ham, Bentinck had written that it was to be expected that the affairs in England 'would burst into extremities, in which case we cannot sit still, but have to do our best, or the Republic and Religion is lost'.[175] Thus, to Bentinck religion and liberty were inextricably connected, and the multiple crises of 1688 of rising Catholicism and absolutism had to be met with resolution.[176]

VI

This chapter has yielded three conclusions on different levels. Firstly, with regard to Bentinck's own role it can be concluded that by 1688 he had developed into a confident soldier and diplomat. The years of experience he had gained in diplomacy, military organisation and foreign affairs seemed to have prepared him for the challenges during the summer and autumn of 1688. Like Nassau-Zuylestein and Dijkveld he was involved in the establishment of a secret intelligence network in England, which he gradually took over during the course of 1688. He also became involved in the logistical preparations of the invasion, taking care of food supplies and ammunition and drafting marching orders for the actual embarkation of the troops. During his diplomatic missions to Germany he mustered military support and was engaged in constructing an anti-French alliance. If diplomacy and military affairs constituted his core responsibilities, Bentinck was involved in virtually all other aspects related to the preparations. He discussed the size and configuration of the invasion fleet. Together with Dijkveld and Fagel he was engaged in establishing political consensus and raising funds. Although Bentinck commented on the text of the *Declaration* and discussed it with William's other advisers, his role in the propaganda campaign was concerned with logistics rather than with contents; he mainly took care of the distribution of pamphlets. Bentinck therefore emerged as William's only confidant to become involved in all aspects of the operation, and would be the only one permanently at his side.

Secondly, it has shown the importance of paying more attention to William's Dutch confidants and favourites, most of whom have suffered from historiographical neglect. There are almost no modern biographies available of the members of

---

der Europäischen Angelegenheiten von 1660–1714 (14 vols, Vienna, 1875–88), IV. 68–72; Grew, *Bentinck*, 112–20.

    173 See also Baxter, *William III*, ch. 16.
    174 Ham to Bentinck 1/11 August 1688, NUL, PwA 527.
    175 Bentinck to Ham 20 July 1688, Japikse, *Correspondentie*, XXIV. 132, transl. from Dutch.
    176 Cf. Groenveld, "'J'equippe une Flotte très Considerable' ", 241.

William's foreign entourage.[177] Although William tended to act independently, he relied more on the advice and support of his closest aides than has often been thought. The activities of extremely able men like Fagel, Nassau-Zuylestein, Bentinck and Dijkveld contributed in large measure to the successes which were obtained.

A last conclusion is that it is important to study the events of 1688/1689 in an international context. In the spring of 1688 the Dutch were as much focused on Germany and France as on England. Bentinck spent considerable time conducting talks with the German allies and diplomatically intervening in the Cologne disputes. At the same time he maintained lines of communication with the opposition in England. As from June events in Germany and England both dictated the use of force. From then on Bentinck was tirelessly engaged in preparing German alliances and the invasion. This chapter has analysed Dutch strategic considerations in 1688 and placed them within a European framework.

---

177 Fagel and Heinsius are only cursorily studied in A. de Fouw, *Onbekende Raadpensionarissen* (The Hague, 1946). But see A.J. Veenendaal, 'Who is in Charge here? Anthonie Heinsius and his Role in Dutch Politics' in: A.J. Veenendaal and J.A.F. de Jongste (eds), *Anthonie Heinsius and the Dutch Republic 1688–1720* (The Hague, 2002), 11–24; E. Edwards, 'An Unknown Statesman: Gaspar Fagel in the Service of William III and the Dutch Republic', *History*, 87 (2002), 353–71.

Chapter 3

The Consolidation of the Williamite Settlement (1689–91)

The successful Dutch invasion that initiated the Glorious Revolution had unintentionally resulted in a vacancy of the English throne. William's position in this regard was still being debated. Moreover, his position in Scotland and Ireland was still by no means secure, and his kingship there might have to be assured by force. His absence from two of his kingdoms and the United Provinces, and his concentration on the war that had broken out on the continent, weakened his grip on affairs in these parts of his realms. The revolution settlement was especially unstable during the first two years of William's reign. While he struggled to maintain his prerogatives in the three kingdoms, there was also opposition in the United Provinces, and from outside there was the continuous threat of a French-Jacobite invasion.

Jonathan Israel has argued that the period 1689–91 should be regarded as an essential and distinct phase in William's reign during which he consolidated his position in Britain partly with the help of Dutch military forces. There was, then, a connection between events in these realms. The establishment of this composite monarchy provoked considerable opposition and complications. According to Israel, William's 'position in Britain and Ireland was precarious and his position in the United Provinces potentially so. One defeat in Ireland might well mean the collapse of the entire shaky edifice, Glorious Revolution and all'.[1] It took until the end of 1691 to firmly consolidate the revolution settlement and to subjugate the Scottish and Irish rebels.

This chapter does not seek to provide an exhaustive analysis of the first years of William's reign, but to show how events in the three kingdoms and the republic were intimately connected. Bentinck played an important role in several key issues that threatened the settlement, and as such was involved in stabilising and consolidating the Williamite settlement, both in the British kingdoms and the United Provinces.

I

Until recently historians have paid little attention to the Dutch role leading up to the Convention.[2] Few historians now believe that William's aim had been to steal the crown from his father-in-law, but it would be difficult to argue that his invasion had

---

1 J.I. Israel, 'The Dutch Role in the Glorious Revolution' in: J.I. Israel (ed.), *The Anglo-Dutch Moment. Essays on the Glorious Revolution and its World Impact* (Cambridge, 1991), 105–62, 154.

2 But see ibid. 129–30.

been wholly altruistic. The Prince was now in actual control of the administration, his main advisers laboured for his elevation and the Dutch army virtually occupied the capital (the English troops having been ordered to leave the city). Did the Prince influence the proceedings of the Convention?

At first sight evidence seems to support the idea that William abstained from any interference either before or during the Convention.[3] It is extremely difficult to find any direct evidence of William's intervention, but as early as August 1688 he had intimated to Bentinck that he was particularly reluctant (though not unwilling) to grant Parliament the initiative.[4] However, William was now effectively in control, and English politicians made anything but a positive impression. Moreover, the French had declared war and moved their troops to the Dutch borders, and a decisive stand was crucial. It would be hard to believe the Prince did not play his hand.[5] In fact, a careful reconstruction of the conduct of the Dutch suggests three ways in which William may have strengthened his position.

Firstly, as Dutch troops swarmed the London streets, the invaders were in effective control of the city and did not allow interference or criticism. The general mood was initially pro-Dutch. Sir John Reresby noted upon his arrival in London that

> the streets were filled with ill lookeing and ill habited Dutch and other strangers of the Prince's army. And yet the Citty was soe pleased with their diliverers that they did not or would not perceave their deformity nor the oppression they laid under, which was much greater then what they felt from the English army.[6]

The notorious removal of the King from his palace by the Blue Guards had been highly controversial; despite William's popularity and widespread rejection of the policies of the King, the latter could still count on significant sympathy from his subjects. William did not make the same mistake again, and there would be no more obvious displays of power. Nevertheless, the Dutch army remained an independent force outside the control of the Convention, and was, as such, an occupying force. In December several local townsmen complained to the Earl of Clarendon about disorders caused by Dutch soldiers. When the Earl spoke of it to Bentinck, he dismissed the complaints and intimated that Clarendon had no right to question such matters. Henry Capel had to explain to Bentinck the reasonableness of Clarendon's request, telling him that the Earl was in his 'own country, and therefore people made application to [him]. Bentinck shews his temper betimes'.[7] Although the Dutch army seems to have behaved properly on the whole, such tensions with the civilian

---

3 G. Burnet, *History of his Own Time* (6 vols, London, 1725), III. 1380; 30 January 1689, *Memoirs of Sir John Reresby. The Complete Text and a Selection from his Letters*, ed. W.H. Speck (London, 1991), 546.

4 William to Bentinck 29 August 1688, Japikse, *Correspondentie*, XXIII. 49.

5 Cf. Israel, 'Dutch Role', 134–6.

6 22 January 1689, Speck, *Memoirs*, 545.

7 5 December 1688, *The Correspondence of H.H. Earl of Clarendon and of his Brother, Laurence Hyde, Earl of Rochester; with the Diary of Lord Clarendon from 1687 to 1690 ... and the Diary of Lord Rochester during his Embassy to Poland in 1676*, ed. S.W. Singer (2 vols., London, 1828), II. 217.

population were inevitable. Bentinck's unbending attitude towards his peers caused additional friction. The evident joy at the arrival of the 'liberating' army soon turned into resentment. It seems, though, that for that very reason William withdrew some of his troops from the City during the Convention. The Prince understood very well that military force would only harm his case and could not legitimize his presence and claim.[8]

Secondly, although apparently William did not directly influence the proceedings of the Convention, throughout December and January the Williamites actively tried to sway public opinion; public prayers and sermons were delivered. In his study on the 'godly revolution', Tony Claydon has identified the strategy of divines such as Gilbert Burnet, to present the Prince as a deliverer for the Protestant cause.[9] Such attempts not only served to legitimize any claim the Prince had to the throne, they also in some sense sacralised such a claim and served to mobilise popular Orangism. William himself, though shunning crowds, firmly reinforced that view. During his march to London, 'the people flocked to see him, and prayed to god to bless him. As he passed by them, he put off his hat, and said, thank you, good people: I am come to secure the protestant religion, and to free you from popery'.[10] On 10 February, as the Lords in the Convention fiercely debated William's position, a national Thanksgiving Day was organised. Undoubtedly, popular pressure was exerted on the Convention to crown the Prince. Reresby noted that

> the lords that were for conferring the crown immediately upon the Prince, fearing the contrary interest of makeing him only regent, or crowning him in right of his wife, might prevaile, sent some instruments to stir up the mobile who came in a tumultuous manner with a petition, offering it both to the Lords and Commons this purpas: to crown both the Prince and Princess of Orang, to take speedy care of religion and property, and for the defence of Ireland.[11]

Most significant, however, was an active lobbying effort to confer the crown upon William in which Bentinck was particularly instrumental. There has been much speculation about William's motives for invading England, mainly because concrete evidence is scarce and ambiguous. The journals of Constantijn Huygens and Nicolaas Witsen, not often used by historians, provide interesting insights into the mindset and motives of William's Dutch counsellors. Gaspar Fagel's death and Lord Dijkveld's absence robbed William of two of his most senior advisers during the invasion and part of January 1689. Bentinck, then, played a disproportionately important role as William's adviser during these crucial weeks of the Glorious Revolution.[12] Arguably,

---

8   Dispatch Witsen 11 January 1689, GA, 5027/7; It appears therefore that Jonathan Israel's plausible suggestion that some pressure was exerted by the army's presence cannot be substantiated. Israel, 'Dutch Role', 126 ff.; BL, Eg Mss 2717, f° 426r°.

9   A.M. Claydon, *William III and the Godly Revolution* (Cambridge, 1996); 4 December 1688, Singer, *Diary of Clarendon*, II. 215.

10 Singer, *Diary of Clarendon*, II. 256.

11 2 February 1689, Speck, *Memoirs*, 548–9.

12 Dijkveld arrived in early January with the Dutch extraordinary embassy. Fagel had died in December.

the Prince being hesitant, Bentinck – much more ambitious and tenacious – was the driving force behind his decision to settle for the sole executive power.[13]

Clearly William's councillors knew that it was important to uphold the *Declaration* in public. With regard to the purpose of the expedition, Bentinck had assured Clarendon during a conversation on 4 December 1688:

> ... his Highness had given a sincere account of it in his declaration; and that he had proceeded in pursuance thereof ever since his landing. Though ... there are not ill men wanting, who give it out that the Prince aspires at the crown; which is the most wicked insinuation that could be invented; that though three kingdoms would be a great temptation to other men, yet it would appear, that the Prince perferred his word before all other things in the world, and would pursue his declaration in endeavouring to settle all matters here upon a true foundation.[14]

Surely Bentinck understood that Clarendon would be satisfied with this statement, but there is reason to believe he was not just being disingenuous. Around that same day William's staff discussed the difficulties of the Hungerford negotiations. When some of the Prince's entourage informally expressed doubts about the legitimacy of the Prince of Wales, Bentinck became highly irritated. The favourite pointed out that they 'had nothing to do with those things, that all affairs had to be examined by Parliament and that His Highness [William] was to stick to his declaration'.[15]

The situation had obviously changed after James's flight. Some of William's staunchest supporters were dismayed by his apparent passivity during the Convention, but behind the scenes there was frantic lobbying. Nicolaas Witsen, with Dijkveld member of an extraordinary embassy that arrived in London in February, wrote:

> While the Convention was in session, the Prince kept silent, not enticing the members by promises, like many had expected. The 11th [of February] the Prince speaks to Dijkveld in secret, who subsequently speaks with the Lords of the Convention. Still the Prince asks for nothing, neither promises nor threatens, but his friends labour.[16]

It was mainly Bentinck and Dijkveld who laboured. In early February Lord Yester wrote his father the Earl of Tweeddale:

---

13   The Prince had written to Waldeck that he did not find the crown appealing: J.K. Oudendijk, *Willem III, Stadhouder van Holland, Koning van Engeland* (Amsterdam, 1954), 235–6. But the lobbying had started even before James's actual flight, see Bishop of St Asaph to Bentinck, 17 December 1688, J. Dalrymple (ed.), *Memoirs of Great Britain and Ireland etc.* (2 vols, London, 1790), II. 336–7. Cf. Ronquillo to Cogolludo 7 January 1689: 'one way or another they will bestow upon the Prince a supreme authority', *Correspondencia entre Dos Embajadores, Don Pedro Ronquillo y el Marques de Cogolludo 1689–1691*, ed. Duque de Maura (2 vols, Madrid, 1951), I. 63, transl. from Spanish.

14   4 December 1688, Singer, *Diary of Clarendon*, II. 215.

15   12 December 1688, Huygens, *Journaal*, I-i. 34, transl. from Dutch. Cf. William to Danby 12 December 1688 OS, Japikse, *Correspondentie*, XXVIII. 84.

16   Dijkveld 'strongly continued the work of the elevation in January', N. Witsen, 'Verbaal' in: *Geschied- en Letterkundig Mengelwerk*, ed. J. Scheltema (6 vols, Utrecht, 1818–36), III. 135, 139. Transl. from Dutch.

Mr Seymoor told here that he had it from Monsr Beintheine that the Prince was not satisfyed with the restrictions and limitations these were putting upon the crowne and that if it had been left to himself he would have done better and more for theire securitye, this almost fired the house but much more the lords, where it was said by Nottingham that the Prince ought to consider that the Crown of England with whatever limitations was far more then any thing the States of Holland were able to give him.

When Henry Sidney was despatched to the Prince, the latter 'said such a thing was far from his mind'.[17] The next day Dijkveld had a conversation with the Tory Earl of Nottingham, who was willing to accept William as a regent, but not as king. Dijkveld had replied that there was very little difference between those two, implying that the Prince was interested in the executive power rather than the dignity itself.[18]

If Dijkveld and Bentinck were involved in the lobbying for the crown, another issue was the question as to whether William should rule alone or share the sovereign power with Mary. When the Marquis of Halifax suggested that William should be offered the crown, Bentinck

> spoke of it to me, as asking my opinion about it, but so, that I plainly saw what was his own. For he gave me all the arguments that were offered for it; as that it was most natural that the sovereign power should be only in one person; that a man's wife ought only to be his wife; that it was a suitable return to the Prince for what he had done for the Nation; that a divided sovereignty was liable to great inconveniences: and, tho' there was less to be apprehended from the Princess of any thing of that kind than from any woman alive, yet all mortals were frail, and might at some time or other of their lives be wrought on.[19]

Burnet defended the rights of Mary as a full reigning sovereign, and the two men discussed the matter until deep in the night, unable to agree. Bentinck sounded out a number of Williamites. When Herbert furiously rejected his views, the next day Bentinck spoke to Burnet again and agreed that Mary's rights had to be respected.[20] Others took this lobbying behind the scenes very ill as well. Burnet reported that with regard to his authority both Bentinck and the Prince 'spake to a great many upon this subject in a style of such earnestness and positiveness that all this tended to increase the jealousy'.[21]

Although Dijkveld reportedly laboured constantly for William's elevation, he seemed more willing to accept a compromise than was Bentinck. Witsen, on various occasions, remarked that Bentinck was the driving force behind the Prince's decision to insist on the sole executive power:

---

17   Yester to Tweeddale 11 February 1689, House of Lords archives, The Willcocks Collection Section 6.
18   12 February 1689, Huygens, *Journaal*, I-i. 80.
19   Burnet, *History*, III. 1377.
20   M.E. Grew, *William Bentinck and William III (Prince of Orange). The Life of Bentinck, Earl of Portland, from the Welbeck Correspondence* (London, 1924), 150–51.
21   *A Supplement to Burnet's History of my Own Time etc.*, ed. H.C. Foxcroft (Oxford, 1902), 334.

Dijkveld had arranged for the Princess to be elected next to the Prince, although someone (probably Bentinck) had strongly laboured to have only the Prince elected ... Bentinck and Dijkveld had laboured hard, the former with great vehemence, be it on his own account or not.[22]

This evidence suggests that there were no indications of a conscious design by William to aim for a specific settlement. Between December and February William's advisers were divided amongst themselves and making up their minds as events unfolded.

II

On 13 February in Banqueting Hall the crowns were offered to William and Mary, who were to be Joint Monarchs. The coronation took place on 11 April. A few days later Bentinck took his seat in the House of Lords as 1st Earl of Portland, Viscount Woodstock and Baron of Cirencester.[23] William was now King of three kingdoms and 'eminent head' of a republic. The sheer complexities of William's new wide-ranging prerogatives rested uneasily with his inclination to personally retain control.[24] He had difficulty overseeing and co-ordinating his different realms, and Bentinck emerged as virtually the only adviser to transcend a national perspective. William could consult him in relation to the co-ordination of his realms, rendering his role extremely important.

While the Glorious Revolution in England took place without bloodshed, the situation in the other kingdoms was much more precarious. In the spring of 1689 a French-Jacobite army had landed in Ireland, whilst in Scotland the upheaval resulted in the virtual breakdown of existing political frameworks. The revolution in Scotland had a more radical character and deeper impact than in England. The Convention stated on 4 April 1689 that James had 'forfeited' his throne, whereas the Episcopalian settlement collapsed and prelacy was condemned as an 'insupportable grievance'. Armed opposition in favour of the exiled king materialised under the leadership of Viscount Dundee. In March 1689 William decided to employ two of his most trusted commanders, Hugh Mackay and the Duke of Schomberg, to crush the Jacobite forces in Scotland and Ireland respectively.[25] Mackay and his Anglo-Dutch regiments were despatched to Edinburgh to take possession of the castle

---

22   Witsen, 'Verbaal', 135, 147, 159–60, transl. from Dutch. 'When the Conditions upon which the Crown was to be conferred upon him were under Debate, Mynheer Benting told some of those he judged most fit to transmit his Master's Mind to the leading Members of his Party, that if they intended to clog the Crown with such Limitations, they little understood the Disposition of the Prince', [N. Johnston], *The Dear Bargain, or, A True Representation of the State of the English Nation under the Dutch. In a Letter to a Friend* in: Somers, *Third Collection*, III. 253.

23   HMC, *The Manuscripts of the House of Lords 1689–1690* (London, 1889), 84; *House of Lords Journals*, XIV. 175. All these dates are in Old Style.

24   Cf. J. Carter, 'Cabinet Records for the Reign of William III', *English Historical Review*, 88 (1963), 95–114, 104; S.B. Baxter, *William III* (London, 1966), 272.

25   Citters to the States General 18 March 1689, BL, Add Mss 17677, f⁰ 26vº–7rº.

which the Duke of Gordon held for James. The occupation of Edinburgh castle proved short lived, but the Jacobite army under Dundee's leadership was roaming the Highlands and would not be easily subjugated. Embarrassingly, Mackay suffered a defeat in the battle of Killiecrankie in July, and though Dundee himself perished, the Jacobites embarked on a prolonged guerrilla war.[26] William was eager to prevent a bitter struggle and willing to offer indemnity to those ready to abandon their cause and swear allegiance.[27]

Portland was to play an important role in the political affairs of Scotland, as will be discussed in chapter 5. He was also involved in military affairs in Scotland. Throughout the summer and autumn of 1689 he was directly involved in the logistic aspects of the campaign and issuing instructions to Mackay.[28] His primary concern, characteristically, was the military safeguarding of the precarious new settlement. Portland had few doubts that Scotland could be pacified, but the main problem was that it created an undesirable diversion from the more perilous situation in Ireland, as he wrote to Hugh Mackay on 25 April from Whitehall Palace:

> I hope that you will be entirely safe now that our troops are marching, and I doubt not that you will now have received news of the fleet off your coasts. We have received bad news from Londonderry which make us fear that the plague there will make our affairs in Ireland very difficult. It is surprising that the Convention takes such a long time deciding who should be sent there, and that meanwhile they do not let the King know anything about what they have done.[29]

Portland's contribution to the stabilisation of the revolution settlement in Scotland consisted of his involvement in the planning of the military campaign in the Highlands, but also in overcoming factional struggles that hampered the campaign. Evidence of his actions is fragmentary, but two affairs related to the Highland campaigns are illustrative. He became increasingly dissatisfied with his client, the Scottish Secretary of State, George Melville, when military strategy fell prey to partisan animosity. In the spring of 1690 Hugh Mackay had frequently asked for military and financial support from London in order to clear out the Highlands. Would it not be in the King's interest, he wrote to Portland, if Scotland were to be pacified by the time the King went to Ireland?[30] Portland was slow to reply, other matters pressing abroad, but before he had left for The Hague he had given positive orders that Mackay be provided with ships and supplies. When Mackay realised that Melville would not support his strategy and London seemed apathetic, he wrote directly to Portland

---

26 Israel, 'Dutch role', 146–7.

27 Instructions William to Lord Melville 7 March 1689 in: *Leven and Melville Papers. Letters and State Papers chiefly Addressed to George Earl of Melville, Secretary of State for Scotland, 1689–1691*, ed. W.L. Melville (Edinburgh, 1843), 1.

28 Buchan to Nairne 5 September 1689, Melville, *Leven and Melville Papers*, 271.

29 Portland to Mackay (?) 25 April 1689 (Whitehall Palace), Melville, *Leven and Melville Papers*, 16, transl. from French.

30 Mackay to Portland 5 June 1690, H. Mackay, *Memoirs of the War carried on in Scotland and Ireland 1689–1691* (Edinburgh, 1833), 92.

in The Hague.[31] Portland quickly realised that Melville was obstructing Mackay's efforts, and strongly reprimanded the otherwise successful Secretary:

> I recently asked Mr Carstares to speak to you about General Major Mackay, who you know is a very honest man, and very zealous in his service to the King our master, who can be entirely relied on with regard to military matters. Sir, it is very necessary that you get on with him well, that is to say that you show him your confidence, that you act in concert with him about all the said affairs, and that you provide all possible support without delay.[32]

When Portland was in Ireland during the summer of 1690, Scotland was shocked by the discovery of the Montgomery plot, a grotesque Jacobite conspiracy initiated by disgruntled politicians such as Montgomery, Annandale and Ross; it discredited the Club and consequently strengthened the Court. Portland received copies of letters Melville and Carstares sent to the Queen, informing her of the particulars. He needed to be fully informed even though he was not in a position to fully occupy himself with Scotland.[33] As a result of the disastrous naval defeat at Beachy Head in the summer of 1690 William's army was locked up in Ireland. Fears of a Jacobite plot for a rebellion following a French invasion caused panic in Scotland, and Melville was eager to have the army near Edinburgh rather than in the Highlands. But the plot signified little, and Portland angrily wrote to Melville from Ireland, criticising his decision to keep troops around Edinburgh whilst they were needed by Mackay: 'You would squander the fruits of his enterprise there'.[34] The Secretary turned to the Queen, complaining about the ill-directed efforts of the General-Major. Mary forwarded the letter to Portland, and one may presume that he became disillusioned with Melville over the summer.[35]

Portland again intervened when Melville seemed to undermine the 1691 mission of the Earl of Breadalbane, commissioned to spend £12,000 to get the rebellious chiefs to lay down their arms and swear allegiance to William. As in Ireland, William adopted a stick-and-carrot policy, in that at the same time he ordered Thomas Livingstone (who had replaced Mackay on Portland's recommendation)[36] to march to the borders of the Highlands. Breadalbane was supported by Dalrymple who leaned on the English Tory Secretary of State, the Earl of Nottingham and Queen Mary, both

---

31   Mackay to Melville 9 November 1689, 21 December 1689. Mackay to Portland 13 March 1690, 9 April 1690, Mackay, *Memoirs of the War*, 298, 312, 173–6. Cf. *The Register of the Privy Council of Scotland*, XV, ed. E.W.M. Balfour-Melville (3rd series, Edinburgh, 1967), 20.

32   Portland to Melville 9 June 1690 ('Daupres de Haylake'), *Leven and Melville Papers*, 442–3, transl. from French.

33   William Carstares to 'Sir', NUL, PwA 2349; Melville to Mary 23 June 1690, NUL, PwA 2336.

34   Portland to Melville 23 July 1690/2 August 1690 ('Champ du Carick'), Melville, *Leven and Melville Papers*, 475, transl. from French.

35   Melville to Mary 17 August 1690, NUL, PwA 2344.

36   Mackay to Portland 4 November 1690, Mackay, *Memoirs*, 216–17; Cf. Balfour-Melville, *The Register of the Privy Council of Scotland*, 516.

favouring the Episcopalians for religious reasons.[37] The Duke of Hamilton convinced the Presbyterian faction in Edinburgh that Breadalbane's success would lead to a change in the ministry in favour of the Episcopalians, with the result that Melville now tried to sabotage the Breadalbane mission. When Nottingham complained to Portland that Hamilton had ordered Livingston to march to upset the talks, Portland clearly gave his support to Breadalbane's mission:

> As I am persuaded that the negotiation of Mylord Breadelbane was for the service of the King I have helped him to the extent of my abilities. The affair has been achieved and His Majesty has accepted the submission of the Highlanders of Scotland ... God willing the peace and tranquility will be established in that kingdom.[38]

Not until the end of 1691 was the Scottish settlement secure. Due to the December 1691 settlement the pacification of Scotland could be undertaken and troops would become available for the new campaign on the continent. Until all of the Highland chiefs had been subdued, however, troops would still be needed there. During the winter of 1691/1692 Portland was overseeing the troop movements around Inverness.[39]

III

Part of the reason Portland had been slow to reply to Mackay's cries for assistance in the spring of 1690 was his absence from Court. The United Provinces had been in upheaval after the departure of the Stadholder to England and the death of the Grand Pensionary Fagel, while French troops moved towards the Dutch borders in an all-out war that had been declared in November 1688. The Stadholder's absence facilitated latent opposition to the stadholderly system and dissatisfaction with the implications of the new alliance. These surfaced in the spring of 1690 during a constitutional conflict between William and Amsterdam in which Portland became embroiled. Only fragmentary information is available on Portland's role in Dutch politics after 1688, but the conflict with Amsterdam, the most important constitutional conflict in the United Provinces during William's reign as King-Stadholder, is well documented.

Many regents tried to take advantage of the absence of the Stadholder, as they expected that his grip on Dutch affairs would weaken. Opposition against William was widespread and also visible on provincial and local levels. Portland's own position as Bailiff in Breda was challenged. Tromer was alarmed when the Breda sheriffs encroached upon the authority of his apparently feeble vice-bailiff: 'Unless Your Excellency', he wrote to Portland, 'forcefully maintains his authority and office there the foundation will be crushed out of the lawful interest as well as the

---

37   P. Hopkins, *Glencoe and the End of the Highland War* (Edinburgh, 1998), 272 ff.
38   Portland to Nottingham 17/27 August 1691 ('Du Camp de St Gerard'), Dalrymple to Nottingham 17/27 August 1691, HMC, *Finch Mss*, III. 211, 213–14, transl. from French.
39   NUL, PwA 2435.

prerogative of your office of bailiff.'[40] Another creature of William, Halewijn, had been attacked in the States Assembly by Amsterdam.

There was, however, also anxiety among Republicans that William as King would be able to increase his authority as Stadholder, though Orangist pamphleteers argued that William's absence would weaken his position.[41] Moderates, such as the Amsterdam burgomaster Nicolaas Witsen, were faced with a dilemma. They had supported the expedition to England but were disappointed in some of its consequences. Paradoxically, they were dissatisfied with the Stadholder but needed the support of the King. The burgomaster, who returned from his embassy to London in November 1689, had become disgruntled by his exclusion from William's inner circle and his failure to gain commercial advantages for Amsterdam. Portland had been authorised to offer him a barony, hoping this would give him satisfaction. Witsen declined the offer, as it would give the false impression of harmony between Amsterdam and the Stadholder.[42] Meanwhile, the balance in Amsterdam temporarily swung in favour of the Republicans. The City Council had become subject to faction struggles and for the moment it seemed that the Republicans, most notably burgomaster Johan Huydecooper van Maarseveen and the Pensioner Cornelis Bors van Waveren, had the upper hand over the Orangist elements.

Meanwhile, the autumn of 1689 had also seen the diminishing influence of William's creatures in the Council of State (*Raad van State*), the executive body of the Union mainly responsible for military affairs. The Council of State consisted of representatives from each province. Naturally those of the regions which were firmly under William's control (Overijssel, Utrecht and Gelderland) could be counted on, and an attempt was made to secure Waldeck a seat in the Council of State.[43] Van Reede van Amerongen, however, the Utrecht representative and father of Ginckel, tied to William's cause as a trusted diplomat, warned Portland in December 1689 about the recent disharmony in the Council of State. He was unable to establish a majority vote on many important issues and favourable decisions were either prevented or delayed.[44] Portland thought little of Amerongen, and Waldeck complained that the Gelderland deputy Jacob Schimmelpenninck van der Oije lacked vigour in the Council of State.[45] In early January 1690 Amerongen complained to Portland that the *Staat van Oorlog* (State of War, the yearly budget for military expenses) was

---

40   Tromer to Portland December 1689, Japikse, *Correspondentie*, XXVIII. 139, transl. from Dutch.

41   E.g. *De Gelukkige Aanstaande Gevolgen uit de Unie en Verbintenis tusschen Haar Majesteiten Willem III. en Maria II. ... en de Ho. Mo. Heeren Staten Generaal der Vereenigde Nederlanden* (The Hague, 1689). Cf. G.N. Clark, 'The Dutch Missions to England in 1689', *English Historical Review*, 35 (1920), 529–57, 533.

42   William to Portland 31 January 1690, Japikse, *Correspondentie*, XXIII. 85; Witsen, 'Verbaal', 165.

43   29 May 1689, Huygens, *Journaal*, I-i. 133.

44   Amerongen to Portland 30 December 1689, Japikse, *Correspondentie*, XXVIII. 138; William to Heinsius 27 September 1689, *Het Archief van den Raadpensionaris Antonie Heinsius*, ed. H.J. van der Heim (3 vols, The Hague, 1867), II. 13–14.

45   Waldeck to William 26 July 1689, Japikse, *Correspondentie*, XXVIII. 120.

still under discussion.[46] A majority in the Council of State had blocked the *Staat van Oorlog* from being brought before the States General for approval pending an amendment concerning the Dutch troops in England. Amerongen, Anthonie Heinsius (the new Grand Pensionary) and Waldeck opposed the amendment because they thought the Council of State had no right to give such a pre-advice.[47] Thus, at the start of a new campaign, the military preparations were subject to severe delays, causing William considerable anxiety.

Due to the absence of the Stadholder, the Orangists (the 'Williamite party' in the United Provinces) lacked leadership and commitment. In January 1690 Amsterdam decided that the time was right to mount a direct attack on the Stadholder himself, refusing to send him the list from which he was entitled to elect the *schepenen* (magistrates) in the City Council. A resolution from 1581 served as a pretext to send it instead to the *Hof van Holland* (the Court of Justice, imbued with executing several stadholderly prerogatives) during the absence of the Stadholder. William was indignant over the affront and threat to his prerogative. 'I am so alarmed by the conduct of Amsterdam', he wrote to Anthonie Heinsius, 'seeing what its consequences might be, not just for me, but for the welfare of the whole of Europe, that I have thought it proper to send the Earl of Portland to The Hague'.[48] Not a parochial concern for the intricacies of Dutch politics, as Marion Grew has asserted, but the enfolding drama of wide opposition and delays in the ways and means prompted William to reassert his authority.[49]

The matter was especially alarming because a new campaign against the French army in the spring 1690 was impending. In Portland's view, 'if we would not have been in such a dangerous time as we are now, I would regard that behaviour with indifference, because they have never acted in a more extraordinary fashion against reason and order of government'.[50] William's dilemma was not easy to solve. On the eve of his own campaign to Ireland he badly needed the funds Amsterdam could provide, and a good working relationship with the city was worth a compromise. Reflecting on the situation, Portland indignantly wrote to General Godard Reede van Ginckel on 3 January:

> It seems that there are plenty of people in the land who are not of your sentiment that the state has suffered a great loss in the person of the King, because they try to dispute with him about the just and due authority which he has exercised in the service of our beloved fatherland. May God forgive them for the difficulties they create for him in attempting, through their conduct, to change the tender inclination the King has for the country, and who in this conjuncture is the only one who can keep us and make us prosper ... After

---

46 Amerongen to Portland 3 January 1690, ibid., 141–2.
47 Amerongen to William 13 January 1690, ibid., 146–8.
48 William to Heinsius 8 January 1690, *Archives ou Correspondance Inédite de la Maison d'Orange-Nassau*, ed. F.J.L. Krämer (3rd series, 3 vols, Leiden, 1907–9), I. 46, transl. from Dutch.
49 Grew, *Bentinck*, 170–71.
50 Portland to William 11 February 1690 (The Hague), Japikse, *Correspondentie*, XXIII. 101, transl. from French.

that which touches directly on the King, the dissention in the Assembly and the army is the worst that can happen.[51]

The matter was discussed in detail between William and Portland at Kensington Palace, the latter's first letter from Sheerness reflecting on the course of action to be taken.[52] An expedient had been proposed by Heinsius and Dijkveld, one which Portland had misgivings about. He counselled his master:

> In truth, it seems to me to be a very dangerous consequence if Your Majesty allows short-term measures to the first who commit evil acts. It is true that these are dangerous times to let things go to extremes, but what to do, if Your Majesty, without that, loses that which he esteems more than those gentlemen on the other side of the sea can imagine, they only think about themselves and fear the quarrels, for which they are not too much to be blamed.[53]

William agreed with his adviser:

> The more I think about the affair of Amsterdam, the more I am having difficulties, although I am entirely convinced that I should not accept an expedient ... because by doing that I am giving away by provision a right which I pretend to have for myself.[54]

Although the contents of the terms are unknown, Portland comes across as the more uncompromising of William's advisers.

Portland's mission was to bolster and mobilise the Orangists and his arrival was eagerly awaited, Amerongen writing to William that he hoped 'that with the coming of the Earl of Portland this affair will be settled'.[55] His opponents in Amsterdam were also expecting him, and at his arrival 'the smoke almost transformed itself into flame'.[56] The City Council had passed a resolution on 14 January proposing that the States of Holland deny the Earl access to the Assembly of the States of Holland because he was in the service of a 'foreign potentate'. They based their phrasing and argument upon the 1581 resolution, when the clause had obviously referred to the King of Spain.[57] Although aimed at the Stadholder, the assault threatened Portland's own position. The *Ridderschap*, from which Portland operated and of

---

51   Portland to Ginckel 3 January 1690 (Kensington Palace), Japikse, *Correspondentie*, XXVIII. 142, transl. from French.

52   Portland to William 5/15 January 1690 (Sheerness), Japikse, *Correspondentie*, XXIII. 65–7; 10 January 1690, Huygens, *Journaal*, I-i. 223.

53   Portland to William 5/15 January 1690 (Sheerness), Japikse, *Correspondentie*, XXIII. 65–6, transl. from French.

54   William to Portland 16–17 January 1690, ibid., 67, transl. from French.

55   Amerongen to William 13 January 1690, Japikse, *Correspondentie*, XXVIII. 147, transl. from Dutch.

56   *Hollandsche Mercurius, behelsende het Gedenckweerdigste in Christenrijck voorgevallen, binnen 't gansche Jaar 1690* (Haarlem, 1691), XLI. 12, transl. from Dutch.

57   Resolution of the Amsterdam *Vroedschap*, 12 January 1690 printed in: *Hollandse Mercurius 1690*, 12–14. Cf. *An Account of the Passages in the Assembly of the States of Holland and West-Friezeland concerning the Earl of Portlands Exclusion from, or Admission into that Assembly* (London, 1690).

which Heinsius, in his capacity as Grand Pensionary, was spokesman, was the first to object to the conduct of Amsterdam in the States Assembly. Portland conferred with some of the nobles, the Lords Van Noortwijk, Van Wassenaar-Duyvenvoorde and Van Wassenaar-Obdam, who unanimously decided to support their compeer.[58] Having reaffirmed Portland's position within the *Ridderschap*, the nobles now declared that by excluding Portland from the Assembly, Amsterdam interfered with the internal affairs of the *Ridderschap*.

There seems to have been a genuine concern for 'English counsels' in the Dutch assembly.[59] A similar protest would be registered in 1715 when the position of Arnold Joost van Keppel, then Earl of Albemarle, was questioned.[60] But Portland himself had pointed out that there were other members of the Holland States Assembly who were in the service of other monarchs, and one delegate even suggested that such contacts could contribute to a better relationship with other governments.[61] However, the objection of the Amsterdammers in 1690 had not been entirely without legal basis. In fact, rather than dismiss it, the *Ridderschap* retorted that an exception should be made for Portland given his record of service to the country. It stated that

> His Majesty had undertaken the aforementioned expedition [to England] only with the previous communication and full approbation of the State ... that this State had not decided otherwise than that this must certainly lead to a closer and tighter bond of those realms with this State.

For this reason, Portland, who had accompanied William on that expedition, should be received with respect into the Assembly.[62]

Portland wrote to William that he would 'prepare the towns to be reasonable' and that Amsterdam had to be brought to reason. His client in Haarlem, Willem Fabricius, had launched an attack on Amsterdam accusing the city of arrogant behaviour.[63] That same day the States of Holland adopted a resolution, again ordering Amsterdam to send the nomination to London. The magistrates ignored it and, moreover, refused to pay their quota to support the army pending a decision in their favour. It soon became apparent that Amsterdam was quite isolated. Portland confidently wrote to William:

> All the towns without exception ... justified themselves beyond my expectations and, with many obliged expressions towards me, they reacted with indignation against the conduct of the gentlemen of Amsterdam ... .[64]

---

58   Portland to William 20 January 1690 (The Hague), Japikse, *Correspondentie*, XXIII. 71.
59   E.g. L. van Waarmont, *Missive van een Oprecht Patriot, Aen een Lidt van de Regeeringe, over de Geschillen wegens de Gepretendeerde Sessie van W. Benting, Grave van Portlandt* (s.l., 1690).
60   BL, Add Mss 15866, f° 242.
61   Dispatch of the Amsterdam deputy, 20 January 1690, GA, 5029/90.
62   *Hollandse Mercurius 1690*, 14, transl. from Dutch.
63   Portland to William 20 January 1690 (The Hague), 25 January (The Hague), Japikse, *Correspondentie*, XXIII. 72, 77, transl. from French.
64   Portland to William 20 January 1690 (The Hague), ibid., 71, transl. from French.

Apart from Amsterdam, the whole assembly seemed willing to support his position. If the matter could be decided before the members dispersed to their respective cities for consultation (in which case the faint-hearted might after all incline to Amsterdam's side) Portland considered the state of affairs reassuring.[65] In fact, that same day the States of Holland did pass a resolution reaffirming Portland's right to take his position in the Assembly. Amsterdam refused to give in, however, and out of protest her deputation decided to withdraw from the Assembly, leaving only the secretary, Bors van Waveren, as an observer.

Meanwhile Portland started organising the Orangist factions to counter Amsterdam's resistance. He was in close correspondence with Dijkveld and Halewijn and was instructed by William to confer with Waldeck and Heinsius.[66] Some of his correspondents, the Delft regent Gerard Putmans, the *Hof van Holland* delegate Cornelis van Halewijn and the Utrecht nobleman Everard van Weede van Dijkveld, had informed him of the state of affairs.[67] Hieronymus van Beverningk, deputy of Gouda, was considered an unreliable client, but Portland believed he could keep him in the Orangist camp. Portland managed to reconcile rival factions in Haarlem.[68] Van der Dussen was a strong supporter, though Portland failed to secure him a position in the Rotterdam Admiralty.[69] Portland was doubtful as to the firmness of the *Hof van Holland* but was aided by Halewijn, William's client in that body.

The most immediate task was to initiate preparations for the coming campaign, in which he thought the Council of State had been negligent.[70] Waldeck was signalling his difficulties in maintaining his position, which was being challenged by General Slangenburg, and the *Staat van Oorlog* now required urgent action. When the Deputies of the Holland States Assembly went into recess to discuss matters with the city councils, Portland started organising the Orangists in the Council of State. To the dependable councillors, the delegates from provinces dominated by the Stadholder, Gelderland (Schimmelpenninck van der Oije), Utrecht (Amerongen) and Overijssel (Borger Bernard van Welvede), he proposed pushing through a decision in line with William's wishes during the absence of ill-disposed members.[71] He convened a meeting of those in the *Gecommiteerde Raden* (the daily government of Holland) and the Council of State who were in the interest of the Stadholder, 'so that they do not absent themselves too often and they always have a majority, and also that they can prevent the disputes caused by pressure, and this is what I work on to the best of my abilities'.[72]

---

65   Portland to William 20 January 1690 (The Hague), ibid., 71–3.
66   Portland to William 20 January 1690 (The Hague), ibid., 71–3; e.g. Portland to William 3–4 March 1690 (The Hague), William to Portland 16–17 January 1690, ibid., 67–9, 131–4.
67   Portland to William 5/15 January 1690 (Sheerness), ibid., 65–7.
68   Portland to William 11 February 1690 (The Hague), ibid. 102.
69   Portland to William 20 January 1690 (The Hague), 15 February 1690 (The Hague), ibid., 72, 108.
70   William to Portland 17 February 1690, ibid., 109.
71   Portland to William 20 January 1690 (The Hague), ibid. 72–3.
72   Portland to William 4 February 1690 (The Hague), ibid., 92, transl. from French.

William was adamant that no compromise regarding the *Staat van Oorlog* would be acceptable.[73] Since it was imperative that the Council of State be managed properly, Portland was not unwilling to use threats and bribery in order to obtain his goal. 'I do not know why Vrijbergen [the Zeeland deputy in the Council of State] cannot be won over, either by threats or certain bribes', he wrote to William.[74] A few weeks later, however, he confirmed that he thought he had won over Vrijbergen.[75] But as for Huybert, the other Zeeland deputy whom Nassau-Odijk ought to have managed: 'I believe one can easily gain influence over him, but a thing of this nature should not be started lightly nor be stopped halfway through.'[76] Portland sent the Stadholder a draft letter on how to deal with Zeeland.[77] Amerongen was, he thought, old, ineffective and losing his vigour, but the Frisian Stadholder seemed co-operative now.[78]

> It is certain that Mr Amerongen does not act according to what he must do and promises, and the other well intentioned let themselves be swayed by people whose doings should all be suspicious to them, I am obliged to talk a bit clearly here.[79]

But meantime the only thing Portland could do was to put pressure on the Council of State to reach a speedy decision.[80] On 7 February the Council completed the *Staat van Oorlog*, and a week later it was brought into the States General, to the satisfaction of Portland.[81] The Orangists were gaining the upper hand in two vital bodies:

> As for the *Gecommiteerde Raden*, I have promises of engagements of the majority that they are taking care of preventing all that can cause harm to the public, diminishes your authority or creates problems for the Prince of Waldeck. Mr van den Honart who has to preside in the absence of Mr van Noortwijk has promised me that. As for the Council of State, I think that it will be easy enough to form a party so strong to prevent it from causing evil.[82]

In the meantime, Amsterdam still refused to go along with the States' resolution. Portland fulminated against 'those who by their capriciousness wish to let the Republic perish and debunk the foundations of the government'.[83] If William was hesitant to let

---

73 William to Portland 27 January 1690, ibid., 81.
74 William to Portland 27 January 1690, ibid., 80, transl. from French.
75 Portland to William 4 February 1690 (The Hague), ibid., 92.
76 Portland to William 4 February 1690 (The Hague), ibid, transl. from French.
77 Portland to William 11 February 1690 (The Hague), ibid., 103.
78 Portland to William 4 February 1690 (The Hague), 7 February 1690 (The Hague), 15 February 1690 (The Hague), William to Portland 27 January 1690, ibid., 92, 99, 107–8.
79 Portland to William 11 February 1690 (The Hague), ibid., 103, transl. from French.
80 Portland to William 4 February 1690 (The Hague), ibid., 92.
81 Portland to William 18 February 1690 (The Hague), ibid., 111.
82 Portland to William 11 February 1690 (The Hague), ibid., 102, transl. from French.
83 Portland to William 4 February 1690 (The Hague), ibid., 90, transl. from French.

the conflict with Amsterdam escalate, his favourite was adamant that William should defend his prerogatives. Among the Stadholder's associates, Portland and Heinsius played a leading role, and their decision not to settle for an accommodation, was taken without informing Waldeck and Dijkveld. William had shown himself much more conciliatory, urging Portland to establish a good relationship with Amsterdam rather than to alienate her. The key figure was Nicolaas Witsen, who assured Portland of his goodwill, but, the Earl wrote with some misgivings, 'I will believe in a saint when I will see miracles'.[84]

Portland and Heinsius started building up a party among the well-disposed cities in Holland.

> I have commenced to establish a correspondence between the great cities with one man in each of these, who will be responsible for correspondence in concert with the Pensionary. I only fear the feebleness and division of the other cities and those who spare neither money nor promises of office in their effort to seduce the magistrates in the smaller cities of the north of Holland.[85]

In late February he thought he was about to reap the fruits of his efforts, writing to William that those in the city councils who had seemed to have been drawn into Amsterdam's sphere of influence had been regained.[86]

A breakthrough came in early March when the faction of Hudde and Witsen gained the ascendant in the Amsterdam city council.[87] The latter came to The Hague to confer with Portland and propose an expedient. Portland did not give a definite answer, believing that accepting a compromise, a 'plastered accommodation', would leave fundamental problems unsolved.[88] He blamed the 'moderates' for losing six weeks of precious time debating and negotiating, during which the preparations for the coming campaign had been seriously delayed. Witsen meanwhile promised that the nomination would indeed be sent, but demanded that all references to Amsterdam's conduct be erased from the registers.[89] The only compromise Portland was willing to make, was, as it was formulated, to separate his personal from the public interest. This in effect meant that his position remained ambiguous. He was tolerated in the assembly, but Amsterdam did not acknowledge his right to take his seat.[90] Moreover, the compromise on which the parties finally agreed was rather

---

84   Portland to William 4 February 1690 (The Hague), ibid., 91, transl. from French.

85   Portland to William 7 February 1690 (The Hague), ibid., 98, transl. from French.

86   Portland to William 22 February 1690 (The Hague), ibid., 114.

87   J.F. Gebhard, *Het Leven van Mr. Nicolaas Cornelisz. Witsen (1641–1717)* (2 vols, Utrecht, 1882), I. 390; J.I. Israel, *The Dutch Republic, its Rise, Greatness and Fall 1477–1806* (Oxford, 1995), 855–6.

88   Portland to William 7–8 March 1690 (The Hague), Japikse, *Correspondentie*, XXIII. 138, transl. from French.

89   Portland to William 10 March 1690 (The Hague), Japikse, *Correspondentie*, XXIII. 142–3.

90   'the issue of the Earl of Portland silently passed over', quoted in Gebhard, *Witsen*, I. 394; 23 March 1689, Huygens, *Journaal*, I-i. 98, transl. from Dutch.

equivocal. The city would send the nomination to the States of Holland – since the Stadholder was absent – who then forwarded it to London.[91]

Portland acknowledged that it would have been better had the resolution ordering Amsterdam to send the nomination directly to London been upheld,

> ... but it seems to me to be clear proof that the Members of the States judge that it must be sent across the sea, and it is very good that Your Majesty will see to it, since you are in England, that they declare unanimously that they want to maintain Your Majesty in those rights and prerogatives.

But since the matter was not resolved in a satisfactory manner, Portland suggested that the Stadholder send a formal letter of complaint – a draft of which he provided.[92] The magistrates' controversy has often been regarded as proof that the Stadholder's authority had increased due to his kingship, but little attention has been paid to the difficulties he experienced as a direct result of his absence.[93] The disputes of the spring of 1690 took place when the King-Stadholder was in a vulnerable position.

English and Dutch opposition movements were not isolated phenomena but served to reinforce each other. Republicans and country gentlemen on both sides of the Channel opposed the King-Stadholder, and there is some evidence that they established contact. In the aftermath of William's conflict with Amsterdam in 1690, Portland's secretary informed him that 'it has come to my attention [that Amsterdam] is underhand still making secret movements against the King, in order to make these not only here but also in England effective, for the intention of the ill intended both here and there'. He pointed out that a pamphleteer had contacted the English opposition and tried to have some of his writings translated for their benefit.[94] A few months later William achieved a great victory in Ireland, which worked wonders in the United Provinces. Schuylenburg wrote to Portland in late July 1690 that the news of the victory at the Boyne had resulted in

> ... a great calm among the evil people, so much even, that a number of the ill disposed from Amsterdam have become divided out of apprehension of the coming of the King, so much even that it is argued that the interest of Amsterdam is not so much different from that of the Stadholder, on the contrary, that there is a mutual good intelligence.[95]

IV

Portland returned to England in June 1690, only to prepare himself for the campaign in Ireland. Indeed, the most serious threat to the revolution settlement came from

---

91 Resolution States of Holland 12 March 1690, *Hollandsche Mercurius 1690*, 82.
92 Portland to William 14–15 March 1690 (The Hague), Japikse, *Correspondentie*, XXIII. 146, transl. from French.
93 But see Baxter, *William III*, 258 ff.
94 Schuylenburg to Portland 30 June 1690, Japikse, *Correspondentie*, XXVIII. 168, transl. from Dutch.
95 Schuylenburg to Portland 28 July 1690, ibid., 172, transl. from Dutch.

Ireland and was of a predominantly military nature. Whereas Scotland was mostly plagued by rebel skirmishes, in Ireland a French–Jacobite army had landed near Kinsale in the spring of 1689 intent on reconquering the island for King James. The Duke of Schomberg had been appointed in July to command the troops in Ireland. The campaign of 1689 had not been successful, and the King felt obliged to command the forces in Ireland personally the following year. Portland had tried to prevent him from doing so, not just out of fear for his personal safety but also because his opponents would profit from his absence, a matter of particular concern during the disputes in Holland.[96] 'It is a terrible mortification for me', William admitted, 'that I can contribute so little this year to the public good and that I am obliged to go to Ireland, where I will be out of touch with the world.'[97]

William and Portland left London on 4 June 1690. William's army crossed the Irish Sea and arrived on 14 June; 300 transport ships carried 15,000 crack troops bringing the Williamite army to 36,000, some 10,000 more than the Jacobite–French troops commanded by James. The army marched towards Dublin, and confronted James's army halfway, taking up lines of defence behind the Boyne. On 12 July battle commenced, the Duke of Schomberg and the Dutch Blue Guards crossing the river to build a bridgehead, after which the main army advanced. Portland joined the division of Count Schomberg that attacked the right flank of the Jacobite army. Heavily outnumbered and of inferior quality, the Jacobite army was defeated and dispersed. Portland's suggestion that 3,000 cavalry should be despatched to destroy the retreating army was dismissed by those who considered the terrain unsuitable for pursuit.[98] The King in exile fled to western Ireland. In a letter to Dijkveld, two days after the battle, Portland expressed the hope that the victory would balance the losses in the Low Countries, 'but we have to take the good and bad such as the good God sends us'.[99]

William asked Portland to write an account of the battle, presumably because the Earl had had a good overview and an experienced eye. The relation was immediately written and translated into English as *News from the Army in Ireland*, so that it could be printed, distributed and read in the House of Lords. Robert Southwell thought it 'too modest ... a very cold account of what the King had acted that day'.[100] Indeed,

---

96   Portland to William 4 February 1690 (The Hague), Japikse, *Correspondentie*, XXIII. 93.

97   J.G. Simms, *Jacobite Ireland 1685–1691* (London/Toronto, 1969), 134. William to Maximilian Emanuel, Elector of Bavaria 24 March 1690, Japikse, *Correspondentie*, XXVIII. 158, transl. from French. J.G. Simms, 'Williamite Peace Tactics 1690–1691' in: D.W. Hayton and G. O'Brien (eds), *War and Politics in Ireland 1649–1730* (London, 1986), 181; William III to Heinsius 27 May/6 June 1690, Van der Heim, *Archief*, II. 10.

98   Grew, *Bentinck*, 178.

99   Portland to Dijkveld 4/14 July 1690 (Beltrawy), HMC, *Appendix to the Eighth Report*, II (s.l. 1881), 560a, transl. from French.

100   A copy can be found in Melville, *Leven and Melville Papers*, 459–61n. See also his letter to Melville of 4/14 July 1690 (same pages), and Southwell to Nottingham 2 July 1690, 4 July 1690, HMC, *Finch Manuscripts*, II. 328, 338. Part of the account was not written by Portland himself, he was not always at the right spot. Kaye to Wentworth 8 July 1690, HMC, *Manuscripts in Various Collections* (8 vols, London, 1901–14), II. 405.

it was far too dry and factual a description for such a glorious victory, and Portland, much more concerned with the military situation, failed to fully appreciate to what extent the victory could be exploited for political means.

William had hoped that his success would end the war in Ireland, but unfortunately his demand for unconditional surrender, prompted by an overconfident attitude, met with a rebuff.[101] He resisted pressure from his ministers in London, apprehensive of a French descent after the defeat at Beachy Head, to return to England, and marched to Limerick to reduce the remainder of the Irish army. A sequence of incidents enabled Limerick to withstand her besiegers, and William left Ireland in an unsettled state.[102] Portland himself was in Dublin in early September to settle some disputes among officers, and travelled back to England to arrive in Kensington Palace on 24 September 1690.[103]

Portland discussed with the King the distribution of offices in Ireland, but his main concern was the campaign.[104] The preparations for the 1689 campaign had been discussed between Portland and Secretary of State Nottingham. In August 1689 Portland had travelled to Chester, from where the army would cross the Irish Sea, to discuss preparations with (or, according to one observer, to press) Solms and Schomberg.[105] The Secretary-at-War for Ireland, Sir George Clark, was appointed and kept in Ireland at his recommendation, and together with the Commander-in-Chief, the Duke of Schomberg, and the generals, Solms and 's Gravenmoer, Portland planned the Irish campaign in 1690. He also functioned as a channel of communication between the military in Ireland and the King.[106] From the autumn of 1690 Portland retook responsibility for superintending the logistic preparations. 's Gravenmoer, Solms and Schomberg reported to him all problems with the supplies.[107] After the battle of the Boyne and William's return to England, command was taken over by Godard van Reede van Ginckel, who was benefiting from Portland's favours and

---

101 Simms, 'Williamite Peace Tactics', 184; Troost, 'Treaty of Limerick', 25.

102 Troost, 'Treaty of Limerick', 26.

103 Nottingham to Southwell 4 September 1690, HMC, *Finch Manuscripts*, II. 445; Portland to Ginckel 17 September 1690 OS (Kensington Palace), Japikse, *Correspondentie*, XXVIII. 183.

104 Memorial discussing the appointment of high officials in Ireland in his handwriting, NUL, PwA 2074.

105 Portland's instruction 13 August 1689, Japikse, *Correspondentie*, XXIII. 63–4; Portland to Nottingham 26 July/5 August 1689 (Hampton Court Palace), HMC, *Finch Manuscripts*, II. 229; Portland to Schomberg 2 August 1689 (Hampton Court Palace), *CSPD 1689–1690*, 195; 24 November 1689, *Négociations de M. le Comte d'Avaux en Irlande, 1689–90* (Dublin, 1934), 551.

106 HMC, *Manuscripts of F.W. Leyborne-Popham Esq.* (London, 1899), 271, 275. E.g. Schomberg to Portland 12 September 1689 NUL, PwA 1127, Solms to Portland 16 September 1689, NUL, PwA 1163.

107 Schomberg to Portland 16 September 1689, Solms to Portland 16 September 1689 and *passim*, NUL, PwA 1128, PwA 1163.

dependent on royal directions communicated through the favourite.[108] On occasion Portland would give Ginckel personal advice on what strategy to adopt.[109]

The most important matter was to bring the war to a successful conclusion before the spring. Efforts were made during the winter of 1690/1691 to reach a peaceful settlement. Ginckel and Portland decided to relax the uncompromising stance William had initially taken. They realised that an expedient might be necessary in order to facilitate a speedy conclusion to the war.[110] John Grady, an intermediary, was interviewed by Portland during the autumn, and returned to Ireland in October 1690, Portland stressing to Ginckel the importance of his mission.[111] He insisted that it might be necessary to make concessions and offer pardons, if that could prevent the war from continuing through the following spring. 'You can certainly go further than I have done, permitting him to offer more favourable conditions, as you judge fit as to the importance of that affair', he wrote to Ginckel.[112] Nothing was more important than to end the war before the spring campaign, so that troops would become available for the continent, as Portland pointed out.[113] The peace party among the Jacobites proved too weak, however, and by February 1691 Grady requested to be relieved. His mission had failed.[114]

The negotiations in Ireland broken off, Ginckel and the Lords Justices in Dublin decided to test the waters by issuing a declaration that would form the basis of the Treaty of Limerick and offered a pardon and a certain degree of freedom of worship for Catholics.[115] The offer was rejected, and the 1691 campaign commenced, the King impressing upon Ginckel that the fate of Europe depended on his victory.[116] The campaign proceeded successfully, and it is significant that in spite of this Portland continued to insist on reaching a speedy negotiated settlement. Although he had travelled with the King to the Low Countries in May he was still supervising the negotiations. Portland had good hopes that this campaign might be victorious, the Jacobites apparently not receiving any funds from France and their army being in a poor state. He wrote to Ginckel from Het Loo:

---

108 Portland to Ginckel 4/14 October 1690 (Kensington Palace), Japikse, *Correspondentie*, XXVIII. 187.

109 E.g. Portland to Ginckel 15/25 November 1690 (Kensington Palace), ibid., 191.

110 For a good analysis of these negotiations, see Simms, 'Williamite Peace Tactics', 182 ff.; Simms, *Jacobite Ireland*, 187 ff.

111 Portland to Ginckel 25 October 1690 (Kensington Palace), Japikse, *Correspondentie*, XXVIII. 188.

112 Portland to Ginckel 25 October 1690 (Kensington Palace), 13/23 December 1690 (Kensington Palace), ibid., 188, 196, transl. from French. Sidney to Portland 7 November 1690, NUL, PwA 1330. Cf. Simms, 'Williamite Peace Tactics', 188.

113 Portland to Ginckel 20/30 December 1690 (Kensington Palace), Japikse, *Correspondentie*, XXVIII. 197–8.

114 Simms, 'Williamite Peace Tactics', 190.

115 Ibid., 191.

116 William to Ginckel 1/11 May 1691, Japikse, *Correspondentie*, XXVIII. 235.

> If the Irish wish to think about surrender, which you have some cause to hope for, it is no good hesitating in giving them conditions, although they are a bit advantageous, because nothing would be more advantageous to us than to see an end to the war in Ireland.[117]

Such optimism was crushed with the arrival of French reinforcements at the Irish coast in May 1691. Portland, now in Flanders, was unpleasantly surprised, pointing out to Ginckel that no money or reinforcements could be provided at this moment. He hoped that Ginckel would succeed none the less, 'without which the affairs of the whole of Christendom will become much more difficult'.[118] It became imperative now, he anxiously wrote, 'that we must attempt to make an end to this war, in any way possible'. Sidney had been ordered to write to the Lords Justices not to proceed with confiscations of those who had succumbed to the King.[119]

Ginckel's progress was swift and successful. Athlone was besieged during the last week of June and fell on the 30th. The army marched further west and defeated the Jacobite army near Aughrim. On 21 July 1691 Galway surrendered, and only Limerick held out as a Jacobite stronghold. Portland's comment on these events is significant; he congratulated Ginckel on his victory, though 'the English say that you have granted conditions too favourable'.[120] Final victory seemed certain now and he had good hopes that the Jacobite commanders, Tyrconnel and Sarsfield, would accept the terms. But August ended and September dragged on without Limerick falling, and William and Portland's optimism lapsed into anxiety when they left Flanders for Het Loo without having received any positive news.[121] Ginckel had decided to bombard rather than attack Limerick, giving the Jacobites hope that they could prolong the siege and take the campaign into the following year. Portland and William were alarmed by Ginckel's tactic, the King thinking it of '…such a great importance to take this city before the winter, which will bring an end to the War of Ireland, and I will be in a position to bring over the troops here which are absolutely necessary for the conservation of this state and all its allies'.[122] Limerick capitulated, however, on 3 October. 'Thanks be to God', Portland wrote to Ginckel from The Hague, 'which gives me occasion so soon after to rejoice with you about the happy and glorious end of the war in Ireland'.[123] The Treaty of Limerick provided for a general pardon and permitted the Jacobite army to retreat to France. By the middle of December all Jacobite forces, some 12,000 troops, had been shipped off to France, and William was now free to fully concentrate on the war on the continent.

---

117 Portland to Ginckel 11/21 May 1691 (Het Loo), ibid., 236, transl. from French.
118 Ginckel to Portland 18/28 May 1691, Portland to Ginckel 7 June 1691 ('Camp de Anderlech'), ibid., 238–40, transl. from French.
119 Portland to Ginckel 18 June 1691 ('Camp de Bethleem'), ibid., 241, transl. from French.
120 Portland to Ginckel 13 August 1691 ('Camp de Court'), ibid., 249, transl. from French.
121 Portland to Ginckel 27 August 1691 ('Camp St Gerard'), 18 September 1691 (Vilvoorde), ibid., 251–2.
122 William to Ginckel 27 September 1691, ibid., 258, transl. from French.
123 Portland to Ginckel 19 October 1691 (The Hague), ibid., 263, transl. from French.

V

Portland was instrumental in the success of the Glorious Revolution in the spring of 1688/1689, but also in the consolidation of the revolution settlement during the first two years of William's reign. In England and Holland, the maintenance of William's authority mainly required decisive but delicate political manoeuvring. Portland was engaged in London in the spring of 1689 to gain support for William's claim to the crown. In Holland, William's authority was challenged when Republican factions tried to take advantage of the Stadholder's absence. Portland's role in the Amsterdam magistrates' controversy provides a unique insight into the political skills of the Stadholder's favourite. Portland mobilised supporters in vital bodies, such as the Council of State, the *Gecomiteerde Raden* and the various city councils.

While the skirmishes of English and Dutch politics thus caused William and his favourite considerable difficulties, conditions in Scotland and Ireland proved far more precarious as the Williamite settlement in these kingdoms was under military threat. Although occasionally dealing with strategy or tactical manoeuvres, Portland's main responsibilities remained of a logistic and organisational nature. He was involved in the preparations for the war in the Scottish Highlands and oversaw negotiations with the clan chieftains. He was also engaged in the preparations for and participated in the Irish campaigns and supervised the subsequent negotiations with the Jacobite and French leaders.

His correspondence reflects his pre-occupation with the war in Flanders which clearly influenced his decisions on Scotland and Ireland. By the end of 1691 the revolution settlement had been stabilised; on 22 December the last Jacobite forces left Ireland, whereas on 31 December the deadline expired for the Highlanders to swear allegiance to the King. The conclusion of the Jacobite wars had made possible a decisive military shift towards the continental campaign. William's successes had immensely strengthened his position, both on the continent and in the British Isles – as Richard Hill aptly observed in December 1691: 'I think our isle is at anchor and is safe enough'.[124]

---

124   Hill to Trumbull 8 December 1691, HMC, *Downshire Mss*, I-i. 389.

Chapter 4

'Lord Portland takes all': The Re-emergence of the Favourite

In *The French Favourites* (1709) the author resolved to critically investigate the phenomenon of the favourite, in order to show 'who they are that Reign without Right, without Merit, and without a Crown'.[1] The pamphlet used extracts of anti-Mazarin literature, but the date of publication coincided with the death of the Earl of Portland and the zenith of the career of the Duke of Marlborough, pointing to the fact that the favourite had become a well-known actor again on the English political stage. In late-Tudor and early-Stuart England the favourite had been all too familiar. Elizabeth's favourites played an important role in the administration and faction struggles at Court. The Duke of Buckingham, the favourite of James I and Charles I, most resembled the archetypical image of the all-powerful favourite who ruled on behalf of the monarch, like the Cardinals Richelieu and Mazarin in France, and the Dukes of Lerma and Olivarez in Spain. Buckingham exerted an influence that after his day would never be available to Archbishop Laud and the Earl of Strafford, let alone the parliamentary managers of the Restoration period. Charles II and James II made use of parliamentary managers, such as the Earls of Clarendon, Danby and Sunderland.

If the favourite was in decline after the middle of the seventeenth century, Portland's ascendancy as a royal favourite marked the re-emergence of the favourite on the English scene. According to Linda Levy Peck, 'By 1659 a paradigmatic shift had taken place in both the position and analysis of minister-favourites, one that focused less on the court and more on the state'.[2] However, even if Portland's influence did not match that of Buckingham, ostensibly he resembled his illustrious predecessor (with whom he was occasionally compared) as he operated from the Royal Household rather than Parliament as the political managers of the Restoration had done.[3] A recent historiographical reappraisal of the phenomenon of the favourite has also situated its decline in Europe around 1660, when bureaucracies had been

---

1 *The French Favourites: or, the Seventh Discourse of Balzac's Politicks* (London, 1709) in: Somers, *First Collection*, II. 482–6, 483.

2 L. Levy Peck, 'Monopolizing Favour; Structures of Power in the early Seventeenth-Century English Court' in: J.H. Elliott and L.W.B. Brockliss (eds), *The World of the Favourite* (New Haven/London, 1999), 54–70, 66–7.

3 Elizabeth's favourites also came to power through their position in the royal household. P.J. Hammer, 'Absolute and Sovereign Mistress of her Grace? Queen Elizabeth I and her favourites 1581–1592' in: Elliott and Brockliss, *The World of the Favourite*, 38–53. Cf. Peck, 'Monopolizing Favour'. I am grateful to Andrew Barclay for this suggestion.

established and a protracted phase of large-scale warfare had ended.[4] But the re-emergence of the favourite in England between 1689 and 1710, a period of major changes, rests uneasily with this view. The Earl of Portland, Albemarle to a lesser extent, but certainly Marlborough, played an important role during the last two decades of Stuart England.

J.R. Jones has described Portland as the 'mainstay of William's government in its first five years'.[5] This chapter aims to substantiate this claim and estimate the extent of Portland's influence as favourite. It will analyse his influence in William's various realms (England, Scotland, Ireland and the United Provinces) and pay attention to the different spheres of his influence at Court, the councils and the political assemblies. It aims to show how the re-appearance of the apparently reactionary phenomenon of the court-favourite could coincide with the major changes that swept the British Isles during this period.

I

In recent historiography on the Glorious Revolution and its aftermath, the 'modern' aspects of the Williamite settlement, such as the ascendancy of Parliament and the Financial Revolution, have been emphasised. There has been less interest in its conservative, even reactionary elements, such as the continued importance of the Court and, indeed, the re-emergence of the court-favourite. Portland had played a material role during the Glorious Revolution and afterwards emerged as a prominent favourite of the King-Stadholder. This development was not obvious. Gilbert Burnet assured the Earl of Clarendon in December 1688 'that Bentinck was an old servant, was bred up with his master, and had much of his kindness; but, if it pleased God to bless the Prince, Bentinck would not be in the station of a favourite minister'.[6]

However, the new king rewarded his confidant generously; offices and grants were showered upon him after the offering of the crown in Banqueting House. A warrant issued on 27 March 1689 granted Bentinck the titles of Baron of Cirencester, Viscount Woodstock and Earl of Portland. He was made Keeper of the Privy Purse, Groom of the Stole and First Gentleman of the Bedchamber.[7] William created for him an office of superintendence for all the gardens belonging to the royal palaces.[8] As early as January two Dutch competitors for William's favour, Everard van Weede van Dijkveld and Willem Adriaan van Nassau-Odijk, noted that his ascendancy excited great jealousies among the English. Constantijn Huygens remarked that the English

---

4   J. H. Elliott, 'Introduction' in: Elliott and Brockliss, *The World of the Favourite*, 4.
5   J.R. Jones, *The Revolution of 1688 in England* (London, 1972), 325.
6   *The Correspondence of H.H. Earl of Clarendon and of his Brother, Laurence Hyde, Earl of Rochester; with the Diary of Lord Clarendon from 1687 to 1690 ... and the Diary of Lord Rochester during his Embassy to Poland in 1676*, ed. S.W. Singer (2 vols, London, 1828), II. 217.
7   14 February 1689, 27 March 1689, *CSPD 1689–1690*, 2, 43–4.
8   Royal Warrant 1 May 1689, *CTB*, IX-i. 102, cf. IX-iii. 1095–6.

'already held a grudge against Bentinck because he had so much authority'.[9] The ostentatious display of favouritism made Portland the object of scorn and malicious rumours, one popular satire remonstrating that 'Lord Portland takes all'.[10]

Competition for William's favour was severe among his Dutch confidants, but most contestants quickly receded. Willem van Nassau-Zuylestein, for instance, told Constantijn Huygens that

> ... he had no pretensions to have any part in the grand deliberations. That in England it was customary that the Favourites and Counsellors were accused and punished if the King had done wrong. That he would not care whether the Prince would make him a Lord, unless it was to make him serviceable in Parliament.[11]

Neither Everard Van Weede van Dijkveld nor Willem Adriaan van Nassau-Odijk, two of William's closest veteran advisers who came to London on a special embassy in the spring of 1689, received office or a peerage. They returned to the United Provinces in the autumn, where they remained influential in provincial management. Reportedly Nassau-Odijk had been highly dissatisfied.[12] Hendrik van Nassau-Ouwerkerk was given the important Mastership of the Horse, but notwithstanding his enmity to Portland he did not seem to consider himself a competitor for the King's favour.[13] In fact, most Dutch kept a low profile at Court. By the late spring of 1689 Portland remained William's undisputed favourite. The Spanish ambassador Pedro Ronquillo wrote in March 1689 that the First Gentleman of the Bedchamber was William's 'valido'.[14]

Perhaps Portland's greatest rival was his friend Henry Sidney. According to Burnet, William's favour was initially equally divided between the two, but Sidney's sway with the King soon waned.[15] There may have been a moment of severe competition. Huygens reported in October 1689 that Sidney had outrivalled Portland briefly during that summer, when the favourite had apparently fallen out with William. Huygens seems to suggest that Portland and the King had quarrelled over Elizabeth

---

9   8 January 1689, 8 February 1689, Huygens, *Journaal*, I-i. 57, 77, transl. from Dutch.

10   Quoted in G. van Alphen, *De Stemming van de Engelschen tegen de Hollanders in Engeland tijdens de Regeering van den Koning-Stadhouder Willem III 1688–1702* (Assen, 1938), 230.

11   30 January 1689, 14 March 1689, Huygens, *Journaal*, I-i. 70–71, 93, transl. from Dutch. Cf. 'Monsieur de B.', 'Mêmoires ... ou Anecdotes, tant de la Cour du Prince d'Orange Guillaume III, que des Principaux Seigneurs de la République de ce Temps', ed. F.J.L. Krämer, *Bijdragen en Mededelingen betreffende de Geschiedenis der Nederlanden*, 19 (1898), 62–124, 93.

12   'Monsieur de B.', 'Mêmoires', 113; H. Horwitz, *Parliament, Policy and Politics in the Reign of William III* (Manchester, 1977), 19–20.

13   Van Alphen, *Stemming van de Engelschen*, 86.

14   Ronquillo to Cogolludo 4 March 1689, *Correspondencia entre Dos Embajadores, Don Pedro Ronquillo y el Marques de Cogolludo 1689–1691*, ed. Duque de Maura (2 vols., Madrid, 1951), I. 100.

15   'The King's chief personal favour, lay between Bentinck and Sidney', G. Burnet, *History of his Own Time* (6 vols, London, 1725), IV. 8.

Villiers, who had taken up residence near Kensington House, which William had bought from the Earl of Nottingham.[16] By the autumn, however, Sidney and Portland were very close, and they maintained the friendship they had established before the Revolution, reflected in their cordial correspondence over the years. Portland entrusted him with the wardship of his children and the management of his affairs in England in the eventuality of his death.[17]

When Portland arrived in England in 1688, as a Dutch nobleman and favourite he was already a wealthy man. He possessed two large estates, Rhoon and Sorgvliet, and just before embarkation, in October 1688, William had granted him several Dutch lordships: the county of Leerdam and the baronies of Acquoy and IJsselstein.[18] Safe investments, mostly in bonds and stock, were made during the 1680s. In May 1685, for instance, he bought ƒ40,700 worth of bonds. In June 1688 William had granted him ƒ26,000 in bonds, mediated by Don Manuel Belmonte, followed by ƒ41,000 in bonds in June 1689, mediated by Baron Lopez Suasso. In Holland he does not seem to have invested much in land, in fact the only acquisitions in the 1690s were two orchards purchased in 1691 to extend his Rhoon and Pendrecht lordships.[19] At his death in 1709, his possessions in the United Provinces would be valued at ƒ1,562,669. 7st., or £142,060 in English currency.

It is not easy to get a clear sense of his financial position, for various reasons. A number of his yearly accounts have survived, but quite often they do not give an overview of both his Dutch and English possessions. Another complication arises from the fact that much of his accounting was done by Willem van Schuylenburg, who was also accomptant of the Nassau Demesne Council, which handled the affairs of William's private estates.[20] Lastly, certain amounts of money were credited to Portland's account to cover expenses of his offices. For instance, in April 1696 the King delegated full responsibility over the royal gardens to Portland, allotting him a yearly sum of £4,800, with which he had to meet the costs involved.[21]

If Portland had amassed riches by 1688, in England his capital would astronomically increase. On balance, his superintendency yielded some £200 yearly.[22] As First Gentleman of the Bedchamber, he obtained an annuity of £2,000.[23] He received the yearly sums of 20 marks and 20 pounds to support the dignities of his noble titles.[24] More tokens of the King's favour materialised after the coronation.

---

16   11 June 1689, 23 October 1689, Huygens, *Journaal*, I-i. 138–9, 193–4.

17   Portland to Eleanora van Ittersum-Nijenhuis, 30 March 1691, Japikse, *Correspondentie*, XXIII. 164–6.

18   Testamentary disposition by William III, 16 October 1688, Japikse, *Correspondentie*, XXVIII. 47.

19   BL, Eg Mss 1708, f° 56r°, 172 ff.

20   Many of his Dutch affairs were handled by Christoffel Tromer, see Portland to Eleanora van Ittersum-Nijenhuis 30 March 1691 (Breda), Japikse, *Correspondentie*, XXIII. 164–6.

21   30 April 1696, *CTB*, XI-i. 116.

22   1 May 1689, *CTB*, IX-i. 102.

23   11 December 1689, *CTB*, IX-ii. 329.

24   27 March 1689, *CSPD 1689–1690*, 43–4; 13 April 1689, HMC, *The Manuscripts of the House of Lords 1689–1690* (London, 1889), 84; *House of Lords Journal*, XIV. 175; Tromer to Portland 8/18 April 1689, Japikse, *Correspondentie*, XXVIII. 110–11.

Together with gratifications, Portland received some £3,000 yearly from his offices. But it was not the income from his offices that enriched him. Throughout his reign the King conferred numerous grants upon his favourite, mostly in the form of land and estates. In 1695 Portland received enormous grants of land in Wales, comprising the lordships of Yale, Bromfield and Denbigh, which the King however was compelled to withdraw after a parliamentary outcry.[25] To compensate for the losses, Portland received in May 1696 less conspicuous estates scattered over England with a yearly revenue of £4,332. 3s..2$^{1}/_{4}$d. and an estimated value in 1709 of £86,643. 3s. 9d.[26] The Irish grant conferred upon his son Woodstock, the Clancarty estate (repealed by the 1701 Act of Resumption), comprised about 135,000 acres and must have had a yearly income of some £25,000.[27] In 1697 Portland received fee farm rents in Kent, presumably in an attempt by the King to prevent his resignation.[28] Towards the end of his Paris embassy in 1698, a generous grant in Westminster was conferred upon the Ambassador, yielding £9,800 yearly, but the property rose in value and had an estimated value in 1709 of £376,027. 10s.[29] Throughout the 1690s, numerous financial grants were conferred by the King, most of which are listed in his inventory. In England he invested £10,000 in the New East India Company but the vast substance of his capital consisted of land.[30] Portland possessed a number of country estates, town houses and apartments. He was allocated spacious apartments in Kensington Palace, Hampton Court Palace and Whitehall Palace, next to those of the King.[31] In 1689 he received Theobald's House in Berkshire, including the surrounding parks of over 2,500 acres and worth £1,767 per annum.[32] Reportedly he had a mansion in the Pall Mall, and in about 1709 he bought for £3,300 a house at St James's Square for his son Lord Woodstock.[33] Later that year Woodstock would inherit the bulk of his father's English possessions, then valued at an astounding £850,150. 3s. 9d., about six times the value of his Dutch estates that would pass to his second son Willem.

---

25 *CTB*, X-ii. 1046–52.

26 BL, Eg Mss 1708, f° 277v°.

27 J.G. Simms, *The Williamite Confiscation in Ireland, 1690–1703* (London, 1956), 87. An overview of the Irish grants is in HMC, *The Manuscripts of the House of Lords 1699–1702* (London, 1908), 33–8. This grant was nullified by the Resumption Act.

28 29 December 1697, *CTB*, X-iii. 47–8. Cf. 8 December 1697, 9 December 1697, 22 December 1697, ibid., 44, 172, 190–91.

29 BL, Eg Mss 1708, f° 277; C.L. Kingsford, *The Early History of Picadilly, Leicester Square, Soho and their Neighbourhood* (Cambridge, 1925), 65.

30 J.V. Becket, *The Aristocracy in England 1660–1914* (Oxford, 1986), 80–81.

31 E.g. H.M. Colvin, (ed.), *The History of the King's Works 1660–1782* (London, 1976), 184; R.O. Bucholz, *The Augustan Court. Queen Anne and the Decline of Court Culture* (Stanford, 1993), 316n.

32 30 April 1689, 1 May 1689, *CTB*, IX-i. 101–2.

33 25 April 1696, N. Luttrell, *A Brief Historical Relation of State Affairs from September 1678 to April 1714* (6 vols, Oxford, 1857), IV. 50; 30 April 1689, 1 May 1689, *CTB*, IX-i. 101–2. An overview of his estates is in *CTB* X-ii. 1018–26; *Biographia Brittanica, or, the Lives of the Most Eminent Persons Who have Flourished in Great Britain and Ireland etc.* (London, 1747), I. 733; NUL, PwV 106.

Portland's possessions, estimated at his death in 1709
Source: British Library Egerton Manuscripts 1708, f° 277–80

State and inventory of all the goods in England

- May 1689 Theobald's with park and lands, annual rent valued at £1,916. 10s. The house would now be worth £44,079. 10s.
- In April 1698 received various lands in the freehold of Westminster in Middlesex, yearly income of £9,800, though if more houses would be built even £25,068. 10s. Would now be worth £376,027. 10s.
- In May 1696 as donation of the Crown: Grantham in Lincolnshire, lordship Penrith in Cumberland, Rudheath and Dracklow in Chester, Ferrington in Norfolk, Burstall Garth, Hornsey, Thwing, Barnsley and Leven in Yorkshire, Pevensy in Sussex, together a revenue of £4,332. 3s. 2$^{1}/_{4}$d. per year. Would now be worth £86,643. 3s. 9d.
- March 1695 ground and houses for 42 years, £2,000 yearly, is worth £3,000
- Lordship of Bulstrode, would be worth £20,000 now at sale
- Annuities £1,900 yearly, worth £30,400
- Gift to Woodstock at his wedding, to the amount of £115,000
- Left £150,000 in bonds
- Movables £25,000

Total £850,150. 3s. 9d. (ƒ9,351,664. 17st. 0p. in Dutch currency)

Account of possessions in Holland, English translation

- Lordships of Rhoon and Pendrecht, total value now ƒ198,583. 8st.
- House in Voorhout, bought for ƒ48,000, extended and repaired between September 1699 and August 1704, total value now ƒ124,987. 10st.
- Sorgvliet, bought for ƒ21,000 valued at ... [note '373,269. 7st. still at Sorgvliet']
- Farmhouse behind Sorgvliet ƒ10,642. 9st.
- Old seat of Emelaer above Amersfoort ƒ23,756
- Two seats under the jurisdiction of Houten en Goij and Wijck te Duurstede ƒ15,300
- Weibnum bond ƒ8,000
- Bonds of Lord Schoonheten, dated 26 February 1706 ƒ16,000
- Likewise bond 17 January 1708 ƒ7,500 (In both cases no interest as yet paid)
- Annuities ƒ4,000
- Bond Lord Lec 13 June 1701 ƒ70,000
- Various interests and bonds ƒ311,000
- Bonds ƒ275,000, ƒ266,900, ƒ106,000, ƒ94,000

Total ƒ1,562,669. 7st. (£142,060 in English currency)

Total: ƒ10,914,334 in Dutch, or £992,212 in English currency

In Holland Portland normally resided in Sorgvliet. This country house was in close proximity to William's palace of Honselaarsdijk. It was an independent residence that provided the favourite with opportunities to assert his status, which undoubtedly increased due to his powerful position in England after 1688. Surprisingly, in England it was only after the Nine Years War that he found the time and opportunity to maintain a country seat, although William had granted him an estate as early as the spring of 1689. The crown estate of Theobald's, which had belonged to Robert Cecil and the Duke of Albemarle, was in close proximity to Hampton Court Palace. There is little evidence that Portland ever resided there and it seems he mainly kept to his palatial apartments. In March 1697 Portland was made ranger of Windsor Park, an office worth £1,500 per annum that he continued to keep until the death of William III.[34] The Ranger's Lodge, close to Windsor Castle and Hampton Court Palace, became his favourite residence. He spent vast sums of money to improve the Lodge and its surroundings.[35] In 1702 he moved to Bagshot in Surrey, and only in 1706 did he purchase Bulstrode in Buckinghamshire which became his primary seat in England.[36]

Surprisingly the favourite did not purchase an impressive country house for himself, which his financial means and his status both dictated and facilitated. In a time when the English nobility built themselves grand estates, Portland's houses were rather inconspicuous. Bulstrode fell far short of the magnificence of the Duke of Marlborough's Blenheim Palace in Oxfordshire, the Duke of Devonshire's Chatsworth in Derbyshire and Castle Howard in Yorkshire of the Earls of Carlisle. While such lasting monuments of Christopher Wren, William Talman – one-time aides of Portland – and John Vanbrugh still manage to stun visitors today, the modesty of Bulstrode – torn down in the nineteenth century – generally disappointed contemporary observers. It may also have been the result of a personal inclination for modesty; none of his town houses and palace apartments abounded with luxury. The inventory of Portland's Dutch estate at the time of his death suggests that he had expensive tastes, but his city house hardly breathed the atmosphere of grandeur one might expect from a royal favourite. A large collection of silverware, profuse silk ware, ebony chairs and cabinets could be found in his town house in The Hague

---

34   9 March 1697, Luttrell, *Brief Historical Relation*, IV. 195.

35   G.M. Hughes, *A History of Windsor Forest Sunninghill and the Great Park* (London/Edinburgh, 1890), 284–6.

36   Henry Lord Woodstock to Portland 11 November 1702, 18 November 1702, 25 November 1702 NUL, PwA 103–5. O. Manning and W. Bray, *The History and Antiquities of the County of Surrey* (3 vols, London, 1804–14), III. 84 and E.W. Brayley, *A Topographical History of Surrey* (5 vols, London, 1841–48), I. 234 suggest that Bagshot had been granted to Portland by William, but there are no records for this. Portland leased Bagshot until 20 May 1705, and possibly the lease had started just after the loss of Windsor Lodge on 12 May 1702. Arran to Portland 31 August 1705 NUL, PwA 218; Buckinghamshire County Archive D/RA1/60. I am thankful to Ms Caroline Knight for alerting me to this document. W. Page (ed.), *Victoria History of the Counties of England – Buckinghamshire* (5 vols, London, 1905–25), III. 208; G. Lipscomb, *The History and Antiquities of the County of Buckingham* (4 vols, London, 1947), IV. 506.

and at Sorgvliet,[37] but it was not a display of magnificence. In fact, one visitor to Sorgvliet thought that it was 'a House where, if the Productions of Art had been but half so plentiful as those of Nature, it would be one of the most charming Seats of the Universe'.[38]

Indeed, it was Portland's gardens, rather than his country houses, that attracted some attention. He was a knowledgeable and dedicated gardener, and had been an enthusiastic collector of rare plants and seeds for many years.[39] Though no scholar, he had taken a keen interest in garden architecture and acquired knowledge through extensive reading of Italian and French works on this subject.[40] John Maurice had advised him by writing down his *Consideratien op Sorghvliet*, and he had received advice as well from Christiaan and Constantijn Huygens.[41] Having become something of a connoisseur, in 1699 Portland had advised the Prince de Condé on his garden design.[42] André Lenôtre, the French royal garden architect, considered Portland as 'someone with excellent taste'.[43] Portland showed an interest in all aspects of the humanist ideal of garden architecture, combining botanical and scientific knowledge with an appreciation of classical sculpture.[44]

Just before William's visit in 1691 Portland had reconstructed the gardens of Sorgvliet, and a series of prints were commissioned afterwards bearing witness to the splendour of the cascades and topiary.[45] The gardens were famed for the application of the latest techniques, such as the building of an orangery in 1676.[46] Huygens reported as early as 1677 that rare citrus trees were growing there, and in 1689 Portland reportedly brought some pine apple trees from Sorgvliet to the Hampton Court gardens.[47] A catalogue (the *Codex Bentingiana*) was made, later used by Leonard Plukenet, Royal Professor in Botany and gardener to Queen Mary, in his *Phytographica*.[48] The gardens were seen as an example of modern garden

---

37   BL, Eg Mss 1708, f° 172–275 *passim*.

38   *Letters to a Nobleman From a Gentleman Travelling thro' Holland, Flanders and France etc.* (London, 1709), 24.

39   E.g. *CTB*, IX-iii. 866.

40   E. de Jong, *Natuur en Kunst. Nederlandse Tuin- en Landschapsarchitectuur 1650–1740* (Amsterdam, 1993), 70–73; E. de Jong, 'Netherlandish Hesperides. Garden Art in the Period of William and Mary 1650–1702' in: J.D. Hunt and E. de Jong (eds), *The Anglo-Dutch Garden in the Age of William and Mary. De Gouden Eeuw van de Hollandse Tuinkunst* (Amsterdam, 1998), 29.

41   De Jong, *Natuur en Kunst*, 73; John Maurice to Bentinck 28 February 1675, Japikse, *Correspondentie*, XXVII. 14.

42   Condé to Portland 17 May 1699, NUL, PwA 208.

43   Lenôtre to Portland 11 July 1698, Japikse, *Correspondentie*, XXIV. 291, transl. from French.

44   De Jong, 'Netherlandish Hesperides', 30.

45   Hunt and De Jong, *The Anglo-Dutch Garden*, 168; J. van den Avelen, *Sorgvliet* (Amsterdam, 1700?).

46   D. Jacques, et al., *The Gardens of William and Mary* (London, 1988), 38–40.

47   Jacques, *Gardens*, 197; Hunt and De Jong, *The Anglo-Dutch Garden*, 176.

48   D.O. Wijnands, 'Hortus Auriaci: de Tuinen van Oranje en hun Plaats in de Tuinbouw en Plantkunde van de late Zeventiende Eeuw' in: Hunt and De Jong, *The Anglo-Dutch Garden*, 77–83.

architecture. One traveller described it as 'a place so neatly composed that here Art and Nature seem to go hand in hand'.[49] Sorgvliet became a well known garden among connoisseurs. One visitor wrote that 'the Garden, ... the green House, Forreigne Plants and other Curiousitys in that Art is counted one of the best in these parts'.[50] Sir Francis Child, who visited Sorgvliet in 1697 wrote:

> The house is very small and as old, but this Lord Portland has made some additions to it. Before the house is a handsome orangery of fifty large windows and of a half-moon form. In the middle of it is a good hall well-painted. Behind the house are many gardens, fine groves and a vast many shady walks, some terrace ones, various fountains with surprising waterworks, curious arbours and several alleys under arbours, good statues, a large aviary, two high mounts with an infinite number of evergreen trees cut in several shapes. In short, the gardens are prodigious large without two things alike in them all, and ought to be seen by everyone who comes to The Hague.[51]

Portland had superintended the projects in the Prince's gardens and continued to do so in England.[52] In his capacity as Superintendent of the Royal Gardens, Portland was responsible for the extensive building programme and design of the royal gardens. In 1697 he was appointed Ranger of Windsor Park.[53] He was also the Prince's deputy forester in Holland, an office reconfirmed by the States in 1702.[54] Both offices were honorary, although Portland took a keen interest in both garden architecture and the maintenance of the King's estates. Part of his responsibilities was the maintenance of the game, William and Portland himself being avid huntsmen.

Despite what historians have often suggested, William was a dedicated patron of the arts and spent vast sums of money on gardens, palaces and paintings in England as well as Holland.[55] As superintendent of the Prince's gardens and buildings, Portland had been responsible, in conjunction with such artists as Romeyn de Hooghe, Daniel Desmarets and Daniel de Marot, for the building works at Het Loo. One may assume that the professionals had the artistic lead, but there are several indications that Portland was involved with both the layout of the gardens and some of their iconographic aspects.[56] Portland's aides in England were Deputy Superintendent George London, Comptroller William Talman, (both of whom were to co-operate

---

49 BL, Harley Mss 3516, f° 14v°.

50 Hunt, *The Anglo-Dutch Garden*, 293; Cf. K. van Strien, *Touring the Low Countries – Accounts of British Travellers 1660–1720* (Amsterdam, 1998), 196, 200, 205.

51 Quoted in Van Strien, *Touring*, 196. 'the Garden, for the green House, Forreigne plants and other Curiositys in that Art is counted one of the best in these parts, but compared with the Duke of Beauforts at Bodmington and several others in England, it ought not to be mentioned', quoted in J.D. Hunt, 'Anglo-Dutch Garden Art: Style and Idea' in: D. Hoak and M. Feingold (eds), *The World of William and Mary – Anglo-Dutch Perspectives on the Revolution of 1688–1689* (Stanford, 1996), 188–200, 197.

52 De Jong, 'Netherlandish Hesperides', 29.

53 E.g. 26 January 1699, Luttrell, *Brief Historical Relation*, IV. 476.

54 NUL, PwA 2866; BL, Egerton Charter 105.

55 As argued by A.P. Barclay, 'The Impact of King James II on the Departments of the Royal Household' (unpublished PhD thesis, Cambridge University, 1993).

56 De Jong, *Natuur en Kunst*, 68–74.

closely in laying out the gardens for his own estate in Buckinghamshire) and his secretary Frederick Henning.[57]

Portland's superintendency was thus not simply an honorary dignity. A dispute in 1695 with Christopher Wren, the King's Building Master, over the appointment of the Master Bricklayer, suggests the direct role he assumed.[58] He paid attention to and was actively involved in the day-to-day activities of the gardeners, but also the layout and composition of the gardens. He had viewed the gardens of Louis XIV in Versailles extensively and with great interest during his embassy in 1698, and reported about them in elaborate detail to William. Notes in his archive record his observations of the elaborate waterworks of Versailles with calculations on the transport of water.[59] In vain he tried to persuade Lenôtre to accompany him to England, but the latter sent his nephew Claude Desgotz instead.[60] In July 1698, just after Portland's return to England, he and the King viewed the grounds of Windsor with Desgotz and George London, Portland's deputy, and work on the Lodge's garden must have proceeded shortly after.[61]

With the exception of his elaborate gardens, most of Portland's private wealth was not on display but consisted of bank stock, invested sensibly with little risk in safe enterprises, such as the Dutch and English East India Companies and tallies.[62] All this may suggest that he consciously tried to keep a low profile in England. Unlike most favourites, Portland remained rather inconspicuous, choosing not to assert himself by residing in a grand country estate. Nevertheless, his importance was already recognised during the Revolution, when the Earl of Bristol presented William and his favourite with some magnificent horses.[63] He was frequently visited by petitioners. Peers were seen to be lining up at his apartments to be received.[64] An invitation by the royal favourite to dine was highly regarded.[65] Often the company was limited to a small, exclusive, group. On 23 November 1691, for instance, Portland, his son-in-law Essex, the King, Sidney, Marlborough and Godolphin dined in Montagu's quarters in Whitehall Palace.[66] On occasion the King visited the apartments of the favourite for dinner.[67]

An essential prerequisite for playing his role as an Anglo-Dutch favourite, Portland – together with his children – was included in an Act of Naturalisation passed by the Commons on 8 April 1689. Others followed later that month, such as

---

57   J. Harris, *William Talman, Maverick Architect* (London, 1982), 19.
58   Colvin, *History of the King's Works*, 27.
59   NUL, PwA 2067.
60   Hunt and De Jong, *The Anglo-Dutch Garden*, 158; Lenôtre to Portland 21 June 1698, 11 July 1698, Japikse, *Correspondentie*, XXIV. 289–91.
61   2 July 1698, Luttrell, *Brief Historical Relation*, IV. 401.
62   BL, Eg Mss 1708, *passim*.
63   9 December 1688, Huygens, *Journaal*, I-i. 32.
64   Horwitz, *Parliament*, 89. N. Witsen, 'Verbaal' in: *Geschied- en Letterkundig Mengelwerk*, ed. J. Scheltema (6 vols, Utrecht, 1818–36), III. 141.
65   E.g. 12 December 1690, Huygens, *Journaal*, I-i, 374; HMC, *Seventh Report*, 202a.
66   HMC, *Seventh Report*, 207a.
67   E.g. 20 November 1692, 12 February 1693, Huygens, *Journaal*, I-ii. 146, 173; 11 February 1691, Luttrell, *Brief Historical Relation*, II. 355.

Nassau-Ouwerkerk and Nassau-Zuylestein. However, naturalisation was a measure William rarely applied. Nassau Odijk seems not to have been included, and such close aides and confidants as the Huguenot officers Henri Massue de Ruvigny and the 3rd Duke of Schomberg, as well as the Utrecht nobleman and officer Godard van Reede van Ginckel and Mary's secretary Abel Tassin D'Alonne followed only during subsequent years. Arnold Joost van Keppel was naturalised in 1697 in order to receive a peerage.[68] Despite anxiety in England about the influx of high-ranking courtiers, few of those who were actually naturalised or denizised stayed in England.[69] Nassau-Zuylestein, Earl of Rochfort since 1695, took an English spouse – as did most of his children – but returned to his estate in Utrecht after William's death. Keppel, Earl of Albemarle since 1697, married a Dutchwoman and also returned to the Low Countries after 1702. Ginckel, created Earl of Athlone in March 1692, returned to Utrecht and stayed there.

The majority, then, of the Dutch elite in England, partly integrated into English society, but as a community it gradually disintegrated soon after 1689 and had virtually disappeared by 1702. Portland was one of the very few who remained in England. Through his marriage with Anne Villiers he was already married into the English aristocracy, and his family would settle permanently in their adopted country. Both Anne's father, Sir Edward Villiers, had been and her brother would be Knight Marshal of the Household, whereas the latter was also Master of the Horse to the Queen.[70] Andrew Barclay has suggested that Portland chose his noble title because Thomas Weston, the Earl of Portland of the first creation who had died in the spring of 1688, had been related to the Villiers family.[71] The choice of such a title would underline Portland's desire to integrate into the English aristocracy. These Villiers connections therefore provided the new Earl with a ready-made family network at Court from the outset. This image of Portland integrating with the native nobility rests uneasily with his reputation of being an outsider, although he certainly made few other efforts to make himself agreeable. On occasion he was bluntly dismissive of his new compatriots and he once swore to send his son back to the continent so that he would not learn 'debauchery'.[72] Despite such exhortations and a cool personal relationship with many English nobles, evidence suggests that from the start Portland understood that his future career would keep him in England. The

---

68   Cf. *Commons Journal* X. 77, 78, 79, 83, 84, 87, 95, 100, 110, 124, 130; *Lords Journal* XIV. 171, XIV. 196, 199, 201, XVI. 51, 54; *Letters of Denization and Acts of Naturalisation for Aliens in England and Ireland, 1603–1700*, ed. W.A. Shaw (Lymington, 1911), 215, 275 and *passim*.

69   Denization, as opposed to naturalisation, did not lead to full citizenship. Nevertheless it was attractive in that it did not require approval by Parliament, but instead remained the sole prerogative of the King.

70   A. Barclay, 'William's Court as King' in: E. Mijers and D. Onnekink (eds), *Redefining William III. The Impact of the King-Stadholder in International Context* (Aldershot, 2007), 241–61.

71   Ibid., 244.

72   17 April 1692, Huygens, *Journaal,* I-ii. 43–4.

degree of Portland's integration can be measured by his own intimations after 1689 that England was to be his new fatherland.[73]

The momentous events of 1688 had coincided with personal tragedies. Portland's eldest son 'Willemtie' had tragically died in the summer, and his wife Anne had passed away while the Williamite army was marching to London. He had been shattered by the news, but had no opportunity to travel back, arrange his family affairs and comfort his children, a task which was left to Christoffel Tromer, his secretary, Princess Mary and his sister. Two of his daughters arrived in England in April.[74] Most of his children would marry into the British aristocracy and were naturalised Britons. Portland's children from his first marriage had been naturalised by an Act of Parliament in April 1689 and married with English: his son Woodstock would marry with Lady Elizabeth Noel, the daughter of the Earl of Gainsborough, and three of Portland's daughters, Mary, Isabella and Frances Wilhelmina with the Earl of Essex, the Duke of Kingston and William Lord Byron respectively. Mary's marriage to Essex, whom William had made Lord Lieutenant of Hertfordshire, represented a political liaison as well, linking Portland to the influential Capel family.[75] A friend of Essex had strongly advised him 'more than anyone to try to marry Mylady Mary Bentinck because she is so amiable, rich and the daughter of a man who could augment his fortune'.[76] In 1695 Lady Elizabeth, the daughter of Mary and Essex was born: 'I feel ten years older since this morning when I received the news that I am a grandfather … I am sorry that it is a daughter, but Mylord Essex will have to do better next time'.[77] Anna Margaretha married a Dutch nobleman, Arend van Wassenaar-Duyvenvoorde, a prominent member of one of the foremost aristocratic families in the United Provinces and holder of a seat in the Holland *Ridderschap*. Eleanora remained unmarried. Portland had six children from his second marriage. His eldest son from this marriage, Willem, was to inherit his Dutch estates and to become the main adviser of Stadholder William IV. He would marry the Countess of Aldenburg. His second son from this marriage, Charles John, married a daughter of Cadogan. His four daughters all married Englishmen: Sophia with the Duke of Kent, Elizabeth with the bishop of Hereford, Harriet with Viscount Limerick and Barbara with Lord Godolphin.[78]

The distance between London and Hampton Court Palace, the coldness of William and his favourite and their aversion to public display have reinforced an image of the

---

73   Bentinck to Ten Hove 15/25 February 1689 (Whitehall Palace), Japikse, *Correspondentie*, XXVIII. 100.

74   M.E. Grew, *William Bentinck and William III (Prince of Orange). The Life of Bentinck, Earl of Portland, from the Welbeck Correspondence* (London, 1924), 155.

75   Baden to the States General 19/29 Jan. 1692, Hop to the States General 5 February 1692, BL, Add Mss 17677 MM, f° 69v°, 74v°. Cf. Blathwayt to Nottingham 2 October 1692, HMC, *Finch Mss*, IV. 468. The marriage took place at Nijenhuis.

76   HMC, *Seventh Report* (s.l., 1879), 206b, transl. from French.

77   Portland to Capel 18 Aug. 1695, NUL, PwA 245, transl. from French.

78   Shaw, *Letters of Denization*, 215; *Collin's Peerage of England … Greatly Augmented, and Continued to the Present Time*, ed. E. Brydges (9 vols, London, 1812), II. 29–41; D. Schwennicke (ed.), *Europäische Stammtafeln IV Standesherrliche Häuser* (Marburg, 1981), I.

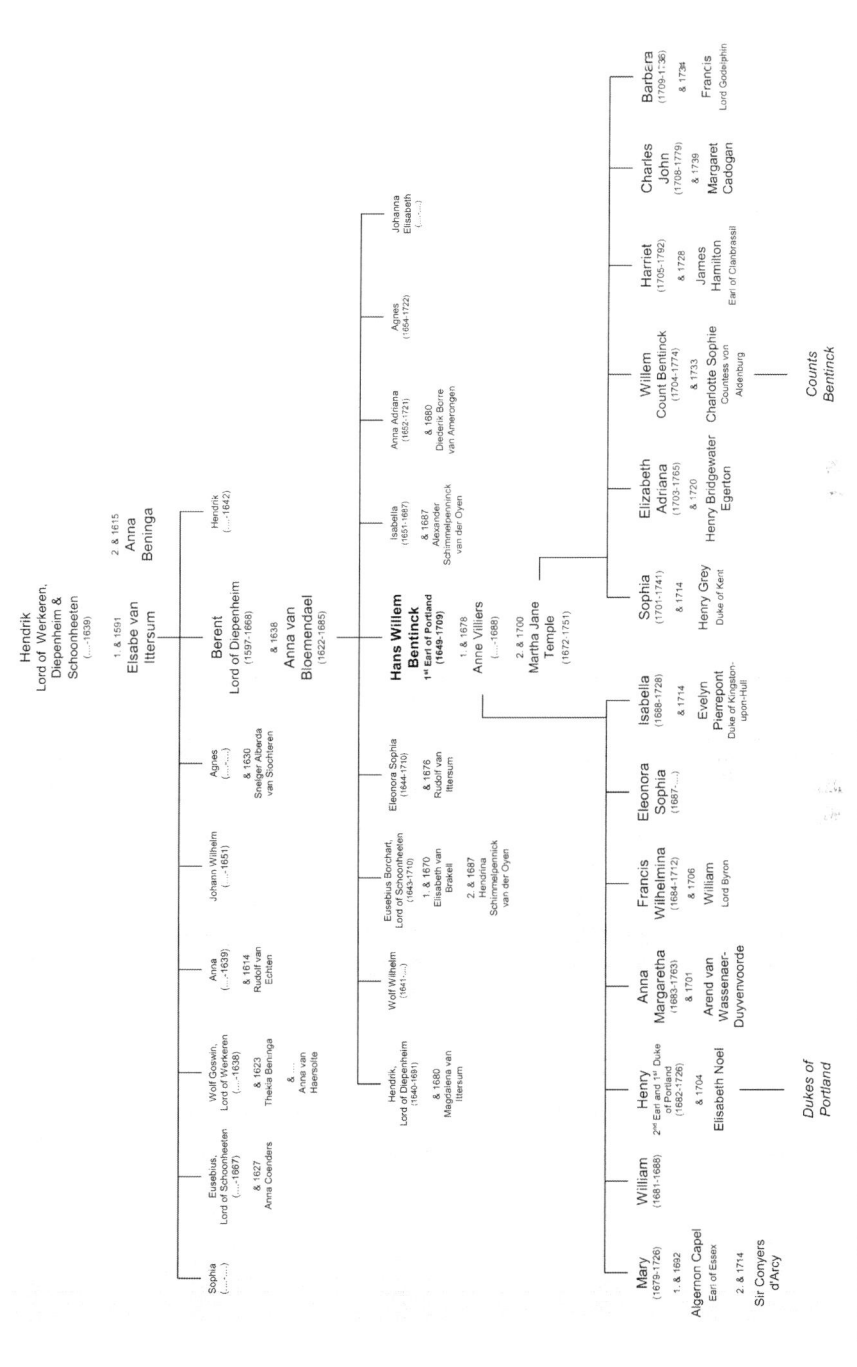

Genealogical Table Compiled by Freya Wolf from *Europäische Stammtafeln IV Standesherrliche Häuser*, D. Schwennecke (ed.) (Marburg, 1981), tables 12 and 17.

King's court as a dull and uneventful place. Undoubtedly the gravity of sustained warfare and the process of the 'godly revolution' made it difficult to maintain a frivolous court, but there were lighter moments. Nine-year-old Lord Woodstock, 'so amiable and with a good body and mind although he is so young', was allowed the unprecedented favour for someone his age of carrying the Queen's mantle into the Church: 'The Queen had a good laugh.'[79] Twelfth Night was celebrated at Court in general merriment, and in 1692 carnival was celebrated with a ball.[80] To celebrate the King's birthday in 1691, another ball was organised at Whitehall Palace, where Mary Bentinck, 'who was the prettiest', was among the dancing couples.[81] William's court was certainly more vibrant than historians have hitherto suggested.[82]

II

Portland, then, became a member of the English polite society, and was certainly not the outsider he is often thought to have been. He maintained cordial relations with many nobles and, by marrying his children to Englishmen and -women, integrated his family with the native aristocracy. But naturally there was envy of the newcomer. 'Great Portland', one pamphleteer wrote, 'at the time of the Revolution was plain Mijn Heer Bentinck'.[83] There may have been little esteem for the Dutch nobility, which had after all more similarities with the gentry; there was no rigid formal division between gentry and nobility in the United Provinces, and the nobility was untitled. But these sentiments did not do justice to Portland's position as such. He held a seat in the Holland nobility, and the barons Bentinck could trace their family tree back easily into the early thirteenth century.[84] At the time of the Glorious Revolution, Portland ranked among the top of the Dutch nobility, in pedigree, wealth and rank.

Due to his title, connections and wealth Portland emerged as a prominent member of the noble elite in England, but it was his position at Court that provided the key to political power. He mainly resided in his apartments in the royal palaces – Whitehall Palace, Hampton Court Palace and Kensington Palace.[85] Having been the Prince's chamberlain, Portland was now First Gentleman of the Bedchamber and Groom of the Stole. As First Gentleman Portland supervised the other Gentlemen of the Bedchamber, in 1689 the Earls of Monmouth, Oxford, Marlborough, Drumlanrigh, Selkirk, Viscount Lumley and Henry Sidney. The Grooms of the Bedchamber were, in 1689, Colonel Peircy Kirke, Hatton Compton, Charles Trelawney, Emanuel

---

79   HMC, *Seventh Report*, 199b, transl. from French.
80   Hop to the States General 18 January 1692, Hop to the States General 19 February 1692 in: BL, Add Mss 17677 MM, f° 42r°, 106r°.
81   HMC, *Seventh Report*, 205b, transl. from French.
82   Cf. Barclay, 'William's Court as King', 249.
83   W. Pittis, *The True-born Englishman: a Satyr, Answer'd Paragraph by Paragraph* (London, 1701), 73.
84   Cf. S.B. Baxter, *William III* (London, 1966), 248–9; P. Schazmann, *The Bentincks. The History of a European Family* (London, 1976), 1–2.
85   E.g. Colvin, *History of the King's Works*, 184. Cf. footnote 100.

Scroop How, John Sayers, James Stanley and the Dutchman Adriaan van Borssele. The hierarchy was reflected in the incomes, Portland earning £2,000, the other Gentlemen £1,000 and the Grooms £500 annually.[86] The grooms were required to perform menial tasks such as assisting the King with getting dressed, and fetching towels and water.[87] As Groom of the Stole Portland could recommend candidates for a few dozen menial offices at Court. The infrastructure of Portland's clientele can only fragmentarily be reconstructed. He himself employed a number of Dutchmen, such as his chamberlain Dorp.[88] Nevertheless, his were not the greatest offices at Court. Indeed, in terms of patronage, his position at court was certainly not as significant as that of the Master of the Horse, Lord Steward or Lord Chamberlain.[89]

The presence of foreigners in William's circle was bitterly criticised, but it is striking how few of them actually held political office or a position at Court. The grand offices went to Englishmen: the Earl of Dorset became Lord Chamberlain and the Earl of Devonshire Lord Steward. According to Bucholz, 'the King's Dutch friends were confined to a very few, though strategic, positions'.[90] This observation is confirmed by the analysis of the Gentlemen and Grooms of the Bedchamber mentioned above, Portland and Borssele being the only Dutchmen attending to the King's personal needs. Moreover, William's court at Hampton Court Palace was not just a royal court; it continued to be a stadholderly court as well. If English courtiers were concerned about foreigners coming to Court, Dutch courtiers at The Hague were equally worried that they might lose their influence due to what was essentially a transfer of the stadholderly court to London. Nassau-Ouwerkerk, for instance, was *stalmeester* to William III, an office which was confirmed in 1689 when the King made him Master of the Horse. Nassau-Zuylestein was essentially a courtier at the stadholderly court in The Hague, and was made Master of the Robes. Portland's offices of Groom of the Stole and First Gentleman of the Bedchamber were not unlike his chamberlainship. Portland was, moreover, the only Dutchman (though not the only foreigner) to be elevated into the peerage in 1689. Several years later, only Albemarle, Rochfort and Athlone would take seats in the Lords, and only Portland's son Woodstock would have a dukedom bestowed on him by George I in 1716.

Portland was also Keeper of the Privy Purse – the office being delegated to his aide, Adriaan van Borssele van der Hooghe.[91] In the autumn of 1691 it was decided that not Portland himself, but his agent Caspar Frederick Henning should be accomptant.[92] As keeper of the Privy Purse, he was responsible for large sums of money; these were mainly meant to cover the needs of the Royal Household. The amounts credited to Portland's account in 1689 amounted to some £9,000, a figure that rose to £23,000 in 1693 and £68,500 in 1695, reaching unprecedented heights

---

86   *CTB*, IX-ii. 330.
87   BL, Add Mss 61419 A, f° 1.
88   26 February 1694, Huygens, *Journaal*, I-i. 319.
89   Cf. Bucholz, *The Augustan Court*, 66–7.
90   Ibid., *The Augustan Court*, 27.
91   'Gedenkschriften van Adriaan van Borssele van der Hooghe, Heer van Geldermalsen', ed. K. Heeringa, in: *Archief. Vroegere en latere Mededeelingen voornamelijk in Betrekking tot Zeeland* (Middelburg, 1916), 67–136, 107.
92   *CTB*, IX-iii. 1095–6.

in 1697 with over £200,000 yearly. A sharp decline set in from 1698, with figures around £83,000, stabilising in 1699.[93] It would be tempting to suggest that Portland was using funds to pay for specific purposes related to William's interest – which the rise during the war years and the sharp decline afterwards seems to support. There are reports of certain irregularities with regard to the use of the Purse, but it is difficult to establish whether these had any foundation. One pamphleteer accused Portland of using Privy Purse money to strengthen the court interest in Parliament.[94] Portland reportedly opposed a parliamentary measure for a separate allowance for the Queen, insisting it should be channelled through the Privy Purse.[95] Huygens was surprised when Portland paid the travel expenses of Job de Wildt, Secretary of the Amsterdam Admiralty and confidant of William, from the Privy Purse.[96] In 1695 Robert Harley, chairman of the Commission of Accounts, complained to Portland about delays in sending him accounts of money received by the Privy Purse. The neglect may not signify much, Portland being engaged in a campaign on the continent at the time.[97] The rise may be explained in terms of the growth of the Royal Household and the additional expenses of a moving household.[98]

Portland's offices were a token of William's favour and financially rewarding, but they hardly provided a basis for the exercise of political power, nor did they entail a significant clientele. Nevertheless, it was Portland's seemingly servile office as Groom which provided him with unlimited opportunities to converse with the King in private.[99] Portland's own apartments always adjoined those of the King and he was in daily consultation with William.[100] Portland's apartments in the palaces symbolised close proximity to the King – just as his retirement would coincide with his decision to live on his country estate. During the summer of 1699, after his retirement, the new favourite Albemarle would take possession of spacious lodgings in Kensington Palace, and receive rooms in Hampton Court Palace linked directly to those of the King.[101] Constantijn Huygens described the long hours the King and Portland spent in his cabinet doing tedious paperwork or discussing matters

---

93 These figures are estimations based on various references in *CTB, passim*.

94 *A True and Impartial Narrative of the Dissenters' new Plot etc.* in: *A Collection of Scarce and Valuable Tracts etc*. IX, ed. W. Scott (London, 1813), 454–5.

95 20 May 1689, Huygens, *Journaal*, I-i. 128.

96 10 June 1694, Huygens, *Journaal*, I-ii. 359.

97 Harley to Portland, n.d. 1695, NUL, Pw2Hy 426.

98 See for instance Godolphin to Portland 21 May 1695, NUL, PwA 473.

99 A. Marshall, *The Age of Faction, Court Politics, 1660–1702* (Manchester/New York, 1999), 26–7; BL, Add Mss 61419, f° 4v°. Cf. D. Starkey, 'Intimacy and Innovation: the Rise of the Privy Chamber, 1485–1547' in: D. Starkey et al. (eds), *The English Court: from the Wars of the Roses to the Civil War* (London/New York, 1987), 71–118.

100 Cf. Horwitz, *Parliament*, 89; Witsen, 'Verbaal', 141; 25 March 1689, Huygens, *Journaal*, I-i. 99.

101 Cf. 11 November 1691, Luttrell, *Brief Historical Relation*, II. 305; HMC, *Seventh Report* (s.l., 1877), 206b; A. Boyer, *The History of the Life & Reign of Queen Anne* (London, 1722), appendix, 50; Brande to States General 14 January 1698, 18 January 1698, Saunière to States General 17 January 1698, BL, Add Mss 17677 SS, f° 10–11, 108r°; Bonnet to the Elector 4/14 January 1698, 7/17 January 1698, BL, Add Mss 30000B, f° 2v°, 6r°.

of importance.[102] The significance of his new position becomes clear from his instruction, stating that the 'Groom of ye Stole (being by his place y^n first Gent of our Bedchamber) hath & shall & ought to have ye sole & absolute charge Command & Governm.' under Us, of our old & new bedchambers, ye great withdrawing room' in all the royal houses and palaces. Only those of royal blood plus a select few, such as Dijkveld and the Lord Privy Seal, the Marquis of Halifax, were allowed to enter the King's bedchamber. The Privy Room could only be entered with the permission of the Groom of the Stole. But it was really the King's bedchambers to which Portland regulated access, where the locus of power was situated. Here the King received only a very select company. Portland thus had significant control over who could see the King.[103] Portland was also used to receive high-placed guests. When the Elector of the Palatinate visited Het Loo, Portland fetched him from his coach and attended him to the King's room.[104]

It is difficult to ascertain to what extent Portland monopolised access to the King, though clearly numerous state officials, even the Secretaries of State, found it difficult to gain an audience.[105] This had just as much to do with William's reluctance to discuss affairs with a larger circle of men and natural inclination to confer with a small circle of confidants. George Melville, the Scottish Secretary, frequently complained that he was unable to see the King, who was 'extreamly throngd with affaires'; the Duke of Shrewsbury, the English Secretary of State, likewise complained to his colleague the Earl of Nottingham.[106] Conditions were no different for those of the King's Dutch entourage. Willem van Schuylenburg, Alexander Schimmelpennick van der Oije and Job de Wildt also experienced difficulties getting an audience.[107] Such problems were hardly alleviated by the transfer of the Court from Whitehall Palace to Hampton Court Palace, at a certain distance from the City and Parliament.

These developments did render the position of his Groom relatively more important. According to Ronquillo one could only see the King 'through the medium of Bentinck, and no-one else'.[108] William often used Portland to shield

---

102 Horwitz, *Parliament*, 204. E.g. Dalrymple to Melville 23 March 1689, *Leven and Melville Papers. Letters and State Papers chiefly Addressed to George Earl of Melville, Secretary of State for Scotland, 1689–1691*, ed. W.L. Melville (Edinburgh, 1843), 3–4; 20 March 1689, 25 March 1689, 30 March 1689, Huygens, *Journaal*, I-i. 96, 99, 102 and *passim*.

103 G.S., First Marquis of Halifax, 'The Spencer House Journals' in: *The Life and Letters of Sir George Savile, First Marquis of Halifax*, ed. H.C. Foxcroft (2 vols, London, 1898), II. 200–52; 9 March 1689, Huygens, *Journaal*, I-i. 91; BL, Add Mss 61419, f° 9v°. Cf. R.O. Bucholz, 'Going to Court in 1700: a Visitor's Guide', *The Court Historian*, 5/3 (2000), 181–221, 208–9.

104 27 April 1692, Huygens, *Journaal*, I-ii. 48.

105 Cf. Shrewsbury to Nottingham 3 October 1689, HMC, *Finch Mss*, II. 252.

106 Shrewsbury to Nottingham 3 October 1689, HMC, *Finch Mss*, II.252; Melville to Hamilton 2 July 1689, 13 July 1689, 25 July 1689, NAS, GD 406/1/3630, GD 406/1/3637, GD 406/1/3640.

107 27 March 1689, Huygens, *Journaal*, I-i. 100.

108 Ronquillo to Cogolludo 18 March 1689, Maura, *Correspondencia*, I. 113, transl. from Spanish.

him from unwelcome petitioners,[109] a convenience that contributed, however, to William's reputation of being distant and cold. Portland soon gained a reputation for being particularly blunt and was regarded by many as an obstacle, rather than an intermediary between the political nation and the King. When, for instance, after Mary's death in 1695 William locked himself up in his quarters, these were tenaciously guarded by Portland who refused to let anyone in. The Marquis of Normanby, a Privy Councillor, had an argument with Portland who refused to let him speak to the King, and there were complaints 'that the King is kept prisoner'.[110] Such behaviour gave rise to sinister insinuations as to Portland's role.

With control over access to the King came the responsibility of channelling petitions. There are numerous examples of solicitations for offices, sometimes minor, sometimes important. Due to his close relationship with the King, Portland managed to become one of the major figures at Court. Indeed, his influence at Court was considerable, such that the Lord Chamberlain – the pre-eminent household servant – complained that 'Myl. Portland had too much power, that too many favours went through his hands'.[111] Portland was often approached by those who desired office at Court. Constantijn Huygens mentions his own frequent attempts to obtain a raise or a new office by asking Portland to intercede with the King.[112] There is plenty more evidence – though often fragmentary – of Portland making recommendations for offices.[113] Exclusion from the inner counsels of the King forced courtiers to solicit sometimes Dijkveld, but mostly Portland, for favours or gaining audiences.

Courtiers were willing to offer substantial amounts of money, should the favourite be able to do them service.[114] Undoubtedly Portland must have created both a clientele and a string of enemies. 'I cannot praise the politeness of his chief favourite, Monsieur Bentinck, since Earl of Portland', the Earl of Ailesbury complained in his memoirs.

> I went to visit him at his appartment next to that of the Prince, and he denied himself twice, although I knew he was in his room. The third time, being in the Prince's drawing-room at noon, and not seeing the favourite there, I went to his side, and his servant told me his master was with the Prince. I told him that was false, and Captain Dorp, whom I knew at Rochester, being there, I requested of him to tell Monsieur Bentinck that I had been there three times, and that by God it should be for the last time, and we never spoke to each other after; a grave bow might pass from one to the other.[115]

Ailesbury was a bitter enemy of Portland's, but still the account may be illustrative for the experience of many courtiers.[116]

---

109   Baxter, *William III*, 273.
110   Ibid., 321; 20 January 1695, Huygens, *Journaal*, I-ii. 447, trans. from French.
111   26 July 1689, Huygens, *Journaal*, I-i. 157, transl. from Dutch.
112   Huygens, *Journaal*, I. *passim*.
113   E.g. 8 April 1689, Huygens, *Journaal*, I-i. 106.
114   E.g. 30 November 1689, ibid., 206.
115   *Memoirs of Thomas, Earl of Ailesbury, etc.*, ed. W.E. Buckley (Westminster, 1890), 227.
116   E.g. ibid., 228.

Portland shielded the King from a multitude of courtiers, but there is no indication that Portland isolated William and surrounded him with his own creatures. In 1691 Portland tried to prevent two Scottish delegates of an opposing faction from having an audience with the King.[117] However, it is significant that Halifax, William's most influential political adviser in England during 1689, never even mentions Portland in his journals recording his private conversations with the King.[118] It seems that in most cases the King kept up lines of communication with a small circle of confidants over which Portland had no influence whatsoever.

It is even more difficult to establish the nature of the relationship between William and Portland behind closed doors. It is doubtful whether his position provided him with influence over the King himself. Such rumours certainly circulated at Court, many regarding Portland as a sinister shadow behind the throne holding some sway over his master. Nicolaas Witsen recorded that according to John Wildman 'the King did nothing without the permission of Bentinck'. At the burgomaster's suggestion that 'maybe he only just takes advice from him', Wildman replied: 'no, we have noticed it ourselves'.[119] Yet most evidence suggests the contrary.

The correspondence between William and Portland is scarce (between 1692 and 1695 almost non-existent), with the exception of 1690 and 1698 when the favourite reported in detail on his missions to The Hague and Paris. It may be that Portland destroyed letters. He had an obsession for secrecy and habitually transmitted instructions in cipher or invisible ink, sometimes directing the recipient to burn the document. Sometimes his orders – when they might be controversial – were transmitted orally via confidants. But he seems to have treasured letters from the King (often affectionately signed with merely 'G' for Guillaume), and the absence of correspondence over the years between 1692 and 1695 may imply an unusual closeness between the two. It was arguably a period when Portland had reached the zenith of his career.

In practice, during the summer of 1689 Portland and William were mainly doing administrative work in the King's closet at Hampton Court Palace. Huygens often caught them working, the King signing documents and issuing orders to Portland. As William was overwhelmed by his new responsibilities, a large share of official correspondence was delegated to the favourite. In actual fact he creamed off material correspondence from the Secretaries of State, the Earls of Nottingham and Shrewsbury, leaving them to deal with routine matters.[120] In this way as well, then, Portland became a channel to the King even for his own ministers. Although it is possible that William on occasion might have kept information from Portland, as Stephen Baxter has suggested, virtually all matters were freely discussed between the two, and the King often intimated that it mattered not whether correspondence was

---

117   P. Hopkins, *Glencoe and the End of the Highland War* (Edinburgh, 1980), 266.
118   Halifax, 'Spencer House Journals'.
119   Witsen, 'Verbaal', 169, transl. from Dutch.
120   E.g. Shrewsbury to Portland 22 October 1689, *CSPD 1689–1690*, 298; Horwitz, *Parliament*, 89; P.W.J. Riley, *King William and the Scottish Politicians* (Edinburgh, 1979), 5; Portland to Nottingham 6/16 Sept. 1689 (Hampton Court Palace). Cf. Portland to Nottingham 24 September 1689 (Hampton Court Palace), HMC, *Finch Mss*, II. 248.

addressed to him or his favourite.[121] Huygens once entered the King's closet during the evening: 'Bentinck handed him a letter or two, and I saw that there was some mighty serious conversation concerning these, sometimes with long silences'.[122]

In the spring of 1695 Portland reached the zenith of his influence; the King was in mourning and his favourite was in virtual control for at least several weeks. Correspondence meant for the King was sent to him, and audiences were postponed or cancelled.[123] In 1696 James Vernon wrote to Secretary of State Shrewsbury that he had 'ordered a copy of the information to be sent to the King, which I shall enclose to my Lord Portland, as supposing it ought to be so'.[124] There are numerous examples of Portland writing or dictating letters as if from the King.[125]

Because he served as intermediary between the King and the political nation, Portland's communicative skills are worth considering. He could read, write and probably speak English tolerably well, having spent some time in England and being married to an Englishwoman. Most of his correspondence, however, is in French, the language he felt most confident in after his native language, and one which few of his peers actively mastered.[126] To George Melville he confided in 1690: 'I am sorry I must write to you in French, I only have this language, I wish instead I would be able to write in English'.[127] Portland's confession was tainted with some false modesty regarding his ability to communicate in English. A document from his hand dated 3 January 1689 is written in near-fluent English. In another draft document from 1688 he switches effortlessly from Dutch to English.[128] A few years later Charles Montagu described his English, with a proper dose of flattery, as 'so just, as you need not change your stile'.[129] In 1696 Portland questioned a number of suspects from the Assassination Plot; his numerous hand-written notes of the complex interrogations are near-fluent with very few idiosyncrasies.[130] It requires skill to take notes during long and complicated interrogations and to write quick

---

121 If William withheld information concerning the prorogation of Parliament, it should be noted that he suspected letters were being intercepted; Heinsius to William 14 January 1695, Japikse, *Correspondentie*, XXIII. 436. Baxter, *William III*, 274–5. Baxter's example refers to a delicate matter involving Albemarle and was atypical. William to Heinsius 20 February 1699, *Letters of William III, and Louis XIV and of their Ministers, etc. 1697–1700*, ed. P. Grimblot (2 vols, London, 1848), II. 279.

122 1 July 1689, Huygens, *Journaal*, I-i. 148, transl. from Dutch. E.g. TNA: PRO, SP 8/6, f° 172r°, SP 8/8 f° 85, 91.

123 E.g. Citters to States General 18 February 1695, BL, Add Mss 17677 PP, f° 14r°; NUL, PwA 1924–30.

124 Vernon to Shrewsbury 24 September 1696, *Letters Illustrative of the Reign of William III etc.*, ed. G.P.R. James (3 vols, London, 1841), I. 1.

125 E.g. 12 August 1694, Huygens, *Journaal*, I-ii. 394.

126 An anonymous writer supposed that he did not understand English: 11 September 1689, *CSPD 1689–1690*, 250; Somers to Portland 14 September 1694, NUL, PwA 1176.

127 Portland to Melville 22 April 1690 (Kensington Palace), Melville, *Leven and Melville Papers*, 429, transl. from French.

128 Japikse, *Correspondentie*, XXIV. 720–21; NUL, PwA 2242.

129 Montagu to Portland 11/21 June 1695, NUL, PwA 936.

130 NUL, PwA 2462–519.

and near faultless English.[131] Nevertheless, his active command of the language may have initially been insufficient to understand the nuances and intricacies of subtle political discourse, and throughout the 1690s he continued to correspond mainly in French.

His reluctance to communicate in English did little to contribute to an understanding with the English nobility, relations with which remained cold in general. Although the hostility towards the Dutch favourite can partly be explained by xenophobia and jealousy, Portland was decidedly more unpopular than the diplomatic Dijkveld or the affable Keppel. Marlborough thought him a 'wooden fellow',[132] his wife Sarah loathed Portland for reasons of her own. The charge of arrogance, made by his opponents, is unsurprising, but even many of his political allies perceived him as cold and distant. It is interesting to note Portland's reflection upon his own character in this respect. To William he once described himself as 'obstinate', which he recognised as a shortcoming, particularly in a diplomat.[133] He also realised he was not affable and easy with people. Perhaps the most illuminating confession was made in a remarkable letter to Shrewsbury of 8/18 September 1696:

> Ever since I had the honour to know you, I have perceived a coldness and reserve towards me, which I wished not to deserve; but rather than attribute it to you, I have concluded that I was myself the cause of it, being sufficiently just to myself, to know part of my failings. But as we cannot control those which arise from nature, and which are born with us, I have deemed the evil incurable, and have merely paid to the minister and secretary of state, the respect which was due to him, without troubling myself farther. But as it is the will of fortune, that you should personally testify to me your approbation of my conduct, and express your satisfaction with it, I assure you, Sir, that I shall return the same cordiality, and that this cold and reserved disposition, which I frankly avow, shall wholly vanish after the candour which you have had the goodness to promise me. I will request some indulgence in regard to my judgment, but none respecting my integrity; and I shall not solicit your friendship, until I shall have taken the first step to render myself worthy of it.[134]

Not even Portland's associates had a high opinion of his intelligence. A not unsympathetic contemporary wrote with some justification that Portland was 'of no deep Understanding, considering his Experience'.[135] Gabriel Sylvius thought his

---

131 There are, of course, some mistakes, and some that can only be made by a Dutchman; a sentence like 'that Blair was but ones in his house in the countrij in march two years ago' displays the usage of the Dutch combination 'ij' for the English 'y', and 'ones' instead of 'once' suggests that Portland may have been better at speaking English than writing it.

132 Godolphin to Marlborough 4 February 1709, *The Marlborough-Godolphin Correspondence*, ed. H.L. Snyder (3 vols, Oxford, 1975), III. 1219. Cf. 21 February 1693, Huygens, *Journaal,* I-ii. 175.

133 Portland to William 13 March 1698 (Paris), Japikse, *Correspondentie*, XXIII. 254, transl. from French.

134 Portland to Shrewsbury 8/18 September 1696 (Het Loo), *Private and Original Correspondence of Charles Talbot, Duke of Shrewsbury etc.*, ed. W. Coxe (London, 1821), 141.

135 J. Macky, 'Characters of the Court of Great Britain' in: *Memoirs of the Life of Sir John Clerk ... 1675–1755*, ed. J. M. Gray (London, 1895), 58.

understanding 'mediocre'.[136] Monsieur de B. commented: 'his mind is rather limited, easy to anticipate and very difficult to lead away from that which he has conceived.'[137] The Earl of Sunderland thought him rather a 'dull animal', whereas Jonathan Swift considered him 'As great a dunce as ever I knew'.[138] Although he patronised various Huguenot scholars,[139] the Earl displayed little interest in scholarship or literature; his library, part of which was transported to London in the autumn of 1689, seemed unremarkable.[140] During a theological discussion with Matthew Prior, Portland commented: 'I am glad, Mr. Prior, to find you so good a Christian. I was afraid that you were an atheist ... I knew that you were a poet; and I took it for granted that you did not believe in God.'[141]

It may very well be that Portland's arrogance towards English courtiers was merely a reaction to such criticism, but it can also be partly explained by factors which seem ostensibly political, but really went back to the revolution. In his view, the English nobility did not show William the gratitude he deserved for liberating their country.[142] Dartmouth recorded Portland saying to William 'that the English were the strangest people he had ever met with; for by their own accounts of one another, there was never an honest nor an able man in the 3 kingdoms; and he readily believed it was true'.[143] It is significant that Portland established friendships almost exclusively with those who had been involved in the revolution, such as Sidney and Carstares.

III

'The government of seventeenth-century England was personal monarchy', Kevin Sharpe wrote, referring to Charles I, warning historians not to 'underestimate the power of the king's person'.[144] Although the political significance of the Court had diminished during the second half of the century, the strong personality of William III and the Court's expansion rendered it still powerful. Hence the role of the court-favourite was potentially significant. Past historiography has sometimes underestimated the role of Portland, because he was favourite to a strong and independent ruler. Stephen Baxter admired William III and infamously dismissed Portland as a 'male-nurse tending a semi-invalid'.[145] Nicolaas Japikse has, on the

---

136 21 February 1693, Huygens, *Journaal*, I-ii. 175.
137 'Monsieur de B.,' 'Mêmoires', 90, transl. from French.
138 *The Prose Works of Jonathan Swift*, ed. T. Scott (11 vols, London 1900), X. 276; J.P. Kenyon, *Robert Spencer, Earl of Sunderland 1621–1702* (London, 1958), 315.
139 Cf. Ch. 5, 6.
140 *CTB*, IX-ii. 337–8.
141 T.B. Macaulay, *History of England from the Accession of James II* (6 vols, London, 1914), VI. 2800.
142 E.g. B. Bevan, *King William III, Prince of Orange, the First European* (London, 1997), 109.
143 Quoted in Grew, *Bentinck*, 158n.
144 K. Sharpe, 'The Image of Virtue: the Court and Household of Charles I, 1625–1642' in: Starkey, *The English Court*, 226–60, 226.
145 Baxter, *William III*, 275.

other hand, overestimated the favourite's importance, but with some justification described Portland as William's alter ego.[146]

Mutual confidence provided an exceptionally solid partnership in which William and Portland could discuss, weigh and consider matters of importance. Undoubtedly, a close friendship forged from childhood years and strengthened over time formed a solid basis for this confidence. Some historians have suggested that there existed a homosexual relationship between the two men, for which, however, only circumstantial evidence has been offered.[147] Despite their friendship, their private correspondence never betrays the sort of intimacy one finds in the correspondence between, for instance, Buckingham and James, or Sarah Churchill and Anne, let alone any sexual connotations. On the contrary, although William's letters clearly radiate his deep friendship and respect for his servant, they are rather devoid of intimate feelings. Portland's letters seem deeply respectful and never assume the familiarity one might expect from someone writing to a childhood friend. He rather presents himself as a loyal servant, aware of the friendship of his master, but never taking it for granted, nor presuming to be an equal. In 1690 he wrote to William:

> It is His Majesty who I take as the sole witness of the actions of my life, and who can be the best judge, in recollecting his memories of my past conduct for more than 26 years. He will undoubtedly have remarked that my ambition has been moderate and fairly reasonable. My private interest has never prevailed over my duty.[148]

When during the Glorious Revolution the Elector of Brandenburg, impressed with Portland after their meeting in Berlin, offered him high office should William perish, he turned the tentative offer down in a dignified manner, arguing that he had served the Prince for so long that he would not even consider an alternative. It may very well be true that Portland's career had been forged by William who made him dependent on him, but having established himself, Portland remained unquestionably loyal, true to the motto of the Bentinck family: 'Fear dishonour'.[149]

In England, as previously in the United Provinces after his entrance into the Holland *Ridderschap*, it was at first unclear whether the favourite would wield any significant power or would be useful to the King. It may very well be true that Portland was initially a 'fixer' rather than a 'favourite'.[150] The King sent his trusted friend on confidential missions or asked him to intervene in matters that required a certain delicacy or seemed related to his personal interest. When, for instance, the Secretary of State, the hypochondriac Duke of Shrewsbury, was inclined to return the seals in the autumn of 1689, Portland was despatched to persuade him to stay

---

146 N. Japikse, 'De Stadhouder en zijn Alter-ego', *Handelingen van de Maatschappij der Nederlandse Letterkunde te Leiden en Levensberichten, 1927–1928* (1928), 20–36.

147 Discussed at more length in chapter 7.

148 Portland to William 19 June 1690 O.S. (Hilsborough), Japikse, *Correspondentie*, XXIII. 158, transl. from French.

149 Cf. D. Onnekink, '"Craignez Honte". Hans Willem Bentinck, Graaf van Portland, en diens Engelse Jaren', *Virtus*, 102 (2001), 20–34.

150 Ms Sonia Anderson suggested to me that perhaps Portland was a 'fixer'.

in office.[151] In 1691 Portland was charged to discuss with the Spanish ambassador his chapel in Whitehall Palace, which by attracting many Catholics caused offence among courtiers.[152] In 1695 Portland was despatched to Germany to find a suitable bride for the King, who had become a widower.[153] Portland's mission to Cleves to meet the Brandenburg princess resulted in failure. He had not given a 'very favourable acc.' of the lady as to her beauty, and the King has no reason to be contented with a wife without it'.[154]

This image of Portland as 'fixer' was reinforced by the Earl of Sunderland who once dismissively commented on the abilities of Portland and Albemarle: 'This young man brings and carries a message well, but Portland is so dull an animal that he can neither fetch nor carry.'[155] And yet contemporaries soon understood that Portland was more than simply the King's messenger. In fact, they realised that they were witnessing the re-emergence of the court-favourite and were quick to point out parallels with the Duke of Buckingham. Like Portland, the Duke had operated mainly from Court and enjoyed the full confidence of the King. Whether a court-favourite could still exert a similar influence during the 1690s is doubtful, as the transfer of the court to Hampton Court Palace meant that it lost significance as a meeting place for the nobility and the King. Moreover, structural developments such as the rise of Parliament rendered the position of the Court less important. It is doubtful whether Portland could have remained an influential favourite had he confined himself to the Court. Indeed, the most significant aspect of Portland's career as favourite was the transformation of the court-favourite into a figure that, though based at Court, was increasingly involved in parliamentary management.[156]

Parliament had led an uncertain existence under the Stuart monarchs, and only under William did it become a firmly established institution. Although by 1689 William was an experienced manager of the affairs of the Dutch political assemblies, he was obviously dependent on the advice of native English politicians, particularly the Marquis of Halifax and the Earl of Danby, created Marquis of Carmarthen. The former, now Lord Privy Seal, proposed suitable candidates for office (he claimed to have been responsible for the appointment of Shrewsbury and Nottingham) and also advised William to conduct his policy of trimming.[157] Portland had had no visible influence on the creation of the 1689 ministry, although he occasionally

---

151   T.C. Nicholson and A.S. Turberville, *Charles Talbot, Duke of Shrewsbury* (Cambridge, 1930), 40–41.

152   HMC, *Seventh Report*, 219a. Cf. ibid. 220b.

153   A list of eligible brides had been drawn up and sent to Portland, NUL, PwA 152.

154   Portland to Shrewsbury 8/18 September 1696 (Het Loo); Prior to Vernon Loo 31 Aug. 1696, L.G.W. Legg, *Matthew Prior. A Study of his Public Career and Correspondence* (Cambridge, 1921).

155   Quoted in Kenyon, *Sunderland*, 315.

156   I am thankful to Andrew Barclay with whom I discussed these matters, and helped shaping my ideas about this transformation.

157   Carmarthen was formerly the Earl of Danby. Foxcroft, *Halifax*, II. 65, 66; A.B. Browning, *Thomas Osborne, Earl of Danby and Duke of Leeds 1632–1712* (3 vols, Glasgow, 1951), I. 429. Cf. Foxcroft, *Halifax*, II. 110; Halifax, 'Spencer House journals', 206 and *passim*.

intervened to strengthen the court party. Increasingly Portland became involved in recommending and selecting ministers. After Halifax's dismissal in December 1689, the Lord President, Carmarthen, was daily closeted with the King and Portland pending a vacancy for the office of Lord Treasurer.[158] Richard Hill suggested to Sir William Trumbull in 1691 that offices were partly in his pocket, though 'the King has few men of capacity whom he and Lord Portland will trust'.[159] In 1692 Portland interviewed Trumbull for the post of Secretary of State. Thus Portland had no leading role, but increasingly an important say in ministerial appointments.[160]

The executive wing of government was formalised in the Privy Council, which had lost its central role, and the compact Cabinet Council, which became the most significant formal governing body during William's reign. Comprising the consequential officials of state, such as the Secretaries of State and the Lord Keeper, it became the nucleus of the King's ministry, as opposed to the expanding Privy Council which lapsed into being an oversized political sounding board of the nation's grandees. The Cabinet's influence was always more limited than that of William's inner circle of informal confidants. On the other hand, the apparent servility of the Councillors has sometimes been overemphasised; capable Secretaries of State, such as Nottingham, wielded considerable influence. Moreover, against William's wishes the Cabinet Council became informally established as well during his absence.[161] One can only speculate about the reason for Portland's apparent willingness, against the advice of the Earl of Sunderland, to further expand the Cabinet Council, which between 1689 and 1693 had doubled to some ten councillors.[162]

Portland's seats in the House of Lords and the Privy and Cabinet Councils – which he retained throughout the remainder of his career – constituted the formal sphere of his political activities. Portland habitually attended the Privy Council and Cabinet Council sessions, the latter held weekly in Kensington Palace or Whitehall Palace.[163] As early as the summer of 1689 there were complaints that the King put his Dutch confidants in key positions in the Councils, a French agent reporting: 'Dijkveld who has as much power in the Council as Bentinck in the Cabinet gives complaints mightily here'.[164] But there is little concrete evidence of Portland playing an important role in the Cabinet Council sessions.[165] The Secretaries' succinct minutes yield only fragments of conversations, and sparse reports mention only an

---

158   Dispatch Parent 12 December 1689, AAE, CPA 171, f° 302r°.

159   Hill to Trumbull 1/11 October 1691, HMC, *Downshire Mss*, I-i. 381.

160   Cf. Ch. 5 *passim*.

161   J. Carter, 'Cabinet Records for the Reign of William III', *English Historical Review*, 88 (1963), 95–114, *passim*.

162   Sunderland to Portland 19 August 1694, NUL, PwA 1241; Carter, 'Cabinet Records', 113.

163   13 August 1689, Luttrell, *Brief Historical Relation*, I. 568; *The Names of the Lords of his Majesty's most Honourable Privy Council* in: Somers, *First Collection*, II. 332–3.

164   Dispatch Parent, 1/11 July 1689, AAE, CPA 170, f° 218, transl. from French.

165   E.g. Nottingham's notes of the Cabinet Council meeting in Hampton Court Palace, 1 September 1689, HMC, *Finch Mss*, III. 428–9; Shrewsbury's minutes for 1694 (erroneously referred to as Privy Council minutes) are more complete, in HMC, *Buccleugh Mss*, *passim*; Carter, 'Cabinet Records', 108.

110   *The Anglo-Dutch Favourite*

occasional disagreement between Portland and other ministers. Only when William did not attend could Portland claim a pre-eminent position in the Cabinet. During the invasion scare of 1692, for instance, the King sent Portland to London as his representative to take charges of affairs.[166] But normally, the King and Portland would both attend; clearly the favourite was not representing his monarch as such in the Cabinet.

Portland's role in parliamentary affairs during the 1690s is difficult to establish due to scant evidence. Confronted with the incessant threat of impeachment, he rarely entrusted his thoughts or instructions to paper but preferred to closet with his associates. When Lord Keeper John Somers initiated a correspondence in 1694, Portland insisted that his letters remain strictly confidential. His most significant correspondence with Sunderland, spanning the length of the 1690s, was partially in cipher and his own letters have not been preserved.[167] His minutes of the interrogations after the Assassination Plot are still in his archive. There are some notes of a 1692 trial case in the Lords, as well as memoranda from meetings of the Holland States Assembly about William's right to elect magistrates in Dordrecht.[168] He sometimes took extensive notes during sessions, many of which must be presumed lost now. The proceedings of the Holland States Assembly and the House of Lords are not well documented, and Portland's role in either body remains rather unclear. The limited evidence available shows that Portland would attend the Lords when matters vital to the King's interest were at stake, or when he was appointed to special committees to prepare Bills. He attended sessions more frequently after 1692, a development coinciding with the ascendancy of the Court Whigs and indicative of his increasing interest in parliamentary affairs.[169]

There are few occasions when Portland actually spoke in the Lords, and no speeches have been preserved. He was certainly a powerful presence and an unyielding defender of the Court. Although Carmarthen does not mention Portland as a supporter of the Court in his list, he evidently was.[170] During his few performances in the Holland States Assembly or House of Lords, however, he often heated up conflicts and his confrontational style was not always fortunate. He was probably not a gifted orator, but would intimate the King's wishes to the Court's defenders in the House. Given his intimate relationship with William, Portland was generally regarded as the King's mouthpiece. Royal instructions were issued by the favourite, and his attitude and remarks in the House of Lords were interpreted as a signal from the King.

Portland had little influence in parliamentary management, which had to be delegated to a seasoned 'chief manager' of native origin. In 1689 the limitations of Portland's influence were explained to Huygens: 'he was not a man who could do the King either service or disservice, having neither considerable possessions nor

---

166   Cf. Ch. 6.
167   Somers to Portland 14 Sept. 1694, NUL, PwA 1176.
168   E.g. NUL, PwA 2382 ff.; BL, Eg Mss 1754, f° 53–4.
169   The evidence is based on a general tendency in the attendance lists printed in the *House of Lords Journals* XIV–XVI.
170   Browning, *Danby*, III. 173–6.

followers and credit in Parliament'.[171] Halifax, and after 1689 Carmarthen, were far more instrumental and experienced in mustering support in the Houses. Nor did Portland initially show an inclination to become involved. He once expressed his low opinion of the Commons, which he thought 'will not doe the King's but their own businesse'.[172] But having had some experience in the Holland States Assembly, during the early 1690s the Earl developed an interest in parliamentary management. When William prorogued Parliament in January 1690 he did so without consulting his favourite.[173] In the spring of 1690, however, Portland asked a friendly MP to block a certain measure in Parliament.[174] In September 1690 Henry Sidney and Thomas Coningsby provided detailed advice to Portland on how to deal with the House of Commons.[175] In October 1692 Dijkveld and Portland discussed the importance of making the members of 'that illustrious body' see the logic of William's foreign policy by informing them of the true state of affairs on the continent. Dijkveld introduced to him Jean de Robéthon, a French Huguenot, who was commissioned to write pamphlets to this purpose.[176] In December 1692 Portland received almost daily reports of parliamentary debates.[177] In November 1692 an agent supposed he would be able to advise the King in these matters.[178] By then he was actively mustering support among placemen in the Commons. In 1695 he complained to Lexington about his exhausting responsibilities in parliamentary management.[179] When in November 1696 the Bill of Attainder was debated, 'My Lord Portland is very hearty and industrious in this matter, and does not stick to speak to any one my Lord Keeper desires'.[180] By the mid-1690s Portland increasingly gained control over parliamentary management in England through his liaison with his client Sunderland.[181]

IV

Greatly adding to Portland's significance as a favourite was his involvement in the administration of the other British kingdoms. He particularly wielded influence in Scotland, one pamphleteer remarking:

---

171 24 October 1689, Huygens, *Journaal*, I-i 194, transl. from Dutch.
172 12 November 1691, Huygens, *Journaal*, I-i. 513.
173 William to Portland 7 February 1690, Japikse, *Correspondentie*, XXIII. 95.
174 Portland to Hop 23 April 1690 (Kensington Palace), Japikse, *Correspondentie*, XXVIII. 164.
175 Coningsby and Sidney to Portland 27 September 1690, NUL, PwA 299.
176 Dijkveld to Portland 26 October 1692, Japikse, *Correspondentie*, XXVIII. 302, transl. from French.
177 NUL, PwA 2385–90 and *passim*.
178 Letter to Portland 1 November 1692, NUL, PwA 2792.
179 Portland to Lexington 17/27 April 1695 (Kensington Palace), BL, Add Mss 46525, f° 101r°; NUL, PwA 2392.
180 Vernon to Shrewsbury 30 November 1696, James, *Letters*, I. 89.
181 E.g. Van Zuylen van Nijvelt to Portland 24 July 1694, BL, Eg Mss 1707, f° 263; Sunderland to Portland 20 June 1693, NUL, PwA 1216; AAE, CPA 178, f° 16r°.

... Benting, who is the Minion and Darling of our Monarch ... has granted unto him as well as Assumed the whole Superintendency of the Kingdom of Scotland & Governs it intirely by his Creatures, who are the only Persons there Trusted with the Administration, and to whom he give such Measures, in Reference both to the Legislative and to the Excutive Part of the Government in that Kingdom ... .[182]

Already in the spring of 1689 the King had decided to delegate Scots affairs almost entirely to Portland, Burnet later remarking that he 'had that nation once wholly in his hands'.[183] He became the sole channel of communication between Scottish politicians and the King and was regarded as his mouthpiece. Lord Advocate Dalrymple wrote to Secretary of State Melville in April 1689, for example, that he had been told 'that the Earle of Portland should wrytt as from the King'.[184] The favourite regulated audiences and virtually monopolised access to the King. Lord Yester, recognising his importance, anxiously tried to get acquainted with Portland in the spring of 1689 when the court party emerged under the latter's tutelage.[185] The major offices were discussed between Portland and the King, the former being actively involved in the creation and management of the ministry. He invited Melville in April 1689 to come to Hampton Court, his 'advyce being so necessary at this tyme, when places ar to be setled'.[186] In the autumn of 1689 he closeted himself for a long time with the Duke of Hamilton, the Scottish Lord High Commissioner, to discuss his continuation in office and the specifics and limits of his authority.[187] When Hamilton neglected to take his seat in the council in January 1693, pressure from Portland forced the sulking Duke to change his mind.[188] Portland's authority was widely recognised and his patronage often sought. In practice, political appointments were regularly suggested by ministers, after which Portland's endorsement would be solicited, the allocation of offices being dependent upon his recommendation to the King.[189] In 1691 for instance, Hamilton, thanking Portland for his 'favers and civillities', asked him to secure a place for his son at the mint.[190]

There may have been several reasons why William had put Portland in charge of Scottish affairs. Firstly, as a close confidant attached to the King, Portland was able to see events within a larger context. It seems imprudent, then, to study Portland's role in the administration of Scotland solely within a Scottish context, as his policy was primarily motivated by events on the continent. Thus Portland was able to

---

182 R. Ferguson, *A Brief Account of some of the late Incroachments and Depredations of the Dutch upon the English etc.* (London?, 1695), 21.
183 *A Supplement to Burnets History of my Own Time etc.*, ed. H.C. Foxcroft (Oxford, 1902), 415. Cf. Riley, *Scottish Politicians*, 5.
184 Dalrymple to Melville 21 April 1689, Melville, *Leven and Melville Papers*, 13.
185 Yester to Tweeddale 16 April 1689, House of Lords Archive, Willcocks Collection, section 6.
186 Dalrymple to Melville 21 April 1689, Melville, *Leven and Melville Papers*, 13.
187 Hamilton to his wife 19 November 1689, NAS, GD 406/1/6587.
188 Johnston to Hamilton 27 December 1692, Carstares to Hamilton 28 January 1693, NAS, GD 406/1/3816, GD 406/1/3769.
189 E.g. Johnston to Carstares 27 May 1693, *State Papers and Letters Addressed to William Carstares*, ed. J. McCormick (Edinburgh, 1774), 184.
190 Hamilton to Portland 27 May 1695, NUL, PwA 375.

intervene in domestic disputes whenever they obstructed royal policy, and support court parties of any identity.

Secondly, as a Calvinist, he would be more acceptable to Presbyterians. But Portland was unwilling to openly commit himself to any party, and his position was initially unclear to all save his closest advisers. He tried to support the Court whilst keeping lines of communication open to the Club, and support the Presbyterians without frustrating the Episcopalians. Portland and Carstares had initially supported a Presbyterian ministry led by Melville, but by 1691 were inclined to broaden its base. By 1692 the King decided to make Dalrymple a second Secretary, followed by a ministerial reshuffle that was meant to represent both the Presbyterian and Episcopalian interest.[191] It had been partly dissatisfaction over Melville's dealing with Mackay and Breadalbane that prompted the King to receive the Episcopalians back into the ministry.

A third reason may have been that a Dutchman in charge was more acceptable for the Scots than an Englishman. He came, however, to be seen as an exponent of English centralism, and there was a real concern that an exclusive court party in Whitehall was giving directions to Edinburgh. As one opposition leader clearly recognised, Portland's main concern was to establish a powerful court party with whomever might serve the King: 'the English Juncto, viz., Hallifax, Denby, Shrewsbury, Nottingham, and Portland, are taking methods for breaking our Parliament.' The phrase 'English junto', here used as an epithet for the Cabinet Council, is reminiscent of the fictitious 'Dutch junto'.[192]

Patrick Riley, in his penetrating study on Scottish politics, concluded that 'The power generally ascribed to Portland was not at all exaggerated. As the man "interposed" between the king and the secretaries, he played a considerable part in Scottish administrative adjustments'.[193] Most Scottish politicians recognised Portland as the 'chief manager' of their affairs, but as most deliberations took place behind closed doors and relevant correspondence is scarce, it is difficult to assess the exact nature and extent of his influence. For practical reasons Portland often had to delegate business to his associates, being overburdened with administrative work. From 1690 Portland was annually engaged in military campaigns, but during the winter season he did take time to closet himself with Scottish politicians; when Cockburn had an audience with Portland in February 1695, they talked fully 'both of men and things'.[194] When Portland arrived in England from the continent in October 1697, the Scottish Secretary of State James Ogilvy 'had the honour and satisfaction to be with the E. of Portland frequently'.[195] But available time was limited. The Scottish Secretary James

---

191   Hopkins, *Glencoe*, 266; Riley, *Scottish Politicians*, 59–60.

192   Forbes to Hume 22 August 1689, HMC, *Manuscripts of the Duke of Roxburghe etc.* (London, 1894), 118. Cf. Ch. 5.

193   Riley, *Scottish Politicians*, 130.

194   Cockburn to Annandale 16 February 1695, HMC, *Manuscripts of J.J. Hope Johnstone Esq. of Annandale* (London, 1897), 73.

195   Ogilvy to Carstares 1 October 1697, 5 October 1697, 19 October 1697, 5 November 1697, McCormick, *State Papers*, 349–52, 356–8, 361.

Johnston, for instance, complained during the 1692 crisis that 'I have scarcely had any time of My Lord Portland since he came'.[196]

Presumably Portland, having never set foot on Scottish soil, was rather oblivious to the intricacies of Scottish affairs and must have initially leaned on his advisers. In practice most Scots business was handled by William Carstares and the Secretaries of State. These were mainly former exiles who had sought refuge in the Netherlands during the 1680s, including Melville and Johnston, who had been close associates of Portland's. Johnston had been involved in Portland's intelligence network as it emerged during 1687–88. He was close to the Presbyterians but basically a Whig, and one who had occasionally flirted with the opposition forces of 'the Club'. Johnston's good relationship with Portland can be traced in their extensive correspondence. Portland had also worked closely with his predecessor, Melville, and most importantly, Carstares, a Presbyterian minister and chaplain to William. H.C. Foxcroft has described Portland and his associates as a 'Scoto-Dutch group' aiming to uphold a Williamite court party in Edinburgh, pacify the Highlands and establish a moderate Presbyterian church settlement.[197]

Scottish politicians were advised to occasionally write to Portland, in fact were instructed to do so with regard to important matters. When the Earl of Annandale took office in 1694, Johnston instructed him to 'writ a letter of compliment to my Lord Portland'.[198] Most of the crucial documents addressed to the King went through Portland's hands.[199] Though he insisted on being meticulously informed, he issued his instructions through Carstares and seldom replied directly. Often, requests to Portland were issued via Carstares as well.[200] The reason for this construction was in many respects a practical one. The Duke of Queensberry told Carstares that he 'thought needless to trouble E.P. with a letter, since I know you will comunicate what you think fit of this to him'.[201] On other occasions, he simply did not know where Portland was.[202] The Scottish Secretary James Ogilvy was not even sure whether Portland would appreciate him writing.[203] In practice most routine business was delegated to Carstares, who discussed matters with him. Secretary of State Johnston for instance once informed Portland that 'I give Mr Carstares a note of some things wch I hope y^r Lordship will gett done'.[204] Occasionally Portland himself would conduct the correspondence, the contents of which would usually be discussed with Carstares beforehand.[205] Portland delegated most business to Carstares but would

---

196   Johnston to Stair 10 May 1692, NAS, SP 3, f° 32.
197   Foxcroft, *Supplement*, 541.
198   Johnston to Annandale 6 December 1694, HMC, *Johnstone Mss*, 67.
199   E.g. NUL, PwA 2436, PwA 2442, PwA 2425 and *passim*.
200   Ogilvy to Carstares 27 April 1697, 10 August 1697, McCormick, *State Papers*, 298, 329.
201   Queensberry to Carstares 29 June 1697, ibid., 313.
202   Queensberry to Carstares 21 August 1697, ibid., 333.
203   Ogilvy to Carstares 10 December 1695, ibid., 270.
204   Johnston to Portland 22 March 1692, NAS, SP 3, f° 16.
205   Carstares to Melville 26 May 1694, 22 November 1694, 22 November 1694, NLS, Ms 3471, f° 20, 24v°, 27.

regularly be informed of matters of importance.[206] Johnston in particular wrote detailed and lengthy reports about proceedings. Characteristically Portland seldom replied, and instructions were usually channelled through Carstares.

Often it seemed that the favourite was evading responsibility, whereas in fact he was merely keeping 'behind the curtain', as Johnston recognised: 'I writ often rather to other than to your self [Portland] because they'll watch opportunities to show you my letters and to put you in mind to procure answers'.[207] In 1692 however Johnston complained to Carstares that 'My Lord P told me at parting not to writ often to him I perceive by his not answering that he is resolved not to medle in our affaires'.[208] Riley has noted that often Portland feigned abstention, all the while keeping a tight grip on affairs. To Tweeddale for instance Portland, probably reluctant after the Glencoe massacre, wrote in 1692:

> I beg you to be persuaded that I meddle as little as possible with affairs which are not of my department, and especially those of Scotland, nevertheless, when the service of His Majesty, or yourself, demands that you take the trouble to write to me, Sir, I will be pleased to receive the honour of your letters ... .[209]

Thus Portland emerged as the intermediary between the King and Scottish politicians.

Portland also became the sole channel for recommendations and established himself as the main distributor of patronage.[210] For instance, the Earl of Argyle demanded office for his brother, Patrick Hume for his son, both soliciting Portland's support.[211] By granting requests, Portland built up prestige and esteem, and bound a court party to himself. 'I have, as directed, offered my mite to serve E. Portland', Argyle wrote, 'I cannot think but he will please to have some regard for me.'[212] The court party acknowledged being tied to Portland's favour and interest: 'I am', Ogilvy assured Carstares, 'entirely submissive to what my Lord Portland shall determine.'[213] The Queensberry ministry managed to establish a powerful court party drawn from the main magnate factions. When faction struggles threatened to weaken the ministry, Portland did not hesitate to intervene. For instance, Queensberry and Argyle had become embroiled with Murray, who tried to build up an independent position with the aid of the former following of Johnston and Tweeddale. Queensberry and Ogilvy

---

206 Johnston to Tweeddale 21 February 1693, NAS, SP 3. During Portland's absence on the continent he would receive copies of official correspondence sent to Queen Mary, Johnston to Carstares 24 May 1693, McCormick, *State Papers*, 183.

207 Johnston to Portland 27 May 1693, NAS, SP 3. Cf. Johnston to Carstares 1 June 1693, ibid.

208 Johnston to Carstares 22 April 1692, ibid.

209 Portland to Tweeddale 23 March/3 April 1692 (Het Loo), NLS, Ms 14407, f° 178–9, transl. from French.

210 Argyle to Carstares 3 September 1698, Ogilvy to Carstares 6 Sept. 1698, McCormick, *State Papers*, 433, 437.

211 Argyle to Carstares 1 April 1696, Hume to Carstares 22 May 1697, Hamilton to Carstares 5 October 1698, ibid., 289, 201, 351–2.

212 Argyle to Carstares 3 April 1699, ibid., 476.

213 Ogilvy to Carstares 10 September 1698, ibid., 441.

tried to oust Murray, and asked for the assistance of Carstares and Portland.[214] When Murray was dismissed in 1698 he accused Carstares of being the evil genius, 'a great instrument with Earl Portland', as he wrote to Hume.[215]

If Portland became a central figure in the government of Scotland, his role in Ireland was less prominent, but he still wielded some influence there. In the autumn of 1690, after the victorious battle at the Boyne, the civil government had taken shape with William's appointment of Charles Porter, Thomas Coningsby and Henry Sidney as Lords Justices of Ireland. Coningsby and Sidney started corresponding with Portland on a frequent basis to keep him informed about events.[216] Portland's political involvement in Irish affairs began with recommendations for prospective candidates for high office in Dublin, discussed in a memorandum he provided for the King. Portland clearly had a say in appointments the King made in the church, army and offices.[217] His political influence in Ireland is even more obscure than his role in Scotland, but titbits of information from his memoranda give an insight into what he may have discussed with the King. An undated memorandum in his handwriting gives an overview of the establishment of a government in Dublin, discussing men fit for office, 'to set up a Commission of nine persons in Dublin to administer all affairs'.[218] Again, such memoranda provide no definitive information about Portland's actual influence on appointments, but seem to indicate that the favourite was discussing such matters of the highest importance with the King. Although Ginckel thought that Portland was well disposed towards Coningsby and Porter,[219] in an undated memorandum, possibly from 1690, the favourite wrote:

> Porter is al too violent and wants too much to be master, therefore his recommendation should not be followed, and as Chancellor he should not recommend councillors nor judges ... Duke of Ormond, Fitzpatrick and others want to recommend all men to sustain their interest ... MLS [My Lord Sidney?] warns that many who stayed with King James until the end still hold political office and make friends in England to be employed again.[220]

His mediation was sought by the Lords Justices who recommended men for office.[221] Portland discussed with the King the distribution of offices in Ireland, but his main concern was the campaign.[222] Not surprisingly, the Secretary-at-War for Ireland, Sir George Clark, was appointed and kept in Ireland at his recommendation, and together with the Commander-in-Chief, the Duke of Schomberg, and the generals, Solms and 's Gravenmoer, Portland planned the Irish campaign. Portland continued

---

214 Ogilvy to Carstares 22 June 1697, 24 July 1697, ibid., 311, 320.
215 Ogilvy to Hume n.d. February 1698, HMC, *Roxburghe Mss*, 146.
216 Portland to Schomberg 21 August 1689 (Hampton Court Palace), Coningsby to Portland 21 September 1690, Sidney to Portland 24 September 1690, NUL, PwA 1126, PwA 298, PwA 1321. Cf. NUL, PwA 2074.
217 Sidney to Portland 24 September 1690, 25 September 1697, NUL, PwA 1320, 1321.
218 Draft notes by Portland, undated, NUL, PwA 2073.
219 HMC, *Fourth Report* (London, 1874), 324.
220 NUL, PwA 2074.
221 E.g. Sidney to Portland 18 October 1690, NUL, PwA 1326.
222 NUL, PwA 2074.

to function as the channel of communication between the military in Ireland and the King.[223]

V

The favourite's involvement in Scottish and Irish affairs was rather remarkable, as the King could have chosen to rely on a confidant of native origin. Less unexpected was Portland's role in managing William's affairs in the United Provinces; his activities on both sides of the Channel exemplify his unique role as Anglo-Dutch favourite. William's position as King and Stadholder after 1688 has often been neglected by historians.[224] Indeed, it may be argued that the integration of William's offices is one of the most under-researched aspects of his reign, and its political and decision-making mechanisms remain obscure. Contemporaries as well were baffled by the complications of his dual position as Stadholder and King, many British disregarding 'the (in Comparison) contemptible Authority of the Stadtholder of Holland'.[225] The underestimation of this highly influential office needs to be redressed, for it is precisely the combination of the offices of the King-Stadholder that lies at the heart of the 'personal union' between Britain and the United Provinces. Throughout his reign William resided in England, only occasionally visiting The Hague or withdrawing to Het Loo. In order to deal with his stadholderly affairs, he appointed Constantijn Huygens as Secretary for Dutch affairs only.[226] Huygens dealt mainly with routine matters, and increasingly William came to rely on Grand Pensionary Anthonie Heinsius, who would emerge as one of William's closest confidants in the United Provinces.[227] But it was Portland who became the only Dutch counsellor residing in England with whom William could discuss his affairs in the United Provinces on a daily basis.

As Stadholder William was formally a servant of the States, but in practice he could exert pressure and was in effective control of many of the local and provincial assemblies. Gelderland, Overijssel and Utrecht were securely in his pocket through *regeringsreglementen* (governmental regulations), but this was not the case in the provinces that mattered most, Zeeland and Holland. In Holland in particular his influence varied from town to town and was perhaps weakest in Amsterdam, often his staunchest opponent. A stadholderly clientele had emerged during the 1670s and 1680s in the various provinces and towns, constituting a string of local factions

---

223 HMC, *Manuscripts of F.W. Leyborne-Popham Esq.* (London, 1899), 171, 175.

224 Baxter paid more attention to Dutch politics after 1688 than Troost and Claydon. Baxter, *William III*; Tony Claydon, *William III* (London, 2002); W. Troost, *William III, the Stadholder-King: A Political Biography* (Aldershot, 2005).

225 E.g. Hop to Heinsius 9 May 1690, *Het Archief van den Raadpensionaris Antonie Heinsius*, ed. H.J. van der Heim (3 vols, The Hague, 1867), I. 30–31; *A Very Remarkable Letter from King William III. To his Favourite Bentinck, Earl of Portland, in French and English, together with Reflections thereon* in: Somers, *First Collection*, I. 365.

226 E.g. 19 February 1689, Huygens, *Journaal*, I-i. 85.

227 Cf. H. Lademacher, 'Wilhelm III. von Oranien und Anthonie Heinsius', *Rheinische Vierteljahrsblätter*, 34 (1970), 252–66.

co-operating with the Stadholder.[228] William made use of provincial 'managers'. Utrecht and Zeeland were managed by his confidants Dijkveld and Nassau-Odijk. Friesland and Groningen were dominated by his relative Stadholder Hendrik Casimir, with whom William was often at odds, but who moved to William's position around 1690. On a lower level a string of regents in key positions in the city councils, provincial and national councils complemented an informal clientele of Orangists committed to support William's foreign policy. The limitations of his formal influence were partly overcome through the mobilisation of these Orangist regents and provincial managers. William could not entirely keep his sometimes unruly and corrupt dependants in check, nor completely subdue their prevalent mutual rivalry. In the summer of 1689, for instance, the recalcitrant and dissatisfied Frisian stadholder had formed a temporary alliance with William's equally disgruntled relative, Nassau-Odijk, to topple Waldeck.[229] Although faction struggle amongst William's favourites was common, it was rarely prompted by diverging views on the central focus and direction of his policy as such. In general they loyally supported his foreign policy and facilitated its requirements.[230]

It is difficult to estimate the nature and impact of Portland's authority in the United Provinces. In an important memorandum dated 1692, the French chargé d'affaires, on the advice of D'Avaux, identified a string of Orangist regents in the Holland city councils: Nicolaas Witsen in Amsterdam, Simon van Halewijn in Dordrecht, Willem Fabricius in Haarlem, Jacob Van Zuylen van Nijvelt in Rotterdam, Maas in Leiden, Gerard Putmans in Delft, Bruno van der Dussen in Gouda, his brother Gerard Van der Dussen in Schiedam, van der Straat in Gorcum, and Brassee in Den Briel. Elaborating on the organisation of this group, he explained:

> All the people there are governed on behalf of the Prince of Orange by his great favourite Bentinck, who for three or four years, or perhaps for much longer, has carried out a policy of not including anyone in the government until they had swore an oath that they would unquestionably do and execute all which they would be ordered on behalf of the Prince of Orange, in affirmation of which each one had to sign an act.[231]

He certainly overestimated Portland's influence, as men like Witsen were neither in his nor in William's control, nor were William's favourites Dijkveld or van Zuylen van Nijvelt 'governed' by Portland. Nevertheless, the memorandum does identify Portland at the pinnacle of the Orangist clientele, and as such his authority in the United Provinces had also clearly increased after 1688.

The memo is relatively accurate in mapping the configuration of his clientele that was mobilised during the magistrates' controversy of 1690. City councils were never entirely in the Stadholder's control, and the maintenance and control over such decentralised and diverse clientage systems required constant attention.

---

228 Cf. S. Groenveld, *Evidente Factien in den Staet. Sociaal-Politieke Verhoudingen in de 17ᵉ eeuwse Republiek der Verenigde Nederlanden* (Hilversum, 1990), 10–13, on the phenomenon of 'provincial factions'.
229 Waldeck to William 5 July 1689, Japikse, *Correspondentie*, XXVIII. 119.
230 Cf. Ch. 1
231 AAE, CPH 158, f° 139r°, transl. from Dutch.

'Lord Portland takes all'

Portland's role, again, is particularly difficult to reconstruct, as presumably his discussions with William occurred behind closed doors. There is, however, plenty of information about the favourite's dealing with the Holland towns during the spring of 1690, when he was despatched by the Stadholder to The Hague to deal with the magistrates' controversy (as described in chapter 3). Portland corresponded with William at length on an almost daily basis, which provides a unique insight into their co-operation. The correspondence confirms what otherwise could only have been surmised from fragments of information, namely that Portland played a pivotal role in mobilising and managing William's clientele in order to support his policy.

The conflict also provides information as to favourite's role in the consolidation and maintenance of the Stadholder's clientele, as illustrated by his pivotal part in the ensuing distribution of favours in the spring of 1690. As early as 25 January he recommended solicitors for posts in the Rotterdam admiralty, receivership of the *Ridderschap*, the Schiedam *Heemraet* (a local governing body), mostly within the Orangist clientele and related to such men as Admiral Bastiaansen and Bailiff Van Zuylen van Nijvelt.[232] On 7 February he recommended someone whose brother had facilitated the 1688 invasion, for a captaincy.[233] Portland and Heinsius jointly examined the names on the list of nominees and sent recommendations to William.[234] Portland's recommendations for offices in Haarlem were accepted by William. Portland had recommended Hermans for *Rector Magnificus* of Leiden university; he was well disposed and a Calvinist.[235] William accepted his recommendation. Lord Van Voorst, who had entered the *Ridderschap* the previous year, and had been supported by Portland, now entered the Council of State, and Lord Noortwijk was recommended for the receivership of the *Ridderschap.* Lord Wassenaar's son was made *Ruwaart* (a local office).[236] Portland recommended to William that all Amsterdam *schepenen* (city magistrates) nominated by the Republican Huydekooper should be disregarded.[237] The Amsterdam list caused some problems, as one of the nominees was a protégé of Witsen. Portland would rather not have him, but that would mean that Witsen might be affronted. William selected him, 'thinking it more important to oblige Witsen than any consideration he might have for the person himself'.[238] Reportedly Portland had quarrelled with Beverningk, who had 'played the beast against Portland' over a vacancy in the Rotterdam admiralty.[239]

---

232 Portland to William 25 January 1690 (The Hague), Japikse, *Correspondentie*, XXIII. 77–8.

233 Portland to William 7 February 1690 (The Hague), ibid., 99.

234 Portland to William 14–15 March 1690 (The Hague), ibid., 147.

235 Actually he was a *liefhebber*, an occasional attendee of the Reformed Church, rather than a member.

236 Portland to William 25 January 1690 (The Hague), 4 February 1690 (The Hague), William to Portland 7 February 1690, 17 February 1690, Portland to William 22 February 1690 (The Hague), Japikse, *Correspondentie*, XXIII. 77–8, 91, 96, 110, 114; Wassenaar to Portland 29 July 1691, Japikse, *Correspondentie*, XXIV. 662.

237 TNA:PRO, SP 8/8, f° 106.

238 William to Portland 22 March 1690, Japikse, *Correspondentie*, XXIII. 152, transl. from French.

239 11 November 1690, Huygens, *Journaal*, I-i. 357, literal transl. from Dutch.

Portland, then, had remained involved in Dutch domestic affairs despite his almost continuous absence. Winter seasons would be spent in England, during summertime he was on campaign in Flanders. Only during the spring and the autumn would he join William during his retreat to Het Loo or stay in The Hague for a few weeks. Portland's important role in the attempt to reinvigorate the Orangists in 1690 during the Amsterdam magistrates' affair can partly be explained by their temporary weakness and incoherence, and his position during the remainder of the 1690s cannot simply be extrapolated from this. According to the French chargé d'affaires, Portland's ascendancy can be dated from around late 1688 and continued until at least 1692, suggesting that he managed to sustain his considerable influence. It also suggests that Portland became more influential after the death of Grand Pensionary Gaspar Fagel, whose successor Anthonie Heinsius was a weaker politician, often co-operating with Portland. It seems likely, however, that he increasingly withdrew from Dutch politics during the course of the 1690s, as he himself suggested to the temporary Grand Pensionary Michiel ten Hove as early as the spring of 1689:

> It appears that the good state of affairs here [in England] shall not leave me much occasion to serve my friends in Holland as a result of my absence, which I hope, however, will not be so continuous as to prevent us from meeting with each other; if one, having reached my age, has to change country, one never forgets the first nor the friends there left behind.[240]

Whether this is accurate is difficult to say, as Portland and William frequently discussed Dutch affairs in Hampton Court Palace as well. In March 1689 Portland had discussed with Schuylenburg in London a vacancy in the Chamber of Accounts and the vacancy for Bailiff of the Hague.[241] In October 1690 the Stadholder instructed Portland to write to the *Hof van Holland* in support of his favourite in Rotterdam, van Zuylen van Nijvelt.[242] Obviously Portland remained involved in affairs related to his own political responsibilities.[243]

The limited evidence that is available suggests that by the mid 1690s William's favourites in the United Provinces addressed themselves to Portland. In 1694, for instance, a list for the nomination of Schielandt magistrates was sent to William. His favourite in that area however, Van Zuylen van Nijvelt, sent his recommendations to Portland to be discussed with the Stadholder.[244] After Zuylen's death in June 1695 a contest for vacant offices commenced; Portland was beleaguered by requests for favours and offices.[245] He had consistently put Orangists in the Rotterdam city council. During the ensuing redistribution of favours, those on good terms with

---

240 Bentinck to Ten Hove 15/25 February 1689 (Whitehall Palace), Japikse, *Correspondentie*, XXVIII. 128, transl. from Dutch.
241 20 March 1689, 25 March 1689, 12 Apr. 1689, Huygens, *Journaal*, I-i. 96, 99, 107.
242 17 October 1690, Huygens, *Journaal*, I-i. 346.
243 E.g. BL, Egerton Mss 1707 f° 148–9.
244 Van Zuylen van Nijvelt to Portland 24 July 1694, BL, Eg Mss 1707, f° 263.
245 Van Hogendorp and Van Beijer to Portland 29 June 1695, NUL, PwA 1902.

Portland and Heinsius emerged successful.[246] Evidence suggests, however, that both William and Portland increasingly left matters of Dutch politics to Heinsius and the impression is one of the erosion of Portland's influence during the later part of the 1690s. In 1699 the Earl of Jersey believed 'that Mylord Portland has no other resource than in Heinsius'.[247]

VI

This chapter has analysed the emergence of the favourite in Williamite England. Portland was undoubtedly pre-eminent at Court, but the first few years of his career as a court-favourite witnessed an important transformation, in which he was also increasingly engaged in parliamentary affairs. This transformation which had started during the winter of 1689/1690, had more or less crystallized by 1692. Initially Portland's influence was particularly manifest at Court only. As Groom of the Stole he was able to control access to the King, but he also had a pretext to spend undisturbed time with the King during which policy was discussed. During those years he also managed the King's clientele. His influence at Court was considerable. He was often solicited for favours and positions. Portland also played an important role in the Privy and Cabinet Councils. Increasingly his influence extended to other spheres, and as from around 1692 he became actively involved in parliamentary affairs, although he usually did so in tandem with experienced managers, most notably Sunderland. He also increasingly managed the placemen in Parliament. In 1695 and 1696 his position was stronger than ever before, developments which will be analysed in more detail in chapter 5. His main goal was to aid the war effort, which will be discussed in chapter 6.

Portland also played a co-ordinating role in the government of William's realms, necessary after the emergence of the Anglo-Dutch union, or more accurately, the conjunction of four separate states headed by the King-Stadholder. It seems no accident that William's favourites were Dutchmen who were naturalised Englishmen as well. In this way Portland could monitor William's affairs both in England and the United Provinces. Portland also supervised the King's affairs in Scotland and, to a far lesser extent, in Ireland. In practice he served as an intermediary between the King and 'regional managers', such as Carstares in Scotland, Sidney in Ireland and Van Zuylen van Nijvelt, Dijkveld and Nassau-Odijk in the United Provinces.[248] The extent to which Portland had these men under control or was rather a figure-head is not always clear, but his position as favourite was undisputed. When the Duke of Newcastle died in 1691, there were some who expected Portland to receive the

---

246 J.A.F. de Jongste, 'The 1690s and After: The Local Perspective' in: J.A.F. de Jongste and A.J. Veenendaal (eds), *Anthonie Heinsius and the Dutch Republic 1688–1720. Politics, War and Finance* (The Hague, 2002), 65–88; Van Hogendorp to Portland 15 August 1695, Paisecoeur, Vethuysen, Van Heel and Groeninx to Portland 17 August 1695, NUL, PwA 1903, PwA 1904.

247 Jersey to Albemarle 9 June 1699, BL, Add Mss 63630, f° 134r°, transl. from French.

248 Cf. Riley, *Scottish Politicians*, 85.

vacant Garter.[249] The Jacobite pamphlet *The Dear Bargain* bitterly concluded that 'Mynheer Bentinck now rules over us'.[250]

---

249   HMC, *Seventh Report*, 565a.

250   [N. Johnston], *The Dear Bargain, or, A True Representation of the State of the English Nation under the Dutch. In a Letter to a Friend*, in: Somers, *Third Collection*, III. 260.

Chapter 5

'The Spirit of Contention': Politics and Parties

After the consolidation of the revolution settlement, William could maintain his authority in Britain and focus his attention on the continental war. Success on the battlefield largely depended on the efficient utilisation of British resources, whereas, vice versa, the war had a tremendous impact on the political and constitutional development of Britain. The King made concessions to Parliament, such as the Triennial Bill, in order to obtain funds to wage his continental war. Revisionist historians have argued that the changes which occurred in England after William's revolution were 'unintended consequences', as they were the result of a dialectic clash between King and Parliament, rather than a conscious choice by the King-Stadholder himself, who was rather focused on the war with France.[1] William took great pains to wrestle funds from his new kingdoms, and in the process became the main instigator of changes on the British Isles.

In chapter 4, it was argued that the career of Portland witnessed an important transformation, as the court-favourite became increasingly involved in parliamentary and ministerial management. The shift reflected the growing importance of Parliament in the 1690s. By 1692 Portland had emerged as the undisputed favourite of William III, mainly engaged in the implementation of royal policy. He acquired substantial political responsibility in order to provide the King with the necessary resources. But to what extent can his efforts be judged a success? In this chapter, Portland's political activities in Britain and the consolidation of his position as favourite will be analysed. He was involved in maintaining the stadholderly and royal prerogative. William's political conduct can only be properly understood within a British and European context. This chapter will adopt an integral approach by examining Portland's activities in the United Provinces, England, Scotland and Ireland and will seek to examine patterns in the nature of the personal union and the alliance that was shaped in the aftermath of the revolution. It will also investigate the constitutional

---

1   It is not clear whether this view is entirely accurate, as William had in fact envisaged a vital role for Parliament even before the Revolution. In December 1688 he wrote to one his closest confidants, Everard van Weede van Dijkveld, that it was his intention to reinstall Parliament, hoping 'that through a Parliament these realms may be made useful in order to assist our State and her allies'. William to Dijkveld 19 December 1688, Japikse, *Correspondentie*, XXVIII. 74–5, transl. from Dutch. Cf. 12 December 1688, Huygens, *Journaal*, I-i. 34. Historians have accused William of neglecting his kingdoms, but in fact, he divided his time between his two most important realms, England and the United Provinces. He twice planned state visits to Scotland (although these had to be cancelled), and was the only reigning English Stuart monarch to visit Ireland.

disputes over the strengthening or maintaining of the King-Stadholder's prerogatives in which Portland was involved and his role in the creation and upholding of court interests on both sides of the North Sea with the purpose of mobilising human and financial resources for the continental campaign. Rather than providing an exhaustive chronological account, this chapter will focus on key moments in Portland's career which will illuminate the nature of his activities.

I

Before discussing Portland political convictions and activities, it is worth paying attention to his religious affinity and political ideas.[2] In his writings Portland seldom reflected on specific theological issues, but frequently displayed his dedication to the Protestant cause to which local or even national concerns must be subordinated. There are surprisingly few clues regarding Portland's religious life, and much rests on circumstantial evidence. He attended Sunday services on a regular basis, and Huygens reveals glimpses of him discussing sermons.[3] He seemed more pious than one would expect from a courtier. Indeed, Burnet marvelled about it: 'He is a virtuous and religious man, and I have heard instances of this that are very extraordinary, chiefly in a courtier.'[4] Even on the battlefield Portland would organise a service and take the Lord's Supper in his tent.[5]

At first sight, then, Portland comes across as a devout Calvinist, and it was obviously no coincidence that William put him in charge of Scottish affairs. He was also a patron of Huguenot exiles, both soldiers and scholars, and Portland had shown himself sensitive to the pleas of Huguenots throughout the 1680s.[6] There were a number of Huguenots in his household and clientele. Woodstock's tutor, Michel le Vassor, was a priest who had published his *De la Véritable Religion* on Catholicism in 1689 but had converted to Protestantism in 1695.[7] His venomous anti-Catholic study of Louis XIII[8] incurred the wrath of the French king, who demanded that Portland dismiss him from his services in 1699. The preface specifically refers to Woodstock and Portland. After initially refusing to bow to Louis's demands, Portland

---

2 Cf. Ch. 2.

3 E.g. Portland to William 29 March 1690 (The Hague), Japikse, *Correspondentie*, XXIII. 157; 23 August 1689, Huygens, *Journaal*, I-i. 167.

4 *A Supplement to Burnet's History of my Own Time etc.*, ed. H.C. Foxcroft (Oxford, 1902), 196.

5 24 July 1695, Huygens, *Journaal*, I-ii. 510.

6 P.J.A.N. Rietbergen, 'William of Orange (1650–1702) between European Politics and European Protestantism: the Case of the Huguenots' in: J.A.H. Bots and G.H.M. Posthumus Meyjes (eds), *La Révocation de l'Édit de Nantes et les Provinces-Unies* (Amsterdam, 1986), 46; *Mémoires d'Isaac Dumont de Bostaquet ... sur les Temps qui ont Précédé et Suivi la Révocation de l'Édit de Nantes* (Paris, 1968), 152.

7 28 December 1699, 4 January 1700, N. Luttrell, *A Brief Historical Relation of State Affairs from September 1678 to April 1714* (Oxford, 1857), IV. 598, 600. D.C.A. Agnew, *Protestant Exiles from France etc.* (2 vols, s.l., 1886), II. 390.

8 M. le Vassor, *Histoire du Regne de Louis XIII etc.* (10 vols, Amsterdam, 1700).

must have sensed that given the ongoing diplomatic negotiations with the French over the Spanish Succession, it was unwise to keep Le Vassor in his service.

There are additional reports supporting Portland's reputation of being an anti-papist. According to the Catholic 'Monsieur de B.', he was a 'passionate enemy of our religion'.[9] In his capacity as *Drost* of Lingen and Breda he had been involved in the expulsion of priests and in measures against 'popish impudences', showing his sensitivity to the demands of the Calvinist classis.[10] According to Count d'Avaux, he, in conjunction with Calvinist ministers, had persuaded William to rid his officer corps and court of Catholics.[11] However, D'Avaux and 'Monsieur de B.' were hardly objective observers, and it is doubtful whether such actions were clear examples of a deep-rooted anti-papism. In 1691 Portland complained to the Spanish ambassador, who had a chapel in Whitehall Palace frequently attended by Catholics.[12] His intervention was rather the result of a desire to tactfully resolve the situation, as courtiers in the King's palace itself were daily confronted with people attending mass, and Portland handled the incident with circumspection.

Portland appeared to entertain a providential view of current events. He was convinced that Divine Providence (a recurring phrase in his correspondence) was guiding the King to protect His church, and he had a tendency to explain political events in such terms. Within such a providential view, Portland frequently assured William 'that the good God will turn [events] to your advantage'.[13] In one of his most insightful letters to William, he reflected on how Divine Providence had guided the King's ways to perfect His plan:

> According to this principle you have seen, Sire, that your enterprises have been blessed on so many encounters, and if you would reflect on times past you see that Divine Providence has given the best of success to the most difficult affairs, and to manifest herself more evidently, she has turned to your advantage those things which were absolutely bound to ruin your interests ... the same God who has so often shown Your Majesty that He draws light from the darkness and who has turned to your advantage that which must harm you, will not leave His work unfinished, but will assist you and sustain you under the weight that presses on you.[14]

What influence such personal convictions had upon his policy is less clear. Portland preferred recommending officials who were members of the public church or

---

9 'Monsieur de B.', 'Mêmoires ... ou Anecdotes, tant de la Cour du Prince d'Orange Guillaume III, que des Principaux Seigneurs de la République de ce Temps', ed. F.J.L. Krämer, *Bijdragen en Mededelingen betreffende de Geschiedenis der Nederlanden*, 19 (1898), 62–124, 124, transl. from French.

10 *Acta der Particuliere Synoden van Zuid-Holland 1621–1700*, ed. W.P.C. Knuttel (6 vols, The Hague, 1908–16), V. 99, 149, 239, 283, 319, transl. from Dutch.

11 D'Avaux to Louis 7 October 1688, AAE, CPH 156, f° 237.

12 HMC, *Seventh Report* (s.l., 1879), 219a.

13 Portland to William 25 January 1690 (The Hague), Japikse, *Correspondentie*, XXIII. 76, transl. from French.

14 Portland to William 22 March 1690 (The Hague), ibid., 153, transl. from French.

so-called *liefhebbers* (occasional attendees),[15] but he supported the strictly Calvinist Voetians over the looser Coccejans. These were factions within the Dutch Reformed Church, adhering to the ideas of the theologians Gijsbert Voetius and Johannes Coccejus respectively, and were in some way descendants of the Contra-Remonstrant and Arminian traditions of the first half of the century.[16] But political considerations prevailed over dogmatic differences. English Dissenters complained about his support of the Anglican Church.[17] Although Portland and Carstares consistently supported the Presbyterian church settlement, Scottish Presbyterians were unsure about his commitment to their Church. Portland ordered Melville in April 1690 to 'establish the government of the Church of Scotland, which is apparently the first thing that you must do'.[18] But Patrick Riley has explained that the Presbyterian and Episcopalian political factions should not be equated with their religious convictions, thus Portland's support for the Presbyterian church settlement was not necessarily a guarantee for the Presbyterian faction.[19] Indeed, Portland realised that there were political liabilities; the Presbyterian settlement could rest uneasily with the situation in England, where the Tory party dominated by Anglicans was in the ascendant from 1690. To Melville he wrote:

> That you can adjust the establishment of the church government without lifting it so high that it will collapse under its own weight, but that it can subsist with the monarchy, and that it will not inspire jealousy in the Anglican Church here [in England], and as such not cause any harm to the Presbyterians of this kingdom.[20]

In England as well Portland took an interest in Church affairs, maintaining a correspondence with divines such as the bishops Stillingfleet and Compton.[21] He was involved in the introduction of the Comprehension and Toleration bills in Parliament on the advice of Nottingham in February 1689.[22] Although the Comprehension Bill failed, renewed efforts to assimilate Presbyterians into the Anglican Church were made during the autumn when a royal commission was appointed to adapt the liturgy to accommodate the moderate wings of both churches. A proposal was sent to Portland, who turned for advice to a number of pragmatic Dutch theologians,

---

15   E.g. Portland to William 4 February 1690 (The Hague), William to Portland 17 February 1690, ibid., 94, 110; N. Witsen, 'Verbaal' in: *Geschied- en Letterkundig Mengelwerk*, ed. J. Scheltema (6 vols, Utrecht, 1818–36), III. 152; Cf. Ch. 4.
16   Cf. F.G.M. Broeyer et al. (eds), *Een Richtingenstrijd in de Gereformeerde Kerk: Voetianen en Coccejanen 1650–1750* (Zoetermeer, 1994).
17   Hampden to Harley n.d. November 1690, HMC, *Portland Mss*, III. 451.
18   Portland to Melville 22 April 1690 (Kensington Palace), *Leven and Melville Papers. Letters and State Papers chiefly Addressed to George Earl of Melville, Secretary of State for Scotland, 1689–1691*, ed. W.L. Melville (Edinburgh, 1843), 428, transl. from French.
19   P.W.J. Riley, *King William and the Scottish Politicians* (Edinburgh, 1979), 6–7.
20   Portland to Melville 15/25 May 1690 (Kensington Palace), Melville, *Leven and Melville Papers*, 435, transl. from French.
21   E.g. Stillingfleet to Portland 1 Aug. 1693, BL, Add Mss 4236, f° 318-19; J.I. Israel 'William III and Toleration' in: O.P Grell, N. Tyacke and J.I. Israel (eds), *From Persecution to Toleration, the Glorious Revolution and Religion in England* (Oxford, 1991), 129–71, 163.
22   NUL, PwA 2321–3.

most of whom were on good terms with the Orange court at The Hague.[23] Informally Portland, though probably a Voetian, inquired about the opinion of Coccejan ministers in Amsterdam, and the impression arises that he took a very pragmatic stance in this matter.[24] The report of the commission, returned to Portland, endorsed most of the proposals for comprehension set out by Archbishop Tillotson. One of the theologians, Samuel Desmarets, a Walloon, argued that such a union would be 'the most mortal blow which papism can receive'.[25] Fredericus Spanheim, neither Voetian nor Coccejan, had reasonably argued that Presbyterian and Episcopalian churches could adapt better to republican and monarchical forms of government respectively.[26]

It appears that Portland's view comes close to this. He was certainly not indifferent, clearly promoted Voetianism in the United Provinces and preferred Presbyterianism in Scotland, but his ideas were broader and it appears he thought rather in the vaguer terms of European Protestantism. In his seminal study on the 'godly revolution', Tony Claydon has shown how, spearheaded by Burnet, a providential explanation that 'consisted of a series of interlocking assumptions about the prince and Protestantism in England, and was based upon a deeply spiritual analysis of history' emerged after 1688. A group of court propagandists adopted this defence of the Revolution Settlement and linked William's foreign policy to the defence of European Protestantism.[27] These notions of European Protestantism come close to Portland's ideas on religion and politics.[28]

II

The political situation in each of William's realms had its own distinct features, but there were also similar patterns. Dutch and British historians have fiercely debated the two-party models (Tory–Whig in England, Orangist–Republican in the United Provinces, and Episcopalian–Presbyterian in Scotland) as instruments to analyse political structures in the 1690s. In English historiography the main current is now to see a two-party system of Tories and Whigs, upset now and then by Court–Country controversies. Dutch historians have emphasized the predominance of factions,

---

23   Quoted in J. van den Berg, 'Dutch Calvinism and the Church of England in the Period of the Glorious Revolution' in: S. Groenveld and M. Wintle (eds), *The Exchange of Ideas. Religion, Scholarship and Art in Anglo-Dutch Relations in the Seventeenth Century* (Zutphen, 1994), 84–99, 94, transl. from French. Cf. J. van Genderen, *Herman Witsius* (The Hague, 1953), 72.

24   Witsen, 'Verbaal', 168.

25   Van den Berg, 'Dutch Calvinism', 95; Letters to Portland Oct. 1689, Lambeth Palace Library, Gibson Manuscript 932, f° 70–75.

26   Hampden's letter to Harley of November 1690 seems to imply that Portland was a member of the Church of England, HMC, *Portland Mss*, III. 451.

27   A.M. Claydon, *William III and the Godly Revolution* (Cambridge, 1996), 51 and *passim*.

28   Cf. Ch. 2.

although at key moments ideologically coherent parties could temporarily surface.[29] The patterns and similarities between partisan struggles in Scotland, England and the United Provinces are of particular interest when these structures are studied within an Anglo-Dutch context. The Earl of Shaftesbury noted in 1705 that those in England who tended to be pro-Dutch were Whigs, yet paradoxically they favoured what he called the Tory interest in the Dutch Republic, namely the Orangists, and opposed the Commonwealth interest, or that of the Republicans. So William, as King of England, had been the saviour of English liberties, but as Stadholder and Captain-General he was rather like any tyrant or absolute monarch.[30] Shaftesbury's statement is somewhat misleading, as from the beginning of the 1690s, the Court Whigs had developed into avid defenders of William's prerogatives. Likewise, there were similarities between Scottish Episcopalians and Presbyterians and English Tories and Whigs respectively, as for instance the French ambassador Count Tallard noted in 1698.[31] Recently historians have also noted similarities between the Court and Country interest in the various parts of William's realms. There were similarities between the Scottish 'Club', the English Country, and the Dutch Republicans; these were hardly 'parties' but rather temporary alliances to curtail the power of the Court.[32] As will be argued, Portland consistently supported the 'court interest' in all of William's realms, whatever their political colours.

Portland has often been associated with the Whigs, but he initially rather inclined to the Tories as staunch defenders of the King's prerogatives. Though he loathed partisan struggles, it is of some interest that the language he used in describing his opponents had a strong moral, partisan, tone. In Holland he frequently referred to the Republicans as 'malicious ones' or 'the malicious party'.[33] But in Britain such partiality was far from obvious. On the contrary, he prided himself in being above

---

29   For debates on party struggles see H. Horwitz, 'The Structure of Parliamentary Politics' in: G. Holmes (ed.), *Britain after the Glorious Revolution 1689–1714* (London, 1969), 96–9 ff.; D.W. Hayton, 'The Country Interest and the Party System 1689 – *c.*1720' in: C. Jones (ed.), *Party and Management in Parliament 1660–1784* (Leicester/New York, 1984), 37–85; T. Harris, *Politics under the late Stuarts. Party Conflict in a Divided Society 1660–1715* (New York, 1993), 147 ff.; G. Holmes, *British Politics in the Age of Anne* (London, 1967); H. Horwitz, *Parliament, Policy and Politics in the Reign of William III* (Manchester, 1977); B.W. Hill, *The Growth of Parliamentary Parties 1689–1742* (London, 1976); H. Horwitz, 'Historiographical Perspectives. The 1690s Revisited: Recent Work on Politics and Political Ideas in the Reign of William III', *Parliamentary History*, 35 (1996), 361–77; S. Groenveld, *Evidente Factien in den Staet. Sociaal-Politieke Verhoudingen in de 17e eeuwse Republiek der Verenigde Nederlanden* (Hilversum, 1990).

30   D. Coombs, *The Conduct of the Dutch. British Opinion and the Dutch Alliance during the War of the Spanish Succession* (The Hague, 1958), 12–13.

31   Tallard to Louis 9 May 1698, *Letters of William III, and Louis XIV and of their Ministers etc. 1697–1700*, ed. P. Grimblot (2 vols, London, 1848), I. 467.

32   Country was a 'persuasion' rather than a 'party', a set of ideas prevalent amongst the landed class and aimed at curtailing the central executive. Country strove to strengthen the role of Parliament through such measures as the Place and Triennial Bills and reduce the standing army. Cf. Harris, *Politics under the late Stuarts*, 147 ff.

33   E.g. Portland to William 5/15 January 1690 (Sheerness), Portland to William 14–15 March 1690 (The Hague), Japikse, *Correspondentie*, XXIII. 65, 147, transl. from French.

party and faction struggle. Referring to partisan animosity in Scotland, in 1691 he wrote to Lord Nottingham:

> I have never listened to that which the animosity of one party did against all that could be done by someone from another party, but I have followed reason without any distinction between people or parties as far as my limited judgement was capable of.[34]

There are very few clues in his correspondence which indicate a predilection for a certain party, but some draft notes in 1693, commenting on a letter from the Earl of Sunderland who was pushing the Whig agenda, suggest a strong predilection for the Tories. The fragment neatly sums up precisely those issues which concerned the favourite: 'Tories who are not Jacobites will always be for the King, therefore as many from the Church of England in Parliament as possible.'[35] The statement was not without justification, as some of the radical Whigs perceived it. Hampden, for instance, lamented:

> Who would have thought so unhallowed a mother as a republic could have produced children that are such heros for episcopacy and the divine prerogatives of Monarchs or that my Lord Portland should become a bulwark of Monarchy, and protector and eldest son of the Church of England.[36]

Portland's preference in later years for the Court Whigs rests uneasily with his support for the Court Tories in these years. In his imposing study on parliamentary affairs, Henry Horwitz classified Portland among the Whig peers, voting consistently in favour of Whig measures in the Lords.[37] But available evidence, based on the so-called division lists, suggests rather that he consistently voted for non-party measures in favour of the Court.[38] He was a staunch opponent of the Triennial Bill, which forced the King to convene a Parliament every three years. Parliament, Portland retrospectively wrote to William in 1698 with disdain, 'is insensible to any other thing but the advantage of parties, this is the effect of the Triennial Bill'.[39] Although Sir William Temple had counselled Portland, who had visited Moor Park to seek his advice, to support the measure, in January 1693 the favourite may have advised the King, who was then unsure about its consequences, to veto the Bill. Jonathan Swift, Temple's secretary, was sent to Kensington Palace to reiterate Temple's reasons for

---

34 Portland to Nottingham 17/27 August 1691 ('Camp de St Gerard'), transl. from French. Dalrymple to Nottingham 17/27 August 1691, HMC, *Finch Mss*, III. 211, 213–14.
35 NUL, PwA 1220, transl. from Dutch.
36 Hampden to Harley November 1690, HMC, *Portland Mss*, III. 451.
37 Horwitz, *Parliament*, 336.
38 E. Cruickshanks, D. Hayton and C. Jones, 'Divisions in the House of Lords on the Transfer of the Crown and other Issues, 1689–1694, Ten new Lists' in: C. Jones and D.L. Jones (eds), *Peers, Politics and Power: The House of Lords, 1603–1911* (London, 1986), 79–110, 94, 108.
39 Portland to William 13 March 1698 (Paris), Japikse, *Correspondentie*, XXIII. 255, transl. from French.

advising the King as he had. William referred the secretary to Portland ('a weak man'), who once more did not seem receptive to his arguments.[40]

The Country Tory Sir Thomas Clarges accused Portland of having counselled the King to veto the Place Bill as well (which aimed to bar placemen, the King's dependants, from taking a seat in Parliament) and even initiated an impeachment procedure in the 1692/1693 session.[41] But the opposition of the so-called New Country Party (a cross-party alliance led by the Tory Thomas Clarges and the Whigs Robert Harley and Paul Foley) did not carry enough weight to bring down the ministry.[42] The Court Tories, led by Portland, Nottingham, Rochester and Carmarthen, carried the day, and even managed to muster sufficient support in the Lords to defeat the Place Bill, by a narrow margin, in December 1692.[43] Portland seems to have spoken in the Lords attacking the Place Bill. He must have played a role of some importance, as the opposition blamed him and Nottingham in particular.[44] Although William ultimately accepted the Triennial Bill in exchange for Shrewsbury's promise to accept office, the Place Bill remained unacceptable and was vetoed again in January 1694. The Place Bill was a non-party measure, and evidence strongly suggests that Portland was a non-partisan defender of the Court.[45]

Portland was essentially a courtier, not tied to the Whig or Tory interest, and it is from this perspective that this chapter will take off. Keith Feiling, in his classic study on the Tory party, also pointed to the fact that parliamentary managers such as Sunderland must be classified as non-party courtiers, though they would still have to deal with the reality of partisan struggles in Parliament.[46] Portland's concern was essentially one of establishing a strong court party of whatever tenet. A problem with understanding his position is the lack of relevant source material. He seldom reflected on policymaking, but a sketchy memorandum from June 1693 suggests the central issues that were on his mind: '... difficulty money. decrease prerogative. ministers being attacked.'[47] Indeed, it was the effectiveness of the Court in raising revenues and maintaining the royal prerogative in order to wage war that concerned Portland. Inevitably this would result in opposition. The issues that concerned the King-Stadholder and his favourite would result in continuous political arm-wrestling with the various assemblies. The favourite would play an important role, and was not inclined to compromise. When the Duke of Shrewsbury, tired of constant difficulties and opposition, backed out and expressed a desire to resign from public office,

---

40   *The Prose Works of Jonathan Swift*, ed. T. Scott (11 vols, London, 1900), XI. 378.
41   Quoted in Horwitz, *Parliament*, 127.
42   NUL, PwA 2387; letter to Portland 1 November 1692, NUL, PwA 2792.
43   HMC, *Seventh Report* (s.l., 1879), 212a.
44   11 December 1692, Huygens, *Journaal*, I-ii. 152.
45   HMC, *Seventh Report*, 209a, 212a; Shrewsbury and Essex were absent, the latter gave his vote to Portland. A.S. Turberville, *The House of Lords in the Reign of William III* (Oxford, 1913), 182; Horwitz, *Parliament*, 110; Cruickshanks, Hayton and Jones, 'Divisions', 94, 108. Cf. HMC, *Seventh Report*, 209a.
46   K. Feiling, *A History of the Tory Party 1640–1714* (Oxford, 1924), 291.
47   NUL, PwA 1220, transl. from Dutch.

Portland commented: 'We live in an age where the spirit of contention reigns, but we have to live in this age.'[48]

III

Portland's political vision transcended national boundaries but it was tempting to see him as a representative of a distinct pro-Dutch policy. The expansion of the Dutch community caused friction, and the initial Orangist euphoria turned into frequent outbreaks of xenophobia.[49] According to Nicolaas Witsen, the Dutch Ambassador Extraordinary, who witnessed this reversal during the spring of 1689, the hostility arose from feelings regarding the invasion: '... many say, that it has been for our own interest, that which we have accomplished.'[50] This deep-rooted suspicion was reinforced by the occupation of London and the arrival of a procession of Dutchmen following William. Whether the Dutch 'spread like locusts', as one pamphleteer complained, is doubtful, but there were certainly many Dutchmen who came in William's train as craftsmen, artisans and labourers and settled down in the south of Middlesex and Soho.[51] Portland, as favourite of foreign extraction, was seen to form the core of the so-called 'Dutch junto'. Some of the more sophisticated pamphlets had hinted at sinister political conspiracies being formed behind closed doors. One of the most infamous, the *Dear Bargain*, argued that:

> The important and essential Consults and Resolutions are all managed by a few Foreigners, in a secret Cabal of Dutchmen; of whom, that he might form a standing Council, no less than five Ambassadors came over from Holland at once, whereas those States never sent above two to any crowned Head in Christendom; with these, and Benting, and some of the consederate Lords who were with him in Holland, (though these last very rarely), he concerted the Scheme and Model of his Government.[52]

A similar pamphlet argued that 'Dutch counsels and Dutch measures of acting are the true source of all these mischieves'.[53] Pamphlet literature immediately after the

---

48 Quoted in D.H. Somerville, *The King of Hearts. Charles Talbot, Duke of Shrewsbury* (London, 1962), 148.

49 On this subject, see G. van Alphen, *De Stemming van de Engelschen tegen de Hollanders in Engeland tijdens de Regeering van den Koning-Stadhouder Willem III 1688–1702* (Assen, 1938) and D. Onnekink, '"Dutch Councils": the Foreign Entourage of William III', *Dutch Crossing*, 29 (2005), 5–20.

50 Witsen to Heinsius 26 May 1689, *Het Archief van den Raadpensionaris Antonie Heinsius*, ed. H.J. van der Heim (3 vols, The Hague, 1867), I. 16, transl. from Dutch.

51 Van Alphen, *Stemming van de Engelschen*, 79 ff.

52 [N. Johnston], *The Dear Bargain; or, A true Representation of the State of the English Nation under the Dutch. In a Letter to a Friend* in: Somers, *Third Collection*, III. 258. Cf. *A Modest Apology for the loyal Protestant Subjects of King James*, in: *A Collection of Scarce and Valuable Tracts*, ed. W. Scott, (London, 1813), X. 403.

53 Quoted in Van Alphen, *Stemming van de Engelschen*, 91. Cf. Grimblot, *Letters*, I. 236n. 'How careful he has been to put the strongest places of Trust into the hands of our Country-Men [i.e. Dutchmen], or at least such as our Ambassadors and the E. Of Portland were secure of, who, in case of a turn of times, will be able to hold them till we can pour in

invasion of 1688 picked up this kind of rhetoric in political debates. References to 'Dutch counsels' were to come up consistently in parliamentary debates and pamphlets throughout the 1690s, many of them commissioned by French or Jacobite agents.[54] They provided fuel for mordant fulminations against the suppositious influence of the King's 'evil counsellors'. Portland figured prominently in these discourses. In a speech in opposition to the Naturalization Bill, he was compared to Joseph, the favourite of Pharaoh, who allocated the best land to and provided for his fellow Israelites during the seven lean years.[55] The aversion to Dutch courtiers was reminiscent of criticism of the Scottish entourage of James I, which had been much more prominent. Similar criticism would be directed at the less influential Hanoverian counsellors of George I.[56]

But most of these critiques were based on conjecture, and little is known about the actual extent to which William's Dutch advisers were influential. The 'Standing Council' to which the *Dear Bargain* referred, was said to consist of Portland and the five Ambassadors, who were only in London until the autumn of 1689. The embassy was appointed by William himself; Nassau-Odijk and Dijkveld were his aides in Zeeland and Utrecht respectively, Alexander Schimmelpennick van der Oije was William's creature in Gelderland and Portland's brother-in-law, and the Zeeland regent Aernout van Citters and Nicolaas Witsen represented the States General and Amsterdam respectively.[57] Yet in practice William disregarded the envoys and let them work out the particulars of the alliance with an English commission. In fact, Dijkveld was the only Dutchman who wielded significant influence in the councils.[58] The Embassy was heavily divided, and resentment over William's ignoring their request to repeal the Navigation Acts actually led to a major clash between Amsterdam and the King-Stadholder the following spring. Sir George Clark noted the 'confusion, friction and dissatisfaction among the statesmen who belonged to the less trusted class'.[59] Even Nassau-Odijk, a prominent aide of the King, resented his exclusion and returned to Zeeland highly dissatisfied. When Witsen, the Amsterdam burgomaster, tried to obtain trade advantages and the revocation of the Navigation

---

fresh supplies.', *Min Heer T. van C's Answer to Min Heer H. van L.'s Letter of the 15th of March 1689, Representing the True Interest of Holland, and what They have already Gained by our Losses*, in: Somers, *First Collection*, IV. 126.

54   Van Alphen, *Stemming van de Engelschen*, 75–9. E.g. *His Majesty's most Gracious Speech to both Houses of Parliament etc.* (1692). On traditional anti-Dutch rhetoric, see S. Pincus, 'From Butterboxes to Wooden Shoes: the Shift in English Popular Sentiment from Anti-Dutch to Anti-French in the 1670s', *Historical Journal*, 38/2 (1995), 333–61.

55   *A Choice Collection of Papers relating to State Affairs during the late Revolution*, I (London, 1703), 522.

56   N. Cuddy, 'The Revival of the Entourage: the Bedchamber of James I, 1603–1625' in: D. Starkey et al., *The English Court: from the Wars of the Roses to the Civil War* (London/New York, 1987), 173–225; R. Hatton, *George I: Elector and King* (London, 1978), 132 ff.

57   William to Dijkveld 9/19 December 1688, William to Hendrik Fagel 9/19 December 1688, Japikse, *Correspondentie*, XXVIII. 74–6.

58   Dispatch of Parent 11 July 1689 NS, AAE, CPA 170, f° 217v°.

59   G.N. Clark, 'The Dutch Missions to England in 1689', *English Historical Review*, 35 (1920), 540.

Act, his requests were brushed aside by William. When Citters protested against the final draft of the naval treaty, William and Heinsius applied pressure and the ambassador gave in.[60] Thus there had never been a standing council, and the embassy disintegrated in the autumn of 1689, when Dijkveld, the only adviser to whom William did pay attention, returned to Utrecht.[61]

The influence of foreigners in Parliament was marginal. This is something the Dutch themselves realised as well. In a private conversation the High Councillor Hubert Roosenboom stated that the Dutch could not hold high office. When Huygens suggested that the King could naturalise some, the former replied that the English already held a grudge towards Portland, and Dutch officeholders would only attract more antipathy.[62] There were no foreigners in the Commons, and less than half a dozen actually took seats in the House of Lords. Portland entered the House in 1689, to be followed only by the Duke of Schomberg, Nassau-Zuylestein and Keppel, both in 1695, as Earl of Rochfort and Earl of Albemarle.[63] The Duke of Leinster and Ginckel, created Earl of Athlone in 1692, were eligible for seats in the Irish House of Lords. The Cabinet Council, established in 1689 on the recommendation of William's closest English adviser, the Marquis of Halifax, only included Portland, in addition to Halifax as Lord Privy Seal, the Marquis of Carmarthen as Lord President, and the two Secretaries of State, the Earls of Nottingham and Shrewsbury.[64] The Privy Council only contained Portland, and later the second Duke of Schomberg.[65]

Criticism of the Dutch can probably better be explained as resentment of those outside the inner circles. It was also a device to covertly criticise the Court or political opponents. John Toland already noted that the English used 'to damn all the Dutch when they durst not expressly curse King William'.[66] An interesting pamphlet, which was presumably written in the spring of 1689 and which reflected on 'the present Administration of Affairs, since managed by Dutch Councils', referred not so much to the Dutch but to the Whigs:

> If you have heard or read of the Changes between 1640 and 1660 you can't be surprised at the Accidents between 78 and 89. The Pretences, the Successes, the Methods used and had in both, are so exactly agreeable, that the last would have been impossible, but that the same Men who did procure the first have occasioned the latter.[67]

---

60 Witsen to Heinsius 23 August 1689, Van der Heim, *Archief*, I. 21.
61 Cf. 18 January 1689, 26 August 1689, Huygens, *Journaal*, I-i. 63–4, 168.
62 8 January 1689, Huygens, *Journaal*, I-i, 57–8.
63 Van Alphen, *Stemming van de Engelschen*, 90.
64 13 August 1689, Luttrell, *Brief Historical Relation*, I. 568.
65 *The Names of the Lord of his Majesty's most Honourable Privy Council* in: Somers, *First Collection*, II, 322–3; Van Alphen, *Stemming van de Engelschen*, 276.
66 Quoted in J.I. Israel, 'General introduction' in: J.I. Israel (ed.), *The Anglo-Dutch Moment. Essays on the Glorious Revolution and its World Impact* (Cambridge, 1991), 1–43, 42. Cf. E. Cruickshanks, *The Glorious Revolution* (Basingstoke, 2000), 73.
67 *A Letter to a Member of the Committee of Grievances containing some Seasonable Reflections on the Present Administration of Affairs, since Managed by Dutch Councils* in: Somers, *Second Collection*, IV. 62.

In this particular case, a Churchman criticised a Commonwealthman, and the attack seems intertwined with debates between Whigs and Tories rather than a protest against Dutch advisers in William's inner circle. The seemingly anti-Dutch rhetoric can thus also be understood within a Court-Country context, the Dutch being a convenient pretext to criticise the King.[68] At the same time it holds true that William did place a disproportionate amount of confidence in a small circle of foreigners, which inevitably incited criticism voiced in numerous pamphlets. One 1695 pamphlet for instance railed about the

> Usurper, with his Bentinks and Ginckles ... [who] are in an apparent Conspiracy with the High and Mighty at the Hague, to reduce these kingdoms to a feebleness and indigency, out of which they have a design we shall never emerge.[69]

However, a heavy reliance on pamphlet material has led historians to take such critical notes perhaps too much at face value without examining deeper layers of the debate.[70] It is doubtful whether there were significant 'Dutch counsels', or indeed whether the 'Dutch Junto' was Dutch at all. Instead, it appears that many of such attacks were inspired rather by faction struggle or rivalry. More importantly, anti-Dutch rhetoric became a convenient method of criticising the government. 'Dutch' was principally a metaphor for William's policy.

IV

Portland was averse to partisan rivalry, but he was inevitably drawn into power struggles between Tories and Whigs. The Court Tories, led by Carmarthen and Nottingham, were in charge of the ministry as from late 1690, and were strengthened in 1691 when the Earl of Rochester and Edward Seymour entered the Privy Council. William had been influenced by Halifax, who had advised him to conduct a policy of trimming: whichever party would be willing to serve the King most would come into office. But William made sure never to be dependent on any one party, and although the Court Tories were strong in the ministry, the Whigs were satisfied with several posts. Portland's commitment to this practice can be seen in his role in the reconstruction of the ministry after Sidney's dismissal as Secretary of State in 1692. The Tory Nottingham being sole Secretary, Portland was sent by the King to interview Trumbull for the Northern Department post. Portland, Trumbull recorded,

> would be glad to know my inclinations; and (among other things) to know of what party I was ... Whig or Tory, as commonly called. For my affection to [the] government he knew that well. But as to the other, would desire me to inform him, the Whigs being many in

---

68 'Lay by your Reason' in: *Political Ballads*, ed. W. Walker Wilkins (London, 1860), II. 28–9. Cf. Ch. 7.

69 *Whether the Preserving of the Protestant Religion was the Motive unto, or the End that was Designed in the late Revolution* (1695), 442.

70 E.g. C. Rose, *England in the 1690s: Revolution, Religion and War* (Oxford, 1999); Van Alphen, *De Stemming van de Engelschen*.

number, rather more than the others, and would expect (upon a removal) to have one they could confide in, and would take it ill if I had not such a one ... .

Trumbull prudently replied that 'as to any party, I had never been of any, that I was of the Church of England'. Portland then inquired if Trumbull thought if he was esteemed by the Whigs. He thought not. It cost him the office, Portland explaining that 'the Whigs must not be made desperate'.[71] By the middle of 1692 Portland moved away from the Court Tories as he bitterly argued with Nottingham about the latter's support of a blue water policy and clashed with Carmarthen over his own defence of the Presbyterian settlement in Scotland.[72] By 1693 cracks had appeared in the Tory ministry itself, Nottingham and Carmarthen being increasingly at odds with each other.[73] Due to ministerial weakness prospects for the management of Parliament were dim and Portland was open to alternatives. Henry Guy, secretary in the Treasury and client of the Earl of Sunderland, had warned him that

> People are posessed of a most dangerous opinion, that England is not taken care of; that must bee cured, or all signifyes nothing, which may bee done, and the Allyes supported to the height; but if it is not done, the confederacy will quickly bee at an end.[74]

In the summer of 1692 Sunderland had contacted Portland from his country retreat Althorp. His reluctant approach was not so much because Portland had 'a thousand important affaires to looke after', but because of his wariness at returning to mainstream politics after his dramatic fall from power in the autumn of 1688.[75] Sunderland's first letter of 5 May 1692 was answered at once by Portland, who seemed very eager to get him involved in parliamentary and ministerial management. It was necessary, Sunderland argued, to oblige 'the Governement to be more vigorous and not to suffer every body to say and do what they please'. The trick lay, he somewhat disingenuously wrote, in making use of experienced parliamentary managers. 'I can assure your Lord.P', he wrote to Portland, 'that the Considerable Part of [the nation] doe not care who are Ministers of State. Whether this man or that', thereby implicitly criticising William's trimming policy and clearing the way for what came to be known as the Whig Junto.[76]

Portland's dispute with the Tories and their failure to provide strong government made him more open to Sunderland's suggestions. These were communicated to the King on Portland's return to Flanders, and contacts must have been more intensive during the winter of 1692/1693. The military defeats on the continent had not been disastrous in themselves – the Duke of Luxembourg had failed to achieve a decisive victory – but they weakened the Court's support in Parliament. Sunderland had not yet specified his ideas. In a retrospective letter to Portland, he suggested

---

71   Quoted in Horwitz, *Parliament*, 77–8.
72   Cf. page 159–61.
73   Cf. Feiling, *Tory Party*, 280; J.P. Kenyon, 'The Earl of Sunderland and the King's Administration, 1693–1695', *English Historical Review*, 71 (1956), 582.
74   Guy to Portland November n.d. 1692, Japikse, *Correspondentie*, XXIV. 37.
75   Sunderland to Portland 16 May 1692, NUL, PwA 1210.
76   Sunderland to Portland 5 May 1692, 16 May 1692, NUL, PwA 1209, 1210.

that the K. must make the foundation of his Governement as broad and as firme as he can, and that all People are to be employed who will serve him. but this Principle, though it is infallible, has with its certainty this likewise common with the Gospell, that everybody turns it to what they please, so that you and I who are both of this mind, may often differ in things, partys and persons.[77]

Indeed, Portland was still clinging to the Court Tories whom he regarded as the stronghold of royal prerogative but who increasingly came to oppose William's continental policy. Sunderland later retrospectively repeated his argument:

Whenever the Governement has leaned to the Whigs it has been strong, whenever the other has prevayled it has been despised, but as I have already said, I have endeavoured soo often to show this ... I wonder you and the K. after so many years doe not see it as it is.[78]

Sunderland's advice was partially accepted. Indicative of William's new direction of policy, in early January 1693 he dined privately with Portland, Sunderland and a number of Whig stalwarts.[79] At the closing of the 1692/1693 session Whigs re-entered the ministry as the King made John Trenchard Secretary of State and promoted John Somers Lord Keeper. In November 1693 Nottingham was dismissed.

The Court Tories being ousted from government or politically sidelined, by 1693 Portland tightened his grip on ministerial and parliamentary management, as Sunderland was more dependent on the King and his favourite. Sunderland was loathed by most sections of the political nation because of his dubious role during James II's reign. When asked how the King could confide in such a man, Portland argued that Sunderland was abler than anyone, and because he was generally hated, would serve the King faithfully.[80] From 1693 the two Earls increasingly co-operated in a manner that foreshadowed the political alliance of the 'du-umvirate' of Marlborough and Godolphin during the War of the Spanish Succession; whilst Portland was on the continent during summers, Sunderland managed the ministry. As to his methods, Portland had argued, whatever Sunderland did, he must take into account that the King treasured his prerogatives and loathed partisan struggle.[81] He condoned his methods of bribing and promising favours to establish a court interest.[82] Sunderland, moreover, was ready to unreservedly endorse a Williamite foreign policy. Dissatisfied with Tory foreign policy, Portland impressed upon him the importance of continental strategy; 'you will not think', the latter assured him, 'that wee would have the businesse of Flanders or Holland neglected, which is of so vast importance'.[83]

---

77   Sunderland to Portland 13 July 1694, NUL, PwA 1238.
78   Sunderland to Portland 5 August 1694, NUL, PwA 1240.
79   7 January 1693, Luttrell, *Brief Historical Relation*, III. 5.
80   Auersperg's report, quoted in O. Klopp, *Der Fall des Hauses Stuart und die Succession des Hauses Hannover in Grosz-Britannien und Irland im Zusammenhange der Europäischen Angelegenheiten von 1660–1714* (14 vols, Vienna, 1875–88), VII. 130.
81   Sunderland to Portland 10 July 1693, NUL, PwA 1222.
82   Sunderland to Portland 10 July 1693, 21 Aug. 1693, NUL, PwA 1222, PwA 1230.
83   Sunderland to Portland 21 August 1693, NUL, PwA 1230.

As Sunderland constructed a ministry made up of Junto Whigs, Portland functioned as broker to obtain royal approval.[84] Thus it was partly under Portland's tutelage that a Whig court party emerged. Although the Whig Junto, as it came to be styled, largely worked through Sunderland's mediation, Somers and Trenchard provided Portland with a continuous flow of information, notwithstanding 'the great weight of business wch must be upon you at this time', Somers wrote to him.[85] In May 1693 the ministers had considered a list of MPs and 'agreed on the best meanes of persuading them to be reasonable', and a roster of persons fit for office was drawn up and sent to Portland.[86] He became the main channel of approach when recommendations were made by the Junto. He was keenly aware, however, that the Whig ministers had an agenda of their own. Sidney Godolphin, the Tory Treasury Commissioner, was alarmed by the pattern in Whig appointments, initiated by the Whig Junto, and Portland was careful not to grant all requests.[87]

The beginning of 1695 in some ways marked the zenith of Portland's career. The Queen had fallen ill with smallpox in late December 1694; after a brief recovery her situation worsened and in the beginning of January she died. The King had to be carried out of the room by Portland and Archbishop Tenison.[88] William's own life was in danger and he could not force himself to face the grave political situation that had accompanied the death of a reigning monarch. He retreated to his quarters, tenaciously guarded by Portland who refused to let anyone in.[89] The situation epitomised the favourite's position between the King and the political nation. Due to the King's apathy Portland now considerably strengthened his already influential position as intermediary between The Hague and London through correspondence with Anthonie Heinsius, which from January 1695 came through his hands. This emerging political liaison would only become closer and illustrates the extent of his influence by 1695.[90]

The summer of 1695 saw the Whig Junto temporarily in crisis, making the favourite more vulnerable to parliamentary attacks. As Henry Guy, accused of

---

84   Sunderland to Portland 4 July 1693, 6 July 1694, 13 September 1694, NUL, PwA 1221, PwA 1237, PwA 1243.

85   Somers to Portland 20 June 1693, Trenchard to Portland 5 May 1693, Russell to Portland 6 July 1693, Sunderland to Portland 3 May 1693, NUL PwA 1171, PwA 1407, PwA 1094, PwA 1212.

86   Sunderland to Portland 25 April 1693, 3 May 1693, 20 June 1693, NUL PwA 1211, 1212, PwA 1216.

87   E.g. Sunderland to Portland 20 June 1693, n.d. May 1694, 6 September 1694, 29 May 1695, 11 June 1695, 18 June 1697, Somers to Portland 24 August 1694, 14 September 1694, 19 June 1696, Shrewsbury to Portland 16 July 1697, Russell to Portland 6 July 1693, NUL, PwA 1216, PwA 1232, PwA 1242, PwA 1245, PwA 1246, PwA 1260, PwA 1175, PwA 1176, PwA 1180, PwA 1389, PwA 1094; Horwitz, *Parliament*, 154; J.P. Kenyon, *Robert Spencer, Earl of Sunderland 1621–1702* (London, 1958), 264–6.

88   Johnston to Annandale 28 December 1694, HMC, *Manuscripts of J.J. Hope Johnstone Esq. of Annandale* (London, 1897), 69; Portland to Lexington 15/25 January 1695, BL, Add Mss 46525, f° 90v°.

89   Baxter, *William III*, 320–21. Cf. 20 January 1695, Huygens, *Journaal*, I-ii. 447.

90   NUL, PwA 558–628, 1915–91.

having accepted bribes, was dismissed from the Treasury, John Trenchard fell ill and retreated from the secretaryship, leaving feeble Shrewsbury under severe pressure. The rest of the ministry was bitterly divided. The Junto Whigs Charles Montagu and Thomas Wharton were revolting against Sunderland's leadership. Sunderland had replaced Trenchard with William Trumbull – an able administrator but not a strong character.[91] By mid-August, however, Sunderland seemed to have things under control and wrote to Portland that the Whigs would be ready to serve the King.[92] In October William decided to visit Sunderland at his estate at Althorp, accompanied by Portland, the Duke of Shrewsbury, Henry Sidney, Sidney Godolphin, Thomas Wharton and Charles Montagu.[93] Meanwhile an attempt was made to reunite the Court and Country Whigs by inviting Paul Foley, a leader of the Country interest. Portland supported such a rapprochement and even allowed Henry Guy to arrange a meeting for him with Robert Harley.[94]

V

The dilemmas William was confronted with in England were not unlike those in Scotland; he had to choose between a party that was devoted to him for religious reasons but encroached upon his prerogatives (the Whigs and the Presbyterians), and one that supported his royal authority but had a different religious outlook and was suspected of Jacobite sympathies (the Tories and the Episcopalians).[95] Moreover, an opposition known as 'the Club', the Scottish equivalent of the Country Party, instantly emerged and severely hampered the granting of supplies, arguably the main concern of the King.[96] According to Patrick Riley, his policy towards Scotland was devoted to 'the maintenance of the royal prerogative and strong executive power. And, in the long run, he sought to tap his northern kingdom as a source of manpower for his armies and of money to defray a fraction of their costs'.[97] Apart from that, William's policy was largely, as Alexander Murdoch wrote, a 'non-policy of neglect'.[98] The first year of William's reign saw the anxious attempts to rebuild a court party that ironically turned out to be even more demanding in terms of the levying of taxes and the establishment of a standing army.[99] Thus the new King strove to establish a court party that would enable him to pursue his foreign policy.

---

91   Kenyon, *Sunderland*, 269 ff.
92   Sunderland to Portland 18 August 1695, NUL, PwA 1249.
93   Spencer to Newcastle 14 October 1695, HMC, *Portland Mss*, II. 174.
94   Guy to Portland 31 May 1695, 14 June 1695, 23 July 1695, 6 August 1695, NUL, PwA 502, PwA 503, PwA 509, PwA 511. Cf. page 186.
95   Cf. Browning, *Danby*, I. 437–8.
96   P. Hopkins, *Glencoe and the End of the Highland War* (Edinburgh, 1986), 134.
97   Riley, *Scottish Politicians*, 1.
98   A. Murdoch, *The People Above. Politics and Administration in Mid-Eighteenth-Century Scotland* (Edinburgh, 1980), 1.
99   Ibid., 2.

The overriding interest in Scotland was to discourage an overzealous Presbyterian party.[100] Despite Portland's known sympathy to the Presbyterians, they feared he was working against them behind the scenes in 'reducing what is doon in our church government upon this ground, that Presbitry is not the generall inclination of the people'.[101] The Presbyterians realised that it was vital to gain his support, and through Carstares they tried to convince the Earl that 'Presbiterian, and King William's friend, are convertable tearmes'.[102] The Presbyterians had good hopes of winning Portland for their cause. One of their most prominent exponents, the Earl of Crawford, ceaselessly solicited him through the channel of Carstares to impress upon him the importance of Presbyterianism, but uncertainty remained.[103] A Presbyterian delegation was received with protestations of goodwill by the King, but in 1690 Crawford was still anxious to know 'how the Earle of Portland stands affected to Dissenters, he being very differently represented upon that head'.[104]

A complicating factor was that Portland's preference for the Presbyterians in Scotland rested uneasily with his support of the Court Tories in England. Although the Episcopalians had come back into the Scottish ministry in 1692, it was still dominated by Presbyterians under James Johnston, who had succeeded George Melville as Scottish Secretary of State. When a bitter conflict emerged between Whigs and Tories over Scottish church matters in December 1692, Portland found himself defending the Presbyterian settlement against the Tory ministers:

> There was a conference two nights past between the M. of Carmarthen, the two English Secretaries of State, the two Scotch Secretaryes of State ... and Lithglow concerning the State of the Clergy in Scotland ... in the conference above mentioned there was also present the Archbishop of Canterbury the Earl of Portland my Lord Lowthian and that Portland stood with all his last efforts for the Presbyterians but was quite baffled by Carmarthen ... .[105]

But Portland's sympathy for the Presbyterian church did not prompt him to necessarily support its political ambitions. William had become highly dissatisfied with the Presbyterians when in January 1692 an Assembly refused to admit Episcopalian ministers into the church, which effectively frustrated a new comprehension scheme, and Presbyterian radicalism so much disgusted Portland that once more he gave the appearance of turning his back on Scottish business.[106]

Despite his predilection for the Presbyterian church, his reluctance to wholeheartedly support the Presbyterian-dominated ministry confused and irritated those who regarded him as a potential ally. In 1693 the Presbyterians ingeniously

---

100   Ibid., 1.
101   Forbes to Hume 22 August 1689, HMC, *Manuscripts of the Duke of Roxburghe etc.* (London, 1894), 118.
102   Crawford to Carstares 12 November 1689, NUL, PwA 2357.
103   Crawford's letters, NUL, PwA 2353–7.
104   Draft letter from Crawford 21 January 1690, HMC, *Johnstone Mss*, 152.
105   Mackenzie to Delvin 29 Dec. 1692, NLS, Ms 1320, f° 28.
106   Hopkins, *Glencoe*, 355.

proposed a Bill to give Portland a Scottish title.[107] 'I see that Parliament has done me the honour to mention me to the King in their last act, which I have not deserved', he wrote to the Duke of Hamilton without apparent enthusiasm.[108] The measure had been contrived by Johnston; 'I drew the reasons for it back to the Revolution that it might not be said in England that we were thanking you for setting up presbitery', he shrewdly wrote to Portland.[109] For some reason the honour was never bestowed on him, but whether he liked it or not, the opposing factions of Dalrymple and Johnston kept pulling him into the maelstrom of Scottish faction politics.

Despite parliamentary opposition, between 1692 and 1695 Portland managed to strengthen his position through his liaison with Sunderland and the Whig Junto. In Scotland, however, he had withdrawn from business during these years; Burnet observed 'that he had let it go out of his dependence'.[110] He lacked a coherent court party and manager of Sunderland's stature, but an important reason must also have been of a practical nature. To a certain extent, to carry out the management of the Scottish parliament was almost unfeasible during the campaigning season. 'He is so very much taken up in consultations with the Generalls', the Scottish under-secretary informed the Earl of Tweeddale, 'and riding about the camp or towards the enemies lines, that I beleive he can spare very little time to any other thing'.[111] Moreover, his associates were quarrelling, making it difficult for him to gain control over ministerial and parliamentary affairs. Those affairs which required his personal intervention were not always handled well. He had great difficulty managing his ministry, for instance with appeasing the frustrated Duke of Hamilton who had desired the chancellorship in 1692.[112] While Portland withdrew from the intricacies of Scots business, more of it went through the hands of Carstares, who handled most of the relevant correspondence with Portland.[113]

The low point was the 1695 session, dominated by the aftermath of the Glencoe affair, and Portland had shown himself a 'trew prophete' by his pessimistic predictions.[114] During the winter of 1691/1692, the clan chiefs who would swear allegiance to the King were exempted from punishment. Those who refused to succumb would be dealt with 'by fire and sword'.[115] The MacDonald clan of Glencoe had hesitated several days too long, and was massacred in January 1692. Though technically the King was responsible, the direct order came from Dalrymple, and the

---

107   15 June 1693, *The Acts of the Parliament of Scotland. A.D. M.C.XXIV–M.DCC.VII*, ed. C. Innes and T. Thomson (12 vols, London, 1814–75), IX. 323. The Bill was accepted and a memorial was sent to the King by Tweeddale, 15 June 1693, NUL, PwA 548.

108   Portland to Hamilton 17 August 1693 ('Camp de Lembech'), HMC, *Supplementary Report on the Manuscripts of His Grace the Duke of Hamilton* (London, 1932), 127, transl. from French.

109   Johnston to Portland 17 June 1693, NAS, SP 3.

110   Foxcroft, *Supplement*, 415.

111   Pringle to Tweeddale 16 June 1695, NLS, Ms 7018–20.

112   Portland to Hamilton 20 February 1692, HMC, *Hamilton Mss Supplementary*, 124.

113   Carstares to Melville 26 May 1694, 22 November 1694, NLS, Ms 3471, f° 20, 27.

114   Breadalbane to Portland 1 June 1695, NUL, PwA 222.

115   William to Livingstone 11 January 1692, *CSPD 1691–1692*, 94.

event is best explained within the context of local clan rivalry. Nevertheless the event left an irremovable stain upon the reputation of the King, who, as in the case of the De Witt murders, was suspiciously reluctant to investigate the massacre. Portland's characteristic hesitation to look into the matter was also unfortunate, but he had his reasons.[116] William had initially instructed Johnston to investigate the atrocities, who took the opportunity to put the blame on his Episcopalian rival Dalrymple. The Presbyterian faction, led by Tweeddale and Johnston, managed to imprison Breadalbane for his supposed involvement, though the underlying motivation was political rather than legal, as Johnston attempted to oust the Episcopalians from the ministry. He also encouraged Parliament to insist on an investigation into the Glencoe affair and make it a precondition for the granting of supplies. To William, this renewed clash between rival factions was extremely distasteful.[117] Breadalbane's imprisonment had also disgusted Portland and he was eager to help the former negotiator.[118] At the same time Portland discredited himself by hindering the inquiry, which could suggest some sort of involvement in the massacre.[119] Although the King was cleared by the parliamentary inquiry, there remained a sinister odour about his role and that of his favourite. Portland was unable to forgive Johnston for his actions and arranged for the removal of his former closest aide from the ministry.

Portland's support for Johnston had begun to wane as early as December 1694, and he courted Melville, now in the Episcopalian camp.[120] Other Episcopalians, including Dalrymple and Linlithglow, were on better terms with Carstares and Portland, and Presbyterian dominance seemed to be eroding.[121] During the summer of 1695 William was petitioned from both sides, but he was unwilling to initiate any changes. By the autumn Portland was instrumental in the changes the King now made. Magnates such as the Duke of Queensberry and the Earl of Argyle had been pressing to come in and oust Johnston's old ally, Tweeddale.[122] Now Tweeddale's position was crumbling fast, and after the Lord Advocate's successful audience with Portland, the Chancellor was dismissed.[123]

A new ministry consisting of all the major noble interests had emerged, this time firmly under Portland's control. Tweeddale was replaced with Patrick Hume, a former exile and one committed to the Revolution settlement. The two secretaries, Johnston and Dalrymple, were replaced with James Ogilvy, a client of Portland's, and John Murray. On Ogilvy's recommendation, some of the high nobility, such as Queensberry and Argyle were placated and given office in the Treasury. 'a new

---

116   Hill to Portland 28 February 1692, *CSPD 1691–1692*, 153–4; Hopkins, *Glencoe*, 338.
117   Riley, *Scottish Politicians*, 95, 101.
118   Breadalbane to Portland 29 July 1695, NUL, PwA 224; Stair to Breadalbane 27 June 1695, Glenorchy to Breadalbane n.d., 29 July/8 August 1695, 2 September 1695 OS, NAS, GD112/39/169/10, GD112/39/169/16, GD112/39/169/35, GD112/39/172/3.
119   Foxcroft, *Supplement*, 544.
120   Carstares to Melville 22 November 1694, NLS, Ms 3471, f° 24.
121   Riley, *Scottish Politicians*, 94.
122   Ibid., 109.
123   Tweeddale to Yester 23 January 1696, NLS, Ms 7030, f° 28; Yester to Tweeddale 19 January 1696, NLS, Ms 14404, f° 335.

set of men are put in', Burnet wrote, 'who will generally depend on Portland.'[124] The Earl now actively intervened in disputes that could destabilise the ministry.[125] Portland persuaded Melville to give up the Privy Seal in order for it to be given to Queensberry.[126] Portland reaffirmed his position as the sole channel of communication to the King.[127] The result was a more stable ministry and a successful parliamentary session in 1696.

Portland was thus responsible for the establishment of a court party that comprised both Presbyterians and Episcopalians.[128] It is therefore worth reflecting on Patrick Riley's portrayal of Portland as an ignorant and partisan favourite. In his opinion, Portland had supported the Presbyterian Secretary of State George Melville because of 'blind loyalty, ignorance and gross miscalculation'.[129] But as has been shown, Portland had been highly critical of the Secretary's role on various occasions and the Presbyterians in general.[130] Most importantly, however, it should be pointed out that two imposing studies of Scotland in the 1690s by Paul Hopkins and Patrick Riley almost solely study Scottish affairs in isolation, despite Riley's accurate introduction in which he argues that William and Portland had to deal with a European crisis simultaneously. The image created of Portland as a lazy and evasive favourite is out of perspective given that the Scottish parliament sat when he was on military campaign in Flanders, making it practically impossible for him to become intimately involved. Nevertheless, Portland clearly intervened when matters vital to the interest of the King were at stake.

VI

Portland's was increasingly influential in Ireland as well. In the summer of 1692, Sidney had written to him from Althorp, the estate of the Earl of Sunderland, who was related to him:

> I beleeve you will not be sorry to heare from me in a place where I am sure you have as good freinds as any you have in England; the Master of the house, Mr Guy, and I have had already long discourses, since wee came hither, by which a stander by might easily see the concerne wee had for the Gouvernement and the Kindnesse wee have for you ... .[131]

This meeting lay at the bottom of the political alliance that was emerging between Sunderland and Portland, assisted by Henry Guy and Henry Capel. After the defeat

---

124 Riley, *Scottish Politicians*, 109 ff.
125 Murray to Portland 12 May 1696, NUL, PwA 952.
126 Riley, *Scottish Politicians*, 113–14; Queensberry to Portland 14 June 1696, NUL, PwA 371.
127 E.g. Hume to Portland 16 May 1696, NUL, PwA 682.
128 Riley, *Scottish Politicians*, 161.
129 Hopkins, *Glencoe*, 265 and *passim*; Riley, *Scottish Politicians*, 70, cf. 57–8.
130 Riley made an error in translating one of Portland's letters, suggesting the Earl was completely unaware of partisan animosity in Scotland. Portland actually wrote that he never paid attention to the wishes of parties, a significant difference. See the quote on page 129.
131 Sidney to Portland 14 August 1692, NUL, PwA 1351.

of the Jacobite forces in Ireland and the conclusion of the peace, William had created his commander-in-chief Ginckel Earl of Athlone and Baron Aughrim, only the second Dutchman to receive a peerage. Another trusted servant, Henry Sidney, was appointed Lord Lieutenant in March 1692, perhaps not the most fortunate choice after his apparent failure as Secretary of State.[132] The appointment of his close friend drew Portland deeper into the vortex of Irish politics. Sidney's main responsibilities were the implementation of the Treaty of Limerick, concluded partly due to Portland's activities, and the preparation for a parliamentary session to raise the revenue for the King in Ireland. Pending its convocation, Sidney remained in London to arrange initial funds to maintain the army in Ireland, meanwhile informing Portland in detail on his progress.[133] Their correspondence leaves little doubt that the first thing to be arranged was for the Irish to 'contribute towards the Expence that is necessary for the maintaining the quiet of that Kingdome'.[134] The first Irish parliamentary session in October 1692, however, was ill managed and the King prorogued Parliament within a few weeks.[135]

Sidney's lenient stance with regard to the Catholics, as stipulated in the Treaty of Limerick, was resented by a number of Protestant MPs. 'I defy them', he wrote to Portland, 'and am sure they can accuse me of nothing but asserting the King's prerogative.'[136] But he failed to effectively manage the Irish parliament, which William decided to dissolve. Sidney was recalled and replaced with three Lords Justices: Henry Capel, Cyril Wyche and William Duncombe. It was mainly through the channel of Sunderland, who was steering Capel, that Portland now kept an eye on Irish policy and the plans to convoke a new parliament.[137] Although little evidence of Portland's direct influence can be found, he was now allied to an influential group of Whigs, consisting mainly of Sunderland, Shrewsbury, Trenchard and Capel, who determined the King's Irish policy.[138]

In 1694 Portland was involved in another ministerial reshuffle in Ireland. Wyche and Duncombe were accused by Secretary of State Shrewsbury of undermining the government's position on the so-called 'sole right' issue, with which the Irish parliament tried to take the responsibility for preparing bills for raising money, thereby infringing on the royal prerogative. A session had to be postponed: 'the time is elapsed', Portland wrote to Shrewsbury, 'for holding a Parliament this year, whence those two [Wyche and Duncombe] who were adverse to a session, have indirectly

---

132 Baden to the States General 2/12 February 1692, BL, Add Mss 17677 MM, f° 89r°.
133 NUL, PwA 1335–53.
134 Sidney to Portland 26 July 1692, NUL, PwA 1344.
135 W. Troost, 'William III and the Treaty of Limerick 1691–1697' (unpublished PhD thesis, University of Leiden, 1983), 55 ff.
136 Quoted in ibid., 69.
137 Sunderland to Portland 25 April 1693, 13 June 1693, NUL, PwA 1211, PwA 1215.
138 Cf. Troost, 'Treaty of Limerick', 156; C.I. McGrath, 'English Ministers, Irish Politicians and the Making of a Parliamentary Settlement in Ireland, 1692–5', *English Historical Review*, 19 (2004), 585–613.

obtained their end.'[139] Capel, strongly supported by Portland and Sunderland, now moved to become Sole Governor. The actual appointment, not made until 1695, had firm backing from Portland, who had made sure that his competitor Coningsby was by-passed. Capel could also count on the powerful support of Whig magnates such as Montagu, Shrewsbury and Sunderland. The court parties in both England and Ireland had become decidedly Whig under the management of Sunderland and the patronage of Portland. The latter instructed Capel to report directly to him any matters of importance.[140] Orders from the King to Capel were, vice versa, communicated through Portland, who hereby had regained a firm grip on affairs in Dublin, together with Sunderland, as Capel wrote to Portland, 'on whose friendship next to Your L.^{s} I intirely depend'.[141] Their political alliance was strengthened by the marriage of Capel's nephew, the Earl of Essex, with Portland's daughter Mary.[142] Bartholomew Vanhomrig, a former resident of Amsterdam and now alderman in Dublin, was employed to act as a messenger between the future Lord Lieutenant of Ireland Capel and Portland.[143]

Capel's appointment had been made possible by a political compromise between the King and his Irish parliament. Sidney had vigorously opposed the 'sole right' claims of Parliament, but had ultimately admitted defeat. Capel was acceptable as Sole Governor, because as a dissenting Whig he had the trust of those Protestants who feared the appointment of a second Tory governor; in turn, this faction had agreed not to push the 'sole right' claim, but in the spring there were some fears, as Portland wrote to Capel, that they might hunt for Sidney's former associates:

> His Majesty has ordered me to write to you about the subject of the affairs in the country in which you are, that as you expect to succeed in the Parliament by the assurances which you have been given by men who largely opposed his service during the times of My Lord Romney, it is to be feared that they will attack those who have advised him to insist on the Sole Right, and in particular Mylord Coningsby, which is what the King wishes you to try to prevent and hinder if possible.[144]

But the 'sole right' compromise seemed to work, and William's request for funds was acknowledged in exchange for a pledge for anti-Catholic legislation.[145] 'I

---

139 Portland to Shrewsbury 6/16 August 1694 ('Camp de Mont St André'), *Private and Original Correspondence of Charles Talbot, Duke of Shrewsbury etc.*, ed. W. Coxe (London, 1821), 64.
140 Portland to Capel 20 November 1694 (Kensington Palace), 17 March 1695 (Kensington Palace), NUL, PwA 230, PwA 233; Troost, 'Treaty of Limerick', 98.
141 Portland to Capel 12 May 1695 (Kensington Palace), Capel to Portland 10 December 1695, NUL, PwA 239, 254.
142 But see Portland to Capel 22 April 1695, NUL, PwA 237.
143 Portland to Capel 15 April 1695, NUL, PwA 236 and *passim*. Cf. Troost, 'Treaty of Limerick', 109. Portland sometimes wrote instructions with the explicit order to destroy them after receipt, e.g. Galway to Portland 15 July 1692, NUL, PwA 1099.
144 Portland to Capel 12 May 1695 (Kensington Palace), NUL, PwA 239.
145 Troost, 'Treaty of Limerick', 114; Capel to Portland 17 December 1695, NUL, PwA 255; Van Homrigh wrote to Portland that Parliament had granted as much money as could be found in the kingdom, 14 December 1695, BL, Eg Mss 1707, f° 308.

infinitely rejoice in the success of your affairs in Parliament', Portland wrote to Capel in December 1695; 'appearances are so good here that we cannot doubt that those in England will have a good session.'[146]

But the court party suffered a heavy blow with the death of Capel in the spring of 1696, and several new candidates addressed themselves to the King and Portland.[147] The appointment of a successor proved troublesome. Charles Porter had stronger support in Parliament than Capel had had, but he was rendered obnoxious to the reigning Whig party in England. William, upon Sunderland's advice, postponed the decision until after the summer, meanwhile instructing Portland to discuss the matter with Sunderland and Shrewsbury.[148] It was Sunderland's associate John Methuen who was made Chancellor of Ireland in 1697.[149] The favourite thus remained influential in Irish affairs, and when the Imperial ambassador Auersperg intervened on behalf of the Irish Catholic priests in 1697, he turned to Portland.[150]

VII

The five years after the consolidation of the revolution settlement in 1691 saw a fundamental shift in William's continental position, changing from a desperate defensive stance to a confident strategy to contain French expansion. This shift had been made possible partly through the profound changes that swept the English political landscape after 1688, most notably the emergence of a 'standing Parliament' providing him with funds. The rise of Parliament made it essential for the King to exercise control over it. Portland was involved in establishing and strengthening court interests in the various parts of William's realms. In 1690 he intervened when the Orangist faction in Holland was weakened. As from 1689 he supported and supervised the Melville administration in Scotland, and to a lesser extent the Johnston ministry that emerged in 1692. He re-affirmed his central position in Scottish politics with the establishment of the Queensberry administration in 1695. After 1690 he was influential in the government of Ireland, and by 1695 his Whig associates and the Irish Lord Lieutenant Capel were in control in that kingdom. He also became increasingly involved in English parliamentary politics through his liaison with the Earl of Sunderland after 1692. He was instrumental in building up a court party, consisting of Junto Whigs, which successfully thwarted opposition measures to weaken the royal prerogative, such as the Triennial and Place Bills.

This chapter has described Portland as a courtier rather than as a party politician. Although historians have on occasion referred to him as a Presbyterian or a Whig,

---

146 Portland to Capel 3 December 1695 OS (Kensington Palace), Japikse, *Correspondentie*, XXIV. 52, transl. from French.

147 Norfolk to Portland 9 June 1696, NUL, PwA 679.

148 Sunderland to Portland 3 June 1696, NUL, PwA 1252; William to Portland 13 August 1696, Japikse, *Correspondentie*, XXIII. 185.

149 Shrewsbury to Portland 11 January 1697, NUL, PwA 1386.

150 W. Troost, 'Ireland's Role in the Foreign Policy of William III' in: E. Mijers and D. Onnekink, *Redefining William III. The Impact of the King-Stadholder in International Context* (Aldershot, 2007), 53–66.

clearly such labels do not adequately describe his position. Portland held a preference for both the Scottish Presbyterians and the English Tories despite their different religious backgrounds. But he also was unwilling to become attached to any party. He moved away from both the Presbyterians and the Tories in 1692 when they could not provide strong government, taking on board Episcopalians in Scotland and Whigs in England. Another reason for his breach with the Tories was the direction of foreign policy. Whereas the Tories preferred a blue water strategy, the Whigs in particular were able and willing to wholeheartedly endorse William's continental policy. Portland therefore became instrumental in William's trimming policy, willing to have a ministry of any colour as long as it provided strong government. He played an important role in mobilising resources for the war on the continent, which will be described in the following chapter.

1 William III and Hans Willem Bentick. 100 x 140 cm. Painting. By permission of Iconografisch Bureau/RKD, The Hague.

2 Anne Villiers. Oil on canvas. By permission of Iconografisch Bureau/RKD, The Hague.

3　Jane Martha Temple. Oil on canvas. By Simon Dubios. 36 x 31 cm, Middachten, De Steeg. By permission of Iconografisch Bureau/RKD, The Hague.

4   Hans Willem Bentick. Oil on canvas. By Simon Dubois. 36 x 31 cm, Middachten, De Steeg. By permission of Iconografisch Bureau/RKD, The Hague.

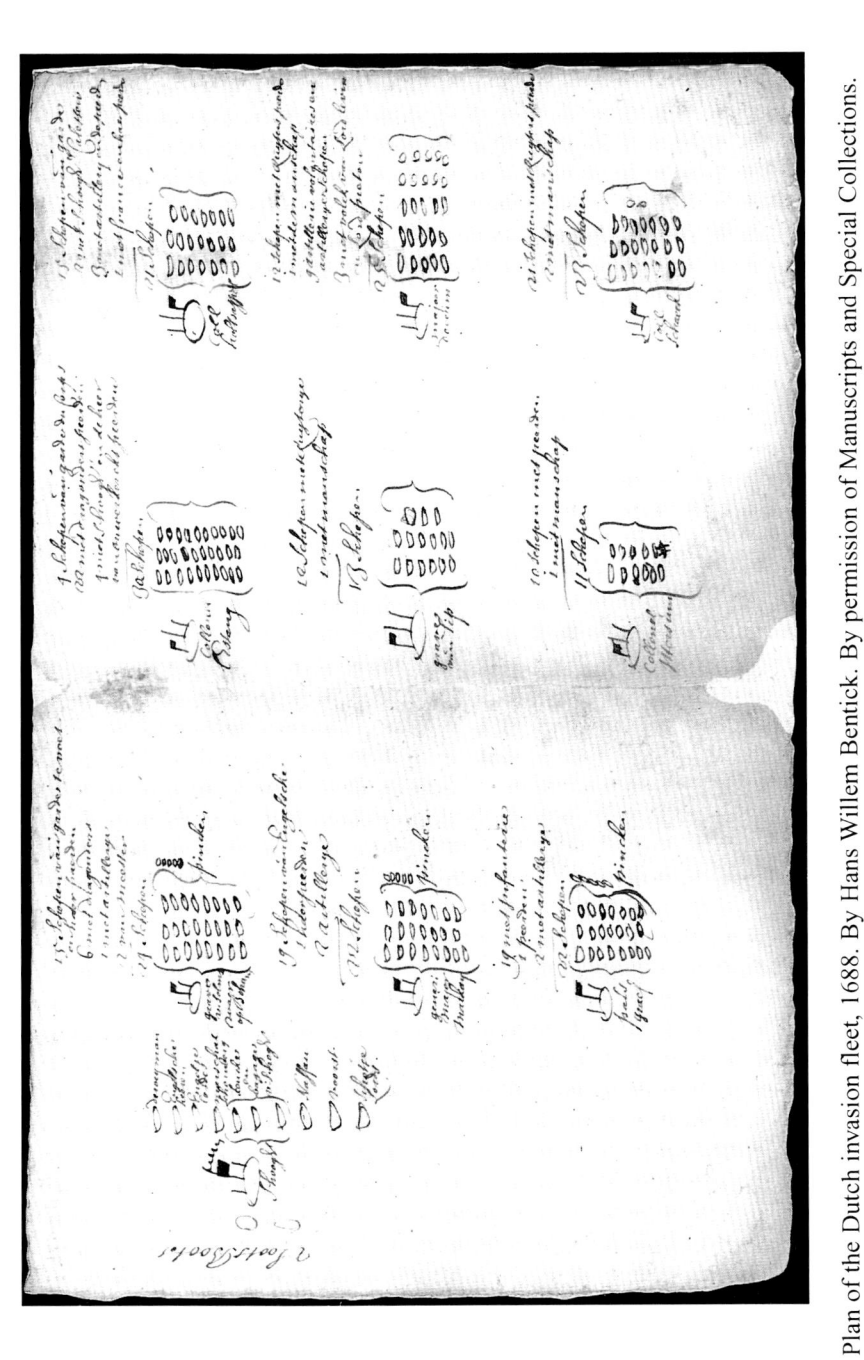

5 Plan of the Dutch invasion fleet, 1688. By Hans Willem Bentick. By permission of Manuscripts and Special Collections. The University of Nottingham (Ref. Pw A 2197/2).

6 'Hollands hollende koe', 1690. By permission of Atlas van Stolk (Ref. 2827).

Chapter 6

'The Great Affair':
War on the Continent

In March 1689 Bentinck informed the *ad interim* Grand Pensionary, Michiel ten Hove, that the English parliament had decided to join the alliance with the Dutch Republic.[1] When in May the Commons vouched their support for the King in his war against France, William declared that this moment marked the real beginning of his kingship.[2] William led his armies in to war in Flanders, thus drawing the British Isles into the mainstream of continental affairs. Arguably, the war occupied the King and his favourite more than any other issue. The Marquis of Halifax thought: 'Hee hath such a mind to France, that it would incline one to think, hee tooke England onely in his way.'[3] The war overshadowed any domestic concerns. When the magistrates of one of the Dutch cities were causing problems in 1690, Portland wrote to reassure William that at least they still supported the war effort: 'they can be relied on in the great affair.'[4]

In chapter 5, the consequences of William's foreign policy for the domestic political scene have been investigated. This chapter studies the role of the Anglo-Dutch favourite in the Nine Years War. The personal union of the three British kingdoms and the United Provinces manifested itself precisely in those spheres which were related to the war: military and diplomatic co-operation. Rather than providing a chronological overview of the Nine Years War, this chapter will concentrate on Portland's role as a military commander and adviser, looking at his contributions to the organisational and logistic aspects of the campaigns.

I

In December 1690 Constantijn Huygens and Portland had a discussion on painting, something they both enjoyed and frequently did. This time, they were particularly interested in a painting by Dirck Maas, depicting the Battle of the Boyne that had taken place earlier that year. The painting could be seen as a mere souvenir, but it

---
 1   Bentinck to Michiel ten Hove 15/25 March 1689 (Hampton Court Palace), Japikse, *Correspondentie*, XXVIII. 107.
 2   N. Japikse, *Willem III – De Stadhouder Koning* (2 vols, Amsterdam, 1930), II. 287.
 3   2 June 1689, G.S., First Marquis of Halifax, 'The Spencer House Journals' in: *The Life and Letters of Sir George Savile, First Marquis of Halifax*, ed. H.C. Foxcroft (2 vols, London, 1898), II. 219.
 4   Portland to William 11 February 1690 (The Hague), Japikse, *Correspondentie*, XXIII. 102, transl. from French.

also signified a glorification of this military victory. Portland, who had fought in the encounter, commissioned the painting and must have seen it as a celebration of one of his most enduring feats.[5]

Throughout his career, the favourite, like the King, regarded himself primarily as a soldier, and he probably felt more at home in a military camp than at Court. But although Portland would become a competent and experienced soldier, he never showed extraordinary talent, and his shining career and rapid climbing through the ranks was mainly the result of his favour with William. In June 1690, days before the dramatic encounter at the Boyne, Portland sat down to write a note to William, in which he reflected upon the 26 years of service to his master, and reminded the King of his promise to appoint him Lieutenant-General of the army, to spare him the fate of having to obey someone of 'lesser merit'.[6] Portland must have exerted more pressure upon William, for in September 1690, at the end of the campaign, the awaited promotion was awarded. In March 1691 he was also made Lieutenant-General of the Dutch forces.[7] He now held high military rank in the British and Dutch armies, the dual rank facilitating his role in the co-ordination of the allied war effort.

The note Portland wrote was, however, never read by William, as he specified for it to be delivered to him 'After my death, should I be killed during this campaign, 1690 in Ireland'.[8] The prospect of perishing on the battlefield must have been continuously on his mind, having fought in the Dutch War and now in the Nine Years War. Portland wrote several wills on the eve of military campaigns, such as in 1692, in which he beseeched the King to take care of his children should he perish – referring to an old promise of William to that effect. In the will Portland reflected upon 'the insecurity of life being such as to remind a God fearing Christian to be mindful of the end', referring particularly to the 'hasards of war'.[9] The will was written in his own hand in the army camp at Merle in the Spanish Netherlands. In 1693 he was wounded at the battle of Neerwinden, illustrating the frequent physical dangers he experienced in battle.[10]

---

5   *Catalogue of the Pictures belonging to His Grace the Duke of Portland, KG, at Welbeck etc.*, ed. R.W. Goulding (Cambridge, 1936), no. 523, 210; 22 December 1690, Huygens, *Journaal*, I-i. 378. Cf. K.A. Esdaile, Earl of Ilchester and H.M. Hake (eds), *Vertue Note Books* (6 vols, Oxford, 1930–55), V. 52.

6   Portland may have referred to the Duke of Schomberg, who had been appointed Lieutenant-General of the Cavalry. Portland to William 19 June 1690 O.S. (Hilsborough), Japikse, *Correspondentie*, XXIII. 159, transl. from French.

7   F.J.G. ten Raa, *Het Staatsche Leger 1568–1795. VI* (The Hague 1940), 234.

8   Portland to William 19 June 1690 O.S. (Hilsborough), Japikse, *Correspondentie*, XXIII. 158, transl. from French.

9   Portland's will 20/30 June 1692, Japikse, *Correspondentie*, XXIV. 710–13, transl. from Dutch. At the eve of the 1691 campaign Portland wrote to his eldest children, Henry and Mary, about his new will, 30 March 1691, NUL, PwA 1699, PwA 1700.

10   *Correspondence of the Family of Hatton, being chiefly Letters Addressed to Christopher, First Viscount Hatton. A.D. 1601–1704*, ed. E.M. Thompson (2 vols, London, 1878), II. 194; 27 July 1693, N. Luttrell, *A Brief Historical Relation of State Affairs from September 1678 to April 1714* (Oxford, 1857), III. 146; Bertie to Lindsey 27 July 1693, HMC,

As a military officer Portland had seen numerous battlefields, and he had gained plenty of experience during the Dutch War. As the Glorious Revolution turned out to be a bloodless event, the regiment under Portland's command did not see any action, though Portland was ordered to undertake a reconnaissance mission on the Salisbury plain on the eve of what could have been a military encounter with the army of James II. A similar mission was entrusted to him in July 1692, when he was to observe the French army with 2,000 cavalry from William's base at Camp Genappe in the Spanish Netherlands.[11] In July 1690 he joined the Duke of Schomberg's assault on the Jacobite army, after having crossed the Boyne. He was the author of the *News from the Army in Ireland*, a factual account of the battle.[12] In July 1692 he took part in the battle of Steenkerken, in which William had unsuccessfully engaged the French army. In June 1695 Portland was ordered by the King to engage French raiders preying on the bread convoy near Gent. With some 1,100 cavalry he charged the enemy with success.[13]

William must have been satisfied with his conduct, for after Steenkerken the Lieutenant-General was delegated operational command for the first time. Portland was ordered by the King to initiate an attack on Dunkerque after the abortive attempts to launch a descent on the French coast. An alternative plan was worked out by the Marquis of Carmarthen to use the troops from England, meant for the descent, for an attack on Dunkerque. Portland was eager to take up the idea, and William had put him in charge of the operation.[14] A lengthy memorandum in Portland's handwriting – a strategic plan for an assault on Dunkerque in September 1692 – reveals him taking detailed care of every aspect of the operation. It included marching orders for Allied battalions taking part in the military operation. Ships had to be employed to transport part of the army. It also contained detailed instructions about the provisioning of supplies, such as ammunition and bread. Lastly, it revealed strategy for the operation and the co-ordinated moves of the navy and army.[15] Portland's talent for military organising and logistic planning and the military experience he had gained during the Glorious Revolution were clearly put to good use.

Nevertheless, Portland never distinguished himself on the battlefield and his appointment as Lieutenant General was a political one inasmuch as William put some of his closest aides in high military positions. Those most talented, such as the Duke of Schomberg, his son the Duke of Leinster, Count Solms and the Prince of Waldeck, who had all gained a tremendous amount of experience, were entrusted with command in Ireland, England or Flanders.

Manuscripts of the Earl of Ancaster etc. (Dublin, 1907), 35; Sunderland to Portland 28 July 1693, Frederick I to Portland 29 August 1693, NUL, PwA 1224, PwA 427.

11   HMC, *Manuscripts of the Rt. Hon. Viscount de L'Isle etc.* (London, 1966), VI. 544; Japikse, *Correspondentie*, XXIV. 628.

12   *Leven and Melville Papers. Letters and State Papers chiefly Addressed to George Earl of Melville, Secretary of State for Scotland, 1689–1691*, ed. W.L. Melville (Edinburgh, 1843), 459–61n. Cf. page 80.

13   J. Childs, *The Nine Years War and the British Army 1688–1697: The Operations in the Low Countries* (Manchester, 1991), 274.

14   William to Portland 10 September 1692, Japikse, *Correspondentie*, XXIII. 172 ff.

15   NUL, PwA 2393.

Portland's talents were more suited to planning than strategy or operational command. He comes across as organised and disciplined and seems to have had a flair for arithmetic. His main tasks included the gathering of intelligence and making logistic preparations for military campaigns. He had considerable logistical responsibilities, as is reflected by the wealth of plans, statistics and maps in his personal archive. When Portland was in The Hague during springtime he dealt with the preparations for the continental campaign. In 1690 he was involved in the hiring of troops from Brandenburg. With the resident of the Duke of Brunswick-Wolfenbüttel he concluded a treaty for the hiring of a regiment infantry and six regiments cavalry.[16] He was also engaged in lengthy conferences with Waldeck on the management of the Congress in The Hague, and with Antonio Alvarez Machado on forage.[17]

Thus, in practice he developed into a military organiser and secretary to the King. In this capacity his broad experience on the battlefield proved useful, enabling him to interpret and evaluate the continuous flow of intelligence. His task was to inform the King of the overall strength and disposition of troops in Ireland, England, Scotland and on the continent. Portland also gathered additional information on naval matters from various sources.[18] The information was discussed with the King in long meetings, which took place frequently. Portland provided William with diagrams and tables on the number of battalions and their disposition. In a draft from 1690 options are discussed to reduce or augment the number of soldiers within each battalion.[19] They may have discussed military tactics as well during these meetings, as Portland's memoranda often contained lists of available regiments, and suggestions on where to move them. The sketchy character of Portland's memoranda suggests that they may very well have been drawn up during discussions with the King in his closet. One instruction for Solms gives an idea of how such talks may have transpired. It was written in an unknown handwriting, and was probably prepared by one of Portland's aides. The document has corrections in Portland's own handwriting, and was presumably discussed with the King.[20] After such a discussion, the King would take a decision and issue an instruction to his confidant, or order him to write to the Secretary of State. Portland would subsequently draw up memoranda stating the disposition of troops and their proposed movements.[21]

But Portland was more than just William's secretary for military affairs, and also emerged as one of his key military advisers. Although William took ultimate responsibility, overall strategy would be discussed with Grand Pensionary Anthonie Heinsius, the Secretaries of State and William's key advisers such as Dijkveld and Portland during winter season. Before the start of the campaign its practical

---

16   Childs, *Nine Years War*, 137; 31 March 1690, Huygens, *Journaal*, I-i. 249.

17   Waldeck to William 14 February 1690, P.L. Müller, *Wilhelm III. von Oranien und Georg Friedrich von Waldeck. Ein Beitrag zur Geschichte des Kampfes um das Europäischen Gleichgewicht* (2 vols, The Hague, 1873), II. 211.

18   Wharton to Portland 13 July 1694, Beckman to Portland 31 October 1695, NUL, PwA 1587, PwA 50.

19   TNA: PRO, SP 8/8, f° 19.

20   Instruction for Solms, Japikse, *Correspondentie*, XXVIII. 308–9.

21   E.g. TNA: PRO, SP 8/17, f° 17–30 and *passim*.

implications would be worked out with the military commanders, usually at Het Loo. Portland would also advise the King on a tactical level. When William's main army was expected to engage in battle in the summer of 1694, as Portland notified Shrewsbury, both he and the Secretary advised a defensive stance. Though advisable from a military perspective, the 1694 defensive strategy was politically undesirable and could harm William's reputation, and it was Portland's responsibility to warn the King about the political implications.[22]

The favourite emerged in various forms as a medium between the King and his Allies and commanders. He often corresponded with the commanders in Allied armies, such as Max Emanuel, Louis of Baden and the Prince of Vaudemont.[23] Portland also maintained a correspondence with the Allied leaders such as the Elector of Brandenburg and the Celle minister Bernstorff.[24] As part of his role as liaison between England and the United Provinces, Portland was instrumental in the co-ordination of movements of the Dutch and English fleets. Normally, when the King would leave for Holland in the spring, he was accompanied by Portland who organised naval conferences in The Hague, attended by Anthonie Heinsius, William Blathwayt and Job de Wildt on the co-ordination of the Anglo-Dutch fleet in the Channel.[25] The latter mainly managed naval affairs whereas in England the Secretaries of State were responsible. The Earl of Nottingham in particular took a keen interest in naval matters, and maintained a voluminous correspondence with Portland.[26]

Within the Anglo-Dutch army, the King would often communicate orders to his commanders, such as Galway or Leinster, through Portland.[27] When Schomberg, Solms and 's Gravenmoer were sent to Ireland in the summer of 1689, instructions were issued via Portland, and they in turn were instructed to keep Portland informed.[28] Normally the favourite's letters merely conveyed royal commands, but on some occasions he seemed to have scope for initiatives. His correspondence concerning the Irish campaign in 1691 clearly shows that Portland was sometimes independently issuing instructions and opinions to Baron Ginckel.[29] In 1692 he discussed strategy with Secretary of State Nottingham, and he began to take a more detailed interest in the conduct of his Whig successors, John Trenchard and the Duke of Shrewsbury. They commenced a correspondence on naval affairs and how best to co-ordinate Dutch and English fleet movements.[30] The Secretaries of State after Nottingham were certainly less independent characters and were more prone to follow instructions.

---

22 Shrewsbury to Portland 10 July 1694, NUL, PwA 1376; Portland to Shrewsbury 26 July 1694 NS (Camp of Mont St André), HMC, *Buccleugh Mss*, I-i. 101.
23 NUL, PwA 30–42, PwA 43–9, PwA 725–823.
24 NUL, PwA 131–47, 421–43.
25 E.g. Minutes of the proceedings of the Lords Justices, 27 May 1695, *CSPD 1694–1695*, 479.
26 NUL, PwA 1869–73. Cf. Nottingham's correspondence in HMC, *Finch Mss*.
27 NUL, PwA 1097–118, PwA 1129–35.
28 E.g. NUL, PwA 2365–75, PwA 463–8, PwA 2312–13.
29 E.g. Portland to Nottingham 20/30 June 1692 ('Camp de Mesle'), HMC, *Finch Mss*, IV. 246–7.
30 E.g. Trenchard to Portland 13 June 1693, 23 June 1693, 27 June 1693, 29 May 1694, 15 June 1694, 13 July 1694, NUL, PwA 1410–12, PwA 1422, PwA 1424–5; Shrewsbury to

Increasingly – and contributing to his efficiency as a staff officer – Portland established a personal network of correspondents who supplied him with intelligence. Baron Lexington, the British ambassador in Vienna, for instance, sent him private letters on strategic decision-making in Vienna with regard to Piedmont and the Rhine frontiers.[31] Furthermore, he was kept informed of enemy movements and strength – either a complete overview or a tactical situation – and based on his intelligence strategic alternatives could be discussed.[32]

It is difficult to estimate to what extent Portland was responsible or was merely executing orders from William, who kept a close eye on military affairs. Probably his true position lay between those two extremes. Essentially a staff officer, his role was well described by the Duke of Schomberg who referred to Portland in 1689 as 'the secretary to write all' concerning military matters.[33] Portland emerged as the pivotal figure in military correspondence, creaming off the most relevant correspondence and leaving Secretary-at-War Blathwayt and the Secretaries of State dealing mainly with routine business.[34]

Thus by the mid-1690s Portland had encroached upon the more important military correspondence of the Secretaries of State and War. Past historiography has underestimated his importance, and focused more on John Churchill, Earl of Marlborough, during the early years of the war – one historian even speaking of 'Churchillian policy'. This is based upon a complaint by Schomberg that 'My Lord Churchill proposes all' concerning military affairs.[35] But Schomberg referred mainly to Marlborough's role in the Irish campaign, and it is by no means certain that his role in other spheres was comparable. Indeed, it was the very lack of influence that prompted him to launch an assault on William's foreign generals in 1692. Portland was less conspicuous but essentially more influential in military affairs. It was ultimately Portland who discussed matters with the King on a day-to-day basis and he was influential in the highest appointments. In 1690, for instance, he recommended Sir Richard Haddock for admiral. Generals like Baron Ginckel were also profiting from Portland's favour, and Count Solms in particular, was a close

---

Portland 1 January 1695, HMC, *Buccleugh Mss*, II-i. 169; minutes of the proceedings of the Lords Justices 31 July 1696, *CSPD 1696*, 312. This practice had begun during the Nottingham administration, cf. Portland to Nottingham 5/15 May 1691 (The Hague), Nottingham to Portland 12 May 1691, 5 June 1691, Nottingham to the officers of the Ordnance 27 February 1691, HMC, *Finch Mss*, III. 16–17, 48–9, 58–9, 98–9.

31   E.g. NUL, PwA 1311–12.
32   E.g. NUL, PwA 1292, PwA 2393–420.
33   Quoted in J. Childs, *The British Army of William III 1689–1702* (Manchester, 1987), 25.
34   Portland to Nottingham 6/16 June 1689 (Hampton Court Palace), 26 July/5 August 1689 (Hampton Court Palace), HMC, *Finch Mss*, II. 212, 229; Childs, *British Army*, 25; Buchan to Nairne 5 September 1689, Melville, *Leven and Melville Papers*, 271; Portland's memorial of 29 March 1690, Japikse, *Correspondentie*, XXVIII. 160–61; *CSPD 1690–1691*, 214; R.A. Preston, 'William Blathwayt and the Evolution of a Royal Personal Secretariat', *History*, February/June (1949), 28–43, 32, 34.
35   M. Glozier, *The Huguenot Soldiers of William of Orange and the Glorious Revolution of 1688. The Lions of Judah*. (Brighton, 2002), 113.

associate.[36] George Clarke claimed that Portland sustained the position of William Blathwayt as Secretary-at-War, whom he had hoped to succeed.[37]

Arguably the army was the main concern of the King-Stadholder and consequently of his favourite. In fact, the vast bulk of Portland's (and later Albemarle's) tasks was in some way connected with the army. William, through his favourite, was able to keep control over the army to a larger extent than has hitherto been suggested. Portland was involved in the mobilisation of human and financial resources needed for the campaigns in Scotland, Ireland and Flanders.

II

Diplomacy was another sphere directly related to the war in which the favourite was involved. Appointments were normally made with Portland's consent. In 1693 Eberhard Danckelmann, the Brandenburg first minister, asked to have George Stepney, envoy in the Empire, as a resident and turned to Portland for his approval.[38] Stepney himself approached Portland's secretary, Jacob van Leeuwen, and wrote to Portland directly, complaining about his 'amphibious' character and asking for his patronage and a settled position.[39] When Abraham Kick, the English consul in Rotterdam, wanted clarity about his position, he wrote to Blathwayt and Secretary of State Trenchard, but indicated that Portland was ultimately responsible.[40] Francisco Schonenberg, the Anglo-Dutch diplomat in Madrid, considered himself a client of Portland's.[41]

The Secretaries of State were handling the day to day diplomatic business, and men like Nottingham were certainly not completely marginalized with regard to foreign affairs, as has often been assumed.[42] Portland's contact with regular envoys was infrequent. He did not discourage diplomats from writing to him. For instance, John Methuen, envoy in Lisbon, reported his audience with the Portuguese king in 1693 to Portland.[43] The favourite only replied in specific cases, however, which was not always understood by diplomats. Stepney had a series of letters unanswered until Portland reprimanded him and made clear that he was to receive instructions from

---

36 E.g. Portland to Ginckel 4/14 October 1690 (Kensington Palace), Japikse, *Correspondentie*, XXVIII. 187; H. Horwitz, *Revolution Politicks. The Career of Daniel Finch, Second Earl of Nottingham 1647–1730* (Cambridge, 1968), 108.

37 HMC, *Manuscripts of F.W. Leyborne-Popham Esq.* (London, 1899), 171, 175.

38 Stepney to Blathwayt 21 March 1693, TNA:PRO, SP 105/58, f° 85–6. For Portland's involvement in diplomatic matters see, for example, Heinsius to Portland 30 January 1693, NUL, PwA 1915.

39 Stepney to Strafford June 1694, Stepney to Portland 20/30 July 1694, TNA:PRO, SP 105/54, f° 32, 47r°.

40 Kick to Trenchard 12 November 1694, TNA:PRO, SP 84/223, f° 51r°.

41 E.g. Schonenberg to Portland 26 May 1695, NA 1.02.04/7.

42 See his correspondence in HMC, *Finch Mss*; e.g. Portland to Shrewsbury 6/16 September 1694 (Camp of Rousselaer): 'Mr. Blathwait has no knowledge of it', HMC, *Buccleugh Mss*, II-i. 128.

43 A.D. Francis, *The Methuens and Portugal, 1691–1708* (Cambridge, 1966), 54.

the Secretaries of State and the Secretary-at-War.[44] To Coenraad van Heemskerck, the Dutch envoy in the Empire, Portland explained that he did not have time to maintain a regular correspondence with diplomats. Van Heemskerck supposed that Portland would receive copies of his letters to Blathwayt.[45] When Van Heemskerck by-passed the ordinary channels of communication, however, and wrote directly to the King concerning a matter that required secrecy, he was reprimanded by Portland, who gave him to understand that all such correspondence to the King was to be addressed to himself.[46]

A portion of the more important diplomatic correspondence went through Portland's hands, but his informal correspondence with envoys was of more significance.[47] To fully reconstruct Portland's intelligence network is problematic, not only because of its secretive nature but also because a substantial part of his archive was lost during the eighteenth century.[48] Part of his network consisted of secret agents engaged in counter-espionage activities. From early 1693, an anonymous agent was stationed in Paris providing him with a steady flow of intelligence of varied value. Evidence suggests that he may also have been part of Portland's intelligence network in 1688.[49] In 1694 Portland and Dijkveld commissioned Francisco Mollo, the Polish resident, to open a channel with the French.[50] Strictly in the diplomatic sphere were a string of clients who informally corresponded with him. Van Heemskerck had been a long-time confidant and kept in contact with Portland during his missions to the Empire. Portland's client in Berlin was the Dutch envoy, Johan Ham, with whom he continued to correspond during the 1690s. In Vienna it was Robert Sutton, Baron Lexington, with whom Portland established a crucial line of communication, marginalizing Stepney. Similarly, Aernout van Citters was sidelined in London and it was Envoy Extraordinary Jacob Hop, a trusted aide of William, who was doing the real work.[51] Only fragments of evidence remain of Portland's direct contact with Francisco Schonenberg, William's representative in Madrid.[52] Godard Adriaan van Reede van Amerongen, on Portland's suggestion despatched as envoy

---

44 Portland to Stepney 12/22 July 1694, TNA:PRO, SP 105/82, f° 225–6. Cf. Preston, 'William Blathwayt', 36–7, 39, 42. On Portland's relationship with George Stepney, see S. Spens, *George Stepney, 1663–1707, Diplomat and Poet* (Cambridge, 1997), *passim*.

45 Portland to Heemskerck 10 July 1692 ('Camp de Genappe'), Heemskerck to Portland 3 August 1692, NA 1.02.01/83.

46 Portland to Heemskerck 21 December 1694 (Kensington Palace), NA 1.02.01/176.

47 Cf. Heemskerck to William 21 November 1694, NUL, PwA 551.

48 See Japikse's explanation in the introduction of Japikse, *Correspondentie*, XXIII. xxix ff.

49 NUL, PwA 2804–60. The formula of the letters was similar, i.e. they appeared to be trivial letters but there was an appendix in invisible ink with important information. The letters were also sent to undercover addresses. One of the aliases, Bonnet, was actually used for Portland in 1688. (NUL, PwA 2804). Cf. Ch. 2.

50 23 June 1694, Huygens, *Journaal*, II-ii. 366.

51 G.N. Clark, 'The Dutch Missions to England in 1689', *English Historical Review*, 35 (1920), 540 and *passim*.

52 E.g. Schonenberg to Portland 18 July 1696, NUL, PwA 1137.

to Copenhagen, corresponded with the favourite.[53] Portland also maintained contact with foreign representatives, such as Gabriel Oxenstierna, the Swedish ambassador in The Hague.[54]

Consequently, Portland stood at the axis of formal and informal Dutch and English intelligence and diplomatic networks. A number of these correspondents provided him with an alternative flow of intelligence outside the formal channels which ultimately through him reached the King.[55] Portland's influence in these matters reached a temporary zenith in early 1695. As the King was in mourning, evidence suggests that Portland dealt with the bulk of diplomatic correspondence directed to the King.[56]

III

The consolidation of the Williamite settlement in late 1691 enabled the King to devise an Anglo-Dutch grand strategy. Centred around the Flanders campaign and aimed at encircling France it was complemented during the second half of 1692 by a blockade of the French coasts and the entrance of an Anglo-Dutch squadron into the Mediterranean.[57] Such a grand strategy could only succeed if the High Allies, Spain and the Empire, would throw in their weight, William not willing to spend Dutch and British subsidies and troops on the Rhine frontier while the Emperor concentrated his resources on Hungary.[58] Unsuccessful invasions into France were undertaken by the Imperial armies along the Rhine, temporarily profiting from the withdrawal of French armies to reinforce the troops in the Spanish Netherlands.

To co-ordinate the joint efforts of the Allies to combat France, the Congress of the Allies, made up of representatives, assembled in The Hague. Portland had been engaged in setting up the Congress during his mission to Holland in 1690.[59] In January 1690, William had instructed Portland to discuss with Grand Pensionary Heinsius, the Dutch Lieutenant Commander-in-Chief the Prince of Waldeck and Dijkveld the co-operation between the Dutch and the English at the Congress, and in particular how to instruct the English ambassador to The Hague, Charles Berkeley.[60]

---

53   Amerongen to William 28 March 1690, Japikse, *Correspondentie*, XXVIII. 158.

54   Portland to William, 22 February 1690, Japikse (Den Haag), *Correspondentie*, XXIII. 114.

55   E.g. Gortz to Heinsius 13 January 1694 NS, Heemskerck to Heinsius 12 March 1695, 6 April 1695, *Weensche Gezantschapsberichten van 1670–1720*, ed. G. von Antal and J.C.H. de Pater (2 vols, The Hague, 1929–34), I. 561, 590, 594.

56   E.g. Heinsius' letters to William, NUL, PwA 1924–30.

57   Cf. J.B. Hattendorf, *England in the War of the Spanish Succession. A Study of the English View and Conduct of Grand Strategy, 1702–1712* (New York, 1987), 80–3.

58   William to Heinsius 19/29 January 1692, but see also Heinsius to Heemskerck 17 April 1692, *Het Archief van den Raadpensionaris Antonie Heinsius*, ed. H.J. van der Heim (3 vols, The Hague, 1867), I. 76–7.

59   Spens, *George Stepney*, 34.

60   William to Bentinck 24 January 1690, Japikse, *Correspondentie*, XXIII. 75.

In The Hague Portland became involved in discussing grand strategy with the Allies, for instance in discussing plans for an invasion into France from Savoy. William thought this was the responsibility of the Emperor.[61] He was not unwilling to approve of the Savoyard diversion as long as it did not weaken the Flanders army.[62] In an important conference held in Vienna in January 1693, the Marquises of Borgomañero and Di Prié, the Spanish and Savoyard ambassadors, argued for a strong diversion into France via Savoy.[63] Savoy had joined the Grand Alliance in October 1690, the negotiations for which had involved Portland.[64] In a memorial to the King, Portland had urged that all possible speed was necessary, not only to assist the Duke financially, but also to press Spain to send troops and order the English envoy in Geneva to endeavour to conclude a treaty with the Protestant Swiss cantons.[65] In May 1690 a plan had been discussed between him, Secretary of State Shrewsbury and Pedro Ronquillo, the Spanish ambassador in London, to draw the Protestant cantons into the alliance, with an eye to succouring Savoy.[66] A plan to assist Vaudois in a revolt was revived. In late March 1691, the King discussed the succour of Savoy with Portland, Nottingham and the Savoyard envoy De la Tour, and decided to subsidise the Emperor to despatch 16,000 Imperial and 6,000 Bavarian troops to Savoy.[67]

The question was, however, whether this would have an impact on the campaign in the northern theatre. A major concern for William was the shift in Imperial resources from the Rhine frontier to the south and east. Count Harrach, one of the Emperor's closest advisers, insisted that the ineffective Flanders army was 'hampered by its own weight'.[68] Portland, in turn, complained about the efforts of Austria, accusing its ministry of a 'great lethargy and inaction, while they have two wars to fight'.[69] Indeed, confronted with a rebellion in Hungary and an ongoing war with the Turks, the Emperor was reluctant to shift his resources to the western front. When he decided to transfer the capable commander, Prince Louis of Baden, from Hungary to the Rhine, however, Portland urged Stepney to remain present at conferences in Vienna on military matters, and assured him that the King was very satisfied with the transfer of Baden, who had done 'more than the whole ministry together'.[70] The Prince's coming promised a decisive shift in Vienna's vacillating

---

61   Nottingham to Paget 2 February 1692, HMC, *Finch Mss*, IV. 11–12; Heinsius to Schomberg 5 January 1692, Van der Heim, *Archief*, I. 217–18.
62   Nottingham to Stepney 17 February NS 1693, TNA:PRO, SP 105/58, f° 68v°.
63   Stepney to Nottingham 21 January 1693, ibid., f° 10v°–19.
64   6 July 1690, Huygens, *Journaal*, I-i. 292.
65   NUL, PwA 151; Portland's memorial September/October 1690, Japikse, *Correspondentie*, XXIV. 393–4.
66   Ronquillo to Fuensalida 5 May 1690 in Maura, *Correspondencia*, II. 164.
67   31 March 1691, Huygens, *Journaal*, I-i. 412.
68   Stepney to Nottingham 21 January 1693, TNA:PRO, SP 105/58, f° 10v°–19, transl. from French.
69   Portland to Lexington 17/27 April 1695 (Kensington Palace), BL, Add Mss 46525, f° 100r°, transl. from French.
70   Portland to Stepney 6 February 1693 NS (Kensington Palace), TNA: PRO, SP 105/82, f° 80–81; Portland to Lexington 17/27 April 1695 (Kensington Palace), BL, Add Ms

policy; he and Count Königsegg, the Imperial Vice Chancellor, supported a transfer of 4,000 cavalry from Hungary, a move opposed however by powerful ministers.[71] Via Van Heemskerck, Portland was also kept informed about the state of affairs in the Ottoman Empire, which would have immediate repercussions on the war on the Balkans. Turkish capacity to continue the war seemed to be on the wane. In 1695 Portland received the alarming news that the 'Great Seigneur must come on campaign in person with a great army',[72] but Van Heemskerck, though sceptical about prospects for peace, assured him that in the Sublime Porte 'there is neither order nor obedience, the militia are without chiefs and the treasury without money'.[73]

If Portland received regular news from Vienna about the Empire, through the King's representative in Madrid, Francisco Schonenberg, he was kept informed about the conduct of the other High Ally, Spain. In January 1695 – when the King was in mourning and wholly uninterested in business – Portland responded furiously to Lexington's message that the Spanish king desired 8,000 extra troops in Catalonia,

> ... which is impossible, they want us to carry the costs of the whole war without doing anything for themselves, and moreover they cry out against peace, and do not want it on any other conditions than those of the Treaty of the Pyrenees, which is extraordinary.

He instructed Lexington to discuss the matter with Borgomañero in Vienna.[74]

From these fragments of information regarding Portland's contacts with diplomats in Vienna and Madrid rises an image of the favourite involved, in various ways, with grand strategy. But his attention was primarily focused on the war in the Low Countries. His diplomatic activities consistently aimed at securing support for the concentration of large forces in Flanders. Plans for a seaborne descent on France had been discussed during the autumn of 1691, although William never intended it to be more than a diversion from the Flanders campaign.[75] But precisely in the following year the Williamite settlement in the British Isles, having been internally consolidated, came under threat from outside. Rumours of an impending descent by the French had circulated for some time during the spring of 1692, and the French marshal Bellefonds had assembled troops in Normandy with ships ready in Dunkerque for transportation.[76] By the end of April the accumulation of evidence had sufficiently convinced William to have the Irish regiments, destined for Flanders, despatched to England and to send Portland to England with several Dutch men-of-war.[77]

46525, f° 100v°, transl. from French.
71   Stepney to Nottingham 7 February 1693, TNA:PRO, SP 105/58, f° 35–7.
72   Portland to Lexington 17/27 April 1695 (Kensington Palace), BL, Add Mss 46525, f° 100v°–101r°, transl. from French.
73   Heemskerck to William 10 December 1694, 22 December 1694, 25 December 1694, NUL, PwA 552–4, transl. from French (Portland handled this correspondence, see Heemskerck to William 21 November 1694, NUL, PwA 551).
74   Portland to Lexington 15/25 January 1695, BL, Add Mss 46525, f° 92r°, transl. from French.
75   Horwitz, *Revolution Politicks*, 88, 98.
76   E.g. William to Heinsius 24 April 1692, Van der Heim, *Archief*, II. 50.
77   Blathwayt to Nottingham 26 April/6 May 1692, HMC, *Finch Mss*, IV. 102.

Portland arrived at Whitehall Palace on 13 May, after which an emergency Cabinet Council meeting was convened.[78] Several informers had come forward connecting the impending descent to a Jacobite rising. Portland had received an anonymous letter providing fairly detailed evidence for its accusation that a number of officers and nobles, including the Earl of Marlborough and the Sidney Godolphin, were involved in the plot; Portland immediately forwarded the letter to Nottingham. William warned Portland that it was a most delicate matter and should be handled with circumspection.[79] The decision to arrest Marlborough was taken by a council of Sidney, Portland, Leinster and a number of officers, and the warrant was prepared by Nottingham. Portland also assumed control of measures to take Jacobite conspirators into custody. A plan was made to systematically search London, inquiries were to be made concerning suspect persons and the main roads to the North and to ports were to be watched.[80] The somewhat inflated hysteria was soon subdued by the news that the French had suffered a shattering defeat at the hands of the combined Anglo-Dutch fleet at La Hogue, which not only destroyed any plans for a descent but also turned out to be a crucial event in the war at sea; after La Hogue the Allies had achieved decisive naval supremacy over the French, who now stuck to privateering.[81] The plot turned out to be unsubstantiated.[82]

On the day of the news of the victory the Queen ordered Portland, Sidney, Rochester and Galway to depart for Portsmouth, ostensibly to congratulate Russell but with the purpose of deciding on how to exploit the naval victory. Because the location and condition of the remainder of the French fleet were not yet known, this could only be discussed in general terms.[83] Plans for a descent had been decided on in the preceding parliamentary session, but when details had to be worked out in the spring only Nottingham seemed enthusiastic.[84] Further preparations had been terminated in the face of the invasion threat, but now options were discussed, troops were concentrated and transport ships had been sent. Portland himself travelled back to the continent and arrived in The Hague on 21 June.[85] Exactly how the victory should be exploited was unclear, the Council of War initially leaving it to the judgement of the naval officers to decide on how 'to annoy yᵉ Enemy'.[86] Ambitious plans for an invasion were narrowed down to a naval descent on St Malo, where part of the French fleet had fled. A bitter dispute followed between Russell and Nottingham; the former had initially proposed an invasion, but because of delays he became sceptical

---

78   3 May 1692, Luttrell, *Brief Historical Relation*, II. 439, 440.
79   William to Portland 26 May 1692, Japikse, *Correspondentie*, XXIII. 171.
80   HMC, *Finch Mss*, IV. 160–61.
81   G.N. Clark, 'The Nine Years War 1688–1697' in: J. Bromley (ed.), *The New Cambridge Modern History* (Cambridge, 1970), VI. 244.
82   Nottingham to Portland 10 June 1692, HMC, *Finch Mss*, IV. 217.
83   J. Ehrman, *The Navy in the War of William III 1689–1697. Its State and Direction* (Cambridge, 1953), 399–400; 28 May 1692, 4 June 1692, Luttrell, *Brief Historical Relation*, II. 465, 473; Nottingham to Russell 26 May 1692, HMC, *Finch Mss*, IV. 185–6.
84   Horwitz, *Revolution Politicks*, 130.
85   Portland to Nottingham 11/21 June (in sight of Goeree), 12/22 June 1692 (On board a yacht between The Hague and Rotterdam), HMC, *Finch Mss*, IV. 223–5.
86   NUL, PwA 1087; Ehrman, *The Navy in the War of William III*, 400 ff.

and even dissuaded from the intended descent. Now the pressure on William's armies in Flanders induced the King to consider using regiments initially meant for the descent for his own campaign. Ehrman has erroneously argued that the King kept aloof from the discussions in his ministry. Portland was fully informed of all proceedings, and discussed the options with Carmarthen, Nottingham, Galway and Leinster, the ministers and military commanders responsible for the descent.[87]

Both Portland and William had been staunch supporters of a descent, but strategic disagreements soon came to the fore between Portland and Nottingham. Not surprisingly, it was the Tory ministry – Nottingham, supported by Carmarthen and Rochester – which favoured a shift in resources away from the army to the navy. It is worth analysing the ensuing correspondence between Nottingham and Portland in some detail as it illuminates their diverging views on strategy, which came into the open that summer. Portland was not unwilling to despatch several Flanders regiments for the descent, as he wrote to Nottingham whilst crossing the Channel on 21 June, but he needed to evaluate the situation first. When he arrived in The Hague, it seemed that although the Citadel of Namur (under attack by the French) was putting on a stout defence, the King was unwilling to despatch either cavalry or infantry. Nottingham was pessimistic about the consequences; a descent would be impossible without reinforcements, and the King should not waste an opportunity to achieve a notable success against France, 'otherwise I may venture to foretell that the Parliament will not be induced to maintain an army abroad'.[88] The decision lay with the King, and not until Portland had arrived in the camp on 26 June could measures be taken.[89] The King, however, was unwilling to compromise and commanded via Blathwayt that the cavalry be sent across the Channel without delay.[90]

Portland insisted to Nottingham that these were not, in fact, necessary for the descent and that infantry should suffice:

In God's name, Sir, let us try to profit from the advantage that we have got at sea, the more so as our fortunes on land are not so good, which is why His Majesty cannot send over any troops that are here, because our allies create so little diversion for the enemies that the latter are not forced to send detachments from their armies here, but keep their forces in this country. Which is why His Majesty demands so strongly to have at least ten squadrons of his cavalry in England sent to the army here.[91]

He suggested that a descent could be carried out 'without setting foot on land'. In his opinion Nottingham asked for too much and delayed matters whilst the French

---

87   Ehrman, *The Navy in the War of William III*, 402. Cf. M. Glozier, *Marshal Schomberg (1615–1690) – 'The Ablest Soldier of His Age' International Soldiering and the Formation of State Armies in Seventeenth-Century Europe* (Brighton, 2005), 160 ff.
88   Nottingham to Portland 14 June 1692, HMC, *Finch Mss*, IV. 233.
89   Meesters to Nottingham 18/28 June 1692, ibid., 245.
90   Blathwayt to Nottingham 16/26 June 1692, ibid., 214.
91   Portland to Nottingham 16/26 June 1692 ('Camp de Melay'), ibid., 241, transl. from French.

had time to mount a strong defence.[92] While Nottingham had argued the contrary, Portland was clearly supported in his opinion by Leinster and Galway, who were both surprised that the Secretary and Carmarthen had asked for 7,000 troops for what they saw as an uncertain expedition.[93] The discussion now touched the deeper strategic considerations involved, and Portland recognised the Tories' efforts to downgrade the Flanders campaign in favour of their naval strategy. In another letter to Nottingham on the same day, not written on the King's command, he elaborated on what the secretary had written to him of the

> ... surely good success in what I propose, and the prospect of it as fair as we could wish, will abundantly compensate for any of those misfortunes, for whether a town more or less be won or lost in Flanders, certainly the advantage or disadvantage is not comparable to the destruction of their fleet, which leave all France open to an invasion and will encourage the Parliament to pursue it with the uttmost vigour and resolution.[94]

Portland took exception to his argument:

> Permit me to say to you that when you speak of one or two more cities lost in this country and the consequence thereof for England, you do not talk very much like a general of the army, nor an able minister of state

Although it would not be unreasonable to try to humour Parliament, given the fact that Namur was about to be lost, why would the King despatch regiments when it was not absolutely necessary?[95] Nottingham chose not to argue with the favourite, and defended himself, saying he had been misunderstood:

> ... I am sure I never said, that England could be safe if Holland were exposed to ruin; 'tis long that I have thought their interests the same; nor did I say that the loss of a town or 2 in Flanders was of little consequence, but rather quite the contrary, that it would be very prejudiciall and mischevious to Holland, and therefore also to us. But I onely ventured to affirm that such a loss would not be so fatall to Holland and us as the destruction of the French fleet would be to France; and I am not yet convinced that I am in an error.[96]

But Portland insisted:

> Perhaps, sir, that in my reply to yours ... I have not explained myself clearly, but you have expressed yourself so clearly in your letter that I could not have misunderstood. When you

---

92 Portland to Nottingham 20/30 June 1692 ('Camp de Meslé'), ibid., 246, transl. from French.

93 Galway to Portland 28 June 1692, Leinster to Portland 28 June 1692, NUL PwA 1097, 1129; Carmarthen to William 14 June 1692, *CSPD 1691–1692*, 326–7. Nottingham claimed that Leinster had intimated his desire for more troops, letter to Portland 15 July 1692, HMC, *Finch Mss*, IV. 316, which was strongly denied by Leinster. Portland knew this, 4/14 July 1692 to Nottingham (Camp of Genappe), ibid., 291–2.

94 Nottingham to Portland 14 June 1692, HMC, *Finch Mss*, IV. 232.

95 Portland to Nottingham 20/30 June 1692 ('Camp de Meslé'), ibid., 247, transl. from French.

96 Nottingham to Portland 28 June 1692, ibid., 286.

say that the loss of one or two cities in Flanders is not as important as the advantage of the destruction of the enemy fleet, I only reply by saying that any city which is lost here might lead to the destruction of the Low Countries ... .[97]

Delays and shortage of transport ships led to the abandonment of the plans regarding St Malo or Brest, causing Portland 'an extreme vexation'.[98]

IV

During the summer the Tories developed what would eventually become their 'blue water strategy', a shift from continental to naval warfare, which was strongly opposed by Portland. The Tories were now caught in a dilemma they were not able to solve. Only if the King would endorse their strategy could they secure a majority in the House of Commons for supplying him in the coming year. Since William dismissed their proposals, however, they had become an ineffective political force. Nottingham's notions on foreign policy and Rochester's suggestions along the same lines met with Portland's thorough disapproval.[99]

Thus Portland and the Court Tories disagreed on continental strategy, and consequently also the application of the standing army. The growth of the army had expanded the state apparatus, and a struggle over its control, patronage and resources was inevitable. This process in which politicians and the military both tried to gain control over the decision-making process has perhaps been somewhat neglected by historians. It was a struggle over influence and money, but also over the direction of the war. In his debate over war strategy with Nottingham, Portland had been supported by generals such as the Earl of Galway, who commanded the army in Ireland, and Schomberg's son the Duke of Leinster, commander of the troops in England, who were disgruntled by Nottingham's involvement despite his lack of expertise. In 1693 Nottingham was removed from office for political reasons. It is significant that after this dispute the competent and headstrong Nottingham was replaced with Secretaries that were either weak, such as the Duke of Shrewsbury, or political lightweights, such as John Trenchard and William Trumbull. Simultaneously, those in military positions gained significance; William Blathwayt, the Secretary-at-War during the campaigning season, became increasingly influential even during winter seasons.[100]

Meanwhile, opposition to William's militarised regime also materialised in Parliament in the form of criticism of his strategy and army. Rochester's and Nottingham's pessimism concerning the 1692/1693 session of Parliament was echoed in an anonymous letter Portland received, informing him that some were:

---

97   Portland to Nottingham 4/14 July 1692 ('Camp de Genappe'), ibid., 291, transl. from French.

98   Portland to Nottingham 11/21 August 1692 ('Camp de Ninove'), ibid., 384, transl. from French.

99   Godolphin to William 13 July 1692, Rochester to William 16 August 1692, Carmarthen to William 9 September 1692, *CSPD 1691–1692*, 365, 410–12, 443–4.

100   Normally, the Secretary-at-War was equal to the Secretaries of State only when on campaign. Cf. Preston, 'William Blathwayt', 28–32.

... upon severall projects to make a division in this next session of Parliam.ᵗ some members are for impeaching your Lord.ᵖ. as advising his Ma.ᵗⁱᵉ to keep up the Dutch Confederacy, & therby expending the English Blood and Treasure beyond sea & doing no good therewith against the ffrench [sic].[101]

The prediction was not unjustified and the Commons were after blood. Though Portland was accused of having sacrificed English troops at Steenkerken, it was Solms who had to bear the brunt of a ferocious attack on foreign officers. 'I think', one MP had argued during the debates,

> it is not consistent with the interest of this kingdom for to have foreign officers over an English army when we have so many brave, courageous men amongst us. The Englishman can have no interest but the good of his own country; what foreigners may have I cannot tell.[102]

The opposition, however, though buoyed by a wave of xenophobia, was unable to carry the day. Even Edward Seymour supported the Crown, arguing that there were no able English commanders to take over.[103]

The small circle of powerful foreign military commanders was, however, widely resented, and it was clear that the dissatisfaction of English officers such as Marlborough had sparked the conflict. The Imperial resident Johann Hoffmann dismissed the criticism:

> They have no reason to complain because apart from several generals like Portland and Nassau-Ouwerkerk, no Dutchmen have established themselves here. The complaints are rather caused by an ingrained antipathy against anything foreign.[104]

The Huguenot, Dutch and German officers, however, occupied some of the highest offices in the army. The German Hermann Schomberg had fought for Louis XIV but changed sides after the King revoked the Edict of Nantes; he became William's Commander-of-Chief of the army in Ireland until he was succeeded in 1690 – after a brief interim command by the German general the Count of Solms-Braunfels – by the Utrecht nobleman Godard van Reede van Ginckel. The Huguenot officer Henri Massue de Ruvigny, Earl of Galway, succeeded Ginckel in 1692 until appointed Lord Justice in 1697. Hugh Mackay had been commander of the Anglo-Dutch regiments in the United Provinces and was despatched to Scotland in 1689. These foreigners were mainly employed for their capacities and experience. William also distrusted some of his English subjects, but this was not the main reason for his reliance on foreign officers, as he was perfectly content to leave the fleet under the

---

101 Letter to Portland 1 November 1692 NUL, PwA 2792. Cf. C. Rose, *England in the 1690s: Revolution, Religion and War* (Oxford, 1999), 129.
102 Quoted in Rose, *England in the 1690s*, 40.
103 Childs, *British Army*, 76.
104 Quoted in G. van Alphen, *De Stemming van de Engelschen tegen de Hollanders in Engeland tijdens de Regeering van den Koning-Stadhouder Willem III 1688–1702* (Assen, 1938), 126, transl. from German.

able command of English admirals.[105] The most prominent members of William's entourage thus tended to be selected for their military capacities.[106]

English diplomats likewise protested against the favour shown to the King's and Portland's Dutch clients. William allowed his English envoys to work side by side with Dutch representatives, but when real business had to be done he chose to rely on the efforts of trusted envoys.[107] Anglo-Dutch diplomatic co-operation during this period was reasonably successful, but relations between British and Dutch envoys were often strained. The Dutch and British resident in Constantinople, for instance, were hardly on speaking terms, and tended to have separate audiences to the Porte of which they did not inform each other. Van Heemskerck encroached upon the British resident's terrain as well, causing widespread resentment amongst British envoys such as George Stepney.[108]

The most vocal protest came from the particularly able and ambitious Stepney, who hoped that the King 'may be desired not to suffer strangers any more to concern themselves with our affairs, which is a scandall to our nation, and cannot but embroile us ... There is no dealing with the King when a Dutchman comes into competition'.[109] Portland was in close correspondence with Stepney's Dutch colleague, Johan Ham.[110] In spite of his envy Stepney confessed that Ham, who had considerable experience having served under Amerongen in Berlin for more than a decade, is 'very diligent and generally very well informed of affaires.' Stepney bitterly complained, though, that Ham was 'a creature of my Lord Portland'.[111] To Strafford he confided that Portland's expressions

> ... were very much a courtier's way of dealing. But at the bottom I must assure you he is the man who has hindered me, not so much out of ill will towards me, as of favour to Ham and Keppell. Mr Blathwayt does as good as tell me so; but wee are not allow'd to speak our minds.[112]

But Portland did not necessarily favour Dutch envoys, some of whom were also excluded from the inner circle, whereas Englishmen like Baron Lexington and Richard Hill can be considered Portland's clients. Stepney's objection must be interpreted with care, and may be better explained as a symptom of ordinary faction struggle rather than xenophobia.

---

105   Childs, *British Army*, 74, 76.
106   D. Rubini, *Court and Country 1688–1702* (London, 1968), 14, 24.
107   These were not necessarily Dutchmen though, as many English envoys complained. Cf. M. Lane, 'The Diplomatic Service under William III', *Transactions of the Royal Historical Society*, 4th series, 10 (1927), 87–109.
108   E.g. Nottingham to Heinsius 23 December 1692, HMC, *Finch Mss*, IV. 530–31; Whitcombe to Trumbull 26 February 1692, 26 March 1692, Cooke to Trumbull 2 April 1692, 9 October 1692, HMC, *Downshire Mss*, I. 398, 402, 404, 413.
109   Quoted in Lane, 'The Diplomatic Service', 103.
110   Portland to Stepney 12/22 July 1694 ('Camp de Rostbeck'), TNA:PRO, SP 105/82, f° 225–6.
111   Stepney to Colt 11 March 1693 NS, TNA:PRO, SP 105/58, f° 77v°.
112   Stepney to Strafford n.d. June 1694, TNA: SP 105/54, f° 32r°. Of course, Stepney was wrong about Keppel.

V

William's reliance on the Court Tories proved ultimately disappointing, but the taking on board of the Court Whigs quickly resulted in success. The Whig Junto managed to obtain an unprecedented £5 million from Parliament during the winter session of 1693/1694, as well as permission to augment the forces by an additional 20,000 troops. As a result the Allies managed to achieve numerical superiority over the French in the Low Countries, offering the possibility to initiate an offensive.

The shift mainly took place in 1695. At the beginning of the campaign William's enlarged army was able to split up, and started investing fort Knokke, while keeping an eye on Namur. The King had decided to undertake his first major offensive of the war, and in early July he marched east to besiege the seemingly impregnable Namur, fallen to the enemy in 1692. Vauban had strengthened the fortress and the French marshal, the Duke of Villeroi, risked leaving it in order to chase the now weakened army of the Prince of Vaudemont throughout the west of Flanders. Allied strategy profited from Portland's intelligence machine working more smoothly now than ever. In July, his aides managed to intercept some letters of the Sun King to Boufflers. Portland forwarded them to Shrewsbury to have them deciphered by John Wallis, an Oxford mathematician. The letters indicated that Louis had ordered Boufflers to hold out in the fortress, whilst Villeroi had received instructions to create a diversion in Flanders.[113] Consequently, Portland was able to reassure William that a siege could continue without the enemy approaching. It was only in late July when Villeroi realised that the siege, with the help of the famed Dutch engineer Menno van Coehoorn, proceeded swiftly and satisfactorily. He now moved to intimidate the enemy and bombarded Brussels. Meanwhile the city of Namur had fallen, and William effectively blocked Villeroi, giving the besiegers a chance to capture the citadel as well. Reporting to Lexington, Portland apologetically wrote that 'We have been in the trenches and on horseback almost night and day'.[114] On 29 August, Portland was despatched to demand the surrender of the defenders, since no army was coming to their relief.[115] Major assaults were launched that day and the following, and on 1 September Portland managed to convince the defenders that their efforts were futile.[116]

Boufflers decided to surrender, and Portland wrote to Lexington that Namur had fallen: 'If this good news does not satisfy you, I will put another grain in the scale, and tell you that our fleet has avenged, in part, on Calais the bombardment of Brussels.'[117] The French army was offered a free exit, but Boufflers himself

---

113 Intercepted correspondence in NUL, PwA 2521; Portland to Shrewsbury 14 July 1695 (Camp before Namur), *Private and Original Correspondence of Charles Talbot, Duke of Shrewsbury etc.*, ed. W. Coxe (London, 1821), 91–2.

114 Portland to Lexington 5 August 1695 ('du Camp devant Namure'), BL, Add Mss 46525, f° 110r°, transl. from French.

115 Stepney to Lexington 20/30 August 1695, TNA:PRO, SP 105/54, f° 155.

116 Stepney to Trumbull 22 August/1 September 1695, TNA:PRO, SP 105/54, f° 157.

117 Portland to Lexington 3 September 1695 ('Camp d'Austin pres Namur'), BL, Add Mss 46525, f°113r°, transl. from French.

was arrested by Portland, pending an exchange for captured allied regiments.[118] Portland was willing to release the marshal and give him a passport to travel to France via any route, if Boufflers could transmit the royal assurance that some Allied regiments would be released.[119] But the regiments were still detained, and Boufflers consequently remained in Maastricht. The encounter between Portland and Boufflers formed a somewhat curious overture to their cordial friendship, from which important political advantages would soon materialise.[120] To Shrewsbury, Portland wrote exhilaratedly:

> This is so glorious a conquest, and at the same time so advantageous, that I think has not been equalled for many years. It will greatly change the aspect of affairs, and puts us in a condition to make either war or peace better, without suffering terms to be imposed on us, as France has hitherto done.[121]

The fall of Namur had no positive effect on the war along the Rhine, however, which Portland noticed almost in despair:

> ... they hesitate along the Rhine with their action as they let us deal with all the French forces, we have to fear a neutrality in Catalonia, and meanwhile the minister of the Emperor cries out against peace, and simply let slip the occasions to make peace, which is an incomprehensible thing of which the end could be fatal for the whole of Christendom, of which God delivers us.[122]

Nevertheless, the campaign of 1695 had proved decisive. The Allies had halted the French offensive, but were unable to reverse it, both because a strategic stalemate had been reached and because the resources of the main belligerents were close to exhaustion.

VI

Central to the recovery of the Allied strategic position and the ultimate success in containing French expansion had been the Financial Revolution in England. The campaigns on the continent had drained English funds, making it imperative for the government to find new expedients to finance the war. The position of the British was visibly strengthened by the improved financial infrastructure after the establishment of the Bank of England.

For some years now Portland had been actively involved in financial affairs. In the summer of 1694 he had tried to raise money for the army in Flanders, and

---

118   Gaultier to Portland 20 September 1695, NUL, PwA 155; Stepney to Trumbull 26 August/5 September 1695, TNA:PRO, SP 105/54, f° 163.

119   Boufflers to Portland 11 September 1695, NUL, PwA 172.

120   Portland to Boufflers 19 Oct. 1695, NUL, PwA 174.

121   Portland to Shrewsbury 6 September 1695 (Camp of Boquette, near Namur), Coxe, *Private and Original Correspondence*, 104–5.

122   Portland to Lexington 29 September 1695 ('Camp de Promilles'), BL, Add Mss 46525, f° 107v°, transl. from French.

from the spring of 1695 he kept in close correspondence with Charles Montagu, Chancellor of the Exchequer and member of the Whig Junto, the chief initiator of the financial reforms. With him Portland co-ordinated attempts to obtain ready money for the Flanders army, and he had had some success in doing so in collaboration with a deputation from the Bank of England to the continent.[123] Montagu was able to promise Portland to send three representatives with an advancement of £50,000 in May 1695.[124]

In 1696 a Recoinage Bill was enacted which called for the replacement of old clipped coins with new currency. By May 1696, however, the government was faced with an acute shortage of money. John Somers had already warned Portland that 'the difficulties about the coyn are very great'.[125] The repercussions were serious, and could force William to remain passive during the 1696 continental campaign. Desperate for cash, Portland had urged Schuylenburg for money, but he could only promise to forward some ƒ100,000 which was not even much for an emergency transfer.[126] William was doubtful whether the States General would agree on a loan, the more so since the Dutch were unwilling to make any deals in England as long as the financial situation was uncertain.[127] Blathwayt pressed Godolphin to send supplies immediately since the army could not be kept together. The Lords Justices, upon hearing the appeals of the Lord Treasurer, stated the 'impossibility they were under to furnish any considerable sum ... . They saw no way for supplying the army'.[128] William anxiously wrote to Portland:

> I have received by the last courier from England a letter from the Duke of Shrewsbury, by which he plainly tells me that he does not see a possibility for the money and credit to re-establish itself, and that therefore my only option is to make peace.[129]

The King decided to send Portland as an envoy with full powers 'to pump the nation': to assist the ministry, convoke the Lords Justices and call Parliament if necessary.[130]

'The arrival of the Earl of Portland yesterday afternoon caused a general surprise here', the Brandenburg envoy Bonnet reported.[131] Except for Lord Keeper John Somers, Portland found no ministers present, and he immediately sent for

---

123   Godolphin to William, 28 July 1694, 31 July 1694, *CSPD 1694–1695*, 242–5. Cf. *CTB*, X-iii. 1443; Montagu to Portland 17 May 1695, 21 June 1695 NS, NUL, PwA 935, PwA 936.

124   Montagu to Portland 17 May 1695, NUL, PwA 935.

125   Somers to Portland 19 June 1696, NUL, PwA 1180.

126   Schuylenburg to Portland 21 July 1696, NUL, PwA 1145.

127   S.B. Baxter, *William III* (London, 1966), 339; William to Portland 14 August 1696, NUL, PwA 1728; Hill to Shrewsbury 6 August NS 1696, HMC, *Buccleugh Mss*, II-i. 373.

128   Minutes of the proceedings of the Lords Justices of England, 14 July 1696, *CSPD 1696*, 296.

129   William to Portland 6 August 1696, Japikse, *Correspondentie*, XXIII. 179, transl. from French; Shrewsbury to William 21 July 1696, *CSPD 1696*, 280–81.

130   A. Pryme, *Diary of my Own Life etc.* (Durham, 1869), 108–9.

131   Dispatch Bonnet 28 July/7 August 1696, BL, Add Ms 30000A, f° 192r°, transl. from French.

Secretary of State Shrewsbury and Sunderland, the latter having retired to his estate Althorp. The next morning (27 July) Portland conferred with Shrewsbury, Somers and the Lords Justices, stated the urgency of his business and was informed of the steps being taken and the expedients proposed. Portland was willing to consider loans (even from the Land Bank, a Country rival of the Whig-dominated Bank of England), general subscriptions, or, as a last resort, convening Parliament.[132] He was accompanied by one of the directors of the Bank of Amsterdam, who was willing to advance £200,000 on stringent conditions.[133] A deal with a number of merchants came to nothing, Portland suggesting that they refused the conditions proposed and that they were probably not able to deliver the requested £46,000.[134]

Portland soon expressed his wish to return to the continent, but was pressed both by the King and the ministry to remain.[135] 'I am angry and ashamed to say how long it is believed necessary that I remain here', he wrote to Flanders, 'until there is something settled or adjusted concerning money.'[136] He arranged a dinner meeting with Paul Foley and representatives of the Land Bank, who promised to advance £40,000, but could not raise it.[137] On 4 August three letters were sent to William from Whitehall Palace, neither very hopeful. Godolphin thought that 'the scarcity of the "species" of money will still disappoint us of finding any considerable sum by any method that can be proposed'.[138] Shrewsbury hoped that 'God delivers us from these present straits'.[139] Portland quarrelled with the Lord Treasurer,[140] and proposed a number of alternatives, determined to succeed in his mission.[141] With the merchants and the Land Bank unable to provide, they could request a loan from the City, raise a general subscription, or raise a sum of money from the Exchequer.[142] The second option failed, the last was blocked by William, since it was too risky.[143] A meeting was held between the Treasury and the Lords Justices to agree on a loan. Land tax was also considered. At the end of August Portland, after having exerted

---

132   NUL, PwA 2017; Portland to William 28 July 1696 OS (Whitehall Palace), Japikse, *Correspondentie*, XXIII. 183–4.
133   Cook to Treby 4 August 1696, HMC, *The Manuscripts of Sir William Fitzherbert ...* (London, 1893), 41–2; Bret to Huntingdon 30 July 1696, HMC, *Manuscripts of ... the Manor House, Ashby-de-la-Zouche* (4 vols, London, 1930), II. 271.
134   Portland to William 31 July 1696 (Whitehall Palace), Japikse, *Correspondentie*, XXIII. 183–4.
135   Shrewsbury to William 31 July 1696, *CSPD 1696*, 310. William to Portland 20 August 1696, Japikse, *Correspondentie*, XXIII. 191.
136   Portland to William 28 July 1696 (Whitehall Palace), Japikse, *Correspondentie*, XXIII. 183, transl. from French.
137   Stockdale to Viscount Irwin 22 August 1696, HMC, *Manuscripts in Various Collections* (8 vols. London, 1901–14), VIII. 82.
138   Godolphin to William 4 August 1696 OS, *CSPD 1696*, 317.
139   Shrewsbury to William 4 August 1696 OS, ibid., 318.
140   Shrewsbury to William 31 July 1696 OS, ibid., 310.
141   Portland to William 4 August 1696 OS (Whitehall Palace), Japikse, *Correspondentie*, XXIII. 187–9.
142   Portland to William 4 August 1696 OS (Whitehall Palace), ibid.
143   William to Portland 20 August 1696, Japikse, *Correspondentie*, XXIII. 191–2.

his influence with the Bank of England,[144] was finally able to communicate the good news that £200,000 had been guaranteed by the Bank due to a general subscription.[145] Measures for another general subscription should still be considered, Portland, suggested; 'strike the iron when is hot'.[146] He left London on 28 August.[147] Though the Bank had promised to immediately advance £50,000, it took some time before the measures took effect, and only in October could Portland reassure paymaster general Richard Hill that bills of exchange were on their way, meanwhile expressing his anger with the delays.[148]

VII

In the spring of 1696 the Williamite settlement was in danger of a threat of an entirely different nature. Rumours about an impending plot against the King's life and an invasion scare caused an upheaval in March. The death of Queen Mary a year earlier had weakened William's constitutional position, at least in the eyes of the Jacobites, who felt that a new attempt on William's life could dramatically alter the state of affairs. A number of plotters had concocted a plan to attack William and his train near Turnham Green, which the King passed on his weekly hunting trip to Richmond. On 23 February, two days before an intended trip, an acquaintance of Portland's, Fisher, told him of a plan to attack and assassinate the King. The plotters planned to send 46 men, thereby outnumbering the King's servants two to one. Portland relayed this information to the King, who remained sceptical; the 1690s were full of plots and rumours, mostly chimerical. The next evening, however, Portland was visited in his office in Whitehall Palace by another reluctant plotter, Captain Prendergrass, who not only confirmed what Fisher had said, but also told Portland that the assassination would be accompanied by an invasion of James II's supporters from Calais and a general insurrection of Catholics and Jacobites.[149] The King still being sceptical, Portland threatened to make the matter public unless the King agreed to cancel his plans; William gave in and the hunt for the next day was called off.[150] Upon receiving the information about the assassination attempt, Portland immediately set things in motion to arrest those involved. 'The names of most of their group of accomplices were known', he wrote to Lexington, 'all those

---

144 J..E.T. Rogers, *The First Nine Years of the Bank of England* (Oxford/New York 1887), 68.

145 Portland to William 25 August 1696 (Whitehall Palace), Japikse, *Correspondentie*, XXIII. 195.

146 Portland to William 25 August 1696 (Whitehall Palace), ibid., 196, transl. from French.

147 Saunière to States General 28 August 1696, BL, Add Mss 17677 QQ, f° 519r°.

148 Portland to Hill 5 October 1696, 26 October 1696, NUL, PwA 653, PwA 655.

149 J. Garrett, *The Triumphs of Providence: the Assassination Plot, 1696* (Cambridge, 1980), 135–6.

150 Brande to States General 6 March 1696, Saunière to States General 6 March 1696, BL, Add Mss 17677 QQ, f° 51–4, 287–90.

who could be found were seized.'[151] After the arrest of the plotters, Portland was engaged for several weeks with prolonged interrogations of the suspects – his notes of which have survived – to uncover the dimensions of the conspiracy.[152]

Portland had been earlier involved in dealing with conspiracies. Reports with regard to the interrogation of suspects of the Montgomery Plot in 1690 were sent to the Queen and the Lord Justices, but also forwarded to Portland who was then on campaign in Ireland. The Earl was similarly informed about the proceedings concerning the Lancashire Plot in 1694.[153] The routine gathering of intelligence about matters of security would be handled by the Secretaries of State.[154] They informed Portland when anything important came up, but he also received intelligence from his own sources.[155] He had agents and informers in city councils, in Parliament and in the streets. He maintained a private correspondence with agents and diplomats abroad and had secret agents in France. He often received anonymous letters or was visited by informers at his office in Whitehall Palace.[156] Portland was also involved in the employment of spies. He built a network of informers that infiltrated suspect groups and searched the streets. In 1695 Somers recommended the services of a certain Chaloner, who had made 'many and considerable discoveries of the dealings of the Jacobites'.[157] The Jacobite Earl of Ailesbury, who was arrested in 1696 during the Assassination Plot, complained that Portland had employed his son's governor Chondan to spy on him in his own house.[158] In 1690 Portland had been approached by Simpson, a spy who double-crossed him as he was involved in the Montgomery Plot; one year later Portland again made a miscalculation by making use of the services of the notorious impostor William Fuller.[159] Indeed, Portland occasionally encroached upon the Secretaries' responsibilities by personally handling aspects of the intelligence business. Referring to certain amounts of money to be paid to an informer, Secretary of State Shrewsbury professed that 'the heads relating to

---

151 Portland to Lexington 3/13 March 1696 (Kensington Palace), BL, Add Mss 46525, f° 119v°, transl. from French.

152 NUL, PwA 2462–519.

153 NUL, PwA 858–60; Trenchard to Portland 13 July 1695, NUL, PwA 1425.

154 Cf. Trumbull to Portland 25 June 1695, NUL, PwA 1435; NUL, PwA 1436.

155 E.g. anonymous letter 11 September 1689, *CSPD 1689–1690*, I. 250; anonymous letter to Portland 13 May 1690, HMC, *Finch Mss*, II. 280. Cf. Somers to Portland 28 May 1695, NUL, PwA 1177.

156 E.g. anonymous to Portland 13 May 1690, HMC, *Finch Mss*, II. 280.

157 Somers to Portland 28 May 1695, NUL, PwA 1177.

158 *Memoirs of Thomas, Earl of Ailesbury, etc.*, ed. W.E. Buckley (2 vols, Westminster, 1890), II. 405.

159 NUL, PwA 446 ff.; 9 December 1691, A. Grey, *Debates of the House of Commons from the Year 1667 to the Year 1694* (10 vols, London 1769), X. 203; Fuller complained that 'Lord Portland hindered and discouraged his discovery so long', Bishop of St David's to Huntingdon 10 December 1691, HMC, *Ashby Mss*, II. 222; P. Hopkins, 'Sir James Montgomerie of Skelmorlie' in: E. Corp and E. Cruickshanks (eds), *The Stuart Court in Exile and the Jacobites* (London/Rio Grande, 1995), 35–59, 45.

matter unknown to her Mat[y] and of which nobody but the King or yourself has any knowledge'.[160]

Alan Marshall has studied the intelligence services in the Restoration period, but surprisingly little research has been conducted to evaluate the response of the Williamite regime to the threats of conspiracies.[161] Evidence suggests that the intelligence services developed and improved. Referring to the Assassination Plot, Portland had written to his friend Lexington: 'We were at the edge of a precipice close to falling when the good God in His providence showed us in what peril we were, and the peril of all of Europe.'[162] However, later that year he wrote to Richard Hill: 'the Jacobites here threaten us again with some sort of hidden plan of the sort they tried last year, but we have prepared ourselves better.'[163] The plan Portland provided in 1692 to systematically search London is of particular interest. It suggested for 'an able person [to] be employed to make a list of all streets in and near London, in alphabetical order. These will be divided in eight parts, each division will be taken care of by one who makes a list of all inns, horses, of persons coming and going'. Inquiries should be made about persons in private lodgings, meeting places of non-jurors, horse markets and gunsmiths were to be checked.[164] Little is known yet about its implementation or impact, and more research is needed to see whether Williamite intelligence really responded successfully to the challenges.

There may have been three reasons why Portland played a pivotal role in the intelligence activities during the 1690s in England. Firstly, given his experience on the eve of the Glorious Revolution, it seemed natural that he would assume responsibility for internal and external security. Secondly, the continuous Jacobite threat undermined the confidence William could have in any of his servants, even his Secretaries of State. There were few courtiers who did not contact St Germain at some stage. Marlborough, for instance, had been suspected of high treason in 1694. Portland obviously could not be suspected of Jacobite sympathies.

A last reason was Portland's involvement in the gathering of intelligence in the United Provinces, as indeed the Williamite settlement was threatened on both sides of the Channel. Dissatisfaction with the war led some to initiate secret negotiations with the French. When William's cousin Hendrik Casimir, the Frisian Stadholder, felt slighted at the appointment of Holstein-Plön as commander, he initiated talks with the French agent D'Asfelt in 1694. These were unimportant in themselves, but the case of Simon van Halewijn (prosecuted for high treason) the preceding year had shown how vulnerable the Republic was to French intrigues. Van Halewijn had turned against William, and had said to be rather dead than '*dobbe dobbe dob* and

---

160 Shrewsbury to Portland 22 June 1694, NUL, PwA 1374.

161 A. Marshall, *Intelligence and Espionage in the Reign of Charles II, 1660–1685* (Cambridge, 1994).

162 Portland to Lexington 3/13 March 1696 (Kensington Palace), BL, Add Mss 46525, f° 118r°, transl. from French.

163 Portland to Hill 10 November 1696 (Kensington Palace), NUL, PwA 658, transl. from French.

164 HMC, *Finch Mss*, IV. 160–61.

march to the beat of the King of England's drum'.[165] Portland put heavy pressure on the Frisian stadholder to explain matters and demanded to know the contents of his conversations with D'Asfelt. Portland's covert employment of the Overijssel nobleman Rutger van Haarsolte, a confidant of Hendrik Casimir, to keep him informed of the Frisian Stadholder's diplomatic escapades, formed another tentacle in his intelligence network.[166] In the summer of 1696, only months after the discovery of the Assassination Plot, High Councillor Hubert Roosenboom informed Portland that an organ player in The Hague, Van Blanckenburg, had been bribed to assist in the assassination of the King while the latter was attending service.[167]

Portland also received information about the state of affairs in the United Provinces from his subordinates. Christoffel Tromer, his secretary and Steward of his Rhoon estate and Postmaster of Breda, played an important role in this, much of which can be gleaned through their correspondence. Tromer was Portland's secretary as early as 1680,[168] and like Portland was briefly in England in 1685.[169] He had not accompanied Portland during the invasion of 1688, but he was in London in the spring of 1689. He must have returned to The Hague later that year to take care of his affairs.[170] There is no doubt that Portland trusted his secretary, as he wrote in a will in 1691, referring his sister to Tromer for a sincere account of his affairs.[171] The Secretary had contact with Portland's Dutch relatives; in December 1689 Tromer reported to Portland that his brothers and sisters had arrived in Sorgvliet to spend some time there. In 1702, Portland's son sent his letters to his father by means of the Secretary.[172] Tromer was actively involved with Portland's secret intelligence network in 1687 and 1688,[173] and he had helped with the preparations for the Glorious Revolution, William writing to Portland from Het Loo asking Tromer to show copies of the *Declaration* to George Melville.[174] In 1698 Anthonie Heinsius sent his letters about the secret negotiations on the Spanish Partition Treaties to Portland via the secretary.[175] Tromer remained in

---

165 Quoted in G. de Bruin, *Geheimhouding en Verraad. De Geheimhouding van Staatszaken ten tijde van de Republiek (1600–1750)* (The Hague, 1991), 544–56, esp. 549. Literal transl. from Dutch, a fancy phrase referring to the sound of a drum.

166 Portland to Haarsolte 26 February 1694 (Kensington Palace), 26 March 1694 (Kensington Palace), Japikse, *Correspondentie*, XXIII. 381–2, 385–6.

167 Saunière to States General 6 March 1696, BL, Add Mss 17677 QQ, f° 289v°–90r°; NUL, PwA 1912; Roosenboom to Portland 21 July 1696, NUL, PwA 1911. Cf. Galway to Portland 30 June 1696, NUL, PwA 1111, PwA 1112.

168 Tromer to Ellis, 16 October? 1680, BL, Add Mss 28875, f° 84r°.

169 Anonymous letter 5 Aug. 1685, TNA:PRO, SP 84/220, f° 9.

170 Tromer to Portland 18 April 1689, 9 September 1689, Japikse, *Correspondentie*, XXVIII. 110, 124.

171 Portland to Eleanora van Ittersum-Nijenhuis 30 March 1691 (Breda), Japikse, *Correspondentie*, 164.

172 Lord Woodstock to Portland 4 February 1702, NUL, PwA 73.

173 Anonymous letter, 18 December 1687, NUL, PwA 2110.

174 William to Portland 29 August 1688, Japikse, *Correspondentie*, 50.

175 Heinsius to Portland 24 March 1698, NUL, PwA 1945.

Portland's service until the latter's death in 1709, as a letter from his brother-in-law, Baron Arent van Wassenaer-Duyvenvoorde, suggests.[176]

Tromer also corresponded frequently with Portland's aide in England, Gaspar Henning, about the affairs of 'our master'.[177] This correspondence was used to transmit sensitive information to Portland, to protect it from the 'curiosity' of some.[178] It also contained regular news about events on the continent, and newsletters were frequently sent to London.[179] Many of Portland's financial affairs were handled by Willem van Schuylenburg, *Greffier* of William's Demesne Council, with whom Portland had to deal professionally, and with whom Tromer kept up a frequent correspondence as well.[180] Van Schuylenburg played an important role in channelling money to the Allies, and had also been involved in financial transactions in the summer of 1688.[181] Like Tromer, Schuylenburg also kept Portland informed of many affairs in the United Provinces unrelated to his private affairs. Tromer and Schuylenburg played an important role in enabling Portland to maintain his Dutch estates whilst in England. Schuylenburg also informed Portland about the state of affairs in Breda, where he was Vice-Stadholder.[182]

Jacob van Leeuwen remained Portland's secretary for Dutch affairs until the end of his career, but seldom resurfaced during the 1690s.[183] Portland also employed a number of informers in several Dutch cities and the Amsterdam Stock Exchange. A few key correspondents notified him of the proceedings in the States Assemblies.[184] In Overijssel Portland's relatives held key positions, and he corresponded frequently with his brother, Lord of Diepenheim.

Portland also patronised a number of Huguenots,[185] including scholars such as Michel le Vassor and Paul Rapin de Thoyras, who would act as governor to his son Woodstock.[186] It would be difficult to consider Portland as a patron of literature, but both Vassor and Thoyras were prolific authors, the former even dedicating a study to Lord Woodstock.[187] But the real significance of these Huguenots in Portland's clientele lay in their practical capacities. Several of them acted as his secretary at various stages of his career. Abel Tassin d'Allonne, for instance, a Protestant refugee, had been the secretary of Mary, but had also been involved in missions to England

---

176 Van Wassenaer-Duyvenvoorde to Portland 11 October 1709, NUL, PwA 1564.
177 Tromer to Henning 3 May 1689, BL, Eg Mss 1707, f° 54, transl. from French.
178 Tromer to Henning 6 May 1689, BL, Eg Mss 1707, f° 56–7, transl. from French.
179 Tromer to Henning 23 August 1689, BL, Eg Mss 1707, f° 69.
180 E.g. Portland's account book, NUL, PwV 49.
181 Landgrave of Hesse-Cassel to Portland 15 July 1694, NUL, PwA 636; Portland to Hill 15 January 1697, NUL, PwA 663, William to Portland 27 May 1688, 7 June 1688, 26 Aug. 1688, Japikse, *Correspondentie*, XXIII. 38, 42, 47.
182 E.g. Van Schuylenburg to Portland 21 July 1696, NUL, PwA 1145.
183 Van Leeuwen to Prior 2/12 July 1698, HMC, *Bath Mss*, III. 233.
184 Portland to Cuperus 7/17 June 1689 (Hampton Court Palace), Japikse, *Correspondentie*, XXVIII. 115–16; Portland to William 25 January 1690 (The Hague), Japikse, *Correspondentie*, XXIII. 77.
185 Cf. page 250–51.
186 Cf. Ch. 4.
187 Cf. Ch. 5.

before the Revolution. In 1697 he prepared Portland's embassy in Paris. A year later Portland managed to give him a post as William's secretary for Dutch affairs after the death of Constantijn Huygens jr.[188] Rene Saunière de L'Hermitage, a French Huguenot who had emigrated to London in 1686, seems to have acted as a governor to Portland's children. He also became an agent of the States General in London,[189] and was well acquainted with Jean de Robéthon.[190] He worked for Portland and Dijkveld in the 1690s and later became a contact of Portland's at the Hanoverian court. Guillaume de Lamberty acted as Portland's secretary between 1698 and 1700, and (like Rapin) became a chronicler of the political events of Europe during this age.[191] Few details about the relationship between Portland and these Huguenots can be established, but it is significant that the Earl managed to surround himself with these men, who had excellent contacts and contributed to establishing an international intelligence network.

VIII

To Stephen Baxter, William's control of the allied armies lay at the heart of what he perceived as a Dual Monarchy between the United Provinces and the British Isles.[192] The diplomatic, financial and military resources of the three kingdoms and the republic were pooled in order to wage the war against France. The Anglo-Dutch favourite played an important role in this development. During the Nine Years War Portland gained operational experience, although he never distinguished himself on the battlefield. He held high military rank in both the English and Dutch armies. Although he was on the King-Stadholder's staff of military advisers, it is difficult to claim that he played an essential role.

Portland's main contribution to the war effort was, however, of an organisational nature. Firstly, he seemed to have acted as William's secretary for military affairs in an informal setting, creaming off some responsibilities from the Secretary-at-War and the Secretaries of State. In this capacity Portland aided William, who was particularly concerned about keeping a tight grip on military affairs, to keep an overview, and they must have frequently discussed military strategy. Secondly, Portland's dual military ranks aided him in his efforts to co-ordinate the Anglo-Dutch war efforts. He discussed military affairs with the Secretaries of State and the Dutch Grand Pensionary and officials of the admiralties, and was present at joint Anglo-Dutch meetings on military strategy. He also kept up a correspondence with Allied commanders, and received information on enemy movements and Allied armies from a network of correspondents, both informal agents and diplomats. This also enabled him to play a role in counter-intelligence. Lastly, he was concerned

---

188 D.C.A. Agnew, *Protestant Exiles from France etc.* (2 vols, s.l., 1886), II. 207–8.
189 See his lengthy and informative despatches in BL, Add Mss 17677.
190 Agnew, *Protestant Exiles*, II. 199.
191 L. Frey and M. Frey (eds), *The Treaties of the War of the Spanish Succession – An Historical and Critical Dictionary* (London, 1995), 237. Cf. page 250.
192 Baxter, *William III*, 281 ff.

with the financial implications of the war effort, being actively involved in securing funds for the armies.

Chapter 7

Ganymede: The Image of the Favourite

Historians studying the reign of William have not paid sufficient attention to the rhetoric on favouritism which frequently surfaced in pamphlets and parliamentary debates. Often critical, it targeted the conduct of the King's foreign favourites, in particular the Earl of Portland. The fear that a powerful individual could rise to a position which rendered the King a mere figurehead was a common theme in English history and deeply entrenched in the collective political mind.[1] Hence a famous pamphlet – published after Portland was granted land in Wales in 1695 – voiced the fear that Britain now had a 'Dutch Prince of Wales', a puissant foreigner who was second in command.[2] Kevin Sharpe and Steve Zwicker have pointed out the importance of studying polemic literature in Stuart England as embedded within a political context.[3] This chapter analyses speeches and pamphlets criticising the favourite, as well as Williamite propaganda, and seeks to re-examine the reputation of Portland. By placing anti-favourite rhetoric within a longer established literary tradition, and by comparing it with criticism of Portland in the United Provinces, its deeper structure can be exposed, providing tools for understanding the criticism of favouritism as a manifestation of political discontent. A dialogue took place on various levels within the political nation in which the core political issues of the post-revolutionary settlement figured.

I

On 5 February 1691 William, returning from England for the first time, entered The Hague in a triumphal procession. The citizens had arranged for arches to be raised along the route through which he and a long train of noblemen entered amid loud acclamations from the public. Portland's status had visibly increased. He sat in his own coach just behind the King-Stadholder's during the entry.[4] Such proximity to

---

1   Of course this was a common theme in continental monarchies as well, but (within the context of this debate) not so in the Republic.
2   This obviously gained significance with William being childless. The title was 'conferred' upon Portland for the grant he received, normally associated with the Prince of Wales. Cf. Ch. 4. *Gloria Cambriae: Or, The Speech of a Bold Britain in Parliament, against a Dutch Prince of Wales, Mr Price* (London, 1702) in: Somers, *First Collection*, III. 98–105.
3   K. Sharpe and S.N. Zwicker, *Politics of Discourse. The Literature and History of Seventeenth-Century England* (Berkeley/Los Angeles/London, 1987), 2.
4   P. Schazmann, *The Bentincks. The History of a European Family* (London, 1976), 88. Cf. G. Bidloo, *Relation du Voyage de Sa Majesté Brittanique en Hollande etc.* (The Hague, 1692), 94, 103.

the monarch symbolised power and influence. When William had left London for Ireland on 4 June 1690, for instance, he had snubbed Prince George of Denmark by offering the seat in his coach to his favourite rather than to the Prince. Two weeks after the glorious entry into The Hague, Portland received the King and several allied princes and noblemen for falcon hunting at his estate at Sorgvliet.[5] A week later, on 25 February, the King

> ... went to take a walk for diversion at Sorgvliet with Their Highnesses the Electors of Bavaria and Brandenburg, the Landgrave of Hesse, and many other princes and gentlemen, which His Majesty entertained there. It was extraordinary to watch the crowds of people strolling to and fro.

In March the favourite hosted a dinner at Sorgvliet again for the King and the Elector of Brandenburg.[6]

The noble entourage that was entertained with falcon hunting at Sorgvliet would have been led by Portland through the garden to the so-called Parnassus Mount – an artificial hill from which both the sea and The Hague could be seen. The guests would have passed a statue of Diana on top of the hill, marking the border between garden and grounds for hunting, one of Portland's passionate pastimes.[7] Portland's gardens at Sorgvliet were famed for their beauty and harmonious mixture of classic art and exotic garden features. The high-placed guests would also have seen in the elaborate gardens a famous artificial cave known as the grotto of Ganymede. Abducted by an eagle, this mythological prince of Troy was forced to leave his home to become cupbearer to Zeus. The grotto was one of the most remarkable features of the Sorgvliet gardens. By presenting himself as Ganymede, Portland could portray his own position as loyal servant to the King. The recurring Ganymede image was evident in the favourite hosting a dinner for the King and his Allies. In the royal palace Portland had been known to stand sometimes behind William's chair to attend to his needs during dinner, embodying the Ganymede image to perfection.[8]

Portland succeeded remarkably well in presenting himself as William's closest confidant. He was almost always in his entourage and usually physically close to the King, as evidenced by contemporary reports, paintings and drawings. In a drawing made of William at Brixham the favourite is at his side.[9] Perhaps the most interesting painting is a double portrait by Isaac Soubre of William and Bentinck in 1675 made just after their recovery from smallpox – a clever image of the master and his loyal servant. The original painting is a portrait of William alone, who clearly occupies the centre of the canvas. Bentinck is later painted behind him so as to make it look like a double portrait. Was it done to acknowledge his loyalty after the event as Noordam

---

   5   Bidloo, *Relation*, 81.
   6   Ibid., 84, transl. from French.
   7   A description of Sorgvliet can be found in J.D. Hunt and E. de Jong (eds), *The Anglo–Dutch Garden in the Age of William and Mary. De Gouden Eeuw van de Hollandse Tuinkunst* (Amsterdam/London, 1988), 163–79.
   8   H.W. Chapman, *Mary II, Queen of England* (London, 1953), 242.
   9   Atlas van Stolk, Cat. No. 2739. Reproduced in W. Troost, *William III, the Stadholder–King: A Political Biography* (Aldershot, 2005), 201.

suggests? Was it Bentinck himself who commissioned the painting?[10] Whatever the initial purpose, the portrait gives a splendid image of the intimacy between the King and his servant.

Portland's collection of paintings was not very extensive, but some were done by leading artists of his time. It is difficult to determine either the location or contents of the original art collection. Portland left few paintings at Bulstrode, but the inventory of Sorgvliet mentions only three minor landscape paintings.[11] He took a keen interest in the visual arts. Constantijn Huygens mentioned a number of conversations they had had about the display of paintings in the royal palaces, and he was ordered by Portland to instruct Godfrey Kneller to make a portrait of the King.[12] Portland was impressed by Gaspar Netscher whom he had commissioned to paint portraits of his first wife Anne Villiers and William III.[13] The main purpose of the art collection was self-aggrandisement, reflecting the status and recounting the achievements of the favourite-soldier. The collection of portraits reads like a gallery of the highlights of his life. In 1697 Sir Godfrey Kneller painted him as Knight of the Order of the Garter, which he had then just received; copies of this work are now in England as well as in Holland. In 1698 Portland sat in Hyacinthe Rigaud's studio in Paris for what would become the most impressive portrait, commemorating his grandest moment as Ambassador Extraordinary, wearing the Order of the Garter in a near-regal pose.[14] Portraits commissioned from Rigaud of the Grand Dauphin and Louis XIV were additional reminders of his grand embassy, during which he also commissioned nine portraits of Ladies of the French court.[15] The latest portrait, dating from 1706, shows Portland amidst his wife and children, a wealthy, retired landed aristocrat.[16]

The propaganda value of art has in recent years been emphasised by students of garden history. Erik de Jong has argued that William's visit to Sorgvliet in 1691 preceding the Congress of The Hague had profound political implications, Portland having made his country house a symbol of Orangism.[17] Knowledge of the classics combined with extensive reading of modern garden literature inspired him to weave symbolic elements into the garden designs. His close co-operation with Romeyn de Hooghe strongly suggests that these designs had some elements of propaganda. De

---

10   *Catalogue of the Pictures belonging to His Grace the Duke of Portland, KG, at Welbeck etc.*, ed. R.W. Goulding (Cambridge, 1936), no. 952, 303. Cf. D.J. Noordam, *Riskante Relaties. Vijf Eeuwen Homoseksualiteit in Nederland, 1233–1733* (Hilversum, 1995), 109. Illus. 1.

11   Goulding, *Catalogue*, x. There are few references to Portland's paintings in his correspondence. Cf. *Vertue Note Books*, eds K.A. Esdaile, Earl of Ilchester and H.M. Hake (6 vols, Oxford, 1930–55), V. 52.

12   10 September 1689, Huygens, *Journaal*, I-i. 175; 24 November 1695, 2 December 1695, 2 March 1696, Huygens, *Journaal*, I-ii. 551, 554, 575. Cf. 24 May 1676, 25 June 1676, Huygens, *Journaal*, II. 95, 107.

13   *Catalogue of the Pictures belonging to His Grace the Duke of Portland, at Welbeck Abbey, and in London*, ed. C.F. Murray (London, 1894), 189.

14   Cf. cover illustration.

15   Goulding, *Catalogue*, 374–5. Cf. NUL, PwA 844–56, *passim*.

16   Goulding, *Catalogue*, no. 993, 311.

17   E. de Jong, *Natuur en Kunst. Nederlandse Tuin- en Landschapsarchitectuur 1650–1740* (Amsterdam, 1993), 65 ff.

Hooghe – undoubtedly with a certain dosage of obliging flattery – acknowledged that 'one can attribute the design of almost everything that is grand and rare' in the gardens of Het Loo to Portland.[18]

Portland influenced the changing styles of the royal gardens, both through the introduction of the so-called Anglo-Dutch garden style and French elements after his embassy to Paris.[19] A number of gardens that were laid out around Hampton Court Palace and especially Kensington Palace included elements that were specifically Dutch; they tended to be smaller, lacked a clear overall structure, but instead consisted of small independent sections with canals, hedges and topiary.[20] This particular style was copied by such men as William Temple, who integrated Dutch elements into his gardens at Moor Park in Surrey. The Whig minister Thomas Wharton did so at his Winchendon House, and Secretary-at-War William Blathwayt at his country house in Gloucestershire. On the other side of the Channel, Arnold Joost van Keppel copied the garden style of Het Loo at his country house Voorst, as did Ginckel, who laid out gardens around Middachten.[21] These men also formed a socio-cultural circle, in which discussions on garden design functioned as a pretext to maintain a correspondence.[22] Such a relationship is evident in Portland's correspondence with Charles Mordaunt, the Countess of Sunderland or Gaspar Fagel.[23] Of course, it did not necessarily imply any political affiliation, as Portland also corresponded with the French nobility on his horticultural activities.

Nevertheless, some of the imagery used in William's gardens had explicit political connotations. Portland had been involved in the designing of the gardens of Het Loo and his own estate Sorgvliet, laid out an Anglo-Dutch garden around Bulstrode and the Lodge of Windsor Park.[24] The design of the gardens of Het Loo contained elements of political propaganda. William III was portrayed as Hercules, used as an image of Christian strength and virtue.[25] This Hercules imagery appeared

---

18   Quoted in ibid., 70n, transl. from French. Cf. page 98–101.

19   E.g. E. De Jong, 'Netherlandish Hesperides. Garden Art in the Period of William and Mary 1650–1702' in: J.D. Hunt and E. de Jong (eds), *The Anglo-Dutch Garden in the Age of William and Mary. De Gouden Eeuw van de Hollandse Tuinkunst* (Amsterdam, 1998), 15–40, 35.

20   J.D. Hunt, 'Anglo-Dutch Garden Art: Style and Idea' in: D. Hoak and M. Feingold (eds), *The World of William and Mary – Anglo-Dutch Perspectives on the Revolution of 1688–1689* (Stanford 1996), 188–200, 194–5 and *passim*.

21   Hunt and De Jong, *The Anglo-Dutch Garden*, 105–269; D. Jacques, et al. (eds), *The Gardens of William and Mary* (London, 1988), 36–61.

22   E. Edwards, 'Horticulture and Diplomacy: Politicians, Diplomats and Gardeners in the Late Seventeenth Century', conference paper, *Inside Out and Outside In: A New Look at the 17th Century Republic of Letters,* 12–13 December 2003, University of Aberdeen.

23   Cf. Ch. 2.

24   Surprisingly little is known about Portland's estate Bulstrode. Officially it was bought in 1706, but Portland's aid Talman seems to have been involved in the outlay of the gardens as early as 1690. Cf. J. Harris, *William Talman, Maverick Architect* (London, 1982), 46n, 49, 89; G.M. Hughes, *A History of Windsor Forest, Sunninghill, and the Great Park* (London/Edinburgh, 1890), 284.

25   Cf. S.B. Baxter, 'William III as Hercules: the Political Implications of Court Culture' in: L.G. Schwoerer (ed.), *The Revolution of 1688–1689: Changing Perspectives* (Cambridge,

on both sides of the Channel and can be found both at Het Loo and Hampton Court. In order to show one's allegiance to the Williamite settlement it became fashionable to imitate this symbolism. The rise of the so called Anglo-Dutch garden style can be traced back to the early 1690s, and must be to some extent attributed to Portland's activities. After 1702 the style was decidedly on the wane.[26]

II

Portland thus used art as Orangist propaganda, and the image of Ganymede in particular to emphasise his close relationship to the King. However, the Ganymede image had a double meaning, as it also symbolised a sodomitic relationship. As such it was employed by pamphleteers hoping to discredit the reputation of the favourite. Sodomy in turn was a metaphor for a number of vices. If anti-Dutch sentiments were exploited by the Jacobite and Country opposition to target the key elements of William's regime,[27] anti-favourite rhetoric was adopted to attack the man who embodied all the evils of the Williamite settlement. Julian Hoppit has aptly observed about King William, that the English could love the 'idea' (the Williamite settlement), but not the man. In Portland's case one could argue that they cared not about the man, but hated the 'idea' (the favourite).[28] In many respects, to the political nation Portland embodied the archetypal image of the 'evil counsellor'. Already in the spring of 1689 it was observed 'that the brunt of hatred and anger fell upon the favourite'.[29] Portland's obvious support for the continental war and his increasing role in ministerial management provided fuel for his enemies to launch assaults on the ministry and, beyond that, on the King himself. Portland realised he was fiercely unpopular with large sections of the political nation and was careful not to provide the opposition with any pretext.[30] Thus unlike the Earls of Danby or Sunderland, he was never impeached or forced out of office, and he remained, for ten years, an unassailable and untouchable force behind the throne. Although Portland tried to remain 'behind the curtain', he was nevertheless continuously attacked in pamphlets and the Commons throughout the 1690s. Indeed, it was essential to his role as favourite to function as a shield to protect the King's reputation; he absorbed criticism directed at his master and might ultimately be sacrificed on the altar of royal power. As Nathaniel Crouch, author of *The Unfortunate Court-Favourites of England*, observed: 'there are certain crises of Government, wherein Princes have

---

1992), 95–106.
    26   Hunt, 'Anglo-Dutch Garden Art: Style and Idea'. Horace Walpole later described Bulstrode as 'a melancholy monument of Dutch magnificence', quoted in: G.W. Keeton, *Lord Chancellor Jeffreys and the Stuart Cause* (London, 1965), 352.
    27   Cf. page 131–4.
    28   J. Hoppit, *A Land of Liberty? England 1689–1727* (Oxford, 2000), 135.
    29   23 March 1689, Huygens, *Journaal*, I-i. 98, trans. from Dutch
    30   He did so with success: only during the 1701 impeachment procedures did Parliament have specific evidence.

been obliged to Sacrifice their darling Ministers either to their own safety, or to the importunity of the People.'[31]

Throughout the seventeenth and eighteenth centuries several works were published studying the favourite as a historical phenomenon. The publication of *The Unfortunate Court-Favourites of England* in 1695 may not have been coincidental, as it marked the zenith of Portland's career and the rise in fortune of his rival, Arnold Joost van Keppel, the later Earl of Albemarle. The book contains no direct reference to William's Dutch entourage, in fact, the last favourites who are studied are those of Charles I; the Restoration parliamentary managers, such as the Earl of Danby, do not seem to qualify as favourites in the traditional sense. But the renewed interest in court favourites could well be explained by the re-emergence of the phenomenon after 1688. Crouch published many cheap and popular works on history and may have sensed that due to this development there would be demand for such a work.[32]

The rise of a new favourite at Court obviously incited renewed interest in historical overviews of favourites. *The Character of an Ill-Court-Favourite* (1681), translated from the French, studied favourites only in sixteenth century Spain and ancient Rome, but contemporaries must have had recent events in mind, as the Earl of Danby had been impeached and imprisoned in 1679. Between 1692 and 1695, during the ascendancy of Portland, at least three works on favourites appeared. In addition to Crouch's work, in 1692, for instance, a tragedy was re-staged at the Theater Royal on 'The Great Favourite, or, the Duke of Lerma', underlining the popularity of the theme. *The History of Prime Ministers and Favourites in England*, published in 1763, calls upon the new King George III not to become dependent upon one minister – an obvious reference to the 3rd Earl of Bute. Robert Walpole's career also witnessed renewed interest.[33] In 1651 the exiled Earl of Clarendon (a

---

31 [N. Crouch], *The Unfortunate Court-Favourites of England, Exemplified in some Remarks upon the Lives, Actions, and fatal Fall of divers Great Men, who have been Favourites to several English Kings and Queens etc.* (London, 1695).

32 R. Mayer, 'Nathaniel Crouch, Bookseller and Historian: Popular Historiography and Cultural Power in late Seventeenth-Century England', *Eighteenth-Century Studies*, 27 (1994), 391–419, *passim*.

33 The genre seems to have been thriving from the early seventeenth century until about the middle of the eighteenth century. Many of these works were published or reprinted in clustered periods, when a favourite or prime minister was at the zenith of his career or had just fallen out of favour. For instance, following the fall of the Earl of Danby (1679–81): J. Crowne, *The Ambitious Statesman, or, The loyal Favourite etc.* (London, 1679); *The Character of an Ill-Court-Favourite: Representing the Mischiefs that flow from Ministers of State when they are more Great than Good, etc.* (London, 1681); J. Banks, *The Unhappy Favourite: or, the Earl of Essex etc.* (London, 1682). During the zenith of Portland's position as favourite (1692–95): R. Howard, *The Great Favourite, or, the Duke of Lerma. A Tragedy* (edn London, 1692); E. de Refuge, *Arcana Aulica: or, Walsingham's Manual of Prudential Maxims, for the States-man and Courtier. To which is added Fragmenta Regalia: or, Observations on Queen Elizabeth, her Times and Favourites. By Sir Robert Naunton* (edn London, 1694); Crouch, *The Unfortunate Court-Favourites* (London, 1695). During the zenith of Marlborough's position as favourite and his fall (1706–12): E. Hyde, Earl of Clarendon, *The Characters of Robert Earl of Essex, Favourite to Queen Elizabeth and George D. of Buckingham, Favourite to K. James I and K. Ch. I with a Comparison* (edn London, 1706); *The Perfect Picture of*

future first minister) had published a work on Buckingham and Essex, in which the favourite of his executed master was vindicated.³⁴

A literary canon was established in which the favourite was endowed with certain characteristics and a set career path. *The Character of an Ill-Court-Favourite* condemns favourites in all manners, and describes a typical career:

> As the first advances of Ill-Court-Favourites are commonly base and shameful, their Progress *vile*, wicked and destructive, their short Continuances attended with Hazards and Anxieties, so their Eclipses are ever more fatal, and their falls desperate, they are generally surprised with Ruin ... .³⁵

Arrogance, greed, corruption and sodomy figured as the main characteristics of favourites. Sudden changes in fortune and a violent ending were often their fate: David Rizzio and the Duke of Buckingham were assassinated, the Earls of Essex and Strafford and Archbishop Laud executed. When Portland was threatened with impeachment in 1701 for negotiating the Spanish Partition Treaties, one MP was said to be reminded of 'the history of Sejanus', the favourite of Emperor Tiberius who was charged with high-treason and executed.³⁶

Crouch's *The Unfortunate Court-Favourites of England* provides a balanced, almost sympathetic analysis of their careers and reaches mixed conclusions:

> some Court-Favourites have justly merited the unhappy fate they met with, for their many Rapines, Insolencies and Enormities, as that others have been ruined meerly from the Caprichio or inconstant Temper of the Prince whom they served.³⁷

The author recounts the lives of such prominent favourites as Gloucester, Wolsey and Buckingham and offers firm judgments. Robert Devereux, Earl of Essex, for instance, is presented as a disinterested servant who had become the victim of the intrigues of court faction. The Duke of Buckingham, on the contrary, is 'cowardly, base in mind, opinion, and deserves not the name of a Gentleman or Souldier'.³⁸ Crouch, a publisher in his own right, was also responsible for a *History of the House*

---

a Favourite:, or, Secret Memoirs of Robert Dudley, Earl of Leicester (edn London, 1708); *Observations and Remarks upon the Lives and Reigns of King Henry VIII. King Edward VI, Queen Mary I, Queen Elizabeth and King James. With Particular Characters, after the Earl of Clarendon's Method, of all their Favourites etc.* (edn London, 1712). During Robert Walpole's ascendancy (1730–32): A. Smith, *Court Intrigues: or, An Account of the Secret Amours of our British Nobility* (London, 1730); J. Adamson, *The Reigns of King Edward II. And so far of King Edward III. As relates to the Lives and Actions of Piers Gaveston, Hugh de Spencer, and Roger, Lord Mortimer, etc.* (London, 1732). The Earl of Bute: *The History of Prime Ministers and Favourites, in England; from the Conquest down to the Present Time: with Reflections on the Fatal Consequences of their Misconduct, etc.* (London, 1763).

34   Clarendon, *Characters*.
35   *The Character of an Ill-Court-Favourite*, 31.
36   *The Parliamentary Diary of Sir Richard Cocks 1698–1702*, ed. D.W. Hayton (Oxford, 1996), 76–9.
37   Crouch, *The Unfortunate Court-Favourites*, 'to the reader'.
38   Ibid., 173.

of Orange and endorsed the principles of the Glorious Revolution.[39] Perhaps his balanced view of favourites was in tacit support of King William's favourite, who was under continuous public attack.

The Unfortunate Court-Favourites of England differed distinctively in tone from the numerous pamphlets that bear witness to the general dislike of the favourite, and in which the semblance of historical accuracy is lost in polemical rhetoric. Anonymous pamphlets had the added advantage that they could specifically name the favourite they were attacking rather than make allusions. Pamphlets published in the 1690s attacking Portland, however, should be interpreted in light of existing traditions. The charges were often imprecise; the 'Portland' of pamphleteers was a fictional, stereotypical character. The pattern of his career seemed all too familiar. A foreign favourite is easily caricatured and pamphleteers could draw inspiration from an available discourse. In a range of pamphlets erupting after 1688 specific charges based on factual information are extremely rare.[40] It was easy to accuse a rich and ambitious man of squandering his integrity, but the charge of corruption could not be substantiated. The evidence presented came from hostile sources and was based on rumour.[41]

Portland, raised into the peerage, was portrayed as a foreigner from a humble background, just like, for instance, the Prince of Eboli, a Portuguese nobleman of lowly origins who became the childhood friend and favourite of Philip II. The importance of the social status and background of the favourite can hardly be overestimated. *The Unfortunate Court-Favourite* has a high opinion of the Earl of Essex partly because of his noble lineage.[42] According to the Country Whig John Tutchin's *The Foreigners* (1700), Portland was 'Of mean descent, yet insolently proud, Shun'd by the Great, and hated by the Crowd; Who neither Blood nor Parentage can boast'.[43] The 'Advice to a Painter' (1697) likewise stated that Portland was 'Of undescended parentage, made great, By chance, his virtues not discovered yet'.[44]

The foreignness of some favourites, such as Eboli and Mazarin, only seemed to underline the abnormality of their careers. The majority of pamphlets referred to Portland as 'Bentinck' or 'Benting', thus emphasising his foreign background rather than using his naturalized English title. Often the name was also used in combination

---

39   Mayer, 'Nathaniel Crouch', 408.

40   E.g. *A Very Remarkable Letter from King William III. To his Favourite Bentinck, Earl of Portland, in French and English, together with Reflections thereon* in: Somers, *First Collection*, I. 356–62; *A Dialogue between K.W. and Benting, Occasioned by his Going into Flanders after the Death of the Queen* (London, 1695).

41   *Memoirs of Thomas, Earl of Ailesbury, etc.*, ed. W.E. Buckley (2 vols, Westminster, 1890). I. 227–8; T.B. Macaulay, *History of England from the Accession of James II* (6 vols, London, 1914), 2490–92; HMC, *The Manuscripts of the House of Lords Mss 1693–1695* (London, 1900), 557; *Cobbett's Parliamentary History of England etc. 1688–1702* (12 vols, London, 1806–12), V. 925; H. Horwitz, *Parliament, Policy and Politics in the Reign of William III* (Manchester 1977), 151–2; satirical verse on Portland, NUL, PwA 2035.

42   Crouch, *The Unfortunate Court-Favourites*.

43   J. Tutchin, *The Foreigners* (London, 1700).

44   'Advice to a Painter' (1697) in: *Poems of Affairs of State. Augustan Satirical Verse 1660–1714, VI: 1697–1704*, ed. F. H. Ellis (New Haven/London, 1970), 16–17.

with 'Myn Heer', the Dutch way of addressing a gentleman, and employed in many pamphlets as a dismissive reference to the Dutch. Thus 'Myn Heer Bentinck' is an abusive phrase referring to the foreigner who obviously does not deserve his English noble title. Targeting such charges, John Oldmixon published a panegyric poem on the occasion of Portland's embassy to Paris, stating that 'True British Graces in the Hero shine'.[45] *The Natives* (1700), a reply to *The Foreigners*, pointed to the fact that Portland was 'among the foreigners the first, By none but [England's] malecontents e'er curst'.[46] The most powerful defence of foreigners came from Daniel Defoe in his magisterial *The True-born Englishman*.[47]

III

Anticipating such xenophobia, William was careful from the start not to raise Dutchmen into the peerage – in fact Bentinck was the only one to receive an earldom in 1689, followed only by about half a dozen foreigners during the course of the 1690s. Notwithstanding the pamphleteers' accusations, Bentinck descended from an ancient noble family, although part of the regional squirarchy from the relatively insignificant eastern province of Overijssel. However, in 1676 William bequeathed to him the estate of Drimmelen, with the express purpose of making him eligible for a seat in the Holland *Ridderschap* – which predictably incited resentment from the Holland magnate families, such as the Noordwijks and Wassenaars. Nevertheless, by 1688 Bentinck was a respected member of that body and among the greatest nobles in the United Provinces, in wealth, influence and social status. *The Reverse: or, the Tables Turn'd* (1700) pointed to the noble backgrounds of Portland and Albemarle in their defence: 'Noble his birth, though foreign is his blood, (For other lands can shew a noble flood)'.[48]

Perceptions by English courtiers of Portland's reputed arrogance must be analysed with care. Macaulay already remarked that character judgements were bound to be negative because of cultural and linguistic barriers. Indeed, they fit in exactly with the standard repertoire of anti-Dutch sentiments – as indeed Portland's perception of the English seems rather stereotypical. The Dutch perceived the English as fickle and undependable, the English saw their neighbours as dull, cold and unimaginative.[49] Whilst acknowledging Portland's arrogant stance, Saint-Simon was positive about the impression he made in Paris:

Portland arrived with a personal splendour, a courtesy, an air of a man of the world and a courtier, with a galantry and a gracefullness which were surprising. With all that, a great

---

45   J. Oldmixon, *A Poem ... addressed to the ... Earl of Portland ... on his ... Return from his Embassy in France* (London, 1698).
46   *The Natives* (London, 1700).
47   D. Defoe, *The True-born Englishman. A Satyr* (London, 1701).
48   *The Reverse: or, the Tables Turn'd* (London, 1700).
49   D. Coombs, *The Conduct of the Dutch. British Opinion and the Dutch Alliance during the War of the Spanish Succession* (The Hague, 1958), 13–15.

deal of dignity, haughtiness even, but his judgments were sound and prompt, without any sense of arbitrariness.[50]

Favourites were typically charged with greed and corruption, as for instance in *The Foreigners* and *The True-Born Englishman Answer'd Paragraph by Paragraph*.[51] Accusations concerning Portland's integrity were also rampant. Rumours about Portland being guilty of corruption circulated at Court as early as 1689, when Nicolaas Witsen was told that Portland had made large profits: 'it has been estimated at thirty thousand rixdollars, on top of the one hundred thousand he has already received. But God knows whether it is true.'[52] The vastness of his clientele predictably incited rumours of nepotism in the bustling coffee houses in the City.[53] In July 1689 Portland and the Earl of Dorset, the Lord Chamberlain, were accused by the Commons of corruption.[54] When evidence emerged in 1695 of bribes offered by the East India Company in order to get the charter prolonged, Parliament ordered an enquiry that soon degenerated into a Whiggish witch-hunt for Tories and court members. The enquiries were pushed further, which, Portland wrote to Lexington, 'could touch their own members … they look to me like a bunch of people who get rather drunk, quarrel amongst each other, bloody each others' noses and then retire'.[55] But the party soon turned against others. Carmarthen, Nottingham, Trevor, Guy and Portland were all accused of having accepted substantial bribes: the ministers between £1,000 and £10,000 each, and Portland reportedly the astronomical amount of £50,000 – an interesting index of their perceived political influence. The accusations were not wholly unjustified; Trevor resigned, and Carmarthen's already doubtful reputation was tainted again. Nottingham and Portland, however, were found to have indignantly refused the bribes, the latter even declaring that if they would repeat their dishonest solicitations, they would find an enemy of their company in him.[56] Even though he was cleared of all charges, Portland showed little relief and remained resentful.[57] 'It is annoying', he wrote to Lexington, 'to be left exposed in this place, where this appalling corruption is only too common'. A bottle of Tockay wine, a present from his friend Baron Lexington, was received with sarcasm, Portland expressing

---

50   *Mémoires de Saint-Simon*, ed. A. de Boislisle (21 vols, Paris, 1879–1930), V. 61, transl. from French.

51   W. Pittis, *The True-born Englishman: a Satyr, answer'd Paragraph by Paragraph*, (London, 1701), 73; Tutchin, *The Foreigners*, 7.

52   N. Witsen, 'Verbaal' in: *Geschied- en Letterkundig Mengelwerk*, ed. J. Scheltema (6 vols, Utrecht, 1818–36), III, 162, transl. from Dutch.

53   E.g. Horwitz, *Parliament*, 33, 151–2; D.B. Horn, *The British Diplomatic Service 1688–1789* (Oxford, 1961), 145; Heemskerck to Portland 30 December 1689, Japikse, *Correspondentie*, XXVIII. 137; Witsen, 'Verbaal', III. 151.

54   Dispatch Parent 4 July 1689 NS, AAE, CPA 170, f° 203v°.

55   Portland to Lexington 22 March/1 April 1695 (Kensington Palace), BL, Add Mss 46525, f° 99r°, transl. from French.

56   Saunière to States General 6 May 1695, BL, Add Mss 17677 PP, f° 244–8; HMC, *House of Lords Mss 1693–95*, 557; *Cobbett's Parliamentary History*, V. 925; Horwitz, *Parliament*, 151–2.

57   Saunière to States General 10 May 1695, BL, Add Mss 17677 PP, f° 252r°.

the hope that 'I won't be guilty of bribery should I accept it and drink it'.[58] Nor was the King pleased with the actions of Parliament, and he granted Portland a manor worth £2,000 per annum to express his confidence in his favourite.[59]

Nicknamed 'the Archbishop of Toledo' (whose wealth was legendary), Portland passed as one of the richest subjects but was still an avaricious man.[60] Even one of his associates, James Vernon, 'was surprised to see one so blinded with his own interest, and consider nothing else, especially having obtained so many grants'.[61] According to another observer he was 'very profuse in Gardening, Birds, and Household Furniture, but mighty frugal and parsimonious in every Thing else'.[62]

There was also considerable concern that 'William the Conqueror' only brought in his cronies to cream off the riches of the country. One of the most famous Jacobite pamphlets, Nathaniel Johnston's *The Dear Bargain; or, A True Representation of the State of the English Nation under the Dutch* (1690), complained about

> The putting the highest Offices of Trust and Importance into the Hands of [William's] own mercenary Foreigners, who have no other Interest, or Being but what depends on his Fortune, like so many Bashaws, or Berglebegs upon the Grand Seignior; such as Schonberg, and Huson, Benting, Solms.[63]

Tutchin's *The Foreigners*, referring to the Welsh and Irish grants of land William bestowed on Portland, complained that 'what he got the [English] Nation lost: By lavish Grants whole Provinces he gains'.[64] *The History of Prime Ministers and Favourites in England* mainly castigates William's favourites for being greedy.[65]

The most notorious case in which Portland's greed seemed apparent was his acceptance of the massive Welsh grants, which William bestowed on him in the spring of 1695. A number of Welsh MPs had heard about the grant and filed a complaint in July 1695. Godolphin told Portland that 'we were all of one opinion in not thinking this a seasonable time, either in respect to his Maj[tys] service or Y[r] Ldships advantage to presse the finishing of this grant'.[66] But the Junto laboured to get the grant through, Henry Guy assuring Portland that 'the King may grant it in ffee to you or any one; notwithstanding any of the objections, which were in the minutes

---

58   Portland to Lexington 23 April/3 May 1695 (Kensington Palace), BL, Add Mss 46525, f° 106, transl. from French.

59   14 May 1695, N. Luttrell, *A Brief Historical Relation of State Affairs from September 1678 to April 1714* (Oxford, 1857), III. 472.

60   Buckley, *Memoirs*, II. 504

61   In reference to Portland's quarrel with Montagu. Vernon to Shrewsbury 19 June 1697, *Letters Illustrative of the Reign of William III etc.*, ed. G.P.R. James (3 vols, London, 1841), I. 271.

62   J. Macky, 'Characters of the Court of Great Britain ... .' in: *Memoirs of the Life of Sir John Clerk ... 1675–1755*, ed. J.M. Gray (London, 1895), 58.

63   [N. Johnston], *The Dear Bargain; or, A True Representation of the State of the English Nation under the Dutch. In a Letter to a Friend* (1690) in: Somers, *Third Collection*, III. 259.

64   Tutchin, *The Foreigners*.

65   *The History of Prime Ministers and Favourites*, 136.

66   Godolphin to Portland 9 July 1695, NUL, PwA 474.

at the hearing before the Lords of the Treasury'.[67] Despite such considerations there was obvious anxiety that Country MPs would take advantage of the situation. Guy astutely contacted Robert Harley, who complained about rumours that Thomas Wharton of the Whig Junto would endeavour to keep him out of Parliament. Guy promised to look into it. He proposed to Portland to arrange a meeting with Harley, not least because the latter was 'a considerable man in the countrey where the affaire of [Portland] doth ly'.[68] Simultaneously he tried to bring Paul Foley closer to the government. Although Portland had his misgivings about Foley, he agreed that the overture could be useful, and Harley showed himself satisfied with Portland's attitude.[69] The rapprochement failed, however, because of animosity between Court and Country Whigs. Thus the Whig Junto was apprehensive and Guy suggested that Portland should lend his personal political weight to the matter of the grant: 'the putting it forward must come from your side as I before advized you; for Lowndes can go no farther of himselfe'.[70] Portland, indeed, decided to pursue the matter and asked John Somers, the Lord Keeper, for legal advice.[71] In retrospect this was a political blunder, as his request would tarnish his reputation.

Despite the apparent understanding between Harley and Portland the long-awaited attack came in the spring of 1696, led by one of Harley's associates.[72] The three lordships of Yale, Bromfield and Denbigh consisted of almost the complete county of Denbigh and measured some 30 miles in extent. The rents yielded an estimated £1,700 annually.[73] But it was not just the vastness of the estates that was problematic. The lordships were traditionally granted to the Prince of Wales, and when Elizabeth bestowed them upon the Earl of Leicester a century before the result had been rebellion.[74] A token of subjugation to the Prince of Wales was the so-called mise, a tax levied for the benefit of the landlord, yielding some £800 yearly. In a famous speech in Parliament, Robert Price skilfully exploited the underlying resentment in the Commons against foreigners, in referring to Portland as a 'Dutch Prince of Wales'.[75] 'If we are to pay these Mises to this Noble Lord upon this Grant', he complained, 'then he is, or is quasi a Prince of Wales ... I suppose this Grant of

---

67 Guy to Portland 25 June 1695, NUL, PwA 505. Cf. Guy to Portland 18/28 June 1695, Japikse, *Correspondentie*, XXIV. 59–60; Trumbull to Portland 26 August 1695, Montagu to Portland 21 June 1695, NUL, PwA 505, PwA 936.
68 Guy to Portland 15 July 1695, NUL, PwA 506.
69 Guy to Portland 23 July 1695, NUL, PwA 509 ff.
70 Guy to Portland 30 July 1695, NUL, PwA 510.
71 Portland to Somers n.d. October 1695 (Althorp), Surrey History Centre, Somers Manuscripts, 371/14/K/7.
72 E. Cruickshanks, S. Handley and D.W. Hayton (eds), *The History of Parliament. The House of Common 1690–1715* (5 vols, Cambridge, 2002), IV. 253–4.
73 An overview of the Welsh grants is in *CTB*, X-ii. 1046–52.
74 Godolphin to Portland 9 July 1695, NUL, PwA 474.
75 *Cobbett's Parliamentary History*, V. 979 ff.; A. McInnes, *Robert Harley, Puritan Politician* (London, 1970), 36. Portland revealed himself to be sensitive regarding this accusation. Sunderland wrote to him: 'I find you are in a great mistake thinking that the Partiality to strangers which I mentioned in some letters had relation to you, which it has not in the least, nor to none neare the King, but to an Opinion is taken up that he has an aversion

the Principality, is a forerunner of the Honour too.'[76] The Commons subsequently petitioned the King to withdraw the grant from 'Lord Portland, who had thought to have been Prince of Wales'.[77] Portland now recognised it was unwise to challenge the Commons, and asked William to give in to their demands.[78]

Despite the wave of protests it is likely that the King would have been able to carry the grant through, but a new expensive campaign was impending and a bitter fight over this issue was inopportune. The protests were obviously exploited to publicly criticise William's favourites as a way of attacking the King and the Whig Junto. Ostensibly Parliament had objected to lavishing grants upon a typical overmighty, greedy favourite. In fact, subsequent grants to Portland went through without a dissenting voice in the Commons. William, infuriated with the behaviour of his parliament, insisted on bestowing numerous other grants, scattered around England, upon his favourite, only months after the incident. These were worth even more than the Welsh grants, yielding over an estimated £3,000 annually.[79] These grants passed almost unchallenged, and it is difficult to see the grants themselves as very controversial. Perhaps Parliament felt that its one-time display of William's favourites on a political scaffold was satisfactory. Country MPs must also have realised that in the spring of 1696 they had caught the King at a weak moment, but by the summer they needed his support for their Land Bank scheme.[80]

Thus the favourite was seen as overmighty, corrupt and greedy, but pamphleteers also frequently accused 'Ganymede' of sodomy. They obviously exploited the resemblance of the relationship between the King and his confidant, to that of James I and George Villiers, the Duke of Buckingham. The association was strengthened through Portland's connection to the Villiers family. Portland was furious when it was rumoured in 1698 that William would make him Duke of Buckingham, because, as the Brandenburg envoy Bonnet wrote, 'that name has always been very odious to the English'.[81]

The charges of sexual promiscuity and sodomy persistently appeared in pamphlets. According to the Country Whig Robert Ferguson's in his *A Brief Account of some of the late Incroachments and Depredations of the Dutch upon the English* (1695), 'Benting … is the Minion and Darling of our Monarch for Familiarities, and

---

and a contempt of English men which I thinke ought to be cured and may very easily be done', Sunderland to Portland 8 September 1695, NUL, PwA 1250.

76   *Speach for repealing Grants in Wales for Bentinck 1696* in: *A Choice Collection of Papers relating to State Affairs during the late Revolution* (London, 1703), 523–30, 526.

77   Edge to Kenyon 21 January 1696, HMC, *The Manuscripts of Lord Kenyon* (London, 1894), 396.

78   Saunière to States General 14 January 1696, BL, Add Mss 17677 QQ, f° 222v°; *Cobbett's Parliamentary History*, V. 986–7n. This must have soured relations between Portland and Harley, although it was now that Guy brought them into acquaintance. Guy to Portland, 23 July 1695, 16 August 1695, Japikse, *Correspondentie*, XXIV. 61, 62.

79   BL, Eg Mss 1708, f° 277v°.

80   Cf. Ch. 6.

81   Dispatch Bonnet 12/22 July 1698, BL, Add Mss 30000B, f° 168, transl. from French.

Privacies which I blush to mention'.[82] 'The Advice to a Painter' (1697) suggested that there was a sexual relationship between William and his two favourites, Portland and Albemarle, the latter having supposedly supplanted the former in William's affection:

> twere insolence too great
> T'expose the secrets of the cabinet;
> Or tell how they their looser moments spend;
> That hellish scene would all chaste ears offend.
> For should you pry into the close alcove,
> And draw the exercise of royal love,
> Keppel and [Bentinck] are Ganymede and Jove.[83]

Thus sexual promiscuity and sodomy in particular seemed widespread at a court which was supposed to be godly and virtuous. *The False Favourite's Downfall* (1692), referring to the Earl of Marlborough's disgrace, sketches a court from which all sexual morality seems to have vanished. 'The peer with one eye [Shrewsbury] does as oft with [Mary] lie as Portland with him I raised so high'.[84] In the particularly scandalous Jacobite pamphlet *A Dialogue between K.W. and Benting* (1695), William asks Portland to fetch him his mistress, Elizabeth Villiers, 'for diversion'. Unwilling to oblige, she suggests Portland should perform the service himself, since the King is a sodomite.[85]

Most historians have dismissed the rumours of sodomy on sensible grounds.[86] Of course, it is not clear what sort of evidence one could expect regarding the sexual behaviour of a man who by all accounts treasured his privacy. Portland's actions in nursing William in 1675 when the latter had caught smallpox is often pointed to in this regard. But it was a well-known medical 'fact' at the time that the ill person could benefit from such an action; the incident was widely publicised in order to show Portland's fidelity, and it would seem highly improbable that it was in fact an act of sodomy.[87]

---

82   R. Ferguson, *A Brief Account of some of the late Incroachments and Depredations of the Dutch upon the English etc.* (London?, 1695).

83   'Advice to a Painter', 17–18.

84   'The False Favourite's Downfall' (1692) in: *Poems of Affairs of State. Augustan Satirical Verse 1660–1714, V: 1688–1697*, ed. W.J. Cameron (New Haven/London, 1971), 332–3.

85   *Dialogue between K.W. and Benting*, 7. A reply to this pamphlet: *The Spirit of Jacobitism; or, Remarks upon a Dialogue between K.W. and Benting, in a Dialogue between Two Friends of the Present Government* (London, 1695).

86   S.B. Baxter, *William III* (London, 1966), 349–51; Horwitz, *Parliament*, 203–4; A.M. Claydon, *William III and the Godly Revolution* (Cambridge, 1996), 92; D.J. Roorda, 'Willem III, de Koning-Stadhouder' in: S. Groenveld et al. (eds), *Rond Prins en Patriciaat: Verspreide Opstellen door D.J. Roorda* (Weesp, 1984), 118–42, 140.

87   The story that Bentinck actually shared the bed with William seems to be a myth, cf. page 9.

A closer look at the source of such accusations makes it clear that they came almost exclusively from Jacobite pamphleteers who often operated from St Germain. The charge had never been made before in the United Provinces, nor was it even hinted at by courtiers who were not otherwise unfamiliar with biting sarcastic portrayals of court life. None of the courtiers and diarists who spent most of their days in the vicinity of the King and Portland hinted at physical intimacy. Huygens, for instance, never surmises there might be more to the relationship between Keppel and the King, though he loathed the former and was quite frank about courtiers' sexual escapades or indeed William's liaison with Elizabeth Villiers. Dutch pamphleteers or diarists never mention a homosexual relationship between Portland and the King, and the topic only came up after 1689.[88] Indeed, it was not until 1697 that Portland wrote a private letter to William in which he was evidently shocked to have heard the rumours surrounding Keppel and the King, which makes it extremely doubtful that sodomy was something he would condone:

> Things I am ashamed to hear, and which I thought you [Your Majesty] to be as far removed of as any man of the world, I would have thought a man of society would have distanced himself from. I thought that only malicious people in England were fabricating these scathing things. But I was thunderstruck to see that the same discourse is given by The Hague and the army ... a similar discourse is going on.[89]

The charge mainly came from English pamphleteers who cunningly exploited an established literary tradition, and this charge was absent from Dutch pamphlets.

Portland himself was very much aware of the satirical verses that were circulating, and he kept some copies in his own archive.[90] He himself was engaged in counter-propaganda. Such artists as Romeyn de Hooghe were commissioned to create propaganda images, and pamphleteers (most notably Daniel Defoe) were employed. Portland asked William permission in 1690 'to give some gratification to those who take up the pen for the justification of your cause'.[91] Portland's patronage of pamphleteers defending the Court also figured in 1692, when he advised Secretary of State Nottingham that

> a good penn be employ'd (in a concise manner) relating to the affaires of the government, to obviate malignant objections and to maintain truth in its owne colours; and those prints to be sent, gratis, to the severall great towns.[92]

In 1696 he provided his papers on his interrogations of the suspects of the Assassination Plot to the Huguenot author Jean Abbadie, who published an account of the events in French, Dutch and English.[93] Thus Portland was not a helpless victim,

---

88 Noordam, *Riskante Relaties*, 117–18.
89 Portland to William 30 May 1697 (Brussels), William to Portland 1 June 1697, Japikse, *Correspondentie*, XXIII. 198–200, transl. from French.
90 E.g. NUL, PwA 2032, PwA 2035, PwA 2036, PwA 2037.
91 Portland to William 11 February 1690 (The Hague), Japikse, *Correspondentie*, XXIII. 102, transl. from French.
92 HMC, *Finch Mss*, IV. 160–61.
93 D.C.A. Agnew, *Protestant Exiles from France etc.* (2 vols, s.l., 1886), II. 226.

IV

Pamphlets criticising Portland have two characteristics in common which are of particular interest. Firstly, they portrayed him as a representative of 'Dutch' government.[94] Gregorius van Alphen, who made an extensive study of these pamphlets, noted that Portland became a metaphor for misgovernment and foreignness.[95] Secondly, they particularly targeted his moral behaviour: he was regarded as corrupt, greedy and sodomitic. Linda Levy Peck has identified charges of corruption as part and parcel of the anti-favourite rhetorical repertoire, providing pamphleteers with a ready vocabulary to prove the immorality of the members of the King's entourage.[96] Tony Claydon has explained how court propagandists had stressed the providential nature of the Williamite settlement; William had been elected as a divine instrument to defend Protestantism both abroad and at home. The purification of the Court of its vices was an essential part of the 'godly revolution'.[97] Those who criticised the Court targeted the immoral behaviour of courtiers, which was particularly appealing to the Country opposition.

Moral satire with political connotations was popular. Mary Delraviere Manley's *Secret Memoirs and Manners of Several Persons of Quality of Both Sexes from the New Atlantis, an Island in the Mediterranean* (1709), for instance, was a collection of fictional court anecdotes based on real events.[98] One of the characters in the book, 'the duke', clearly refers to Portland: 'the young favourite (tho' formerly but of his pleasures) became [William's] first minister. He was always trusted, and extreme habile in the Affairs of State; he follow'd the wise maxims of Machiavel, who aim'd to make his prince great.'[99] Portland's supposed affair with Stuarta Howard, a maid of honour to the Queen, is satirised and elaborated on *ad absurdum* and is evidently fictional, as are the activities of other politicians depicted in this work. Manley's book was regarded as a piece of Tory propaganda and the author was charged with libel by the Whig leaders.[100]

---

94   Cf. page 131–4.
95   G. van Alphen, *De Stemming van de Engelschen tegen de Hollanders in Engeland tijdens de Regeering van den Koning-Stadhouder Willem III 1688–1702* (Assen, 1938), 229.
96   L. Levy Peck, *Court Patronage and Corruption in Early Stuart England* (London, 1991).
97   Claydon, *William III and the Godly Revolution*.
98   M. Delariviere Manley, *Secret Memoirs and Manners of Several Persons of Quality of both Sexes from the New Atlantis, an Island in the Mediterranean* (London, 1709). I am thankful to Ophelia Field for this reference.
99   Ibid., 49.
100   There were, however, rumours of such an affair. 24 September 1692, 27 September 1692, 11 December 1692, 20 December 1692, Luttrell, *Brief Historical Relation*, II. 574, 577, 643, 644; Lady Giffard to Martha Jane Temple 14 September 1698, BL, Eg Mss 1705, f° 23v°.

If loose morals stained the virtuous courtier, they were also indicators of bad government. Sodomy in particular had various connotations. McFarlane, in his study of fiction and sodomy, argued: 'Conceptualized as the embodiment of a disorder at once sexual, cultural, political, and religious, the sodomite represented an anarchic force that threatened to undermine the nation and against which the nation might define itself.'[101] The sodomitic favourite, then, became a manifestation of unnatural behaviour and foreignness. A contemporary poem on King William can illustrate this:

> For the case, Sir, is such, the people think much,
> That your love is Italian, your Government Dutch,
> Ah who could have thought, that a Low-Country stallion,
> And a Protestant Prince, should prove an Italian?

The poem also asserted that 'Billy with Benting does play the Italian', playing on connotations that are easily recognised. The Dutch Protestant prince is a sodomite, an Italian lover; the association with Italy leads the reader to think of Roman Catholicism, but also of foreignness in general. Hence the Dutch Calvinist is the antithesis to Englishness and Anglican religion.[102] *The Unfortunate Court-Favourites of England* played on similar connotations in portraying Buckingham as a sodomite with an undistinguished pedigree who plundered the treasury and sympathised with Catholicism.[103]

Whereas some pamphleteers emphasised the foreign, unnatural aspects of William's reign, others stress the continuity of 'absolute' government. In 'Lay by your Reason' (1691), Portland is no different from other favourites:

> What have we gain'd?
> Grievances retain'd,
> The Government is still the same, the King is only chang'd.
> Was ever such a bargain!
> What boots it a farthing,
> Whether Father Petre rules, or Bentinck and Carmarthen:
> Distresses, oppressed,
> With empty hopes caressed,
> We still remain in *statu quo*, there's nothing yet redressed.[104]

The pamphleteer John Dennis had accused his opponent John Tutchin of attacking Portland in his pamphlet only to strike at the King.[105] Hence pamphleteers in the 1690s, confronted with the apparent re-emergence of oppressive government,

---

101 C. McFarlane, *The Sodomite in Fiction and Satire 1660–1750* (New York, 1997), 78–9.
102 Cameron, *Poems*, 38, 221.
103 Crouch, *The Unfortunate Court-Favourites*.
104 'Lay by your Reason' in: *Political Ballads of the Seventeenth and Eighteenth Centuries*, ed. W. Walker Wilkins (2 vols, London, 1860), II. 28–9.
105 C. Rose, *England in the 1690s: Revolution, Religion and War* (Oxford, 1999), 57.

merely revived a literary tradition as an instrument to express their criticism.[106] The significance of these pamphlets, then, lies not in what they seem to convey, but rather in their underlying purpose. In a sustained propaganda war between the Court and the opposition, the defenders of the Court had stressed the providential nature of the Williamite settlement; the King had been elected as a divine instrument to defend Protestantism both abroad and at home. The 'godly revolution' stirred a nation to revert to piety in general, and to purify the Court in particular of its vices. Attackers of the Court could tap into an available discourse that criticised the conduct of courtiers in order to erode their credibility. Such criticism of court life must have been especially appealing in Country circles. Pamphleteers could employ their acid pens to dissolve the image of moral integrity of the members of William's entourage.

V

This interpretation of anti-Dutch and anti-favourite rhetoric in terms of partisan struggles becomes more convincing once compared to similar discourse in the United Provinces. In England Portland was perceived as a symbol of Williamite, foreign government, but this was also the case in Holland. In England, Portland was hated for being a Dutch adviser, but with regard to his exclusion from the Holland States Assembly in 1690, one English pamphleteer thought that 'Mynheer Benting himself shall be no more admitted to their secret Consultations, since he is become an English earl', realising full well that Portland was anything but a representative of the loathed mercantile rivals.[107] The proceedings in the Assembly in 1690 were published and translated into English as *An Account of the Passages in the Assembly of the States of Holland and West-Friezeland concerning the Earl of Portlands Exclusion from, or Admission into that Assembly*, so there was clearly an interest in Dutch affairs, indicating an awareness of cross-Channel similarities.[108] If Dutch Republicans suffered from an arbitrary ruler and his evil counsellor, the English might feel the effects of the same soon. The Dutch Orangist publicist Ericus Walten, likewise, warned about the similarities in anti-Williamite propaganda on both sides of the Channel in a pamphlet dedicated to Portland.[109]

Referring to Portland, Burnet had once remarked that 'though commonwealths can very ill bear inequality, yet I never heard any that are in the government of

---

106 Cf. L.W.B. Brockliss, 'Concluding Remarks' in: L.W.B. Brockliss and J.H. Elliott (eds), *The World of the Favourite* (New Haven/London, 1999), 279–309, 288.

107 Johnston, *The Dear Bargain*, 234.

108 *An Account of the Passages in the Assembly of the States of Holland and West-Friezeland concerning the Earl of Portlands Exclusion from, or Admission into that Assembly* (London, 1690).

109 E. Walten, *Brief aan Sijn Excellentie, de Heer Graaf van Portland, etc.* (The Hague, 1692). On Walten's ideas on Orangism, see J.I. Israel, *Monarchy, Orangism and Republicanism in the later Dutch Golden Age* (Amsterdam, 2004).

the towns of Holland complain of him'.[110] However, pamphlets criticising Portland started to appear in the United Provinces during the 1690 conflict with Amsterdam. Though less vicious in tone and character than English contemporary pamphlets, Dutch pasquils centre on the theme of Portland, nicknamed *Groot-Hans* ('Great Hans'), assuming too much power in a republic that has equality as an ideal.[111] To the Dutch Republicans Portland personified the disreputable, even tyrannical aspects of stadholderly rule. 'they talk about me as if I were the devil', he laconically wrote to William in March 1690,

> although I have never uttered an immoderate word in the assembly nor outside. If I have anything reproachful to be called to account for, the satires will soon be full of it, and I can not expect to be given any quarter. However, it is in my nature that these considerations make me proceed rather than hold back, because apart from what I have to do in the interest of the country and the religion, there will certainly be nothing that will spur me into action but your service and interest, for which I will not spare the last drop of my blood.[112]

Political opposition had been accompanied by a propaganda campaign. A Republican print, *De Hollandse Hollende Koe* ('The Holland running cow'), satirised Portland's entry into the States assembly in 1690 and complained about William and his 'vice-stadholder' trampling the privileges of Holland cities.[113] Portland is depicted sitting on a blindfolded cow, carrying a banner in his hand saying 'we are Earl and Master of these lands'. The accompanying poem asserts that 'New sovereigns make new laws'; now that William was King, privileges of old would be shattered and trampled on.[114] In the background is an illustration of the people of Troy bringing the wooden horse within their city gates. Evidently their attack on Portland in 1690, William understood, 'only proceeds from the ill they want to do me'.[115] Portland as well realised how anti-favourite rhetoric could be exploited, and suggested to William that he should dissociate his own interest from that of his master:

> I am more and more persuaded that I have done well to separate my private affairs from the great affair, because that has convinced those who are indifferent that I have acted with moderation, and the gentlemen of Amsterdam will be rather embarrassed themselves ...[116]

---

110   *A Supplement to Burnets History of my Own Time etc.*, ed. H.C. Foxcroft (Oxford, 1902), 196.

111   E.g. *Groot-Hans met de Privilegie-soeker* (s.l., 1690); *De Hollandse Hollende Koe* (s.l., 1690).

112   Portland to William 2 March 1690 (The Hague), Japikse, *Correspondentie*, XXIII. 129, transl. from French.

113   *De Hollandse Hollende Koe*. A description of this print is in *Catalogue of Political and Personal Satires*, ed. F.G. Stephens, M.D. George and G.W. Reid (11 vols, London, 1870–1954). Illus. 6.

114   *De Hollandse Hollende Koe*, transl. from Dutch.

115   William to Portland 20 January 1690, Japikse, *Correspondentie*, XXIII. 70, transl. from French.

116   Portland to William 14–15 March 1690 (The Hague), ibid., 146–7, transl. from French.

De Hollandse Hollende Koe also expressed complaints about higher taxation which were directly linked to financial gain by the English and Germans; just under the cow are the silhouettes of an Englishman and a German secretly profiting from the situation. The Englishman, it says, makes about six million, guilders: the amount of the Dutch financial contribution to the invasion, which Parliament had hitherto neglected to repay. Perhaps most interestingly, the pamphleteer says, we are now living under the English yoke, which is worse than the Spanish. Whereas the English regarded Portland as a 'Dutch Prince of Wales' during the affair of the Welsh grants in 1695, the Amsterdam delegation to the Holland States Assembly in 1690 had referred to him as one 'in the service of a foreign potentate'.[117]

This controversy, in which the favourite figured as a foreigner and an instrument of oppression, was thus reminiscent of Portland's perceived position as a 'Dutch Prince of Wales'. The case of the Welsh grants[118] was illuminating as an ostensible attack on an over-mighty, greedy favourite; the controversy can be analysed as a multi-layered cross-section of political discontent. Clearly there was concern about the alienation of Crown lands. Moreover, Robert Price, MP for Weobly but a Welshman originally, channelled genuine local resentment and Welsh patriotism into this attack. Arguing that Portland did not speak Welsh, Price stood up for local and Welsh rights. By the late seventeenth century Welsh political stances in Parliament were rare, and Price brilliantly transformed traditional anti-English sentiments into a protest against the Dutch.[119] 'How can we hope for happy days in England', he complained, 'when this great Man, and the other (tho' naturaliz'd) are in the English, and also in the Dutch counsels ...?'[120] In hijacking the rhetoric of anti-Dutch discourse his case attracted a much wider appeal and mobilised Country MPs. On a personal level, Price had reason to be dissatisfied with the Williamite regime, having been deprived of his attorney-generalship in 1689. He may have also found support amongst fellow Tories who sensed the controversy to be a useful pretext to launch an assault on the Whig Junto. In fact, it is doubtful whether the assault on the ministry could have succeeded without the support of Harley, who ultimately decided to throw his weight behind it. Xenophobic rhetoric was therefore channelled into opposition attacks against the Court. The combination of anti-Dutch sentiments, anti-court opposition and anti-favourite rhetoric proved potent, mobilising various factions against the government.

The affair of the Welsh grants resonated throughout various sections of the political nation, facilitated by the publication of a pamphlet based on Price's speech, *Gloria Cambriae: Or, The Speech of a Bold Britain in Parliament, against a Dutch Prince of Wales*, published only after William's death in 1702.[121] The 'Advice to a Painter' (1697) referred 'To black designs and lust let him remain, A servile favorite, and grants obtain'.[122] When during the late 1690s an enquiry was launched into

---

117 Cf. page 74.
118 Discussed on page 185–7.
119 G.H. Jenkins, *The Foundations of Modern Wales 1642–1780* (Oxford, 1987), 152–3.
120 'A Speech for Repealing Grants', 529.
121 *Gloria Cambriae*.
122 'Advice to a Painter', 17.

the Irish grants which William had bestowed upon his favourites, a similar protest emerged, but Portland had learned from his mistake and had the grant deferred to his son, Lord Woodstock. *The Exorbitant Grants of William the Third Examined and Questioned* (1703) summarised the common complaint that William had lavished grants upon his favourites.[123] After William's reign chroniclers perpetuated the impression that 'The avarice and rapaciousness of foreign favourites was another very great misfortune'.[124]

Both in the case of the Welsh grants and the Amsterdam controversy, the favourite is seen as a manifestation of arbitrary and foreign rule, and opposition rhetoric exhibits similar phrases and patterns, building on distinct national literary traditions. In England the charge of sodomy, for instance, is employed as a familiar charge, which is completely absent in the Dutch context, where the greatest emphasis falls on excess of power. Obviously, Dutch Republicans had other concerns than English Jacobites. But the apparent mixture of xenophobic and anti-Orangist or anti-Williamite rhetoric is similar. In Dutch pamphlets Portland is seen as a representative of English oppression, whilst in English writings he is criticised for his Dutchness. In both cases Portland is the representative of a foreign, arbitrary ruler.

VI

The language of anti-favouritism was adopted in reaction to the accumulation of wealth and power in the hands of a foreigner close to the King, a man who embodied all the evils of the Williamite settlement. *A Very Remarkable Letter from King William III. To his Favourite Bentinck, Earl of Portland* (1690), for instance, presents William and his favourite as discussing their evil design to subject England to absolute rule.[125] To both Country Whigs and Jacobites Portland embodied the archetypal image of the 'evil counsellor'. The rhetoric employed served as a vehicle for pamphleteers to address issues of wider significance which concerned them. Hence the apparent discrepancy between such rhetoric and Portland's actual behaviour is unproblematic when it is taken into account that they merely represented a microcosm of broader debates during the 1690s. The 'Dutch favourite' became a symbol of Williamite government and foreignness. Thus the protests against Portland were fashioned within a more traditional discourse in which the favourite figured as a corrupt, sodomitic, greedy usurper. This is illustrated by the parliamentary debates on the Welsh grants, but also in the controversy with Amsterdam, in which attacking the favourite became a means by which the opposition could attack the Court. In Ferguson's *A Brief Account of some of the late Encroachments and Depredations*, for instance, Portland is blamed for all wrongs under William.[126] The Anglo-Dutch favourite, then, became

---

123 For the Irish grants, see J.G. Simms, *The Williamite Confiscation in Ireland, 1690–1703* (London, 1956); *The Exorbitant Grants of William the III Examin'd and Questioned. Shewing the Nature of Grants in Successive and Elective Monarchies, etc.* (London, 1703).
124 P. Rapin de Thoyras, *The History of England* etc. (5 vols, London, 1789), IV. 324.
125 *A Very Remarkable Letter from King William III*, 356–62.
126 Ferguson, *Brief Account*, 17, 18, 22.

the focal point of a political discourse during the 1690s in which the most important issues, directions of policy and changes were being debated.

Chapter 8

Arcana Imperii: War and Peace (1697–1700)

In this chapter, Portland's position after the Nine Years War and his subsequent retirement will be considered. J.R. Jones described the period 1697–1701 as 'one of the most confused periods in English political history'.[1] As the war ended, opposition against the standing army and the Irish forfeitures mounted, whereas weak ministries failed to provide stable government. William was forced to find an alternative for the crumbling Whig ministry with which Portland was connected. The combination of these factors gradually eroded Portland's influence and political relevance. Despite Portland's retirement in June 1699, however, he remained active as an ambassador and negotiator during the talks over the Treaties of Partition that were to divide the Spanish Empire. After William's death he was still active as a liaison between the ministries of the Maritime Powers during the War of the Spanish Succession. This chapter will reconstruct Portland's role in the negotiations at Ryswick. It will also focus on the interaction between the Partition Treaty negotiations and domestic political events in England, in particular on the connection to the debates in the Commons on the standing army. This chapter and the next form a sequel to chapters 3 through 7, because they analyse the erosion of Portland's influence, the failure of his policy and the increasing opposition against the Anglo-Dutch favourite.

I

Having been active as a military commander during the Nine Years War, towards the end of the war Portland reassumed his role as diplomat. The uneventful campaign of 1696 seemed to signal that peace was imminent. Negotiations for a general peace were resumed in May between the Dutch and French negotiators Everard van Weede van Dijkveld and François de Callières; Portland, though not personally engaged in the talks, was one of the few who was kept informed. On occasion he even advised Dijkveld to discuss certain matters with the Frenchman.[2] The favourite was also instructed to inform the major Allies about the talks.[3] Prudently, Portland initiated a correspondence with Jacob Boreel, sometime burgomaster of Amsterdam.

---

1   J.R. Jones, *Country and Court: England, 1658–1714* (London, 1978), 302.
2   Portland to Dijkveld 5 February [1697] (Kensington Palace), Portland to Dijkveld 26 March [1697] (Kensington Palace), HMC, *Appendix to the Eighth report* (s.l., 1881), II. 559a–b.
3   E.g. Portland to Danckelmann 25 May 1696 (Het Loo), Japikse, *Correspondentie*, XXIV. 186–7.

In order to pacify the city, the King had promised to keep her informed of the secret negotiations with the French.[4] Diplomatic contacts with the Austrians and Spaniards were severely disrupted during this period due to the deaths of the Spanish ambassador in Vienna, Marquis de Borgomañero, and of Count Windischgrätz, the Austrian ambassador in The Hague. Portland's correspondence with Baron Lexington therefore gained significance.[5] Meanwhile Francisco Schonenberg, the envoy of the States General at the Spanish court and William's confidant, had run into a conflict with the Spanish and was forced to leave Madrid. 'The extradition of Schonenberg', according to an agent in Vienna, 'has produced great tensions in the relations between Spain and the Maritime Powers.'[6] The first signs of disintegration of the Alliance thus surfaced.

More alarming was the defection of one of the Allies. Some nervousness as to the attitude of the Duke of Savoy had prompted the Maritime Powers in the spring of 1696 to set up a plan to besiege Pignerol, a fortress of crucial strategic importance.[7] 'I admit', Portland wrote to Richard Hill, 'that the affairs of Piedmont are of such a great consequences that one cannot help being worried.'[8] Referring to the secret dealings between the Duke and the French marshal Catinat, Portland wrote to the Prince of Vaudemont that

> We should be most afraid for the Piedmont, although I admit I don't think it to be very likely that the Duke of Savoy will do that which seemed to be have been generally feared and believed, that he made a separate deal.[9]

But his giving the Duke the favour of the doubt turned out wrong; in June Catinat made an agreement with Victor Amadeus, and with the Treaty of Turin in August, peace was concluded between Savoy and France. The Allies could do little but to accept the neutrality of the Italian theatre. The prospects for peace seemed grim to Portland:

> ... I think it is still more uncertain, since advices from France state, that after the peace of Savoy is positively concluded, it is no longer desired, and that Callières is to continue negotiating, in order to amuse us, and thus increase the disposition of the people towards peace, the more to disgust them with war.[10]

---

4   Boreel to Portland 7 July 1694, Japikse, *Correspondentie*, XXIII. 397–9; Portland to Boreel 10 July 1694 (Camp of Rosbeeck), Japikse, *Correspondentie*, XXVIII. 342.

5   Lexington to Portland 28 December 1695, NUL, PwA 1308.

6   Quoted in Duque de Maura, *Vida y Reinado de Carlos II* (Madrid, 1990), 450–51, transl. from Spanish.

7   Project for the siege of Pignerol, February 1696, NUL, PwA 1311.

8   Portland to Hill 29 June 1696 ('camp de Corbais'), NUL, PwA 667, transl. from French.

9   Portland to Vaudemont 25 July [?] 1695 ('Camp de Corbaisce'), BL, Add Mss 24205, f° 1–3, transl. from French.

10   Portland to Shrewsbury 8/18 September 1696 (Het Loo), *Private and Original Correspondence of Charles Talbot, Duke of Shrewsbury etc.*, ed. W. Coxe (London, 1821), 141–2.

Earlier Portland had been sceptical about French overtures and those in England who favoured a settlement, dismissing Secretary Huygens as 'one of those chaps who want to have the peace'.[11]

Meanwhile the talks with the French proceeded with difficulty, the major obstacles being the restitution of Luxembourg and the recognition of William as King of England, a point stressed rather by the English ministers than by the Dutch negotiators, something Portland discussed with Secretary of State the Duke of Shrewsbury and the Earl of Sunderland when in London in August 1696.[12] By December 1696 however, the French became more conciliatory and proposed preliminaries which were acceptable to William. Arrangements were made to organise a general peace congress the following spring.

In Huis ter Nieuburch in Ryswick, near The Hague, negotiations commenced. A deadlock was reached in June 1697, however, the main issue being that England needed a guarantee that Louis XIV would not support James II or any rebels, either directly or indirectly. To Louis this was unacceptable, but the Allies could settle for nothing less. It was, William wrote to Grand Pensionary Anthonie Heinsius, the most fundamental issue.[13] Heinsius, notwithstanding his reputation of being subtle and conciliatory, opted for pressing the French ambassadors to accept, believing it would test their sincerity. Dijkveld concurred, but the Amsterdam representative Jacob Boreel was alarmed and feared that the French would break off negotiations.[14] Louis's reservation was understood, but would he accept this restriction, if not *de jure*, then *de facto*? It all hinged on trust. Heinsius was far more distrustful of French motives than William. He ordered Francisco Mollo to threaten to break off the negotiations when the latter could not get a more definite answer.[15] The French seemed willing to accept Heinsius's demands in principle, but could not name James in the articles and offered an expedient.[16]

Portland was chosen to break the deadlock and re-open the negotiations with the French. On 1 July 1697 he sent a messenger to Boufflers, whom he had met two years earlier after the siege of Namur, to request an interview. A meeting took place at the village of Brucom, near Brussels, a week later. Portland arrived with several gentlemen, dismounted and conversed with Boufflers in a nearby orchard for some two hours. Portland told Boufflers that William considered Louis's preliminaries at Ryswick reasonable, and that he distanced himself from the obstructive Imperialists. Thus a separate peace was not impossible. Portland was instructed to re-open negotiations on some of the issues on which the talks had been deadlocked. He demanded that Louis recognise William and pledge not to assist James II. Lastly, Portland promised that Huguenots could only settle in the United Provinces with

---

11   13 July 1696, Huygens, *Journaal*, I-ii. 609, transl. from Dutch.

12   D.H. Somerville, *The King of Hearts. Charles Talbot, Duke of Shrewsbury* (London 1962), 115–8; Shrewsbury to Portland 11/21 September 1696, Coxe, *Private and original Correspondence*, 149.

13   William to Heinsius 18 July 1697, *Het Archief van den Raadpensionaris Antonie Heinsius*, ed. H.J. van der Heim (3 vols, The Hague, 1867), III. 243.

14   Heinsius to William 22 June 1697, Japikse, *Correspondentie*, XXIII. 447–8.

15   Cf. page 154.

16   Heinsius to William 22 June 1697, Japikse, *Correspondentie*, XXIII. 447–8.

Louis's permission, but that a pardon to Jacobites would be left to the English parliament.[17] The main goal was achieved; Portland conveyed the message that William was sincere in his efforts to make peace, and was likewise assured by Boufflers of the sincerity of the French king.[18] A last point of discussion was the matter of Orange, about which William was deeply concerned, and to which much attention was paid during these talks. This suggests that Boufflers did not so much regard Portland as a British envoy, but rather as a personal representative of William. Hence they were the envoys of two sovereign princes rather than spokesmen of two different alliances. This alarmed the other Allies. Although Portland's mission had resulted in more flexibility from the French ambassadors at Ryswick, Heinsius wrote to Portland, the Imperial ambassadors demanded to know the contents of the discussions.[19] Both Heinsius and Portland made efforts to withhold from their allies the fact that more issues than the position of James had been discussed.

A second meeting took place exactly one week later at the same place. The initial barrier of distrust had been removed, and thus the meetings had proved successful. Louis would go so far as to promise not to give any support to William's enemies, but James must not be named. Heinsius suggested to Portland that they should go along with French demands, as long as James was clearly indicated in the text.[20] Also, reciprocity had been accepted by the French, and thus since William was recognised as king, James was, by implication, not.[21] Portland and Heinsius worked in tandem on the fine-tuning of the draft articles.[22] Portland showed himself somewhat more lenient, rejecting Heinsius's proposal to insert a clause that Louis would not accept James's presence in France – an error of judgement which would cause him great problems during his embassy to Paris the following year.[23]

The Ryswick talks were back in full swing when the third meeting took place on 20 July, at which both Portland and Boufflers had larger entourages but spoke alone.[24] Portland had insisted that at this stage British ambassadors needed to be included in the talks.[25] At the fourth meeting on 27 July, Portland and Boufflers for

---

17   M.E. Grew, *William Bentinck and William III (Prince of Orange). The Life of Bentinck, Earl of Portland, from the Welbeck Correspondence* (London, 1924), 284 ff.

18   Cf. William to Heinsius 11 July 1697, *Archives ou Correspondance Inédite de la Maison d'Orange-Nassau*, ed. F.J.L. Krämer (3rd series, 3 vols, Leiden, 1907–9), 573–4; Heinsius to Portland 17 July 1697, NUL, PwA 1935.

19   Heinsius to Portland 13 July 1697, 17 July 1697, NUL, PwA 1934, PwA 1935; Hill to Shrewsbury 18 July 1697 NS, HMC, *Buccleugh Mss*, II-ii. 487.

20   Heinsius to Portland 20 July 1697, NUL, PwA 1937.

21   The fact that Britain's interest was taken care of by Dutch ambassadors (for French ambassadors would not recognise William's British representatives) caused some anxiety in Whitehall. Cf. Heinsius to William 20 July 1697, NUL, PwA 1936.

22   E.g. Heinsius to William 20 July 1697, NUL, PwA 1936. Portland had been instructed to write to Heinsius, see his draft notes in NUL, PwA 2577.

23   Heinsius to Portland 20 July 1697, NUL, PwA 1937. This is curious, for it was exactly what Portland pressed during his embassy in 1698.

24   Hill to Shrewsbury 15/25 July 1697, Shrewsbury to Hill 16 July 1697, Jersey to Shrewsbury 2 August 1697, HMC *Buccleugh Mss*, II-ii. 495, 497, 506.

25   Heinsius to Portland 27 July 1697, NUL, PwA 1937.

the first time retired into a nearby house where the latter handed over a written statement from Louis. Portland was not allowed to retain the document, but only to copy it. His demand that Louis would not give any support to James – though he was not mentioned – was accepted.[26] Boufflers's counter-demand – that Portland would put pressure on the Allies to accept – could not easily be consented to. William had instructed the British and Dutch envoys in Vienna, Barons Lexington and Heemskerck, to make clear to the unwilling Emperor that the war needed to be ended. Heinsius thought that Portland now had succeeded in his mission to break the deadlock, though he should keep in correspondence with Boufflers.[27] The ice was broken, an agreement was reached in principal, and presents were exchanged.[28]

However, the task remained to convince the Allies that the talks were still fruitful. On 4 August Portland travelled to The Hague to give a report of affairs to the Allied ambassadors. He unpleasantly surprised them with the French insistence on keeping Luxembourg and Strasbourg, for which they had offered expedients, much against the will of the Imperialists and Spaniards.[29] The English as well were concerned. On receiving the draft articles, Secretary of State Shrewsbury complained that William was not mentioned by name. Portland explained that this was not necessary, and as to the position of James, he decided to trust Louis's verbal promise.[30] Meanwhile the French had set a 31 August deadline for the Ryswick negotiations. Anxiously Portland and William waited, but the deadline passed with the issues still unresolved. The negotiations got stuck on Strasbourg. Louis refused to part with the city and forced the Allies, mainly the Imperialists, to accept this by 20 September.[31] Clearly the ultimatum was too short, and was meant to divide the Allies.

On 3 September Portland contacted Boufflers again, expressing concern that the negotiations had reached another deadlock.[32] He referred to their recent conversations and observed that the talks in Ryswick were not proceeding well. The Emperor, Leopold I, was reluctant to conclude peace, as the approaching end of the Balkan War opened up the prospect that more resources would become available for the Western front. Moreover, the Grand Alliance had pledged to support his claim to

---

26 Portland to Shrewsbury 19/29 July 1697, Coxe, *Private Correspondence*, 353; Hill to Shrewsbury 29 July 1697, HMC, *Buccleugh Mss*, II-ii. 500.

27 Heinsius to Portland 27 July 1697, NUL, PwA 1939.

28 Boufflers to Portland 31 July 1697, NUL, PwA 177. A fifth meeting on 2 August likewise proceeded smoothly; Boufflers ordered the ambassadors in Delft to act constructively. Hill to Shrewsbury 5 August 1695, HMC, *Buccleugh Mss*, II-ii. 523–4.

29 NUL, PwV 68/20; Villiers to Shrewsbury 9 August 1697, HMC, *Buccleugh Mss*, II-ii. 513.

30 It was therefore logical that Portland should insist on this when he arrived in Paris in February 1698. It was the main test of Louis's sincerity. Portland to Shrewsbury 12 August 1697 (Het Loo), Shrewsbury to Portland 28 August 1697, Coxe, *Private Correspondence*, 363–4.

31 NUL, PwA 2588.

32 Portland to Boufflers 3 September 1697 (The Hague), Boufflers to Portland 8 September 1697, NUL, PwA 179, PwA 180.

the Spanish throne, and the end of the war would inevitably mean the dissolution of the Alliance. Portland argued to Boufflers that William was unwilling to conclude a separate peace, but would do so nonetheless if the Emperor insisted on obstructing the negotiations. Though Portland and Boufflers had reached an agreement on French lenience on the deadline, the French ambassadors now refused the Emperor extra time to join the agreement. On 9 September Portland and Boufflers met again to break the deadlock over the Imperialists' refusal to accept an expedient for Strasbourg. It was a tough discussion that lasted for almost five hours, in which Portland expressed doubt as to Louis's sincerity.[33] He demanded that the deadline be postponed, and the equivalent for Strasbourg enlarged, ('the first indispensable, the second obvious').[34] Though Boufflers was sensitive to Portland's complaints about the uncompromising stance of the French ambassadors, no positive commitments could be made, and their meeting was fruitless. Frantic shuttle diplomacy took place in the days before the deadline, Portland travelling between Het Loo and The Hague frequently.[35] On 20 September William grudgingly accepted the French terms. Portland as well was dissatisfied with the way in which the negotiations had proceeded at Ryswick, writing to Shrewsbury:

> Sir; I congratulate you most truly that peace is at length made; such as it is; for, in my opinion, though it is not much to the advantage of France, who purchases it dearly enough, yet we might have had it in a better manner, without permitting France to assume that haughty demeanor which she has manifested since the last of August, had we not testified an immoderate desire, and even a necessity, of making this peace.[36]

II

Portland embarked for England in October, accompanied by a great number of noblemen, with the ratification of the peace.[37] He had optimistically suggested that the peace of Ryswick 'will ease our affairs in England, provided we do not rely on, and trust to it too much, and we place ourselves in a condition to ensure and preserve it'.[38] William still being on the continent, Portland was instructed to estimate the chances of raising more money to maintain a sizeable army in peace time.[39]

The disbanding of the standing army became the most controversial political issue in post-war Williamite England. Party boundaries briefly faded as Tories and

---

33 Hill to Shrewsbury 9 September 1697, 12 September 1697, HMC, *Buccleugh Mss*, II-ii, 543, 547–8.
34 NUL, PwA 2580, transl. from French.
35 Follet to Harley 7 September 1697, HMC, *Portland Mss*, III. 587.
36 Portland to Shrewsbury 14/24 September 1697 (Het Loo), Coxe, *Private Correspondence*, 373–4.
37 17 September 1697, 5 October 1697, 7 October 1697, 12 October 1697, 16 October 1697, N. Luttrell, *A Brief Historical Relation of State Affairs from September 1678 to April 1714* (Oxford, 1857). IV. 276, 287, 288–9, 290, 293.
38 Portland to Shrewsbury, 14/24 September 1697 (Het Loo), Coxe, *Private Correspondence*, 177.
39 William to Portland 27 October 1697, Japikse, *Correspondentie*, XXIII. 210.

Country Whigs, led by Harley and his New Country Party, made combined assaults on the Whig Junto court party. At the end of the war, a great number of troops had to be demobilised, but William was determined to retain a significant defensive force in order to keep up the balance of power with France. The opposition between 1697 and 1702 was unconvinced of the necessity of a large standing army and, urged on by an intense pamphlet campaign, moved to reduce it to its lowest possible size.[40] Contemporary observers divided the newly elected 1698 Parliament into a Court or army party, and a Country or anti-army party, with a slight majority for the former. It indicates that there was potential parliamentary support to retain a strong army.[41]

Initially, Portland had suggested that 30,000 troops be maintained, and set up a project to reform the troops.[42] William thought the plan too optimistic, but nevertheless followed his advice. On his return, however, Portland noted that the 'immoderate desire' for peace manifested itself more forcefully than he had imagined. Scepticism as to the motives of France was shared by the King and his advisers, but not by Parliament. When Portland arrived in London around 19 October, he discussed the preparations of the parliamentary session, the King being expected in early November.[43] William had already intimated that he would ask Parliament to assist him to maintain an army of 25,000 troops.[44] But it was not to be. In vigorous attacks on the ministry, the opposition leader Robert Harley proposed to further reduce the number, and supply for 12,000 troops was voted – a shattering defeat for the Whig Junto. This confrontation was the beginning of a struggle between the King and his Parliament over the army that was to last for almost two years. A powerful anti-standing-army movement in Country circles tried to reduce the army of the King, who did not easily give in.

That the Court failed was largely due to William's ministerial mismanagement and his characteristic predilection for more secretive methods, which ultimately lost him a great deal of credit in the Commons.[45] Portland and Galway had been scheming to find alternative methods to keep up a strong army. One method was to 'hide' troops in Ireland. The idea was to replace depot troops in Ireland with crack troops and veterans from Flanders. This scheme was hatched in utter secrecy, and only the King, Portland and Galway were involved. On 27 November 1697 Portland had written to Galway that this plan would facilitate the bringing over of more troops to Ireland, and Galway concluded that three extra Huguenot regiments

---

40 'Armies represented centralising power, their officers formed a political interest group of placemen, they cost a great deal of money and necessitated heavy taxation, they reduced the power and importance of the sacred militia, and they weakened the independence of the provinces.' J. Childs, *The British Army of William III 1689–1702* (Manchester, 1987), 185; L.G. Schwoerer, *No Standing Armies! The Antiarmy Ideology in Seventeenth Century England* (Baltimore/London, 1974), 155–87, *passim*.

41 H. Horwitz, *Parliament, Policy and Politics in the Reign of William III* (Manchester, 1977), 240.

42 William to Portland 8 November 1697, Japikse, *Correspondentie*, XXIII. 212.

43 Guy to Harley 19 October 1697, HMC, *Portland Mss*, III. 590.

44 Horwitz, *Parliament*, 224.

45 Childs, *British Army*, 192 ff.

could be brought over.[46] But the method William and Portland had employed to delay disbanding by finding pretexts to keep more troops afoot than had been agreed had infuriated Country MPs. In December 1698 Parliament decided to reduce the number of troops even further.[47]

The opposition also insisted that only native-born troops were to be kept afoot, and notwithstanding William's pleas, the Dutch Red Dragoons and Blue Guards were to sail back to the continent that spring. To William's opponents the Dutch regiments symbolised the evils of Williamite belligerent policy. William's Dutch favourites, likewise, were targeted by the opposition, which after the war mainly manifested itself in widespread opposition against the Irish grants.[48] Popular opinion had it that the King had squandered hundreds of thousands of acres of land on grants to foreigners. From the start of the Irish campaign in 1689 courtiers and commanders had been preying on the spoils of war. As early as 1690 Thomas Coningsby, for instance, asked Portland to intercede with the King regarding claims for several farms even though large parts were still 'intirely under ye enemy'.[49] William had always intended to reward his confidants, but also ordered that the profits from the forfeitures be put to public use.[50]

Coningsby had also recommended an estate to Portland, but it was not until April 1697 that a grant to the favourite of the estate of the Earl of Clancarty was finalised.[51] Conscious of the risk of public exposure and criticism, Portland had asked Henry Capel's advice as to the legality of the grant. The latter's reassurances lost some credibility when the Marquis of Winchester, Lord Justice of Ireland, warned that the grants might be disputed in the Irish parliamentary session that autumn. Portland, wiser after the storm aroused by the Welsh grants the previous year, decided to divert the Common's attention by transferring the grant to his son Henry, Lord Woodstock. To doubly secure the grant, he also tried to get it enacted by the Irish parliament.[52]

A commission had been installed to investigate the legality of the Irish grants William had bestowed upon his confidants. Criticism of the grants proved a useful pretext to launch a full-scale attack on the ministry. J.G. Simms has observed that in the Commons 'The line of cleavage was between the court party and the opposition,

---

46   Galway to Portland 7 December 1697, 12 December 1697, NUL, PwA 1114, PwA 1115; Childs, *British Army,* 194–6.

47   Childs, *British Army*, 200–201.

48   Cf. J.G. Simms, *The Williamite Confiscation in Ireland 1690–1703* (London, 1956), 95; *The Exorbitant Grants of William the III Examin'd and Questioned Shewing the Nature of Grants in Successive and Elective Monarchies, etc.* (London, 1703), in: Somers, *First Collection*, III. 106–14.

49   Coningsby to Portland 26 October 1690, NUL, PwA 303.

50   William to Godolphin 27 February 1691, Japikse, *Correspondentie*, XXVIII. 211; Cf. Simms, *Williamite Confiscation*, 85.

51   23 April 1697, *CTB* XII-i. 135, 284, 299; 15/25 September 1697, 8 November 1697, *CTB* XIII-i. 320, 140; 24 April 1697, Luttrell, *Brief Historical Relation*, IV. 215.

52   Simms, *Williamite Confiscation*, 87; Portland to Vernon 15 October 1698, Portland to Capel 23 March 1696 (Kensington Palace), Capel to Portland 30 March 1696, Winchester to Portland 10 August 1697, NUL, PwA 1492, PwA 271, PwA 272, PwA 1012; Winchester to Shrewsbury 5 August 1697, HMC, *Buccleugh Mss*, II-ii. 522.

or country party',[53] The Commission dexterously concentrated on the foreigners benefiting from these grants (they were singled out in a separate list) in order to criticise the Court. The impression was given that William had bestowed the grant upon foreign profiteers who had done nothing to deserve the favour. According to Simms the grants were given to 'mere courtiers and ... civil advisers' – among whom he included Portland. But William had ample reason to bestow the grants on these particular persons: some seven foreigners received 60 per cent of the Irish grants, but almost all of these could claim them as a reward for their efforts in Ireland. The Earls of Galway, Athlone and Rochfort had fought in Ireland, as had Portland, who had moreover been instrumental in the establishment of the Treaty of Limerick.[54] Sidney had been Lord Lieutenant of Ireland. Many soldiers who had fought in the Irish campaign actually received lesser grants. In fact, the Earl of Albemarle was the only grantee who had not been involved in the subjection of Ireland.[55]

The partisan stance of the Commission became clear from its decision to include in the report a grant made to Lady Orkney, which had never belonged to the Irish estates. The document which was included concerning this particular case was signed by only four out of seven commissioners, which reflects the doubtful legitimacy of the decision and the division of the Commission itself.[56] The Commission was divided along partisan lines as it contained two members who were fiercely anti-Huguenot, and a third who was an avowed opponent of the government.[57] Thus, what seemed to be a protest against foreign favourites was rather a measure against the Court, and could only have carried the day during the late 1690s with the collapse of the Court Whig Party and the rise of the New Country Party.

On behalf of the government, Montagu launched a counter-attack by suggesting that the Commission had only included the Orkney grant in its investigation because 'the report would signify nothing without it'.[58] It was to no avail. Neither was the protest of three of the seven commissioners that they had been marginalized and even kept outside certain investigations. In April 1700 a Resumption Bill passed the Commons, stipulating that all grants bestowed by William would be nullified.[59] Portland, Albemarle and Lady Orkney were accused of advising the King to veto

---

53   Simms, *Williamite Confiscation*, 97, cf. 98–9.
54   ibid., 85.
55   HMC, *House of Lords Mss 1699–1702* (London, 1908), 33–8. From a total of 1,060,792, some 656,807 acres went to foreigners of which Sidney received 49,517, Athlone 26,480, Galway 36,148, Albemarle 108,633, Rochfort 39,871, Woodstock 135,820 and Lady 's Gravenmoer 21,006 acres. Most of the other grantees were soldiers who fought in Ireland. Lady Orkney received 95,649 (not included in Irish grants); Cf. BL, Add Mss 4761, f° 64.
56   G. van Alphen, *De Stemming van de Engelschen tegen de Hollanders in Engeland tijdens de Regeering van den Koning-Stadhouder Willem III 1688–1702* (Assen, 1938), 277–9; Horwitz, *Parliament*, 262–3; Simms, *Williamite Confiscation*, 106.
57   Namely John Trenchard, author of the famous pamphlet *A Short History of the Standing Armies in England*, a fierce opponent of the standing army, Simms, *Williamite Confiscation*, 98.
58   Quoted in Horwitz, *Parliament*, 264.
59   *Cobbett's Parliamentary History of England etc. 1688–1702* (12 vols, London, 1806–12), V. 1215, 1217.

the Bill, but it had been William himself who had stubbornly resisted what now seemed inevitable.[60] A constitutional crisis loomed when the Commons decided to tack the measure onto a Land Tax Bill, causing the Lords to return the Bill.[61] William, however, wished to avoid a crisis and gave in. Albemarle was despatched to the Lords to give a signal that William gave his consent to the Bill.[62] Portland and Albemarle, who had both benefited from the grants, complied and voted in favour of the Bill on its next reading.[63]

Such attacks on the favourite can be seen as part of a broader wave of xenophobia. Albemarle, although Portland's rival, seems to have been eager to keep him at Court out of fear 'that he would be the only one remaining and the prime target for the jealousy of the English'.[64] Burnet had argued that William made himself more unpopular by his preference for Dutch things and courtiers.[65] This xenophobia had been resonating throughout the 1690s, but came to the fore with renewed vehemence after 1697, expressed in parliamentary debates and a continuous stream of pamphlets. The unmistakable xenophobic sentiments, however, were channelled into attacks on the Court. One of the more critical pamphlets was *The Foreigners* by John Tutchin, published in 1700. In scathing metaphor, describing 'Bentir' plundering the land of 'Israel', he wrote:

> Bentir in the Inglorious Role the first,
> Bentir to this and future ages curst,
> Of mean descent, yet insolently proud,
> Shun'd by the Great, and hated by the Crowd;
> Who neither Blood nor Parentage can boast,
> And what he got the Jewish Nation lost:
> By lavish Grants whole Provinces he gains;
> Made forfeit by the Jewish Peoples pains;[66]

Portland was defended, however, by the court propagandist Daniel Defoe in his magisterial pamphlet *The True-born Englishman* published shortly after:

> Ten Years in English Service he appear'd,
> And gain'd his Master's and the World's Regard
> But 'tis not England's custom to Reward.

---

60   William to Portland 5 April 1700 OS, Japikse, *Correspondentie*, XXIII. 351.
61   A.S. Turberville, *The House of Lords in the Reign of William* (Oxford, 1913), 201–2. Cobbett's *Parliamentary History*, V. 1217; Horwitz, *Parliament* 231, 255.
62   Simms, *Williamite Confiscation*, 112.
63   Cobbett's *Parliamentary History*, V. 1218; Turberville, *The House of Lords*, 208–9.
64   Tallard to Louis 3 May 1699, AAE, CPA 181, f° 19v°, transl. from French.
65   Horwitz, *Parliament*, 256.
66   J. Tutchin, *The Foreigners* (London, 1700).

The Wars are over, England needs him not;
Now he's a Dutchman, and the Lord knows what.[67]

A flow of doggerels on the same theme followed in which Portland, Albemarle and others were criticised.[68] The criticism against the King culminated in the 1701 Act of Settlement, enacted to safeguard the Protestant succession via the Hanoverian line after the death of the Duke of Gloucester, Anne's only son. The Act decisively undermined the royal prerogative, but in many aspects could have been a scathing criticism of Portland as well. It stipulated that

> no person born out of the kingdoms of England, Scotland or Ireland, or the dominions thereunto belonging (although he be naturalized or made a denizen, except such as are born of English parents), shall be capable to be of the Privy Council, or a member of either House of Parliament, or to enjoy any office or place of trust either civil or military, or to have any grants of lands, tenements or hereditaments from the crown to himself or to any other or others in trust for him.[69]

Although by 1701 no Dutchmen could be found in the Cabinet or Privy Councils, the Bill obviously targeted William's foreign favourites. When the Commons moved to have Portland removed from the Privy Council, he had already retired and was not even attending the meetings.[70] But the stipulation was firmly embedded within typical Country measures such as a limitation of the King's independence in foreign policy and a reaffirmation of the Place Bill.

III

If opposition complicated Portland's role in domestic politics and military management, his role as the King's close adviser on foreign policy remained unassailable. Some even thought in October 1697 that 'my Lord Portland is only entrusted with the *arcana imperii* and some persons of great quality say that the Earl of Pembroke is as much in the dark as any and resents it'.[71] By then, rumours circulated at Court of Portland being entrusted with an embassy to Spain, which were soon refuted. The news that he would undertake an embassy to Paris, however, appeared to be correct. Undoubtedly, the secrets of the realm in which the favourite was involved pertained to the improvement of relations with France and deciding the fate of the Spanish empire. Portland's embassy to Paris seemed a natural sequence

---

67   D. Defoe, *The True-born Englishman. A Satyr* (London, 1701).

68   *The Natives* (London, 1700); W. Pittis, *The True-born Englishman: a Satyr, Answer'd Paragraph by Paragraph* (London, 1701); *The Reverse: or, the Tables Turn'd* (London, 1700).

69   Quoted in *English Historical Documents 1660–1714 VIII*, ed. A. Browning (London/New York, 1966), 134.

70   Van Alphen, *Stemming van de Engelschen*, 276.

71   Johnston to Huntingdon 5 October 1697, HMC, *The Manuscripts of the ... the Manor House, Ashby-de-la-Zouche* (4 vols, London, 1930), II. 299. Pembroke was Lord Privy Seal and Plenipotentiary at Ryswick.

to his secret dealings with Marshal Boufflers. Moreover, by sending his trusted favourite to the French court, William was transmitting a clear signal to Louis that he desired a better mutual understanding. A last reason for Portland's embassy may have been the result of the King's desire to temporarily remove his confidant from Court due to his intensifying quarrel with the rival favourite, the Earl of Albemarle, a development discussed in detail in chapter 9.

Portland received his instructions on 31 December 1697 and left London on 10 January 1698. The journey of the spectacular train escorting the Ambassador received ample attention. Portland left in the morning, arrived at Rochester to dine, and was received in Sittenburn with the ringing of bells. The next day he passed through Canterbury and arrived at Dover, where he was again greeted by the ringing of bells and the firing of cannons. Because of strong winds, the yacht could only leave Dover on 13 January in the morning, arriving at Calais that same evening. The Commander met him at the pier and escorted him to the Governor's house, where he was entertained by the magistrates of that city. Passing through Bologne the next day, he was greeted on 15 January in Montreuil by the firing of cannons and the offering of wine by the magistrates of that town. Most remarkable was his reception in Amiens, where he was greeted at the city gates by the *Intendant* and two regiments of horse. They escorted him to his house through the entire city, Swiss guards being posted along the entire route.[72]

Arriving in Paris on 20 January, he was greeted by his son Lord Woodstock, the secretary Abel Tassin d'Alonne and the Duke of Boufflers. The courtesies paid to the Ambassador were seen to be more than could be expected in these circumstances, and therefore signalled French desire to improve relations with England. Portland was lodged in Paris in the Hotel d'Auvergne, and frequently held sumptuous dinners. He was introduced to the King by Torcy on 25 January, and had private audiences with the Dauphin, the Dukes of Anjou, Berry and Burgundy, the Duke and Duchess of Orleans and the Duchess of Burgundy.

It was only on 9 March that Portland held his public entry into Paris. The Ambassador, seated in the King's own coach, was attended by gentlemen of the horse, twelve pages, 56 footmen, twelve led horses, four coaches with eight horses and two chariots with six horses – a sight unseen since the Duke of Buckingham's embassy.[73] It was probably one of the most expensive embassies, costing William some £48,000.[74] The Parisians were duly impressed. When Portland received his first official audience on 11 March, the crowd in Versailles was so thick that the Ambassador had difficulty passing through to deliver his opening speech.[75] The Sun King reciprocated the magnificent overture with commensurate splendour, receiving

---

72   A full description of Portland's journey and embassy can be found in TNA:PRO, SP 105/26, and *Journal of the Extraordinary Embassy of His Excellence the Earl of Portland in France*, ed. G.D.J. Schotel (The Hague, 1851).

73   A. Boyer, *The History of King William the Third* (3 vols, London, 1702–03), III. 335 ff.

74   Cf. D.B. Horn, *The British Diplomatic Service 1689–1789* (Oxford, 1961), 66; Boyer, *History of King William*, III, 340–41.

75   TNA: PRO, SP 105/26.

the Ambassador with elaborate courtesies and granting him the unprecedented favour of free access. 'The Court has learned with pleasure', Bonnet wrote from London, 'the good reception that Mylord Portland has received in France.'[76]

The Ambassador was now keeping an open table, which according to the journal could have five tables with 90 guests. According to one Dutch observer, Portland made an effort to impress his guests by organising a splendid dinner with rare spices and food for the Dukes of Boufflers and Beauviller, the Dutch ambassador in Paris, Nassau-Odijk, and many others.[77] He frequently entertained other ambassadors, most notably the Danish envoy Henning Meyercron, the Swedish envoy Johan Palmquist, Ezechiel Spanheim from Brandenburg, Johann Bothmer from Zell, Schuylenberg from Wolfenbüttel, Tettau from Hesse-Cassel, and the Dutch ambassadors Nassau-Odijk and Coenraad van Heemskerck: all former allies. But he also entertained (and was entertained by) the *grandes*, such as the Duke of Boufflers, the Princes of Condé and Conti and the Duke of Orleans, the King's brother. That relations were cordial can be seen from the fact that Princes of the Blood, such as Conti and Condé, and the Ambassador would continue to maintain a friendly correspondence after the embassy had come to an end.[78] While Portland had never been popular with his new compatriots, he thus soon established friendly contacts with many of his former enemies. Saint-Simon praised the good manners and judgement of the English ambassador.[79] The Duchess of Orleans found Portland's conversation pleasing, though her husband was afraid that Portland would only try to hear her out.[80]

Indeed, beneath the surface of courtesies and splendour, the former enemies were testing the waters to uncover each other's motives. It was widely believed that Louis was trying to blind the Ambassador by the brilliance of his reception, of which Portland himself was aware, although 'I admit that if everything that I have seen from the King's person is not sincere it is a comedy well played'.[81] Portland was sceptical as to the usefulness of his mission as he distrusted French motives. Throughout his embassy he repeatedly requested permission to return, partly because he must have been uneasy about his absence from Court where the star of his rival, the Earl of Albemarle, was rising. But he seemed to have genuinely doubted whether he was the most appropriate candidate for the embassy. He was obstinate and independently minded which frequently caused him to interpret William's wishes before receiving actual instructions.[82] Moreover, Portland foresaw the difficulties the King would run into with Parliament, and suggested that William should

---

76 Dispatch Bonnet 4/14 February 1698, BL, Add Mss 30000B, f° 31v°, transl. from French.
77 C. Droste, *Overblijfsels van Geheugchenis etc.* (The Hague 1728), 147.
78 E.g. NUL PwA 202, 203
79 Cf. Ch. 4.
80 Madame to the Duchess of Hanover 16 February 1698, *The Letters of Madame the Correspondence of Elizabeth-Charlotte of Bavaria, Princess Palatine, Duchess of Orleans ... 1661–1708*, ed. G.S. Stevenson (2 vols, London, 1924), I. 160.
81 Portland to William 13 March 1698 (Paris), Japikse, *Correspondentie*, XXIII. 256, transl. from French.
82 Cf. Louis to Tallard 5 May 1698, Tallard to Louis 8 May 1698, *Letters of William III, and Louis XIV and of their Ministers etc. 1697–1700*, ed. P. Grimblot (2 vols., London,

... send me someone who can tell in England the true state of affairs, and in whom the members of Parliament can put a little bit more faith than in what I will write. As I will always be considered as a man attached to Your Majesty and who will say only what You want to hear.[83]

Portland's instructions were fairly generally stated. He was to assure the French king of William's desire to maintain a stable peace. His additional and secret instructions stipulated in very general terms that he should endeavour to have James removed from St Germain, and to seek an understanding in case of the death of the Spanish king.[84] Portland's embassy started off somewhat unfortunately with his obstinate insistence on the removal of James from St Germain. The matter had been discussed between Boufflers and Portland before, but not resolved. Although the former had argued that Louis could not remove the exiled king formally, he might agree to do so afterwards as a sign of goodwill. Louis had never intended to do so, but Portland was still under the impression that he would comply with the demand to have James removed to Avignon or Italy, and regarded the matter as a litmus test of the King's sincerity.[85] Boufflers insisted that Louis had never pledged to comply with William's demand. Though it was difficult for Portland to deny this, it increased his suspicions.[86] The presence, moreover, of a number of Jacobites at Court provoked a bitter argument with Boufflers on the matter. 'I have received all possible marks of honour and distinction', he wrote to William, but

> Englishmen attached to King James are being admitted at court every day ... this has increased my suspicion ... if I leave things on this footing, without showing how sensitive I am about this, that this is not in keeping with the union and good understanding that they assure me they want to establish and maintain ... .[87]

Portland may have been too critical, as Louis had ordered the Jacobite Secretary of State Charles Middleton to prevent Jacobites from coming to Versailles when the English ambassador was present. One of those who seems to have withdrawn from public life altogether during this period was Sir Edward Herbert, the Jacobite Earl of Portland and brother of Lord Torrington.[88]

The French seemed to have been receptive to English sensibilities on the matter. When someone referred to William as Prince of Orange rather than King of England in Portland's presence, he was asked to leave.[89] But Louis did not show any inclination to remove James from his protection. William had permitted Portland to

---

1848), I. 448, 461.
83 Portland to William 23 January 1698 (Dover), Japikse, *Correspondentie*, XXIII. 220; transl. from French.
84 Japikse, *Correspondentie*, XXIII. 214–19.
85 Portland to William 16–18 February 1698 (Paris), ibid., 227–32.
86 Portland to William 16–18 February (Paris), ibid.
87 Portland to William 9 February 1698 (Paris), ibid., 224, transl. from French.
88 E. Corp (ed.), *A Court in Exile. The Stuarts in France 1689–1718* (Cambridge, 2004), 153; E. Gregg, 'France, Rome and the Exiled Stuarts, 1689–1713' in: Corp, *A Court in Exile*, 11–75, 54.
89 TNA: PRO, SP 150/26, f° 8.

press the matter, but perhaps not with the tenacious obstinacy his envoy displayed. In an audience on 17 February, Portland insisted that the King remove James, and that William understood an agreement had been so made. He added that Parliament would doubt Louis's sincerity unless this demand were complied with, the more so since a number of suspects of the Assassination Plot had been spotted in Versailles.[90] On the first point Louis refused, arguing that an agreement had never been made, which was formally correct. The King agreed to look into the second point if Portland would provide him with the names of suspects. Portland had intimated that unless Louis complied with the demand, William might not pay the £50,000 pension to Mary of Modena, a threat that Louis dismissed since this requirement was actually inserted into the Ryswick articles.[91] William was dissatisfied with Portland's strong insistence on this matter – though he typically did not reprimand his emissary in the least – and feared that it proved an ill start of his embassy. Portland thought otherwise, arguing that Louis might feel compelled to be more flexible in other matters unless he intended to provoke a break with William.[92] It was not the first time Portland and the King disagreed about negotiations, the favourite being usually less inclined to take an accommodating stance. Portland was now extremely sceptical about the usefulness of the mission:

> Your Majesty sees what kind of foundation the peace provides and to what extent one can believe their protestations when the effects are the contrary. Your Majesty knows that this does not surprise me, since I expected this since you did me the honour of sending me on this mission.[93]

Soon rumours spread about the contents of the talks, and Portland was suspected of trying to make matters public before he discussed them in an audience. Obviously it would have been interpreted as a means to exert pressure on the King, but Portland assured the French ministers that this was not his intention.[94] 'It is very good', he wrote to William, 'that these rumours of refusal proceed from the Jacobites and do not seem to be coming from your people.'[95] Meanwhile Portland commenced a parallel correspondence with William, meant not to be seen by ministers: 'I will convey the true state of affairs as they are, unless perhaps you judge it better for the interest of the affairs of Parliament that I will not show so openly the little Your Majesty can expect here.'[96]

---

90 Portland to William 16–18 February 1698 (Paris), Japikse, *Correspondentie*, XXIII. 230.
91 Louis to Tallard 16 May 1698, Grimblot, *Letters*, I. 485–6.
92 Portland to William 7–8 March 1698 (Paris), Japikse, *Correspondentie*, XXIII. 245.
93 Portland to William 16–18 February 1698 (Paris), ibid. 232, transl. from French.
94 Portland to William 1 March 1698 (Paris), ibid., 237–8.
95 Portland to William 13 March 1698 (Paris), ibid., 255, transl. from French.
96 Portland to William 13 March 1698 (Paris), ibid., 257, transl. from French.

IV

On 14 March Marquis of Pomponne, the Secretary of State, and his son-in-law and heir apparent, the Marquis of Torcy, visited Portland and broached the subject of the Spanish inheritance in order to reach an understanding with William.[97] They warned that Habsburg would be the dominant power in Europe again if the Emperor should inherit Spain, and expedients must be sought in order to prevent that eventuality. William and Portland must have discussed the matter thoroughly beforehand, though his instructions merely stated that he must sound out the King of France in case the King of Spain should die.[98] It has been assumed that Portland and Boufflers had broached the issue during their private talks at Halle in the summer of 1697. There is, however, no trace in Portland's draft notes, and apparently both William and Louis had anxiously tried to avoid the matter in the Ryswick talks.[99]

Portland had claimed to be wholly unaware of William's thoughts on the Spanish Succession and assured Pomponne and Torcy that their overture was unexpected. He was not instructed to deal on this matter but agreed to listen, not as an ambassador but as a private person, and convey their ideas to his master. To William he wrote:

> I did not want to say anything which could give the impressions that I knew Your Majesty's thoughts, especially as they started with little or nothing, which is why I waited to hear Your Majesty's wishes on this matter.[100]

Of course Portland's aim was to let Louis make an overture.[101] By feigning a lack of knowledge (he even asked Pomponne and Torcy to explain the contents of the will of Philip IV) he hoped to force them to lay their cards on the table. In consecutive meetings Portland surprised his opponents by his intimate and substantial knowledge of affairs.[102] It was only after several weeks that Louis suspected that Portland was playing tricks on him. In May he wrote to Tallard that the talks should be transferred to London; whereas Tallard was negotiating in earnest, Portland was only concealing William's thoughts and trying to sound out Louis's intentions.[103]

---

97   For a good analysis of the French side of these negotiations, see J. C. Rule, 'The Partition Treaties, 1698–1700: A European View' in: E. Mijers and D. Onnekink (eds), *Redefining William III: The Impact of the King-Stadholder in International Context* (Aldershot, 2007), 95–109.

98   'he has to sound out whether there is a means to find expedients to prevent a war which could be set off by the death of the King of Spain who is without children'. Secret instruction for Portland in William's handwriting, 8 January 1698, Japikse, *Correspondentie*, XXIII. 218–19, transl. from French.

99   See his notes in NUL, Pw A 2574 ff.

100   Account of Pomponne and Torcy 14 March 1698, Grimblot, *Letters*, I. 294 ff.; Portland to William 5/15 March 1698, Japikse, *Correspondentie*, XXIII. 259–60, transl. from French.

101   Louis thought that since he was a claimant and William not, it would be incorrect to do otherwise.

102   Account of Pomponne and Torcy 14 March 1698, Grimblot, *Letters*, I. 298, in which they reported that Portland seemed 'really ignorant' of the will of Philip IV.

103   Louis to Tallard 5 May 1698, Grimblot, *Letters*, I. 450.

The Spanish Succession had been a source of concern for over three decades. The Spanish king, Carlos II, had been weak as an infant and repeatedly wavered on the brink of death. His childlessness caused the European powers considerable anxiety since a struggle over his inheritance seemed inevitable. Louis could claim the inheritance on behalf of the Dauphin, who was a son of his first wife, Marie Thérèse, a daughter of Philip IV. The Emperor had married a younger daughter of Philip IV and claimed the inheritance on behalf of his second son, the Archduke Charles. A third claimant was a great-grandson of Philip, Joseph Ferdinand, Electoral prince of Bavaria. Both the French king and the Emperor had the means to back up their claims, and as early as 1668 they had agreed to make a treaty of partition dividing the Spanish Empire to avoid armed struggle. In 1689 the Maritime Powers pledged to support the claim of the Emperor, but changed circumstances after the Peace of Ryswick and the dissolution of the Grand Alliance necessitated a new agreement. Various initiatives had been undertaken; the Austrians and the French had sent their ambassadors, Count Harrach and the Duke d'Harcourt, to Madrid to induce the Spanish king, who by all accounts was dying, to make a final alteration to his will in favour of their sovereigns. It was at this critical juncture that Louis made an overture to William. The Emperor was on the brink of concluding a favourable peace with the Turks and would soon be in a position to claim the full inheritance. The Bavarian pretender was no serious party in the negotiations, lacking the strength to bolster his claim alone; a direct agreement with the Spanish king would be contested by both the Maritime Powers and the Emperor. A direct deal with William to partition the Empire and act as joint guarantors of the treaty was thus the most obvious choice.[104]

The talks were influenced by four factors. Firstly, the health of the King of Spain, which was particularly precarious during 1698 and 1699. This put immense pressure on the negotiations, since no one was certain what would happen should the King die during the talks. Secondly, the war in the Balkans was drawing to a close, the peace being in fact signed in 1699. This raised the prospect of a more active Imperial policy in the West, which was unfavourable to Louis. A third factor was the mutual perception of Louis and William of each other's strength. The devastating parliamentary sessions of 1698 and 1699 in England, in which the Country party decimated William's army and finances, were a particularly crucial element in the talks, though the results were paradoxical and unforeseen. Lastly, the negotiations were influenced by mutual distrust. If the parties were sincerely dealing with each other, they would need to exclude the possibility of reaching an agreement with other parties. The fear would linger, however, that one party might be secretly dealing with a third party, and these suspicions would cloud the negotiations.[105] It is difficult to overestimate the complexities caused by these factors, and it counts for something that the two kings, who had been archenemies for three decades, reached a basic agreement within six weeks after the first overture was made.

The talks continued for six months, and can be summarised by comparing the axioms of the contestants, and the manner in which an agreement was accordingly reached. From William's point of view, the Spanish and French crowns must never

---

104 Cf. Louis to Tallard 16 May 1698, Grimblot, *Letters*, I. 476–7.
105 E.g. Tallard to Louis 16 July 1698, ibid., II. 72–8.

be united. He did not believe that having a French prince (rather than the Dauphin) on the Spanish throne would suffice to prevent an actual union. This was difficult to swallow for Louis, who believed that he had a legal right to the Spanish throne. Secondly, William insisted that the Spanish Netherlands must be connected to Spain, otherwise they would be indefensible. Navarra and Guiposcoa, on the south side of the Pyrenees, should remain in Spanish hands. This was also difficult to accept for France as it would imply an encirclement. Louis consistently strove to gain vital strategic positions to defend his territory: Navarra, Guiposcoa (as a gateway into Spain), Luxembourg or the Spanish Netherlands, and Milan, as a stepping stone into Italy. Obviously, what Louis considered vital defensive strongholds were perceived in London and The Hague as potential key offensive positions. Thirdly, the Maritime Powers needed to secure their trade in the Mediterranean and the West Indies through a number of safe ports. To this Louis objected for two reasons. Firstly, the Maritime Powers were not legal claimants and secondly, they would soon dominate the scene and destroy Spanish trade.

In early April Pomponne and Torcy came with their first concrete proposals. Having considered William's fear that France and Spain might come under one Bourbon crown, Louis proposed that his son the Dauphin renounce the inheritance in favour of one of his sons, the Duke of Anjou or Berry, who would be educated in Spain. The Spanish Netherlands would come under the sovereignty of the Elector of Bavaria, and the English and Dutch would receive guarantees for the safety of their trade in the Mediterranean. Louis tried to make it more attractive by offering ports to the Maritime Powers, and the Spanish Netherlands to the Elector of Bavaria.[106] Portland dismissed the proposals on both legal and pragmatic grounds. Conversing as a 'private person', he argued that there were three pretenders, and there was no reason to suppose the Dauphin had a greater claim than the Archduke or the Electoral prince. He then laid down a proposal that would become the basis of a final agreement: that the Electoral prince should have the bulk of the inheritance, that the Low Countries must remain in strong hands and that the Maritime Powers needed tangible proof for the security of their trade. On 2 April Portland first intimated that William might be willing to listen to proposals, and advised him to speak about it to Tallard. After this counteroffer (still by Portland as a 'private person'), both parties could now work towards a *via media*. Portland thus achieved an important diplomatic success: he forced Louis to renounce the bulk of the inheritance in favour of the Electoral prince.

At this stage, William, Heinsius and Portland (who were the only ones informed of the substance of the talks) were in doubt as to whether to pursue the negotiations. It might be possible, Portland suggested to William, to prevent

> ... the jealousies which France could be prone to, even if Your Majesty himself does not propose anything; meanwhile when I go to see the ministers here, I will talk on the same footing and not say anything which will give the least impression that Your Majesty proposes or answers their proposals, which are so far removed from anything reasonable, in such a way as to cause jealousies among our allies ... .[107]

---

106 Portland to William 2 April 1698 (Paris), Japikse, *Correspondentie*, XXIII. 274–8.
107 Portland to William 10 April 1698 (Paris), ibid., 280, transl. from French.

It was a calculated risk. If France were sincere, she would press the talks nonetheless. If she were not, there was a danger that the Grand Alliance would be undermined. Either way, there was always a risk that Louis would strike a bargain with one of the other parties, and the three men decided to continue the talks and see where they might lead.[108]

Indeed, the way in which Louis perceived the strength of the Dutch and English was crucial to the success of the Partition Treaties. If he regarded them as weak and indecisive (as he had thought, in fact, in 1688), he could gamble on Dutch aloofness and English domestic turmoil and claim the full inheritance. In retrospect England's rise to greatness can be traced back to the Glorious Revolution, but to many contemporaries England of 1698 resembled that of 1688. It was headed by a weak monarch, distrusted by the political nation trying to clip his wings both militarily and financially. On his arrival in London late March 1698 Tallard informed Louis: 'the King of England may still be reckoned of much importance, on account of his personal qualities, but this kingdom must be considered as a country destitute of resources for many years to come.'[109] William's position would only weaken, and Louis could profit from the situation as he had with Charles II and James II: he could bind William to his own interests by giving him subsidies, reducing his ability to act independently.[110] Tallard however warned the King not to draw false conclusions; England still had the ability to act militarily.[111] The alternative would be to strike a sincere deal with William, on the basis that England and France could dominate the rest of Europe and force both Spain and the Emperor to accept the Partition Treaty. This option became less desirable when William's position weakened further throughout 1698 and 1699, and Louis continued to waver between the two options. The leaders of the Maritime Powers argued along the same lines. All depended on strength, and Heinsius kept insisting that regardless of what avenue the talks might take, it was imperative to have a strong army and a strong fleet: whether Louis was sincere or not, 'the more we put ourselves in order, the easier the negotiations in Paris will be'.[112] The success, then, of the Partition Treaties hinged on the strength of the Maritime Powers.

When Louis realised that William would not accept the Dauphin as the sole heir he proposed two alternatives. One was in favour of the Electoral prince but with compensation for the Dauphin which he knew was unacceptable to William. A second allotted the bulk to his grandson and favourable conditions for the Maritime Powers – obviously in an effort to tempt William. Portland dismissed both alternatives:

---

108 Portland to William 10 April 1698 (Paris), ibid.

109 Tallard to Louis 31 March 1698, 3 April 1698, Grimblot, *Letters*, I. 323, 343. Heinsius thought that in case the Spanish king were to die, the Dutch would be powerless to resist the French should they wish to claim the full inheritance. Heinsius to William 14 March 1698, Krämer, *Archives*, II. 62–3.

110 This option was seriously considered by Louis, though Tallard warned him that the situation was not entirely the same, since William could also depend on Holland. Louis to Tallard 26 May 1698, Grimblot, *Letters*, I. 511–12; Tallard to Louis 2 June 1698, ibid., II. 13.

111 Tallard to Louis 2 March 1699, ibid., II. 291–3.

112 Heinsius to William 25 March 1698, Krämer, *Archives*, II. 77, transl. from Dutch.

neither one took the real interests of the Maritime Powers into consideration.[113] William however created an opening and accepted the first alternative in principle, allotting the bulk of the inheritance to the Electoral prince, but strove to improve the conditions. Tallard was optimistic and now believed a deal was possible.[114] The French king's reasonable offers came as a surprise, and William, Portland and Heinsius seemed increasingly to consider the possibility that Louis might be sincere. The offer exceeded their expectations, and the stumbling blocks (Luxembourg and ports for the Maritime Powers in the Mediterranean and the West Indies) could be overcome in time.

In several audiences, throughout late April and May, Portland insisted on more concessions from the French in the Mediterranean and the West Indies. On 17 May he had a long private audience with the King in which they discussed the stumbling blocks to an agreement. Firstly, Portland argued that the Emperor would never be allowed to be dominant in Italy, and so Louis's fears in this regard were unfounded. Secondly, he demanded substantial strongholds in the Mediterranean and the West Indies to safeguard Dutch and English commerce. Thirdly, Luxembourg could not be restituted, indeed, the Barrier had to be enlarged. Lastly, the position of James remained a stumbling block to a good mutual understanding. 'I am very much convinced', Portland wrote to William, 'that if Your Majesty remains very firm on all matters in question, he will be mainly content, if not completely. I believe they sincerely desire to attach themselves to you.'[115] He added that Louis repeatedly said that if he and William would come to an agreement, the rest of Europe had to follow.[116] Portland's final audiences were concerned with bickering about fortified places in the Mediterranean and the West Indies, in which he consistently rejected the offers.[117] It would be intriguing to know what had been discussed in a meeting Portland had in the King's closet just days before he left for London. To William he wrote that the discussion had been too important to entrust its report to paper.[118]

By now Portland's negotiations were no longer productive. He had tried to sound out the King as much as possible without giving too much away. Portland 'will not facilitate any thing', Tallard thought. 'This comes rather from his obstinacy ... than

---

113 Louis to Tallard 17 April 1698: First alternative: to cede to the Electoral prince: Spain, Indies, Low Countries, Majorca, Minorca, Sardinia, Philippines, and other countries except for Naples, Sicily and Luxembourg for the Dauphin, Milan to Archduke; Second alternative: the whole inheritance for a French prince, with the Low Countries for the Electoral prince, Naples and Sicily for Archduke and Tuscany ports. Milan for Savoy. Grimblot, *Letters*, I. 384–93; Portland to William 20 April 1698 (Paris), Japikse, *Correspondentie*, XXIII. 287–90.

114 Tallard to Louis 25 April 1698, Grimblot, *Letters*, I. 419–29.

115 Portland to William 17 May 1698 (Paris), Japikse, *Correspondentie*, XXIII. 308, transl. from French. Cf. Portland to William 4 June 1698 (Paris), ibid., 331.

116 Portland to William 17 May 1698 (Paris), ibid., 308; Louis seems to have thought that for that reason, William would clearly see that it was not in Louis's interest to support James. Louis to Tallard 16 May 1698, Grimblot, *Letters*, I. 486.

117 Portland to William 4 June 1698 (Paris), Japikse, *Correspondentie*, XXIII. 331–3.

118 Portland to William 17 June 1698 (Paris), ibid., 334–5.

from ill will.'[119] Louis found out soon enough it was easier and more advantageous to deal with William directly.[120] Louis was also convinced – and justly so – that Portland and Heinsius were more sceptical than William.[121]

Portland arrived in London on 29 June and reported immediately to the King in Kensington Palace.[122] His embassy had been widely reported on and made him the subject of speculation, criticism and praise. Rumours about his position at Court were particularly confused during the summer. In July Tallard thought that the favour of his rival Albemarle was increasing, but he changed his mind by the autumn. After the conclusion of the First Partition Treaty in November Portland had re-established himself as the pre-eminent favourite at Court. Albemarle threatened to resign and sulked in the countryside for weeks.[123] Meanwhile, during the summer rumours had been spreading that William would dispatch his favourite immediately to Madrid on another embassy. This probably meant that the highly secret talks on the Spanish inheritance Portland had conducted had leaked, as Matthew Prior, secretary of the Paris embassy, reported the rumour first. Secretary of State James Vernon dismissed the rumours, as did Louis, who thought it was devised to thwart the negotiations.[124]

Reflecting upon the achievements of his embassy, contemporary chroniclers both hailed and despised the Ambassador. John Oldmixon published a poem praising Portland as 'Mighty in the Arts of Peace'.[125] Abel Boyer, in his 1703 *History*, was not unsympathetic to Portland but dismissed the embassy as futile and costly. Surprisingly, Paul Rapin de Thoyras, who became tutor of Portland's son Woodstock in 1701, likewise criticised Portland's conduct.[126] Less novel was the recurrence of anti-favourite rhetoric. As Portland's embassy resembled that of Buckingham, a familiar rumour resurfaced in the aftermath of his embassy. Portland, Bonnet reported, 'has shown much indignation for those lying persons saying that he would become Duke of Buckingham'.[127] Portland never obtained the dukedom; it would have been the only honour left William could bestow on him, after the Garter in 1697 and the massive Westminster grants in 1698. By 1698 Portland's position at Court was already eroding, as will be discussed in the last chapter, but outwardly the embassy to Paris had been the zenith of his career.

---

119 Tallard to Louis 8 July 1698, Louis to Tallard 4 July 1698, Grimblot, *Letters*, II. 56, 53.
120 Louis to Tallard 5 May 1698, ibid., I. 446 ff.
121 Tallard thought that 'Heinsius will incline [William] to war', Tallard to Louis 22 July 1698, Grimblot, *Letters*, II. 79.
122 TNA: PRO, SP 105/26.
123 Cf. Ch. 9.
124 Louis to Tallard 24 July 1698, Grimblot, *Letters*, II. 81–3; Vernon to Prior 2 July 1698, Prior to Vernon 3 July 1698, HMC, *Bath Mss*, III. 225–7.
125 J. Oldmixon, *A Poem ... addressed to the ... Earl of Portland ... on his ... Return from his Embassy in France* (London, 1698).
126 Boyer, *History of King William*, III, 340–41. P. Rapin de Thoyras, *The History of England etc.* (5 vols, London, 1789), IV. 245.
127 Dispatch Bonnet 12/22 July 1698, BL, Add Mss 30000B, transl. from French.

Meanwhile Portland took charge of the negotiations with Tallard in London and during the summer at Het Loo.[128] By this time the negotiations had slowed down again. Louis was convinced the delay was due both to Portland (who persuaded William to take a firmer line) and the Commons, who still discussed the matter of demobilisation.[129] Again, William, Heinsius and Portland realised that success would depend above all on the strength of the Maritime Powers. Heinsius insisted 'that all efforts are being made to make the Allies put themselves in a good posture of defence; this point is the most difficult, but the only one to bring this negotiation to a good end'.[130] Tallard reported to Louis in late July that Portland seemed eager for a deal.[131] The talks continued through July and August, both parties realising it was a skirmish for the final crumbs. The last major stumbling block, Milan, was overcome. On 8 September an agreement was reached. On 26 September Portland and Tallard signed the treaty, deputies from the States General followed some two weeks later.[132]

It was only weeks before the conclusion that Portland confronted the ministers in London with a virtual *fait accompli*. He wrote that the talks were in a preliminary stage and that he was in need of their advice.[133] He instructed James Vernon to disclose the contents of his message to only a very select group; Charles Montagu, John Somers, the Duke of Shrewsbury and Edward Russell were subsequently notified. His message took Vernon by utter surprise, though

> ... it was not doubted but your Lord[sp] would bee principally, if not solely relied on, that the nature of the business & the Secret that was to bee observed would necessarily require the putting it into the hands of one that was in the highest confidence with the King.[134]

The Secretary feared that Louis was only 'amusing' them, but Portland seemed to think that an agreement could be solid if supported by force: 'Kings, princes and States do make and have ever made treaties and kept forces for the maintenance of them.'[135] Within days a commission under the Great Seal was sent to Holland, Portland emphasizing that the utmost speed was required; should the King of Spain die, France had the power to put herself in the possession of all the territories.[136]

---

128 This was partly for practical reasons as well; William feared that too many audiences of Tallard might rouse suspicion, Tallard to Louis 8 May 1698, Grimblot, *Letters*, I. 461.
129 Louis to Tallard 4 July 1698 and *passim*, Grimblot, *Letters*, II. 48–54.
130 Heinsius to William 8 July 1698, Krämer, *Archives*, II. 231, transl. from Dutch.
131 Tallard to Louis 30 July 1698, Grimblot, *Letters*, II. 87–92.
132 The First Partition Treaty allotted the bulk of the inheritance to the Electoral prince, Milan to the Archduke and Naples and Sicily to the Dauphin. Cf. Grimblot, *Letters*, II. 483 ff.
133 Portland to Vernon 24 August 1698 (Het Loo), NUL, PwA 1474.
134 Vernon to Portland 2 September 1698, NUL, PwA 1482.
135 Copy letter Portland to Vernon 7 October 1698, NUL, PwA 1491.
136 Portland to Vernon 5 September 1698 (Het Loo), NUL, PwA 1483.

V

In February 1699 Portland received the devastating news from the Elector of Bavaria of the death of his son, rendering the First Partition Treaty obsolete.[137] Portland must have been shocked, and almost upon receipt instructed his successor in Paris, the Earl of Jersey, to sound out Louis as to his opinion.[138] Jersey informed him that Louis seemed intent on renewing the treaty, but said that 'wee must look over the mapp to see, what would be most convenient ... [this] made me thinck'.[139] The subsequent negotiations were mainly conducted between Portland and Tallard; though Heinsius was intimately involved, William seemed more reluctant to enter into the debates.[140] In fact, according to Tallard, Portland had 'all the confidence in that affair. He convinces and determines the King his master in any thing he desires. He is allied to the Pensionary'.[141]

The negotiations for the Second Partition Treaty would prove much more complicated. This was partly because of the complexities of the death of the Electoral prince as well as the involvement of the Emperor, but historians have not always realised that an important source of the difficulties was the spectacular domestic clash between William and Parliament over the army, rather than deteriorating relations with France. This is also suggested by the unpublished and neglected correspondence between Portland and Heinsius, which provides further insights into the complexities of the talks and the parameters within which these were conducted.[142] Portland was concerned about the military potential because between December 1698 and April 1699 the Commons forced the King to reduce the army to almost unprecedented low numbers and send home his treasured Blue Guards, including Portland's horse regiment.[143] Initially Portland had been more optimistic about the attitude of Parliament. When the debates on the army had commenced in the spring of 1698, he supposed that the 'weather' would soon be changing: 'Sunshine after rain'.[144] But by the new session that autumn the situation had become decidedly grimmer. In despair, Portland wrote to Heinsius in January:

> The affairs have come this far here that a change in the Commons is not to be expected, and will be very difficult in the Lords, so that we cannot foresee very well which measure must be taken to redress matters, without great inconveniences one way or another, without our

---

137 Max Emanuel to Portland 8 February 1699, NUL, PwA 48.
138 Portland to Jersey 9 February 1699, Japikse, *Correspondentie*, XXIV. 375.
139 Extract from a letter of Jersey 15 February 1699, NA, 3.01.19/2189.
140 E.g. Portland to Heinsius 10 March 1699 (Kensington Palace), ibid.
141 Tallard to Louis 5 February 1700, AAE, CPA 185, f° 21v°, transl. from French. Cf. Tallard to Louis 22 April 1699, AAE, CPA 180, f° 214v°.
142 NA, 3.01.19/2189. Japikse did not include this correspondence in his volumes. Japikse, *Correspondentie*, XXIII. vii. Cf. Schwoerer, *No Standing Armies!*, 158.
143 Cf. Ch. 6.
144 Portland to William 1 March 1698 (Paris), Japikse, *Correspondentie*, XXIII. 240, transl. from French.

Lord God giving us the means in our hands which we cannot yet foresee, so great is the blindness of the people, and that which is required for their own preservation.[145]

Prior echoed Portland's concern when he wrote: 'how do we think to be respected or make alliances, whilst we can not give one Man to any of our Neighbours upon occasion? ... our friends at St Germains are drinking the house of C[ommons] health.'[146]

Heinsius genuinely feared that this time Louis might prefer a deal with Leopold if the Maritime Powers were to stick to their objections.[147] Portland had always been sceptical about the chances for the success of the treaties. He would have agreed with Sunderland who thought that 'the K. must treat with every body abroad as if all things went well here'.[148] But the domestic political situation was deteriorating. On 20 March 1699 the Commons resolved to disband the Blue Guards, after having rejected William's plea to retain his cherished Dutch elite troops.[149] On the day that the Blue Guards embarked for Holland, Tallard raised his demands. 'The affairs in Parliament are as before', Portland wrote to Heinsius, 'the guards embark today ... it becomes clear that [the French] regulate their measures according to the conduct of Parliament.'[150] Two days later he wrote: 'The affairs in Parliament are getting worse and I fear the French will accordingly become more difficult.'[151]

Portland witnessed the breakdown of William's policy with abhorrence. Between March and May 1699 the Whig Junto finally collapsed, Country MPs made violent attacks on the government and the army was reduced to 7,000 troops. In pamphlets Portland was seen as advising the King to prorogue Parliament in order to maintain the army: 'prorogue 'em I advise you, Or else I fear they'll Sacrafice you.'[152] This was the situation in which Portland was instructed to negotiate a treaty about which he felt increasingly sceptical. There was also a clear difference in opinion as to what line to take during the talks. William seemed intent on making more concessions, Portland, initially, held on to the principle of three claimants. In a memorandum he wrote: 'My opinion is that France will not break off the negotiations, but His Majesty does not want to hazard it.'[153] His professed dissatisfaction with William's tactic preceded his letter of resignation by only five weeks. Only one day after Portland's retirement, Tallard reported to Louis that 'every thing is in such a mess in

---

145 Portland to Heinsius 20 January 1699 (Kensington Palace), NA, 3.01.19/2189, transl. from Dutch. The French ambassador however warned Louis that despite the difficulties the English would 'give their last penny for their defence', Tallard to Louis 2 March 1699, Grimblot, *Letters*, II. 293.

146 Prior to Portland 11 February 1699, NUL, PwA 1036.

147 NUL, PwA 2681.

148 Sunderland to Portland 4 March 1699, NUL, PwA 1277.

149 Schwoerer, *No Standing Armies!*, 172.

150 Portland to Heinsius 24 March 1699 (Kensington Palace), NA, 3.01.19/2189, transl. from Dutch.

151 Portland to Heinsius 31 March 1699 (Kensington Palace), ibid. transl. from Dutch.

152 'A Dialogue Between K[ing] W[illiam], L[or]d Portl[an]d and Sunderland occasion'd by sending the Dutch Guards back to Holland', n.d., NUL, PwA 2034.

153 Notes of Portland 24 March 1699, NUL, PwA 2683, transl. from Dutch.

this country that no one knows to whom to apply on the slightest matter, and there is no one in office who will regulate or decide, or sign any thing whatever'.[154]

As will be discussed in more detail in the following chapter, Portland's decision to retire has often been explained by his quarrel with William over the position of his rival favourite, the Earl of Albemarle. But as will be argued, his retirement can also be related to the failing foreign policy making his position uncomfortable. In this light his explanation to Sunderland that his resignation was simply due to an unwillingness to accept responsibility for William's policy gains significance.[155] Portland now realised that he would only harm the King's interest by remaining in office, explaining to William that 'circumstances ... had been found to cause him annoyance in his public career'.[156] Charles Davenant classified Portland and the ministers who accepted the Partition Treaties among 'these authors of our misfortunes', but Portland, 'at least, did at length think it decent to retreat'.[157] Only because of William's direct request did he consent to continue the negotiations.[158]

William seems to have been surprised and suspicious about French eagerness to conclude the treaty.[159] Perhaps Portland was more aware of the drawbacks of this negotiation, Tallard concluding that 'one cannot do anything more advantageous for our interests than to conclude a treaty with [William] at this conjuncture'.[160] Portland also realised – as he had warned William earlier – that he now personified a foreign policy to which the Commons were averse. Parliament, intent on reducing the army, had not been insensitive to William's plea to retain his beloved Blue Guards. However, because Portland's regiment was part of the Blue Guards, Parliament was determined to return them to the United Provinces.[161]

It was to be expected that Louis would once more claim the bulk of the inheritance for his son, as he had done at the start of the talks a year earlier. Portland had then brushed aside the argument and defended the claim of the Electoral prince. Tallard must have sensed immediately that this time Portland was negotiating from a position of weakness; days after the death of the Prince, Portland visited Tallard to see whether he thought the Elector to be heir to the Prince his son. Louis rejected the Elector's claim on legal grounds, but also because the situation had changed; the Emperor had become stronger now that a peace with the Turks had been concluded. Louis asked for the Dauphin's part to be augmented with Milan, allotting the bulk

---

154 Tallard to Louis 2 May 1699, Grimblot, *Letters*, II. 316.
155 Sunderland to Portland 20 March 1699, NUL, PwA 1279.
156 Tallard to Louis 15 May 1699, Grimblot, *Letters*, II, 329.
157 C. Davenant, 'An Essay upon the Balance of Power' in: *The Political and Commercial Works of ... Charles D'avenant*, ed. C. Whitworth (5 vols, London, 1771), III. 299–360, 330.
158 Tallard to Louis 15 May 1699, Grimblot, *Letters*, II. 329. Most observers, including Tallard, Vernon and indeed the King himself, attributed Portland's decision to retire to a personal grudge rather than a political decision. E.g. Tallard to Louis 2 May 1699, ibid., 319: 'It is not a national cabal that desires to drive him back to Holland. It is himself that is desirous to withdraw.'
159 William to Portland 8 May 1699, Japikse, *Correspondentie*, XXIII. 339.
160 Tallard to Louis, 3 April 1699, AAE, CPA 180, f° 141r°, transl. from French.
161 Tallard to Louis 31 January 1699, Grimblot, *Letters*, II. 245.

of the Empire to the Archduke, with the exception of the Low Countries.[162] Portland and William discussed the matter in London, the latter expressing surprise as to 'why the pretensions of the Dauphin would have been enlarged because of the death of the Electoral Prince'.[163] Indeed, Portland complained to Tallard that Louis 'is trying to take such a great advantage from the death of the Electoral prince of Bavaria that it will be very difficult to come to a happy conclusion'.[164] He argued that if the Dauphin were to receive Milan as well as Naples and Sicily, the balance of power would be upset. Moreover, the proposed separation of the Spanish Netherlands from Spain was unacceptable.[165] An alternative proposal was swiftly hatched. In a memorial Portland handed to Tallard on 10 March, he accepted that the Archduke would receive Spain, but insisted that the Spanish Netherlands needed to be attached to it, and that Milan must fall into neither French nor Austrian hands.[166]

The talks continued more or less without interruption, although they were transferred to Het Loo where William and his favourite had retreated to that summer. Tallard was surprised that the Earl was making so many difficulties, being convinced that the Maritime Powers were eager to reach a settlement at all costs. Despite mutual distrust the talks proceeded more swiftly now, in fact a basic agreement had been made as early as 11 June 1699. But it would take almost a year before the treaties were signed, which shows the instability of the agreement, but also the additional complexity as a result of the Emperor's involvement. Tallard frequently blamed William, but especially Portland, for delaying the talks, but it was the Emperor who made the most difficulties.[167] If the Spanish king were to die before an agreement had been reached, the Maritime Powers may have had to support his claim. Hence Portland was overoptimistic when he assured Tallard in July that the Emperor had agreed to the principle of a partition and would seek an understanding with William.[168] In fact, while Tallard and Portland were fine-tuning the articles of treaty, most of the time was wasted waiting for the Imperialists. The Emperor regarded Italy as the most important part of the Spanish inheritance and refused to cede his claim over Milan.

Tallard bitterly complained, however, that 'the Pensionary and Mr Portland always gave me general and meaningless talk and decided on nothing'.[169] Trying to speed up the talks, Tallard visited Portland at Sorgvliet in mid-September, days before the deadline for Imperial adherence to the treaty. Portland, he wrote,

---

162 Portland must have understood this was formally not the case. The First Partition Treaty stipulated that the Elector would inherit the Spanish Empire from his son, but since the Prince had never been in the actual possession of the inheritance (since the King of Spain was still alive) there was nothing to inherit. Louis to Tallard 13 February 1699, Grimblot, *Letters*, II. 259–60.

163 Portland to Heinsius 27 February 1699 (Kensington Palace), NA, 3.01.19/2189, transl. from Dutch.

164 Tallard to Louis 26 March 1699, AAE, CPA 180, f° 111r°, transl. from French.

165 Portland to Heinsius 24 March 1699 (Kensington Palace), NA, 3.01.19/2189.

166 NUL, PwA 2677, PwA 2678.

167 Tallard to Louis 26 March 1699, AAE, CPA 180, f° 114v°.

168 Tallard to Louis 29 July 1699, AAE, CPA 182, f° 73r°.

169 Tallard to Louis 13 September 1699, AAE, CPA 183, f° 65v°, transl. from French.

replied to me that the King his master could not make up his mind before he had taken note of the news which was expected, but that he knew well that the sentiment of this Prince was still to first have a response from Vienna before he could sign the treaty with us.[170]

Portland continued to reassure Tallard that the treaty would be signed within days, but the latter suspected treachery. Quite likely William was unwilling to sign without Imperial support. Amsterdam certainly was, which also delayed Dutch adherence when the 25 September deadline came and passed. The Dutch accused the Imperialists of spinning out the negotiations whilst awaiting the King of Spain's death. Word reached Vienna that Portland had said that the Emperor would either adhere or be left out, but either way the treaty would proceed, a rumour which was ill-received.[171] The Imperialists bitterly accused Portland whom they perceived as the 'author' of an Anglo-French rapprochement, 'of which he, through his talks with Boufflers, Tallard and the King, laid the foundation, through the warm reception received there [in Paris], which made him better French than beforehand'.[172] Throughout the winter Portland kept on postponing signing the treaty for England, whilst Tallard kept on believing it was imminent.[173]

The Second Partition Treaty was signed only in March 1700, allotting the bulk of the inheritance to the Archduke (Spain, the Indies, the Spanish Netherlands), with compensation for the Dauphin (Naples, Sicily, Finale and the Tuscan ports, augmented with Lorraine). The Duke of Lorraine would receive Milan in return.[174] It was a curiously complicated arrangement. The strengthening of France in Italy would increase the possibility of a war on that peninsula, whereas the Emperor lacked the means to defend the Spanish inheritance properly for his son. Moreover, the Elector of Bavaria felt slighted by the terms, whereas the Spanish king vehemently opposed a division. 'I pray to God', Portland confessed to Heinsius, 'to bless it [the treaty] and to prevent the inconveniences which will have to be feared from it, that through it a peace in Europe may be confirmed.'[175] But this was not what happened. When Carlos died in the autumn, Louis decided to accept his will in favour of the Duke of Anjou, thus rejecting the treaty, and initiating a chain of events that would lead to the War of the Spanish Succession in 1702.[176]

---

170 Tallard to Louis 17 September 1699, ibid., f° 79v°, transl. from French.

171 Hop to Heinsius 16 September 1699, *Weensche Gezantschapsberichten van 1670–1720*, eds G. von Antal and J.C.H. de Pater (2 vols, The Hague, 1929–34), II. 111.

172 Hop to Heinsius 19 September 1699. Cf. Hop to Heinsius 22 May 1700, Antal and De Pater, *Weensche Gezantschapsberichten*, II. 114, 159, transl. from Dutch.

173 E.g. Tallard to Louis 12 October 1699, AAE, CPA 183, f° 169v°.

174 Though the treaty may seem uneven: unlike the Dauphin, the Archduke had no direct prospect of succeeding his father, and the Habsburg territories would remain divided.

175 Portland to Heinsius 23 April 1700 (Whitehall Palace), NA, 3.01.19/2189, transl. from Dutch.

176 On the circumstances leading to Louis's decision, see Rule, 'The Partition Treaties'.

VI

By then Portland had retired from active business, the conclusion of the Second Partition Treaty being his final political act. But his retirement was not to be undisturbed. The particulars of the Partition Treaty had caused an uproar when they came to the attention of the Commons soon after their conclusion. Portland refused to answer any questions, stating that he needed permission of the King first, but on 15 March 1701 he agreed to explain in the Commons his involvement. Initially it was thought that only Jersey and Portland (the signatories of the Second Partition Treaty) had been implicated, but the matter became more confused when Portland mentioned that he had first asked the advice of several key ministers. He moreover stated that he had been called from his country house in Holland by the King, and had asked counsel from the ministers as to whether he should be employed in this matter.[177] Such a gross distortion of events irritated the Whig ministers, who correctly argued that although they were notified of the talks, they had never been involved in them.

If William was unpleasantly surprised by the frontal attack on his foreign policy, the French were baffled by such parliamentary audacity. Tallard had thought that Portland had little to fear, 'Because it is an incontestable right of the Kings of England until now that they can make treaties and alliances, and the only thing that Parliament can do is not to give support.'[178] But the Commons initiated an impeachment procedure and on 12 April Portland was formally charged with 'high crimes and misdemeanour' for concluding in an unconstitutional manner a treaty which was thought to involve Britain in a new war. With the exception of a captain of the guards, no one came to his defence. It was easy to see why. René Saunière de L'Hermitage observed that even his friends did not have the courage to speak out, since the Earl was generally hated as a foreigner.[179] Nor did he, after his resignation, have much influence left, and there seemed little point in enraging the majority. It would seem pointless to impeach a retired foreigner, but most observers realised that this was only a means to an end: 'The great plan was not to get rid of this lord, they only started with him to prepare the road for the destruction of Baron Somers, who is terrifying to the Tories. Mylord Portland, however, has no party whatsoever.'[180] Hence the impeachment procedures fell prey to partisan struggle. Bonnet thought that it was absurd to impeach Portland and not Jersey (the latter now inclining to the Tories): '... this is purely a partisan affair, and not an act of justice.'[181]

As was expected, Portland's attitude had rather enraged Parliament. In an attempt to regain the initiative, he carelessly referred to some older documents from 1698, thus bringing into the light the discussions on the First Partition Treaty, the existence of which Parliament had hitherto been unaware. Portland's mistake was to have

---

177 Pembroke, Lonsdale, Marlborough, Somers, Halifax, Montagu and Vernon were mentioned.

178 Tallard to Louis 14 June 1699, AAE, CPA 186, f° 135r°, transl. from French.

179 Dispatch Saunière 12 April 1701, BL, Add Mss 17677 WW, f° 212.

180 Dispatch Bonnet 1/12 April 1701, BL, Add Mss 30000E, f° 120v°, transl. from French.

181 Dispatch Bonnet 1/12 April 1701, ibid., f° 121v°, transl. from French.

serious repercussions. The first treaty had been discussed whilst the Junto Whigs were still in power. The Tories now saw an opportunity to implicate the former Whig ministry and demanded copies of the correspondence of Vernon and Portland, which were brought in by the former (Portland claiming his were in Holland) to be translated by committee. On 26 April an address was sent to the Lords to impeach the four lords (Portland, Somers, Halifax and Orford).[182] Incredibly, the commission forgot to include Portland in its address to the King.[183] The Lords viewed the proceedings in the Commons with disdain, and considered the accusations against their compeers unjust. An address was sent to the King to halt the impeachment, and a constitutional deadlock was reached. In May the matter curiously faded away. The Commons failing to produce the actual articles of impeachment, the Lords decided to dismiss the charges against Portland on 24 June.

It was not the first time that Portland had been threatened with impeachment. In 1695 a commission had looked into charges of corruption, and had to conclude that his record was spotless. Portland had ridiculed the procedure, as he did in 1700 when rumours of new charges circulated:

> their threats have not prevented me from continuing in my sentiments and conduct, while I have done so out of the service of the King, having little to fear, the only reason they could find to accuse me was that my son had received a grant from the King, which is ridiculous.[184]

The confrontation between Portland and the Commons was, however, not essentially generated by a concern over procedural misdemeanours. For a decade the Commons had loathed Portland's role in strengthening royal executive, muzzling Parliament by blocking the Triennial and Place Bills, and showing frequent disdain for the honourable gentlemen. During the impeachment procedures of 1701 Portland was directly confronted by the Commons for the first time, and they once more clashed over conflicting ideas about government and foreign policy.

Curiously, the actual substance of the Partition Treaties was never seriously discussed, although Portland did take the opportunity to speak of it in the Lords. The impeachment procedures serve to illustrate the contrast between a European-minded, warmongering Portland and an introspective, pacific parliament. Whilst the first clamour of war had started in the spring of 1701, bills for taxes and troops were neglected. It seems appropriate, therefore, that Portland's final public act was an important speech in the Commons in which he explained and defended his actions and the course of Williamite foreign policy:

> That the Treaty of Partition has not produced the Will of Carlos II, but that it was the French faction and the Cardinal Portocarrero which has made use of the pretext that Spain had to do it to ward off the threats from France, and that England's inability to support the Spanish has facilitated the Will. That the fear of that which has occurred, and the secret

---

182 Dispatch Bonnet 15/26 April 1701, ibid., f° 141 ff.
183 Dispatch Bonnet 25/6 May 1701, ibid., f° 156r°.
184 To Heinsius he confided that he had little to fear now that he had retired. Portland to Heinsius 23 April 1700 (Whitehall Palace), NA, 3.01.19/2189, transl. from Dutch.

intelligence of the French negotiations to have Spain in favour of one of their princes, and the danger that she would become too powerful, had been motives which have inspired the Treaty of Partition.[185]

There was a significant sting in his argument. Not he, but the policies of Country MPs and of the disbandment of troops had caused the will of Charles II to be altered in favour of the Duke of Anjou.

If the content of the Partition Treaties was hardly commented on in the parliamentary debates, political writers were quick to discuss these matters. According to one pamphleteer,

> Things being in such a state, might not the King think that what was left for him to do, was to make the best Bargain he could. How bad soever the Partition may be, it seem'd still more desirable to yield up some parts of the Spanish Monarchy, than to let France Conquer it ... .[186]

Jonathan Swift, though he loathed Portland, commented positively upon his efforts in a rather complicated political tract (his first), comparing the favourite to the Athenian general Phocion who withstood Alexander the Great and restored Athens to liberty.[187] Daniel Defoe, as well, in his *Legion's Memorial* (1701), defended the Partition Treaties.[188] The Whig historian John Oldmixon thought that 'The Treaty of Partition was not only a Dream, which never had any Effect, but if it had been effected, it would, without all Doubt, have preserv'd the Peace of Europe'.[189] Charles Davenant, however, in *An Essay upon the Balance of Power*, argued that the treaty would have empowered France and therefore would have dangerously disturbed the existing equilibrium in Europe.[190] As the Partition Treaties were never implemented, however, their conclusion remains among the most significant non-events in European diplomatic history.

VII

Portland became the main instrument in changing the direction of William's foreign policy. For almost three decades William had believed in a balance of power strategy,

---

185 Dispatch Bonnet 17–18 March 1701, BL, Add Mss 30000E, f° 92v°–93r°, transl. from French.

186 *Two Letters to a Friend, Concerning the Partition Treaty, Vindicating His Majesty, King William, From all Reflections; And Answering the Arguments of a late Designing Party, that were for Surrendring to the French King the Whole Spanish Monarchy* (London, 1702), 5.

187 *The Prose Works of Jonathan Swift*, ed. Temple Scott (11 vols, London 1900), I. 244, 245, 259; F.P Lock, 'Swift and English Politics, 1701–1714' in: C. Rawson (ed.), *The Character of Swift's Satire* (London/Toronto, 1983), 127–50, 128.

188 D. Defoe, *Legion's Memorial* (1701) in: *Political and Economic Writings of Daniel Defoe, II: Party Politics*, ed. J. A. Downie (London, 2000), 39–46, 43.

189 J. Oldmixon, *The History of England ...* (London 1735), 226.

190 Davenant, 'An Essay upon the Balance of Power', 330.

but now he was reverting to an older concept of a system of collective guarantees. This chapter has analysed this major transformation in William's foreign policy, one that has hitherto received little attention from historians who have typified it as a consistent but inflexible anti-French strategy. The failure of the treaties must then be explained from the persistent animosity between William and Louis. More recently some historians have emphasised mutual misunderstanding.[191] This chapter has challenged both views. William and Louis genuinely aimed at reaching an understanding. What seems clear from Portland's correspondence is that neither mutual stubborn enmity nor a misunderstanding had caused the failure of the Partition Treaties. Rather, it was William's weakening position in England which made him an unreliable and undesirable partner to Louis.

In 1698 Portland, as Ambassador to France, received his most distinguished commission, and being involved in the negotiations to partition the Spanish empire made him one of the most influential and renowned statesmen of this period. This chapter has also analysed Portland's role after his retirement, during which he was still active as a diplomat. The King refused his offer of resignation in 1697 and employed him during the First Partition Treaty negotiations. When the talks over the Second Treaty were in full swing, the by then retired favourite still managed to sideline Albemarle completely. Nevertheless his position in domestic politics had been crumbling. The weakening of the army reduced the relevance of his usefulness to the King, whereas the opposition attacks against the Anglo-Dutch favourite contributed to the unpopularity of the Whig regime and William's war policy with which he was now associated. Perhaps Defoe's reproach that 'The Wars are over, England needs him not', contained more truth than he realised.[192] To what extent Portland's retirement in 1699 was the result of personal motivations, political judgement or a quarrel with the Earl of Albemarle will be the subject of the final chapter.

---

191   W. Troost, *William III, the Stadholder-King: A Political Biography* (Aldershot, 2005), 292. Troost mainly refers to the ideas of Andrew Lossky and Ragnild Hatton.

192   Defoe, *True-born Englishman*.

Chapter 9

The Vestiges of Power (1697–1709)

In the spring of 1697 Portland decided to retire from public office. Upon the King's request he refrained from doing so, but in June 1699 the favourite laid down all his offices and retired to his country house. The reasons for his retirement are still unclear, as little is known about his motivation or the precise circumstances. Most historians have argued that Portland's decision to retire was the result of a conflict with William over his rival favourite Arnold Joost Keppel, Earl of Albemarle. According to most literature, Keppel slowly but surely pushed Portland away after 1694 until the latter's final fall from favour in 1699.[1] In this chapter it will be argued, however, that Portland's retirement should be regarded against the background of structural changes in English politics. When the Nine Years War ended, opposition against the standing army and the Irish forfeitures mounted, whereas weak ministries failed to provide stable government.[2] William was forced to find an alternative for the crumbling Whig ministry with which Portland was connected. The combination of these factors gradually eroded Portland's influence and political relevance.

I

Arnold Joost van Keppel may be the most neglected favourite in English historiography, his opaque career having been overshadowed by those of his predecessor and successor, Portland and Marlborough.[3] Twenty years Portland's junior, the dashing, charming and good-looking courtier, descended from Gelderland nobility, had accompanied William in 1688 as page. Keppel became Groom of the Bedchamber in the autumn of 1690, receiving an annual pension of £500 for his new office. Next to Adriaan van Borssele van der Hooghe and Portland he was now the third Dutchman serving in the King's bedchamber.[4] When Keppel accompanied the King on a hunting party, he unfortunately broke his leg. Despite the pain, the young man never complained. Keppel thus impressed William with his bravery, and grew in his favour. After the incident Keppel had regular access to the King and

---

1 E.g. W. Troost, *William III, the Stadholder-King: A Political Biography* (Aldershot, 2005), 234.
2 R. Jones, *Country and Court: England, 1658–1714* (London, 1978), 302.
3 But see M. Kerkhof, 'De Carrière van Arnold Joost van Keppel na de Dood van Willem III', *Virtus*, 5/1 (1998). 13–19.
4 *CTB*, IX-iii. 898.

was employed to handle routine military correspondence.[5] The young favourite took over some Dutch correspondence and gradually marginalized Constantijn Huygens. In February 1693 Huygens reported that as large a number of courtiers attended his *lever* as Portland's. But he also started to encroach on the responsibilities of Portland, whose favour according to one witness in 1694 'was in decline, from this and other things, that [William] had ordered Portland to do some business, in which he had failed, but in which Keppel had succeeded'.[6] In 1695 Keppel's career accelerated and he received more material tokens of the King's favour. In May he was promoted to the Mastership of the Robes, instead of Nassau-Zuylestein who was made Earl of Rochfort, the third Dutchman to receive a peerage.[7] As Master of the Robes Keppel now received an annual income of £2,000.[8]

Portland's position as favourite had not been seriously challenged since 1689, and Keppel's capacity to acquire the affection of the King alarmed him. Moreover, he intensely disliked his rival, Constantijn Huygens noting that the two favourites were 'as fire and water against each other'.[9] Portland and Keppel would be caught up in a continuous rivalry for the King's favour. Courtiers anxiously tried to estimate the position of the new favourite. When Portland was away on a mission, in August 1696, Richard Hill remarked to the Duke of Shrewsbury that 'Baron de Keppel ... needed not the absence of my Lord Portland to be the first minister here'.[10] But, according to the Dutch agent René Saunière de L'Hermitage, only those who judged by appearances supposed the new favourite had overshadowed the old: 'The favour of Mylord Portland is still superior.'[11] Keppel received quarters in Kensington Palace next to those of the King, and William gave him the means to buy the estate of Voorst in Gelderland and lay out elaborate gardens.[12] At the same time, however, William ordered his ministers to bestow upon Portland the massive Welsh grants. In December 1695 Sylvius had confided to Huygens that 'the ascendancy of Keppel over Portland continued; that Portland was very polite to the latter'.[13] In the autumn of 1696, however, it was Portland who emerged victorious from a seemingly juvenile squabble. After a visit to Cleves on the way back, 'there happened a quarrel between Lord P[ortland] and Mr K[eppel]. ... K overtook P and kept the way quite to Deering [Dieren], where P, getting out of the coach, threatened to beat the coachman, and

---

5   E.g. Carasa to Keppel 2 January 1692, Stratmann to Keppel 24 February 1692, Nassau-Saarbrück to Keppel 12 April 1696, Keppel to Marlborough 20 July 1696, BL, Add Mss 63629, f° 17–21, 45–6, 51–2.

6   28 April 1694, Huygens, *Journaal,* I-ii. 337, transl. from Dutch.

7   Saunière to States General 17 May 1695, BL, Add Mss 17677 PP, f° 261r°.

8   *CTB*, X-iii. 1295.

9   25 February 1693, Huygens, *Journaal,* I-ii. 176, transl. from Dutch.

10   Hill to Shrewsbury 10/20 August 1696, HMC, *Buccleugh Mss*, II-i. 380.

11   Dispatch Saunière de L'Hermitage 6 December 1695, NA, 3.01.19/402, transl. from French.

12   J.D. Hunt and E. de Jong (eds), *The Anglo-Dutch Garden in the Age of William and Mary. De Gouden Eeuw van de Hollandse Tuinkunst* (London/Amsterdam, 1988), 193.

13   2 April 1695, cf. 25 December 1695, Huygens, *Journaal,* I-ii. 467, 561, transl. from Dutch. Cf. Stepney to Montagu 1 November 1695, TNA: PRO, SP 105/54, f° 187v°: Keppel 'getts ground daily but is harder of access than the other'.

said he was an impertinent puppy'. After arriving back at Het Loo, both favourites complained to William, and Keppel left for his house in Zutphen to let things cool down.[14]

In the spring of 1697, Portland suddenly decided to lay down his offices and retire. William responded in an emotional letter to 'the cruel resolution they have told me that you have asked to leave my service', urging him to reconsider.[15] Portland had been complaining about Keppel for some time, but his resignation still came as a surprise to William. The immediate cause for his decision was probably the elevation of Keppel into the peerage as Earl of Albemarle that spring.[16] A moving correspondence followed, in which Portland assured the King of his unfailing loyalty, and was assured of the latter's unceasing favour.[17] The King was willing to offer Portland anything, but not the one thing he demanded: Albemarle's dismissal. But the King was willing to compromise, and a few days later Portland was appointed Knight of the Garter, to show, Vernon wrote to Shrewsbury, 'he is still preferred a step above [Albemarle]'.[18] In a heated argument Albemarle accused Portland of 'acting to his disadvantage'. The latter had even drawn his sword in anger in the room right next to that of the King himself, who had to personally part the quarrelsome favourites.[19] On 4 April 1697 Portland was installed in the chapter of Windsor and a pompous dinner was accordingly given in his honour, attended by 60 peers, ministers of state and foreign ambassadors.[20] 'this is the more glorious as he has never asked for it', the Brandenburg envoy Bonnet observed.[21] William's generosity knew few bounds. Portland was charged with the desirable rangership of Windsor Park – in the lodge of which he would spend most of his days – which

---

14   HMC, *Bath Mss*, III. 509. Cf. Prior to Vernon 8/18 September 1696, TNA: PRO, SP 84/223, f° 198v°.

15   William to Portland n.d. March 1697, Japikse, *Correspondentie*, XXIII. 197, transl. from French.

16   Dispatches Saunière 1 March 1697, Brande 29 January 1697, 1 March 1697, BL, Add Mss 17677 RR, f° 230r°, 21r°, 32v°.

17   William to Portland 29 May 1697, Portland to William 30 May 1697 (Brussels), William to Portland 1 June 1697, William to Portland 1 June 1697, Portland to William 2 June 1697 (Brussels), William to Portland 3 June 1697, Portland to William 5 June 1697 ('Camp de Promelle'), 6 June 1697 ('Camp de Promelle'), Japikse, *Correspondentie*, XXIII. 198–203.

18   Quoted in *Letters of William III, and Louis XIV and of their Ministers etc. 1697–1700*, ed. P. Grimblot (2 vols, London, 1848), I. 146n; 25 March 1697, N. Luttrell, *A Brief Historical Relation of State Affairs from September 1678 to April 1714* (6 vols, Oxford, 1857), IV. 201.

19   Eames to Huntingdon 6 March 1697, HMC, *Manuscripts of the ... Manor House, Ashby-de-la-Zouche* (4 vols, London, 1930), II. 288. Cf. Jersey to Albemarle 12 March 1697, BL, Add Mss 18606, f° 37v°–38r°.

20   Dispatches Saunière 5 April 1697, Brande 5 April 1697, BL, Add Mss 17677 RR, f° 273, 45.

21   Dispatch Bonnet 23 February/5 March 1697, BL, Add Mss 30000A, f° 272r°, transl. from French. For Portland's position within the peerage, see House of Lords Manuscripts Department, Garter Roll 29, 1697.

provided him with a £1,500 annuity.[22] On top of that he was granted the Irish estate of the Earl of Clancarty.[23]

By late May 1697, however, the matter had still not been resolved, notwithstanding the mediation of the Prince of Vaudemont who was on close terms with both. Whilst the King was on campaign, Portland had sulkily retreated to Brussels pleading illness. He explained that it was not self-interest which had prompted him to take his decision: 'It is your honour which was my deepest concern, and the good will you have for a young man and the way in which it seems that you authorise these liberties and this arrogant behaviour.'[24] William was obviously shocked by his suggestion that rumours of sodomy between Albemarle and the King were circulating both in London and The Hague, and he must have been suspicious about Portland's ulterior motives in this matter.[25] William was unwilling to dismiss Albemarle but open to compromise if only Portland would agree to stay in his service longer. Portland accepted, but 'I have taken the decision only after a great struggle in my mind and against myself'.[26]

The reasons for Keppel's astounding and quick success are not entirely clear. Stephen Baxter has argued that with the death of Queen Mary – who had been fond of Portland – and the expulsion of Elizabeth Villiers, William's mistress and Portland's sister-in-law, two links between Portland and the King were severed.[27] William, struck with remorse, married off Elizabeth Villiers to the Earl of Orkney. Deeply grieving for his beloved wife, he felt emotionally shattered and lonely for months, and increasingly felt comfortable in the entertaining company of Keppel. The young favourite became a central figure in William's affection after Mary's death. If William lost a wife, he gained a son. This view is confirmed by the chronology of Keppel's career. Appointed Groom in 1690 and already high in the King's favour by 1693, it was not until immediately after Mary's death that he received a significant office at Court. At the same time, however, William increasingly relied on Portland who took over business from the weary king during the early months of 1695 – for which he was generously rewarded with the Welsh grants. Moreover, Elizabeth Villiers's exile was no misfortune for the Earl; she had long been his bitter enemy and her removal rather strengthened his position.

Baxter has also argued that Portland lost influence due to his negligence in maintaining links with the Tories, whereas, moreover, Grand Pensionary Anthonie Heinsius and Secretary-at-War William Blathwayt were increasingly taking over Dutch and military correspondence respectively.[28] This analysis looks plausible but is also problematic. Baxter's point does not explain Keppel's ascendancy in relation

---

22 Dispatch Saunière 19 March 1697, BL, Add Mss 17677 RR, f° 257; 9 March 1697, Luttrell, *Brief Historical Relation*, IV. 193.
23 Cf. Ch. 5.
24 Portland to William 30 May 1697 (Brussels), Japikse, *Correspondentie*, XXIII. 199, transl. from French.
25 William to Portland 1 June 1697, ibid., 200. E.g. NUL PwA 2715.
26 William to Portland 1 June 1697, Portland to William 6 June 1697 (Brussels), Japikse, *Correspondentie*, XXIII. 200, 202, transl. from French.
27 S.B. Baxter, *William III* (London, 1966), 326–7.
28 Baxter, *William III*, 326–7.

to Portland's sustained and even increased influence around 1695. Although Keppel may have profited from Portland's neglect to maintain links with the Tories in later years, Portland's patronage over the ruling Whig Junto had considerably strengthened his position during the mid-1690s.

The main reason for Keppel's success may be more complicated. William loathed being dependent on his advisers. During his first year as king, he had confided to Halifax, one of his closest advisers, that 'hee would discourage the falling too much upon particular men'.[29] For this reason he divided influence between his main advisers, Halifax and Carmarthen, and held the main offices, such as Lord Treasurer, in commission. It is likely therefore that he should watch Portland's unchallenged ascendancy with some concern, whilst at the same time he realised that he would be difficult to replace. There was nothing unusual about a monarch wishing to employ more than one favourite, however, or at least trying to keep the ruling favourite unsure of his position, and there is no reason to suggest that William was an exception. In this analysis, rather than being indicative of a decline in Portland's influence, Keppel's ascendancy marked its continuance. Thus, by the mid-1690s the King decided to have a second favourite. In 1689, there had been few or no Dutch courtiers who had been either willing or capable; Nassau-Ouwerkerk and Nassau-Zuylestein, the two most prominent courtiers, never aspired to the position of favourite. William's English courtiers could not be employed to maintain relations with the United Provinces. The most obvious choice was an insignificant Dutchman – who had to be naturalised – who like Portland would become the King's creature. The King's choice fell on Keppel.

William's sincere friendship with Portland has been partly responsible for the myth that theirs was a natural companionship, but mutual friction and irritations were understandable after years of intense, almost stifling friendship. William and Portland had had quarrels before, but the King was clearly increasingly irritated at what he perceived as his favourite's arrogance. In April 1694 William publicly complained that Portland, standing behind him during dinner, 'knows so little the respect he is owing me'.[30] William may have been satisfied with the conduct of his favourite, but at the same time he must have been apprehensive of Portland's authority, reports of which had been common in court circles for years. In 1689 John Wildman had even suggested that William was taking Portland's advice in all matters of importance.[31] In October 1699 the King complained to Matthew Prior that some people had entered 'blindly into all the sentiments of my Lord Portland'.[32] Portland had become far more influential, even in relative terms, than he had been in Holland. This degree of monopolisation of his master's favour as well as political influence had never been attained even before 1688, when, moreover, he was less experienced amongst elder counsellors. Now he was a senior adviser himself, assured of the King's favour and

---

29 G.S., First Marquis of Halifax, 'The Spencer House Journals' in: *The Life and Letters of Sir George Savile, First Marquis of Halifax,* ed. H.C. Foxcroft (2 vols, London, 1898), II. 202. Cf. Baxter, *William III*, 249, 274.
30 28 April 1694, Huygens, *Journaal,* I-ii. 337, transl. from Dutch.
31 Cf. page 103.
32 L.G.W. Legg, *Matthew Prior. A Study of his Public Career and Correspondence* (Cambridge, 1921), 114.

singular position within his entourage, and accustomed to exercise authority. After Sidney's decline in influence in late 1689, Portland's position as William's favourite seemed virtually unchallenged.

The idea that William consciously 'set up' a second favourite is endorsed by Burnet. The King started to train Keppel precisely in those areas in which Portland was engaged.[33] The French ambassador Tallard thought that William cynically exploited the rivalry between his favourites: 'I have seen Mylord Albemarle being sacrificed to Mylord Portland when I was at Het Loo, now this happens to the latter.'[34] Rivalry was not new to the ambitious Portland, as he had frequently quarrelled during the 1670s and 1680s with other favourites.[35] The King had to be careful, however, to achieve some sort of balance, as he needed Portland's services. This is confirmed by James Vernon's observation. When Portland's client was appointed Dutch Secretary in 1698, he supposed that 'it must cost the King something considerable to set the balance even'.[36]

Portland knew very well that he was indispensable, as Albemarle was inexperienced and, reputedly, lazy. William explained to Van Borssele that he 'praised the attachment with which his first favourite Mylord Portland had served him, and complained about the negligence of the second, Mylord Albemarle'.[37] Secure in this knowledge, there was a certain cunning in the manner in which Portland offered his resignation. In 1697, although almost continuously in the company of the King or in correspondence with him, he never personally informed the King of his decision. William clearly wrote that *he was told* that Portland wished to retire in 1697, and thus did not receive the news first hand; Portland was publicly sulking in Brussels even after having received the Garter that spring.[38] Though he could not persuade William to remove Albemarle from Court, his actions had forced William to publicly reaffirm his position. This game was recognised very well by courtiers: 'You will laugh', one courtier wrote to another, 'when I tell you that before you get this, you will hear that some new mark of favour is put on my Lord Portland, or that he has left the court or both.'[39]

The King may have needed a second favourite for another reason as well, as Portland was increasingly burdened with parliamentary management and financial responsibilities. William anxiously tried to keep control over government in the hands of a small circle of confidants, and Albemarle would be a useful additional instrument of royal policy. Some of their responsibilities seemed to be overlapping,

---

33   G. Burnet, *History of his Own Time* (6 vols, London, 1725), IV. 429.

34   Tallard to Louis 22 April 1699, AAE, CPA 180, f° 223, transl. from French.

35   E.g. N. Japikse, *Prins Willem III – De Stadhouder-Koning* (2 vols, Amsterdam, 1933), I. 359.

36   Vernon to Shrewsbury 29 October 1698, *Letters Illustrative of the Reign of William III etc.*, ed. G.P.R. James (3 vols, London, 1841), II. 209.

37   'Gedenkschriften van Adriaan van Borssele van der Hooghe, Heer van Geldermalsen', ed. K. Heeringa, in: *Archief. Vroegere en latere Mededeelingen voornamelijk in Betrekking tot Zeeland* (Middelburg, 1916), 67–136, 122, transl. from French.

38   William to Portland n.d. March 1697, Japikse, *Correspondentie*, XXIII. 197.

39   Johnston to Annandale 10 April 1699, HMC, *Manuscripts of J.J. Hope Johnstone Esq. of Annandale* (London, 1897), 108.

which resulted in faction struggle, something William had constantly tried to avoid. The French ambassador was quick to seek ways to exploit their mutual rivalry.[40] But often courtiers were at a loss over whom to turn to. 'I am in doubt as to whether I should address myself to Mylord Albemarle after having spoken to the Earl of Portland', Bonnet complained.[41] Hence the King now had two favourites, a French report stating that William's 'favour seems to be shared only by the Earls of Portland and Albemarle'.[42] But Burnet was more perceptive when he noted that 'the one had more of the confidence, and the other much more of the favour'.[43] Portland's position as parliamentary and ministerial manager, as well as diplomat, remained unchallenged, whereas Albemarle's responsibilities were largely restricted to the control over royal patronage.

Pamphleteers were quick to explain Albemarle's rise. According to *The Foreigners*, for instance, he was 'Mounted to Grandeur by the usual Course, Of Whoring, Pimping or a Crime that's worse'.[44] Most courtiers differed in opinion as to the causes of Albemarle's success. Burnet thought Albemarle's success 'quick and unaccountable', but James Vernon considered him 'a fine gentleman [who] deserves the favour he is in'.[45] Part of Albemarle's success can be attributed to those personal qualities which Portland did not possess. Portland could be a polished courtier; one witness – although distrusted by the favourite – noted that he 'treated me with abundance of respect and civility, so that if there be anything concealed within, he has a greater command of countenance than I can perceive'.[46] However, most observers found him haughty and tactless, whereas Albemarle was an affable and easy-going courtier.

As yet Albemarle was inexperienced, but William was training him in those areas in which Portland himself had been involved at the early stages of his career: military correspondence and diplomacy. Whereas Albemarle's diplomatic career never took off, his control over royal patronage increased rapidly. Of course, Portland witnessed the ascendancy of this young favourite with a mixture of jealousy and concern – jealousy of this competitor for the King's favour, concern about the influence which the in his eyes reckless and inexperienced courtier exerted. But he found compensation by strengthening his position in other areas, such as ministerial management in England and Scotland, finance, patronage in diplomatic circles and correspondence with Allied foreign commanders. Albemarle did not develop any political or diplomatic activities, and was not in the Cabinet or Privy Council.

---

40   Tallard to Louis 22 January 1699, Grimblot, *Letters*, II. 234–7.
41   Bonnet to the Elector 9 January 1699 NS, BL, Add Mss 30000B, f° 298r°, transl. from French.
42   Instruction 2 March 1698, Grimblot, *Letters*, I. 249.
43   Burnet, *History*, IV. 430.
44   J. Tutchin, *The Foreigners* (London, 1700).
45   Vernon to Stepney 26 August/5 September 1694, TNA:PRO, SP 105/82, f° 235–6; Burnet, *History*, IV. 429.
46   Kingston to Trumbull n.d. 1695, HMC, *Downshire Mss*, I. 601.

II

If by the spring of 1697 Albemarle seemed to have threatened Portland's position, by the summer the elder had re-established himself as the foremost in the King's favour. Portland received credit for being 'so successful an instrument in ye effecting' the peace of Ryswick.[47] The Junto Whigs were hailing their patron for his success which seemed to strengthen their position in the parliamentary session.[48] On his return to England in October 1697 Portland was a celebrated figure being 'very much courted'.[49] The King's confidence in him was undiminished; he gave him permission to prepare the parliamentary session, manage the ministry in his absence and deal with royal correspondence.[50]

When William in the autumn decided to dispatch him to Paris as Ambassador Extraordinary, reactions were mixed. It was undoubtedly a distinguished appointment, but some considered it an 'honourable kind of banishment' as it would leave Albemarle to consolidate his position at Court.[51] The Bishop of St David's thought that 'The year begins with the fall of a great favourite and great palace' – referring also to the fire that broke out in Portland's Whitehall apartments and destroyed most of the palace. It delayed his journey by several days.[52] The favourite himself was not content with his ostensibly honourable assignment, threatening William again in a letter written from Dover on his way to France to resign his commissions.[53] Although William may have been partly motivated by his desire to separate the quarrelling favourites, Portland's critics were probably mistaken, for it was precisely through his role as negotiator that he managed to maintain his position as William's most prominent favourite after 1697. Rumours of Portland having fallen into disgrace had also circulated at Court in the spring of 1690 when he was despatched on a mission to The Hague, and appeared to be wholly unfounded. Referring to Portland's embassy to Paris in 1698, the Scottish Secretary of State, James Ogilvy, wrote to William

---

    47   Bishop of Exeter to Portland 8 November 1697, NUL, PwA 1406. Cf. Gaultier to Portland 9 August 1697, Sunderland to Portland 10 August 1697, NUL, PwA 163, PwA 1267.

    48   Montagu to Portland 27 July 1697, Guy to Portland 17 September 1697, NUL, PwA 939, PwA 517.

    49   Ellis to Williamson 22 October 1697, TNA:PRO, SP 84/223, f° 396r°.

    50   Vernon to Williamson 19 October 1697, *CSPD 1697,* 434; William to Portland 27 October 1697, Japikse, *Correspondentie*, XXIII. 210.

    51   Pringle to Carstares 10 February 1698, *State Papers and Letters Addressed to William Carstares*, ed. J. McCormick (Edinburgh, 1774), 369; Hill to Shrewsbury 20/30 September 1697, HMC, *Buccleugh Mss*, II-ii. 556–7. Cf. Van Leeuwen to Carstares 28 April 1698, McCormick, *State Papers*, 373.

    52   Bishop of St David's to Huntingdon 6 January 1698, HMC, *Manuscripts of the ... Manor House, Ashby-de-la-Zouche* (4 vols, London, 1930), I. 305; A. Boyer, *The History of the Life & Reign of Queen Anne* (London, 1722), appendix, 50; 4–11 January 1698, Luttrell, *Brief Historical Relation*, IV. 327–30. Cf. Bonnet's dispatches of 14 and 17 January 1698, BL, Add Mss 30000B, f° 1–6.

    53   William to Portland 31 January 1698, Japikse, *Correspondentie*, XXIII. 221.

Carstares: 'It is certainly a mark of great trust; and perhaps it may be profitable enough. All I dislike in it is, that he will be so long absent.'[54]

Indeed, if Portland was in some way at the zenith of his reputation, there were worrying signs as factions at Court were shifting and the influence of the Whigs in Parliament diminished. Moreover, after the end of the war the Whig Junto became internally divided and irritated with Sunderland's continuing tutelage. The latter had a number of pivotal clients, such as John Methuen, William Duncombe and Henry Guy, but also maintained contacts with the Country leader Robert Harley, as well as with the increasingly influential Marlborough-Godolphin interest.[55] By late 1697 the co-operation between Portland and Sunderland still functioned adequately, as the Whig Junto and Shrewsbury were dominating the ministry under their supervision. Cracks between the Junto and the Portland-Sunderland interest became apparent in December 1697, however, when Portland and Sunderland initiated a major ministerial reshuffle. Secretary of State Trumbull had been by-passed in 1692, but had gravitated into the Portland-Sunderland interest since then. But he wanted out, complaining he had been used as a 'footman' rather than a minister of state.[56] On 1 December Portland and Sunderland had tried to persuade him to stay, but he refused and was finally dismissed by the King. Before the Junto had learned what happened, their candidate Thomas Wharton was by-passed and Sunderland managed to get James Vernon appointed.[57]

At the same time, however, their interest suffered severe blows, as Sunderland relinquished the lord chamberlainship in December 1697 and Portland was appointed Ambassador Extraordinary to Paris, in which capacity he would have to leave Court for several months at a critical juncture. The crisis had deepened when the Duke of Shrewsbury, a cornerstone in the government, expressed an ardent wish to retire. Shrewsbury was tired of office and fearful of the repercussions of Sir John Fenwick's accusations, in which he had been associated with a Jacobite plot. Portland had tried to persuade him from doing so in the autumn:

> ... even if I had the intention of retiring, I would not do it ... to give occasion to my enemies for saying, that I could not resist this accusation, of which the falsity is so evident, and which, indeed, destroys itself ... if this should occur to me, I swear to you, that I should laugh at it, and you have cause to do the same.[58]

The irony of these remarks would not become apparent for another year when Portland would himself retire.

---

54 Ogilvy to Carstares 5 October 1697, McCormick, *State Papers*, 351.
55 E.g. J.P. Kenyon, *Robert Spencer, Earl of Sunderland 1621–1702* (London, 1958), 303.
56 Quoted in ibid., 295.
57 Ibid., 296; Portland to Shrewsbury 4/14 December 1697 (Kensington Palace), HMC, *Buccleugh Mss*, II-ii. 586.
58 Portland to Shrewsbury 14/24 September 1697 (Het Loo), *Private and Original Correspondence of Charles Talbot, Duke of Shrewsbury etc.*, ed. W. Coxe (London, 1821), 177; Portland to Shrewsbury 8/18 December 1697 (Kensington Palace), HMC, *Buccleuch Mss*, II-ii. 587.

Portland was well prepared for what might happen, and the following day he summoned Sir John Lowther to come down to London, apparently to have him available as a candidate for the impending vacancy.[59] He was clearly in Portland's pocket, being insecure of the King's favour and Portland having secured a post in the Exchequer for his cousin.[60] Portland and Sunderland weathered the storm by persuading Shrewsbury to keep the seals of the secretaryship on the condition that James Vernon, a 'little man', would do the work.[61] In practice, this was a victory for the Portland-Sunderland interest. Although the Junto could not but be content with Shrewsbury's staying, their antipathy towards Sunderland for keeping out Wharton was deep. It explains the latter's approach to Lady Orkney to oust Sunderland. Portland's attempt to let the Tory Lonsdale succeed Shrewsbury also must have alarmed the Whig Junto.

Thus far co-operation between the Junto Whigs and Portland had been mutually beneficial and relations had been cordial. In May 1697, for instance, Portland had lent his apartments in Hampton Court Palace to Charles Montagu, who had 'fitted them and the offices a little better than they were before'.[62] The relationship between Portland and the Junto Whigs had already soured somewhat, however, during the course of 1697. Edward Russell had been annoyed by being passed over for the Garter, and in September Montagu had complained that Portland's grants were 'likely to be destructive of a grant in which I have some concern'.[63] During that same summer John Somers became embittered when a royal grant to support his barony was found to be overlapping with one of Portland's. Though the latter's claim preceded that of Somers, and he was prepared to find an expedient, his ultimate refusal to relinquish his own claim soured mutual relations.[64]

By the beginning of 1698 Portland still hoped that the Junto and Sunderland could be reconciled, but the Court Whigs actively sought to replace or by-pass both Portland (now in Paris) and Sunderland as liaison to the King. Wharton contacted Lady Orkney in an attempt 'to make my lord Albemarle the minister'. On 6 February Somers, Russell and Montagu met the young favourite for dinner, Shrewsbury lurking in the countryside but keeping a close eye on events. Albemarle, Montagu wrote to Shrewsbury, 'renounces the absent [Sunderland], and pretends the king approves of the steps he makes', insisting that 'this is the juncture to press it'.[65] The Junto was pleased with Albemarle's manners, but doubtful as to his experience, Somers judging

---

59 Kenyon, *Sunderland*, 297.
60 Lonsdale to Portland 5 December 1697, 9 December 1697, 13 December 1697, NUL, PwA 827, PwA 828, PwA 829.
61 Portland to Shrewsbury 4/14 December 1697 (Kensington Palace), 3/13 January 1698 (Kensington Palace), HMC, *Buccleugh Mss*, II-ii. 586, 594.
62 Portland to Shrewsbury 8/18 September 1696 (Het Loo), Coxe, *Private Correspondence*, 141–2; Montagu to Portland 18 May 1697, NUL, PwA 937.
63 Montagu to Portland 17 September 1697, NUL, PwA 941.
64 Somers to Shrewsbury 15/25 June 1697, Coxe, *Private Correspondence*, 483–6; Somers to Portland 21 May 1697, NUL, PwA 1182; Portland to Somers 14/24 May 1697 (Zuylestein), SHC, Somers Mss, 371/14/K/8.
65 Portland to William 13 March 1698 (Paris), Japikse, *Correspondentie*, XXIII. 255; Montagu to Shrewsbury 11 February 1698, Coxe, *Private Correspondence*, 533.

The Vestiges of Power 239

him 'too light for the great seal' of the chamberlainship. If Portland was alarmed, he did not show it, although he must have also realised that it was inadvisable for a favourite to accept public office and expose himself in such a manner.[66] The King himself tried to play matters down in a letter to Portland, informing him that 'nothing is heard anymore of Mylord Sunderland as if he is no more in the world, although there are people who try to make projects in the air of which I inform you in the enclosed'.[67]

The Junto never went ahead with the scheme, but Albemarle continued to build up his own interest at Court with the help of Lady Orkney and her brother Edward Villiers, later Earl of Jersey, Portland's brother-in-law. The latter had been courting Albemarle for some time, though he managed – like so many others – to walk the fine line between the two favourites for a while.[68] When Albemarle suffered a bitter setback in the summer of 1697 – when shortly after his elevation Portland received the Garter – Jersey tried to soothe him: 'I see very well in your last that you are annoyed,' he wrote, and continued to elaborate on 'those who you can trust to be your friends'.[69] Jersey was Albemarle's most influential and capable ally, and built up an interest comprising his sister, the King's former mistress, and Matthew Prior.

Inevitably, the power struggle continued, and emerged firstly over the ability to appoint clients to key positions. Here Portland did lose influence, and to many observers it seemed that Albemarle was gaining the upper hand. The control over what may be styled a 'young court', a number of up and coming ambitious men such as the diplomats George Stepney and Matthew Prior, wheeled out of Portland's grasp, as his vacillating behaviour had led them to approach the rival favourite to safeguard their future. Lexington, a key client in the diplomatic service, had done so by late 1698. But these men were never entirely in Albemarle's interest, in fact Prior continued to regard Portland as his patron as well.[70] Reputedly Portland opposed Marlborough's governorship of Gloucester, whereas Albemarle successfully supported the Earl.[71]

Albemarle was fortunate in having Jersey, British ambassador to The Hague, as his main ally. Portland had dangerously neglected to maintain his clientele in the United Provinces, and Albemarle seems to have built up an interest amongst Dutch

---

66 Cf. Kenyon, *Sunderland*, 304. In the summer of 1698 Albemarle bought Twittenham Park: 'I believe he will affect the contrary party to his rival, and seem to make a fine seat and settlement in England.' Montagu to Shrewsbury 16/26 July 1698, Coxe, *Private Correspondence*, 543.

67 William to Portland 13 February 1698, Japikse, *Correspondentie*, XXIII. 226, transl. from French.

68 Jersey to Keppel 22 January 1697, Jersey to Portland 8 March 1697, BL, Add Mss 18606, f° 6v°–7r°, 34r°.

69 Jersey to Albemarle 12 March 1697, BL, Add Mss 18606, f° 37v°–38r°.

70 Lexington to Blathwayt 24 December 1698, BL, Add Mss 46528C, f° 284r°; Prior to Vernon 20 May 1699, BL, Add Mss 40773, f° 341v°; M. Prior, 'An History of the Negotiations of Matthew Prior, Esq' in: M. Prior, *Miscellaneous Works* (2 vols, London, 1740), I. 39.

71 B. Bevan, *King William III, Prince of Orange, the First European* (London, 1997), 156.

officers, such as Field-Marshal Nassau-Saarbrück.[72] After the war opposition against Portland became more outspoken. Dijkveld was inclined to topple Portland, and in the autumn of 1698 Portland and Nassau-Ouwerkerk reportedly 'had a quarrell at Loo & the last they said had used him like a dog ... . This they say has extreamly exalted another person'.[73] In November 1698, whilst the King was residing at Het Loo, Portland had managed to get his client, Abel Tassin d'Alonne, appointed as the King's Secretary for Dutch affairs, a post which had become vacant after the death of Constantijn Huygens Jr. The appointment had been a bitter blow to Albemarle, but as part of a compromise agreement D'Alonne was obliged to work under his supervision. Albemarle's excessive anger at the decision, however, prompted the King to temporarily banish him from Court. ' ... it is assuredly a striking proof that the Earl of Portland gets the upper hand', Tallard thought.[74]

But it was Albemarle who managed to get his clients in the English ministry, whereas meanwhile Portland's political relevance was rapidly eroding when the Whig Junto ultimately collapsed after a string of resignations, and he failed to re-establish his position in the emerging ministry. Sunderland had resigned in December 1697, Shrewsbury did so exactly one year later. Bonnet implicitly suggested that the timing of Portland's retirement was no coincidence. Describing the events leading to his retirement, Bonnet continues to note 'These great changes in the ministry'.[75] Two Junto lords, Montagu and Russell, resigned in the same month as Portland. Albemarle's client Jersey, a Tory, was made Secretary of State in April. By the summer of 1699 a new ministry had emerged.[76]

The erosion of Portland's power had also manifested itself after the Peace of Ryswick, which rendered the Anglo-Dutch connection as well as diplomatic relations and military and political co-ordination with the Allies less important. These were exactly the areas in which Portland had been influential. In January 1699 the foreign troops were sent home. On 3 March Portland's own regiment departed.[77] The Disbanding Act of 26 March 1699 stipulated the return of all remaining Dutch troops back to the continent. On 10 April the army in Ireland was reduced to 12,000 men. Ten days later, Portland decided to resign. With the disbanding of the army, in Portland's view William's post-Ryswick policy had failed. It also implied an immense loss of influence, for he was clearly connected to those who had 'great places in

---

72   E.g. Ranelagh to Albemarle 13 June 1699, BL, Add Mss 63630, f° 144r° and *passim*.

73   Giffard to Temple 14 September 1698, BL, Eg Mss 1705, f° 23; Tallard to Louis 6 July 1699, AAE, CPA 182, f° 36v°.

74   Tallard to Louis 3 November 1698, 17 November 1698, Grimblot, *Letters*, II. 182–4, 188–9; 22 November 1698, Luttrell, *Brief Historical Relation*, IV. 453.

75   Dispatches Bonnet 12/22 May 1699, 16/26 May 1699, BL, Add Mss 30000C, f° 104–7, transl. from French.

76   Dispatches Bonnet 21 April/1 May 1699, 12/22 May 1699, 16/26 May 1699, BL, Add Mss 30000C, f° 87, 104, 106–7. Ranelagh succeeded Portland as Superintendent of the King's gardens and buildings, *CSPD 1700–1702*, 90.

77   Dispatch Saunière 3 March 1699, BL, Add Mss 17677 TT, f° 106r°.

the court and the army'.[78] It was no coincidence that his patronage also eroded in diplomatic circles. Moreover, quarrels with Dutch favourites such as Dijkveld and Nassau-Ouwerkerk, which had been latent during the war, now came into the open. His influence over Dutch correspondence was openly challenged by Albemarle as his neglected clientele in the United Provinces seemed to rapidly dissolve. On the other hand, Portland managed to find compensation as he would now be used by William as negotiator in the Partition Treaty talks, as described in chapter 8, from which Portland effectively managed to exclude Albemarle.

III

Portland finally retired from public service in June 1699, but he had been making arrangements beforehand. In February 1699 he had ordered £10,000 to be transferred to his Amsterdam account.[79] A few weeks later he asked Willem van Schuylenburg to make enquiries about the house of Lord Sommelsdijk, situated on the Voorhout, the most fashionable street in The Hague, close to the Binnenhof where the States of Holland and the States General assembled and the stadholderly quarters were located. The house was accordingly bought in August and would serve as his city residence.[80] It seems that Portland had already made up his mind, and only the exact timing of his retirement was dependent on certain events. The first public sign had been his decision not to join the King on his trip to Newmarket in April, pleading illness. Several days later he withdrew to Windsor Park instead. René Saunière de L'Hermitage wrote that 'it is said that he wishes to retire in order to free himself from all kinds of affairs, so that he can enjoy more rest'.[81] In the first week of May he came to London briefly, only to return to Windsor within days. By 19 May 1699 Saunière could confirm the rumours that Portland had resigned all his commissions.[82] Two days later he came to London and was closeted with the King, who tried everything in his power to retain the Earl in his service. But Portland could not be persuaded, and relinquished all his offices, staying in London only to deal with private affairs and vacate his apartments in Kensington Palace.[83] The King made yet another effort to persuade him to change his mind, and sent Abel Tassin d'Alonne, whom they both trusted, to Windsor. Instead, Portland gave him the key of the Groom of the Stole, to be handed over to the King as a sign of his resignation.[84]

---

78   Quoted in J. Childs, *The British Army of William III 1689–1702* (Manchester, 1987), 201.
79   BL, Eg Mss 1708, f° 28.
80   Schuylenburg to Portland 24 March 1699, BL Eg Ms 1708, f° 29–30; BL, Eg Mss 1708, f° 279–80.
81   Dispatch Saunière 24 April 1699, BL, Add Mss 17677 TT, f° 148, transl. from French.
82   Dispatch Saunière 19 May 1699, ibid., f° 169r°.
83   Dispatch Saunière 19 May 1699, 22 May 1699, ibid., f° 169r°, 170r°; dispatch Bonnet 12/22 May 1699, BL, Add Mss 30000C, f° 104r°.
84   Dispatch Saunière 19 May 1699, BL, Add Mss 17677 TT, f° 169r°.

Nevertheless, it was common knowledge that the King still had great esteem for his confidant. Portland insisted on retiring but explained to William: 'The feelings that such a separation cause in our hearts is known to us only, and the secret will never leave mine.'[85] Up to a point one can speculate on that secret. The fact that the personal relationship between William and Portland had not visibly deteriorated (they were still seen dining and hunting together) indicates that Portland was most likely not referring to their friendship. Undoubtedly Portland had developed a lasting loyalty and deep commitment to William and his political goals during his long service. William's favour to Albemarle was felt by Portland to have broken the monopoly he had had for so many years. Few favourites served their masters for such a long time, and William did not hide his 'extreme sorrow' in a short but deep-felt reply.[86] Although Portland was determined to retire this time, the friendship was never broken and the two men frequently met until their final parting at William's deathbed.

The tidings of his resignation caused panic amongst his clients; ' ... immediately upon my Lord Portland's retiring', Matthew Prior lamented, 'down with Mr. Prior; so when the pillar is removed the ivy that depended on it falls.'[87] Rumours of his retirement had caused panic amongst the court party in Scotland, Patrick Hume complaining that it was 'prejudicall to the King's affairs, and of no advantage to your selfe'.[88] It was also prejudicial to the members of the court party themselves. Patrick Hume and James Ogilvy feared the inevitable collapse of the Queensberry ministry without Portland's support; he had been 'a true friend to us all, and has had a great hand in our present settlement and his interest was sufficient to have supported it'.[89] Secretary of State John Carmichael threatened to resign should Portland lay down his offices.[90] The opposition rejoiced, but although Portland had retreated from Court, his influence in Scots business seems to have been undiminished throughout the summer and autumn of 1699, which somewhat reassured his party.[91]

Many observers were puzzled by Portland's decision to retire. 'It loocks and is though theer is some misterie in this', Thomas Livingstone thought, 'for it appears od that so long in favour and done so great services should so of a suddain retyer;

---

85 Portland to William 1 May 1699 (Windsor), Japikse, *Correspondentie*, XXIII. 337, transl. from French.

86 William to Portland 28 April 1699 OS, ibid., 339.

87 Prior to Portland 13 July 1699, HMC, *Bath Mss*, III. 255–66. Ms Grew was mistaken when she wrote that Portland did not have a court party, *William Bentinck and William III (Prince of Orange). The Life of Bentinck, Earl of Portland, from the Welbeck Correspondence* (London, 1924), 278. Cf. P.W.J. Riley, *King William and the Scottish Politicians* (Edinburgh, 1979), 130; Prior to Montagu 20 May 1699, Prior to Portland 20 May 1699, HMC, *Bath Mss*, III. 343; Sunderland to Portland 4 March 1699, Vernon to Portland 1 August 1699, NUL, PwA 1277, PwA 1498; Prior to Vernon 20 May 1699, BL, Add Mss 40773, f° 341.

88 Hume to Portland 21 June 1699, NUL, PwA 684.

89 Quoted in Riley, *Scottish Politicians*, 130.

90 Carmichael to Carstares 7 August 1699, McCormick, *State Papers*, 487; Hume to Portland 21 June 1699, NUL, PwA 684.

91 Ogilvy to Carstares 17 August 1699, Carmichael to Carstares 8 August 1700, McCormick, *State Papers*, 492, 601.

but court maters are misterius.'[92] James Vernon wrote to Portland: 'I am sorry to hear any mention of your solitude when it is in your owne power to put an end to it.'[93] Obviously there were personal reasons for his retirement. Like William (who had threatened to abdicate himself), he was 'so tired of the world that if there were monasteries in our religion I believe I could retire there', he complained to Matthew Prior only weeks before his resignation.[94]

Traditional historiography has mainly sought explanations for his retirement in the triangular personal relationship between William and his two favourites, and therefore neglected to look into the deeper causes.[95] In chapter 8 it has already been argued that the end of the war and the demise of the Whig Junto played a crucial role in his decision. Portland was well aware, of course, of the rumours surrounding his resignation, but he refused to comment on them, no doubt partly because of their personal and emotional nature. But to Matthew Prior he wrote that none of the rumours contained any truth, clearly indicating that his decision was not motivated by private considerations.[96] He hinted at an ulterior motive to the Earl of Sunderland, arguing that he felt obliged to lay down all his offices, just like the latter had done a year before. The parallel Portland makes is revealing, for Sunderland's reasons had been twofold. First, opposition in Parliament had become so virulent that Sunderland feared impeachment. When rumours circulated that the King had asked for Portland's return in the autumn of 1699, and he refused, 'Some say he does so, foreseeing stormes; others that he knowes the Commones here beare him at ill will and that if he showld againe enter upon bussieness they wold have a fling at him'.[97] Second, his position was crumbling and he refused to take responsibility without his monarch's undivided backing, just like Sunderland had complained that William virtually ignored him.[98]

Despite Portland's retirement, as Saunière wrote, 'This earl says that the plan he has formed to rid himself of his charges does not hinder him, should the King have need of his services, to busy himself with the same zeal and attachment he has always had'.[99] Portland agreed to conclude the negotiations on the Spanish Succession at William's request. Indeed, it would be difficult for the King to find an alternative. There were more skilled diplomats, but none with the stature of the royal favourite. Moreover, Portland had developed into an experienced negotiator with a profound knowledge of affairs. It was the one area in which Albemarle had had no experience at all, and no other diplomat could claim to represent both the Maritime Powers.

---

92   Livingstone to Annandale 11 May 1699, HMC, *Johnstone Mss*, 129.
93   Vernon to Portland 22 August 1699, NUL, PwA 1500.
94   Portland to Prior 2/12 March 1699 (Kensington Palace), HMC, *Bath Mss*, III. 322, transl. from French.
95   With the notable exception of Baxter, *William III*.
96   Portland to Prior 1 June 1699 NS (Windsor), HMC, *Bath Mss*, III. 349. Portland to Heinsius 1 May 1699 (Windsor), NA, 3.01.19/2189.
97   Unknown to Annandale 25 November 1699, HMC, *Johnstone Mss*, 113.
98   Sunderland to Portland 20 March 1699, NUL, PwA 1279. Cf. Tallard to Louis 15 May 1699, Grimblot, *Letters*, II. 329.
99   Dispatch Saunière 22 May 1699, BL, Add Mss 17677 TT, f° 170v°, transl. from French.

Weeks after his retirement Albemarle tried to work himself into the Partition Treaty negotiations. His closest ally, the Earl of Jersey, had returned from his embassy to France and was appointed Secretary of State. In this new configuration Albemarle and Jersey could expect to oust Portland from the talks, and their failure to do so indicates the extent of the latter's control over the negotiations.[100] Portland must have been aware of the advantage his position as negotiator gave him over Albemarle; according to Tallard, it was Portland himself who 'begged' William to leave the negotiations to him.[101] Thus although Portland had now ostensibly been side-lined by his rival Albemarle, in actual fact his influence endured because of his position as negotiator.

Some thought that Portland would return, as he had done in 1697. James Johnston thought there was all a trick to it: 'that a man shall throw up his places, and yet resolve to continue in business is nonsense, nor does any man of sense here believe it. Its more likely that he come into places again.'[102] Another observer wrote: ' ...The king (it is saied) has had Earl Portland with him and has beene ernist with him to enter againe into bussieness, but that he refuses it.' He connected his retirement to the 'stormes' he may have foreseen.[103] By this he may very well also have hinted at the outcry in Scotland about the collapse of the Darien scheme, which almost exactly coincided with Portland's retirement. This Scottish scheme to found a colony in Central America had failed partly because of English and Dutch resistance to new competition, and William came under heavy attack in the autumn session. In October 1699 one anonymous writer warned Portland that the Darien failure would be discussed in Parliament, and already Portland was blamed.[104] But the affair was also embarrassing to William, as the Scottish presence in Spanish-dominated territory disturbed relations whilst negotiations about the Spanish Succession were proceeding.[105] In May 1699 Portland had already received a complaint from the Spanish ambassador with regard to Scottish activities in Darien.[106]

Although Portland continued to exert some influence in Scotland from the background and the Queensberry administration prevailed, it seems to have been

---

100 Tallard to Louis 31 May 1699, AAE, CPA 181, f° 152r°; Tallard to Louis 29 July 1699, AAE, CPA 182, f° 70r°.
101 Tallard to Louis 15 May 1699, Grimblot, *Letters*, II. 328–9.
102 Johnston to Annandale 5 June 1699, HMC, *Johnstone Mss*, 109.
103 Anonymous to Annandale 25 November 1699, HMC, *Johnstone Mss*, 113. Cf. page 243.
104 Anonymous to Portland 31 October 1699, McCormick, *State Papers*, 505–6. Cf. *A Supplement to Burnets History of my Own Time etc.*, ed. H.C. Foxcroft (Oxford, 1902), 544. Portland in House of Lords during Darien debate 'always pays attention to the affairs of that kingdom by order of the King', dispatch Saunière 16 June 1699, BL, Add Mss 17677 TT, f° 189r°, transl. from French.
105 Cf. William to Portland 13 September 1699, Japikse, *Correspondentie*, XXIII. 343–4. Cf. C. Storrs, 'Disaster at Darien (1698–1700)? The Persistence of Spanish Imperial Power on the Eve of the Demise of the Spanish Habsburgs', *European History Quarterly*, 29 (1999), 5–38.
106 NUL, PwA 2675–6.

mainly to finish some business.[107] It was unknown whether he would be replaced. Albemarle does not seem to have been considered a credible alternative.[108] He showed little interest in Scotland, although during Portland's supremacy he had tried to court some of the opposition, most notably Livingstone, with whom Portland was then quarrelling.[109] Attempts made to install Albemarle in Portland's stead after the latter's retirement failed.[110]

Obviously opportunism prevailed amongst courtiers, as one contemporary historian wrote: 'This change did at first please the English and Dutch; the Earl of Albemarle having made several powerful Friends in both Nations, who out of envy to my Lord Portland, were glad to see another in his place.'[111] But Albemarle's moment of triumph was marred by Portland's continuing influence. He was unfortunate as well, in that the initial rejoicing over Portland's retirement, which had temporarily redounded in Albemarle's favour, had turned into a growing opposition against the new favourite that became more vehement than anything Portland had experienced.[112] When Albemarle received the Garter in May 1700, many of the nobility (including Portland) declined to attend the ceremony, although William tried to make it go down better by giving the Earl of Pembroke the Garter simultaneously.[113] Albemarle continued to bring down Portland's old clique, however, and was involved in the fall of the Whig Lord Somers. But even after Portland's retirement Albemarle was confronted with the remnants of his rival's clientele.[114] Sidney, Portland's closest ally, remained in office, and Shrewsbury's client Vernon repeatedly urged Portland throughout the summer of 1699 to return to Court, meanwhile meticulously reporting the latest news.[115]

One observer thought that Albemarle had 'nou both Dutch and English businesse more in his hands than I thinck he cares to mind'.[116] The new favourite had been successful in the United Provinces, where he managed to find support from those opposed to Portland's interest.[117] After Portland's retirement Albemarle had Nassau-Ouwerkerk's son promoted to the Mastership of the Robes, and there seems little doubt that they had been in league in eroding Portland's influence.[118] Van Borssele suggested that William still employed Portland after his retirement to administer the affairs of Overijssel through D'Alonne. In March 1699 Heinsius had assisted

---

107 Riley, *Scottish Politicians*, 130.
108 Unknown to Annandale 15 June 1699, HMC, *Johnstone Mss*, 109–10.
109 Riley, *Scottish Politicians*, 130; Carstares to Melville 4 December 1697, 23 December 1697, NLS, Ms 3471, f° 64–5.
110 Riley, *Scottish Politicians*, 130.
111 Quoted in J. Oldmixon, *The History of England etc.* (London, 1735), 179.
112 *Biographia Brittanica, or, the Lives of the Most Eminent Persons Who have Flourished in Great Britain and Ireland etc.* (London, 1747), I. 729.
113 A. Boyer, *The History of King William III* (3 vols, London, 1702–03), III. 451; Bodleian Library, Rawlinson Manuscript D924, f° 429.
114 Oldmixon, *History of England*, 209–10.
115 Vernon to Portland 4 July 1699, NUL, PwA 1497 ff.
116 Johnston to Annandale 10 April 1699, HMC, *Johnstone Mss*, 163.
117 Oldmixon, *History of England*, 179.
118 Dispatch Bonnet 13/23 June 1699, BL, Add Mss 30000C, f° 124.

Portland in making the latter's nephew *Drost* of Valkenburgh, bypassing Dijkveld's candidate with the support of Portland's 'common friends' in Overijssel.[119] But after Portland's retirement, the bulk of Dutch affairs was monopolised by Albemarle in combination with regional confidants, such as Nassau-Odijk and Dijkveld in Zeeland and Utrecht respectively.[120] According to Jersey, Portland's sole ally had been Heinsius, and the Grand Pensionary remained close to Portland throughout the Partition Treaty negotiations. After Portland's retirement William tried to establish a similar relationship between the Grand Pensionary and Albemarle.[121]

William's lesser Dutch courtiers struggled over the control of Dutch correspondence, as obviously 'The King hardly has anyone with him who has any knowledge of the affairs of the Republic'.[122] In fact, Albemarle's capable secretary Carel Willem van Huls, who would remain an influential courtier during the whole of Queen Anne's reign, took most business out of Albemarle's hands. Van Huls systematically made sure Dutch affairs would be channelled through Albemarle and blocked appointments to office for those outside the new favourite's clientele. Van Borssele, like Albemarle a former Dutch Gentleman of the Bedchamber and an obvious candidate, fell victim to this exclusion policy.[123]

Traditionally, favourites fell from favour or were removed from the King's entourage, either through impeachment or force. Portland's retirement, after having served William for 35 astounding years was thus a rather unique end to a favourite's career. Despite the fact that his position had been successfully challenged, Portland still wielded power and there were no signs that William intended to sideline his favourite altogether. It was only after his retirement that the threat of impeachment loomed large during the debates on the Partition Treaties. One MP, Sir Richard Cocks, wrote in his parliamentary diary,

> could not but reflect upon the instability of humane affairs that that great Lord that so lately had so many obeysances from the Gent. of this house so many respects paid him that even gent of good quality thought it a high honour to drink chocolate with his footmen and that now this great man had not one freind to speak him this was in imitation of the history of Sejanus this caused some heats and reflections.[124]

But unlike this illustrious favourite of the Roman Emperor Tiberius, who was charged with high treason and executed, Portland emerged unscathed and acquiesced in his voluntary retirement, and even remained influential behind the scenes. Portland never 'fell' as a favourite, and he still commanded influence with the King in the field of foreign policy making.

---

119 NUL, PwA 55.
120 Heeringa, 'Gedenkschriften', 130.
121 Tallard to Louis 6 July 1699, AAE, CPA 182, f° 36v°; Jersey to Albemarle 9 June 1699, BL, Add Mss 63630, f° 134r°.
122 Heeringa, 'Gedenkschriften', 128, transl. from French.
123 Ibid., 122–3, 129; Tallard to Louis 5 June 1699, AAE, CPA 181, f° 162.
124 *The Parliamentary Diary of Sir Richard Cocks, 1698–1702*, ed. D.W. Hayton (Oxford, 1996), 76–9.

Commenting upon the fate of the favourite, one anonymous commentator complained bitterly about the fate of Portland,

> ... who all along has shown such prudent and wonderful management amongst the confederates, besides his great metal in discharging so ticklish an embassy with the French king upon which the peace of Europe depended; as likewise his undaunted courage when he was wounded in his Majesty's view at many bloody battles; when milksoaps did not appear, and are now creeping up and down courte, when there is no fear of war or danger. And shall all this great soul's actions, either by himself, or any other way, be extinguished like the snuff of a candle? God forbid. It will make a very bad exite to future generations in history.[125]

Most of those who were now 'creeping up and down courte', however, hardly lamented the retirement of the favourite.

IV

When the Imperial envoy in London, Count Leopold of Auersperg, asked Portland how he could bear to retire after having been involved in public affairs for such a long time, he professed to have become reconciled to country life, 'but throughout all his talk and philosophising he involuntarily sighed deeply many times'.[126] After having served a demanding master for three decades Portland became emphatically attached to his retirement, not willing to 'meddle', as he frequently put it. But behind the scenes he remained actively interested in public affairs, a role perhaps better suited to his qualities and character than being in the limelight. Portland's friendship with William had not appreciably lessened, but their interaction became less frequent. After a clearly emotional disruption in June 1699, their ordinary friendship had soon re-established itself. Portland now focused more on his family and estates, but frequently visited the King and there never was a break between the two men. Portland's retirement from daily political life was just what it purported to be: a retirement. Up until April 1700 he often spoke to the King on behalf of affairs connected to the Partition Treaty. In the winter of 1701 the King had confided to his friend, whilst strolling through the garden of Hampton Court that, his health declining fast, he did not think he would survive the winter.[127] No doubt Portland remembered this when only months later he was called to the King's deathbed in March 1702.[128]

---

125 Anonymous to Carstares 15 August 1699, McCormick, *State Papers*, 486.
126 Quoted in Grew, *Bentinck*, 369.
127 *Biographia Brittanica*, I. 732–3; Burnet, *History*, V. 582.
128 Portland arrived late, after the King's voice had failed, and – according to Burnet – William 'took him by the hand, and carried it to his heart with great tenderness.' *History*, V. 585. Another witness, William's physician Bidloo, gives a variation on this story. According to Bidloo, William whispered some words into Portland's ear just before he lost consciousness. G. Bidloo, *Verhaal der Laaste Ziekte en het Overlijden van Willem de IIIde etc.* (Leiden, 1702), 106. Unlike some historians have suggested, this was no reconciliation, since there had never been a break as such. It was a last farewell.

Having finished the Partition Treaty negotiations, the Earl clearly prepared himself for the life of a landed aristocrat when he remarried in May 1700. Throughout the 1690s there were persistent rumours of an impending remarriage, and both his influence and wealth made him among the most desirable matches. There was a rumour in 1692 that Portland was to marry the daughter of the Duke of Newcastle. There is, moreover, circumstantial evidence that he might have had a mistress; the name of Stuarta Howard circulated for some time and some expected him to marry this lady-in-waiting of Queen Mary. Whatever truth there was in these rumours, between the autumn of 1698 and the spring of 1699 the liaison must have been broken off,[129] and Portland informed an acquaintance, the Duchess of Somerset, that a lady was recommended to him 'with the Character of all those quailitys that can be desierd in a wife'.[130] In May 1700 he married the widow of Lord Berkley of Stratton, Martha Jane Temple, the niece of Sir William Temple, who brought with her a dowry of £20,000.[131] Meanwhile he devised a Grand Tour for his son Lord Woodstock in 1701.[132]

After the accession to the throne of Anne, Portland lost his last office when she gave the rangership of Windsor to Edward Seymour. This was rather a blow to Portland, who was quite attached to the Lodge. The decision was probably inspired by Sarah Churchill, who loathed Portland, and perhaps also needed to assert herself as the new royal favourite.[133] Her antipathy can be traced back to the favourite's role in the arrest of her husband in 1692, but she had also considered Portland a major stumbling block to any reconciliation between William and Anne after Mary's death. 'I never heard of any one that opposed the reconcilement but the Earle of Portland', she wrote, 'upon which my Lord Sunderland spoke very short to him, as ... he had a very good talent when he thought people were impertinent.'[134] Still, Portland's relationship with Anne cannot have been beyond repair. The Duchess of Orleans claimed that he had been instrumental in commencing a correspondence between her and Anne.[135]

The relationship with the new monarch was further soured with a lawsuit. Queen Anne sued Portland for an alleged £91,000 fraud, which the Earl claimed were

---

129 24 September 1692, 27 September 1692, 11 December 1692, 20 December 1692, Luttrell, *Brief Historical Relation*, II. 574, 577, 643, 644; Clarges to Harley 22 September 1692, HMC, *Portland Mss*, III. 501; NUL, PwA 2798; Lady Giffard to Martha Jane Temple 14 September 1698, BL, Eg Mss 1705, f° 23v°; I am thankful to Ms Lynda Crawford of Nottingham University Library for alerting me to Ms Howard.
130 Duchess of Somerset to Portland 26 May 1699, NUL, PwA 1013.
131 4 May 1700, Luttrell, *Brief Historical Relation*, IV. 641.
132 Cf. BL, Eg Mss 1706.
133 12 May 1702, Luttrell, *Brief Historical Relation*, V. 172; F. Harris, *A Passion for Government. The Life of Sarah, Duchess of Marlborough* (Oxford, 1991), 87; Anne to Sarah 19 May 1702, *The Marlborough–Godolphin Correspondence*, ed. H.L. Snyder (3 vols, Oxford, 1975), I. 66.
134 Quoted in Harris, *A Passion for Government*, 75. Cf. 63.
135 *The Letters of Madame: the Correspondence of Elizabeth-Charlotte of Bavaria, Princess Palatine, Duchess of Orleans ... 1661–1708*, ed. G.S. Stevenson (2 vols, London, 1924), II. 83.

tallies bought during William's lifetime. After the hearings, in which his secretary Frederick Henning, and John Smith and Francis Eyles came forward with favourable statements, the crown lost the lawsuit against Portland. Apparently the case had been initiated by his former rival, as Portland informed Robéthon in June 1704 that he had won 'finally that unfortunate and great trial that Mylord Albemarle has caused'.[136]

Soon after Anne's accession to the throne, Portland left England to spend the summer at Sorgvliet, a pattern which would annually be repeated. His visits to the Republic became shorter after 1706 when he bought the estate of Bulstrode in Buckinghamshire. He was an exception, as the remnants of what had been William's Dutch inner circle in England were now mostly dispersed. Athlone became Commander-in-Chief of the Dutch army under the allied command of the Duke of Marlborough, and died in 1703. Nassau-Ouwerkerk became Field Marshal and succeeded Athlone. Nassau-Zuylestein had retired to his estate in Utrecht. Albemarle accepted a post in the Dutch army as Lieutenant General and would serve during the course of the War of the Spanish Succession.[137]

Despite his retirement from Court, Portland did not entirely retreat from active politics. On the afternoon after William's death Portland – though 'very depressed' – attended the session in the House of Lords signalling his determination to perform his duties in Parliament.[138] He was still infrequently seen at Court and was on speaking terms with Sidney Godolphin, First Lord of the Treasury, and the Duke of Marlborough, now Commander-in-Chief of the Anglo-Dutch forces in the field. But his connections with the new administration were few, as it consisted mainly of former opponents such as Robert Harley and the High Tories, the Earls of Nottingham and Rochester. 'You see', Portland wrote to Heinsius, 'the sentiments of many people here, which will not be to the taste of many people in Holland.'[139]

In most of the Dutch provinces the stadholderate was once more abolished after William's death, the Nassaus remaining in office in the North. William's favourites consequently ceased to play a dominant role. Even before his retirement Portland had lost many connections of political significance in the United Provinces. He was no longer part of the inner decision-making core-group that was 'in the secret of the government'.[140] But he still had some important contacts. He remained in close

---

136 D'Alonne to Portland 8 May 1703, 16 May 1704, NUL, PwA 317, PwA 318; TNA: PRO, E 133/153/5, E 133/153/6; 27 June 1704, Luttrell, *Brief Historical Relation*, V. 439; Portland to Robéthon 27 June 1704 (Whitehall Palace), BL, Stowe Mss 222, f° 253, transl. from French.

137 Albemarle to Heinsius 11 April 1702, *De Briefwisseling van Anthonie Heinsius 1702–1720*, ed. A.J. Veenendaal (20 vols, The Hague, 1976–2001), I. 88–9.

138 Saunière to Heinsius 24 March 1702, Veenendaal, *Briefwisseling*, I. 28, transl. from French.

139 Portland to Heinsius 4 December 1703 (Whitehall Palace), Veenendaal, *Briefwisseling*, II. 566, transl. from French.

140 Cf. G. de Bruin, *Geheimhouding en Verraad. De Geheimhouding van Staatszaken ten tijde van de Republiek (1600–1750)* (The Hague, 1991), 352; R. Hatton, *Diplomatic Relations between Great Britain and the Dutch Republic* (London, 1950), 21–9; J.G. Stork-Penning, 'The Ordeal of States – some Remarks on Dutch politics during the War of Spanish Succession', *Acta Historiae Neerlandica*, 2 (1967), 107–40, transl. from Dutch.

correspondence with Heinsius, and was related to Wassenaar-Duyvenvoorde who, like himself, held a seat in the Holland *Ridderschap* and was a member of one of the most influential and affluent Dutch noble families.[141] Portland's relationship with Albemarle remained strained, and in 1706 he clashed with his former rival Nassau-Ouwerkerk in a contest over offices after the death of Lord Catwijk in 1706.[142]

On occasion Portland was still involved in politics. In the summer of 1704, for instance, he discussed possible support for the rebellion of the Camisards in the Cevennes with the Savoyard ambassador in London, Count Annibale Maffei.[143] The French Secretary of State, the Marquis of Torcy, still seems to have considered him as a desirable candidate for negotiations.[144] Despite such occasional activities, by 1702 Portland's active political career had largely come to an end. Jean de Robéthon suggested to Heinsius that Portland might be willing to act as a tutor to the young Frisian Stadholder, Johan Willem Friso, but the plan came to nothing.[145]

However, his contacts on both sides of the North Sea still rendered him useful. He was well informed, and corresponded with an extensive network of agents, mainly former aides and secretaries.[146] These were now also establishing lines of communication between the Allied ministries. René Saunière de L'Hermitage was a prolific supplier of information to Grand Pensionary Heinsius and the States General from London beginning in 1692 when he became an agent. He seems to have been a tutor to Portland's children and was acquainted with Jean de Robéthon.[147] In subsequent years the latter would become an agent for Hanover through whom Portland remained in touch with the electoral court.[148] Guillaume Lamberty likewise served as an agent for Hanover in The Hague from 1706, but had formerly been a secretary to Portland.[149] Abel Tassin d'Alonne had acted as secretary to Portland and was made through him Dutch Secretary to William afterwards. During the War of

---

141   Though it should be remembered that the nobility of Holland was a relatively weak order. See for an analysis of the nobility: J. Aalbers, 'Factieuze Tegenstellingen binnen het College van de Ridderschap van Holland na de Vrede van Utrecht', *Bijdragen en Mededelingen betreffende de Geschiedenis der Nederlanden*, 93 (1978), 412–45, 412–17 ff.

142   See the extensive correspondence between Portland and Wassenaar-Duyvenvoorde, Japikse, *Correspondentie*, XXIV. 459 ff. Cf. Wassenaar-Duyvenvoorde to Portland 17 July 1703, Japikse, *Correspondentie*, XXIV. 469–71.

143   11 July 1704, Luttrell, *Brief Historical Relation*, V. 443–4; Stanhope to Harley 25 July 1704, TNA:PRO, SP 84/226, f° 462.

144   Meyercron to Portland 27 January 1703, NUL, PwA 928.

145   'no person is more suitable than Mylord Portland to be close to that young prince and form him in affairs, both of war and government', Robéthon to Heinsius 21 March 1702, 24 March 1702, Veenendaal, *Briefwisseling*, I. 11–12, 26, transl. from French.

146   Cf. pages 171–3.

147   See his lengthy dispatches in BL, Add Mss 17677; Dijkveld to Portland 26 October 1692, Japikse, *Correspondentie*, XXVIII. 302. Cf. Ch. 3.

148   Robéthon also forwarded to Portland extracts of certain diplomatic correspondences, see for instance his letter of 19 September 1702 to Heinsius, Veenendaal, *Briefwisseling*, I. 430.

149   L. Frey and M. Frey (eds), *The Treaties of the War of the Spanish Succession – An Historical and Critical dictionary* (London, 1995), 237.

the Spanish Succession he was secretary to Heinsius and was active in the counter-espionage Black Chamber.[150]

V

Anthonie Heinsius in particular regarded Portland an important medium between the Dutch and English ministries. The two men had habitually corresponded over the preceding years, a practice which was to continue throughout the rest of Portland's life on a regular basis.[151] This confidential correspondence acquainted Portland with the deliberations of Dutch policy makers, but vice versa provided the Grand Pensionary with a view of sentiments in Whitehall.[152] On occasion Heinsius asked Portland to support Dutch interests and obstruct Tory policy. In January 1703 he asked him to contribute to a speedy dispatch of English troops to the continent and prevent the sending of a fleet to the West Indies, but there is no evidence that Portland was able to comply with Heinsius's wishes.[153] Obviously Portland had to act with circumspection. When Heinsius requested detailed intelligence about Anglo-Dutch military co-operation 'with which he could be of use to the common good', he urged Portland not to let it be known that he had received documents from The Hague. Both men must have realised that Portland's hands were tied. The High Tories would certainly criticise the machinations of this 'Dutch Lord'.[154]

Portland's rapprochement with Marlborough materialised after the victory at Blenheim in August 1704, when the fortunes of the Allies had turned and support for the continental strategy was mounting. Secretary of State Nottingham was dismissed in 1704. Despite Portland's antipathy towards the Duchess of Marlborough, he drew closer to the Marlboroughs and Godolphin who were now dominating the ministry. Congratulating the Duke on his splendid victory, Portland approached Marlborough in September with the aim of establishing a regular correspondence. In the autumn of 1706 Portland even offered Marlborough the use of Sorgvliet, evidence that their relationship had become cordial.[155] Heinsius, whose correspondence with Marlborough was of crucial importance for the functioning of the alliance, in particular hoped that Portland would frequently speak to the Duke during winter

---

150 K.M.M. de Leeuw, *Cryptology and Statecraft in the Dutch Republic* (Amsterdam, 2000), 2.

151 Most of these letters have been published, either in Japikse, *Correspondentie*, XXIV or Veenendaal, *Briefwisseling*.

152 Heinsius frequently asked Portland to informally speak to ministers or ambassadors to consult them about certain matters or estimate their opinion and asked Portland to lobby, e.g. Heinsius to Portland 31 October 1702, 16 January 1703, Japikse, *Correspondentie*, XXIV. 414–15, 420–21.

153 Heinsius to Portland 16 January 1703, Japikse, *Correspondentie*, XXIV. 420–21.

154 Heinsius to Portland 27 November 1703, 7 December 1703, Japikse, *Correspondentie*, XXIV. 435–6, transl. from French; Portland to Heinsius 4 December 1703 (Whitehall Palace), Veenendaal, *Briefwisseling*, II. 566.

155 Probably because in 1705 Marlborough's residence, the Mauritshuis, had been destroyed by fire.

season in London. Marlborough must have found it useful to open an informal channel: 'Pray let me hear from you some times, and let me have your own thoughts, which I promise you shall be known to nobody but myself.'[156] On occasion, Portland would share information on terrain in the Spanish Netherlands gathered during his campaigns in the 1690s. More often, his letters dealt with matters of diplomacy and contained advice to Marlborough on how to deal with Dutch politicians.[157]

The former Anglo-Dutch favourite on occasion was able to smooth over friction between Allied commanders, mediating to prevent inevitable quarrels from escalating.[158] After an uneventful campaign in 1705 Marlborough, dissatisfied with the restrictions imposed by the quarrelsome Dutch general, Frederik Johan van Baer, Lord of Slangenburg, wished to leave the army as early as August. Portland urged him to remain in the field, however, knowing his departure would have a negative effect and send a wrong signal.[159] After discussing the matter with Heinsius, Portland was able to persuade the Duke.[160] Marlborough sought similar advice from Portland when his presence was requested in Vienna that autumn to concert the next campaign.[161] A more significant matter arose in 1706 when the Dutch and English established a Council of State responsible for the Government of the conquered parts of the Spanish Netherlands. The Imperialists, who had cleverly sowed dissension, resented this so-called Condominium.[162] Earlier that summer an Imperial offer to Marlborough to become governor of the Spanish Netherlands had caused such an

---

156 Portland to Marlborough 13 September 1704 (The Hague), BL, Add Mss 61153, f° 214–15; Heinsius to Portland 26 December 1704, Japikse, *Correspondentie*, XXIV. 437–8. Cf. *The Correspondence of John Churchill, First Duke of Marlborough, and Anthonie Heinsius, Grand Pensionary of Holland 1701–1711*, ed. B. van 't Hoff (Utrecht, 1951); Marlborough to Portland 27 July 1705, HMC, *Portland Mss*, IV. 212.

157 E.g. Portland to Marlborough 1 August 1705 (The Hague), BL, Add Mss 61153, f° 218–19.

158 E.g. Albemarle to Heinsius 12 July 1703, Veenendaal, *Briefwisseling*, II. 337; Portland to Heinsius 20 January 1705 (Whitehall Palace), Veenendaal, *Briefwisseling* IV. 35; Somers to Portland 21 June 1705 OS, Japikse, *Correspondentie*, XXIV. 564–5; letter Galway 28 May 1705, NUL, PwA 1117.

159 Portland to Marlborough 1 August 1705 (The Hague), BL, Add Mss 61153, f° 218; Marlborough to Portland 24 August 1705, 7 September 1705, HMC, *Portland Mss*, IV. 230, 242–3; Portland to Marlborough 12 September 1705 (The Hague), Japikse, *Correspondentie*, XXIV. 560.

160 Portland to Marlborough 12 September 1705 (The Hague), Japikse, *Correspondentie*, XXIV. 560; Portland to Godolphin 18 September 1705 (The Hague), BL, Add Mss 61118, f° 73–4. Cf. D. Coombs, *The Conduct of the Dutch. British Opinion and the Dutch Alliance during the War of the Spanish Succession* (The Hague, 1958), 115.

161 Portland to Marlborough 26 September 1705 (The Hague), Japikse, *Correspondentie*, XXIV. 560–61; Marlborough to Portland 1 October 1705, HMC, *Portland Mss*, IV. 249–50; Marlborough to Godolphin 6 October 1705, Snyder, *Correspondence*, I. 502; Marlborough to Heinsius 22 September 1705, Van 't Hoff, *Correspondence*, 214.

162 R. Geikie and I.A. Montgomery, *The Dutch Barrier 1705–1719* (Cambridge, 1930), 13 ff.

uproar in the United Provinces, that the Duke decided to decline the offer.[163] Portland praised him for his

> ... prudence and moderation with which you have evaded a dangerous mine, and of which the effect would have been fatal, of which you have acquitted yourself because you have, Sir, more honour, consideration and much confidence by refusing instead of accepting that which has been offered to you, which is the sentiment of all the honest people, and of your friends ... .[164]

But Marlborough had been deeply dissatisfied with the Dutch attitude, and although the matter had been thus resolved, the first cracks in the close relationship between Heinsius and Marlborough became visible.[165]

Portland's friendships in England were almost solely confined to Whigs. In November 1702, upon his return to England, he had stayed the night at the house of the 3rd Earl of Shaftesbury.[166] Some two years later, he re-established contacts with members of the ascending new Whig Junto, such as John Montagu, now Baron Halifax. In the summer of 1705 John Somers had asked Portland to intervene in the dispute between the British and Dutch commanders, the Earl of Galway and Baron Fagel, which was impeding the campaign in Portugal. He also expressed concern that the peace party in the Republic was gaining strength, and warned Portland that this was no different in England. The two men clearly developed a mutual understanding that 'affairs are not in such a state that a reasonable and lasting peace can be hoped for'.[167] Thus, having been somewhat sidelined during the first two years of the war, by the autumn of 1704 Portland was re-establishing contacts with key members in the ministry and the Whig Junto.

To what extent these indicated an expression of his political affiliation is unclear. Portland's concept of foreign policy remained what it had been before, as he explained to Robéthon: 'I am too old to change, and too much imbued with the sentiments of the late King my master to deviate from them, moreover I love my religion and hate slavery.'[168] As during the 1690s, he was drawn into a partisan struggle against his will. 'I do not ever want to be Whig or Tory', he assured the Elector of Hanover, but added that circumstances now required him to side with the Whigs.[169] Indeed, according to Geoffrey Holmes's analysis of division lists, Portland

---

163 A.J. Veenendaal Sr, *Het Engels-Nederlands Condominium in de Zuidelijke Nederlanden* (Utrecht, 1945), 29 ff.

164 Portland to Marlborough 15 July 1706 (The Hague), BL, Add Mss 61153, f° 222, transl. from French. Marlborough to Portland 22 July 1706, Japikse, *Correspondentie*, XXIV. 560–61.

165 Veenendaal, *Condominium*, 35.

166 Shaftesbury to Furly 4 November 1702, B. Rand (ed.), *The Life, Unpublished Letters and Philosophical Regimen of Anthony, Earl of Shaftesbury* (London/New York, 1900, repr. 1995), 313.

167 Somers to Portland 21 June 1705 OS, 28 August 1705, Japikse, *Correspondentie*, XXIV. 564–6.

168 Portland to Robéthon 5 September 1702 (The Hague), BL, Stowe Mss 222, f° 150r°, transl. from French.

169 Portland to the Elector and Electress of Hanover, 9 June 1706, NUL, PwA 1198.

voted consistently with Whig peers.[170] In the years following 1705 Portland's support for the Whig Junto would become more outspoken, illustrated by three affairs: the Protestant Succession of the House of Hanover, the Union with Scotland and the Barrier Treaty. To the Junto Whigs, these matters were connected. The Protestant Succession could be safeguarded by the House of Hanover, and the Scottish Union would strengthen the Whig Party.[171] The Barrier Treaty strengthened the alliance with the Dutch, which they thought necessary.

Portland had been a strong supporter of the Protestant Succession and the House of Hanover, and remained in close contact with the Electress.[172] His son Woodstock was cordially received in Hanover during his Grand Tour in 1703.[173] In December 1705 Portland voted in favour of the Bill for the Protestant Succession, a pro-Hanoverian measure supported by the Whig peers.[174] The Elector was naturally pleased, and Jean de Robéthon conveyed his permission for Portland to communicate these sentiments to other members of the Whig Junto.[175] In 1716 King George I would elevate Portland's son to the dukedom as a reward for his services in promoting his succession.[176]

The Protestant Succession was dealt with during a time when discussions about a Union between England and Scotland were speeded up. Portland had remained more than an interested observer of Scottish affairs after his retirement. In October 1700 the Duke of Queensberry asked Portland's 'advice and assistance in the present ticklish circumstances of affaires here'.[177] Scottish Secretaries of State were keen to remain in touch with Portland even after the death of William, and he showed an inclination to support the 'good party'.[178] Like the Whig Junto, Portland supported the Union when Carstares asked him his opinion in January 1706, months before the treaty was signed:

> I believe the succession of Hanover establishes a very good thing. But I think the Union is better, because it comprises the succession, that it is to the advantage of both nations, because it prevents all the future differences, it will cut the roots of a good part of your domestic divisions, and it will remedy bit by bit the shortage of money from which Scotland suffers. [179]

---

170 G. Holmes, *British Politics in the Age of Anne* (London, 1967), appendix A, 431.

171 This complex connection is lucidly explained in Holmes, *British Politics*, 82 ff. The Scottish Union was pushed by Whig peers and opposed by Tories, apprehensive of the incorporation of a Presbyterian entity.

172 See their correspondence in BL, Stowe Mss 222 and 223, and NUL, PwA 1189–201.

173 Sophia, Electress of Hanover, to Portland 13 January 1703, NUL PwA 1193; Portland to Robéthon 2 February 1703 (Whitehall Palace), BL, Stowe Ms 222, f° 182; George Louis of Hanover to Portland 7 March 1703, NUL, PwA 462.

174 Portland to D'Alonne 11 December 1705 (Whitehall Palace), Veenendaal, *Briefwisseling*, IV. 453.

175 Robéthon to Portland n.d. 1706, NUL, PwA 1079, n.d. 1706 NUL, PwA 1080.

176 R. Hatton, *George I. Elector and King* (London, 1978), 408.

177 Queensberry to Portland 8 October 1700, NUL, PwA 373.

178 Carmichael to Carstares 8 August 1700, Portland to Carstares 14 July 1702, Loudon to Carstares 4 December 1705, McCormick, *State Papers*, 601, 717, 739–40.

179 Portland to Carstares 24 January 1706 (Whitehall Palace), 11 April 1706, McCormick, *State Papers*, 742, 749, transl. from French. Portland opposed the idea of a

The re-emergence of the political alliance of Portland and the Junto Whigs grew out of a common perception of foreign policy, but the personal relationships were also cordial. Portland kept up a correspondence with Somers. Halifax regularly visited him at Bulstrode where, undoubtedly, matters of policy were discussed as well.[180] It was perhaps his typical failing that his contacts were restricted almost exclusively to the Whig Junto, and that he maintained few contacts with the Tories. At the time, though, allying with Junto Whigs seemed sensible policy, as they were firm supporters of the Anglo-Dutch Alliance, and were gaining control over the ministry between December 1706 and November 1708.

In Holland as well Portland was still active as an advocate for war. Wassenaar-Duyvenvoorde and Portland were, like Heinsius, in favour of prolonging the war until a favourable, stable and durable peace could be established. This faction within the *Ridderschap* was reinforced by Wassenaar-Obdam, Commander-in-Chief of the Dutch armed forces in the Spanish Netherlands.[181] The war-faction tended to have close relations with the Whigs in England and regarded the Anglo-Dutch alliance as an axiom in Dutch foreign policy.[182]

As war aims between the Maritime Powers were diverging, in May 1706 Marlborough had drawn up a memorandum to invite the Dutch to guarantee the Hanoverian Succession. It became the basis for a mutual agreement in which the Dutch signed the guarantee and the English promised to support a Barrier Treaty.[183] This deal initially met with the satisfaction of both parties, but was to divide the Allies over the years after 1706, a process in which Portland was to play his final mediating role.[184] The years between 1706 and 1708 were marked by stagnating negotiations over the Barrier, and Portland was frequently asked by both sides to intervene or smooth over difficulties.

Despite his occasional lobbying Portland displayed no desire to become openly involved. 'I am content not to meddle at all', he wrote to John Somers in early 1709, 'which is better than to expose myself to blame without being able to expect to do any good.'[185] But perhaps he was also feeling the strain of old age. He spent more time at Bulstrode and less in London, even during parliamentary sessions. To Heinsius he wrote in the spring of 1708 'that our age increases and our forces diminish accordingly'.[186] From early 1709, his ever-neat handwriting started to become uncertain, but his interest in events never waned. His correspondence with Heinsius continued, with Somers intensified. In January 1708 he left Bulstrode for

---

federal union.

180 E.g. Portland to Somers 13 February [1708?] (Bulstrode), SHC, Somers Mss 371/14/K/14; Halifax to Portland 19 February 1708, Japikse, *Correspondentie*, XXIV. 566–7.

181 Cf. Aalbers, 'Factieuze Tegenstellingen', 421–3.

182 Ibid., 419–20.

183 Geiki, *Dutch Barrier*, 38 ff. Cf. Heinsius to Portland 19 February 1709, Japikse, *Correspondentie*, XXIV. 452.

184 Cf. Geiki, *Dutch Barrier*, 47.

185 Portland to Somers 15 April 1709 (Bulstrode), SHC, Somers Mss 371/14/K/24, transl. from French.

186 Portland to Heinsius 4 June 1708 (Bulstrode), Veenendaal, *Briefwisseling*, VII. 297, transl. from French.

London at Heinsius's request to talk to 'many people' in relation to the coming campaign.[187] Undoubtedly, his being sidelined from active politics was something he regretted, confiding to Somers in early 1709: ' ... I am now here like the lazy servant of the Gospel who buried his talent in the ground, where it brought no profit'.[188] He continued to maintain a correspondence with William Carstares, as he was still concerned

> ... about the public good, our sacred religion, liberty, and all that is dear to us, you can be assured, Sir, that I often think of you. The good God be eternally praised for delivering us from fears. One does not dare to think of the consequences of evils, which menace us, without trembling.[189]

Over September and October 1709 he still corresponded intensively with the Junto Whigs and Marlborough on the Barrier Treaty and negotiations for peace with the French which had commenced in Geertruidenberg.[190] Only weeks later he fell ill with pleurisy at Bulstrode.[191] After lying twelve days on his sickbed, he died on 4 December at 5 o'clock in the morning.[192] Ten days later, his corpse, having been brought to London, was 'carried with great funeral pomp, from his house in St James's square to Westminster Abbey, and there interred in the vault under the east window of Henry the VII's chapel'.[193] The funeral took place with magnificent ceremony; there were some 50 carriages, numerous riders, and a great number of nobles attended the service.[194]

VI

At his death in 1709 Portland was fabulously rich. A good indicator is the state of his affairs at his death in 1709, when his possessions were valued at an astronomical eleven million Dutch guilders, roughly equalling one million pounds sterling.[195] It is of some interest that some £900,000 was connected to his possessions in England. Clearly, the Anglo-Dutch favourite had transferred the weight of his career, as well

---

187 Portland to Heinsius 3 January 1708 (Bulstrode), ibid., 4, transl. from French.

188 Portland to Somers 8 February 1709 (Bulstrode), SHC, Somers Mss 371/14/K/16, transl. from French.

189 Portland to Carstares (Bulstrode) 10 April 1708, McCormick, *State Papers*, transl. from French.

190 Portland to Somers 7 September 1709 (Whitehall Palace), SHC, Somers Mss 371/14/K/26; Portland to Marlborough 13 September 1709 (Whitehall Palace), BL, Add Mss 61153, f° 239–40; Townshend to Portland 1 October 1709, Japikse, *Correspondentie*, XXIV. 568.

191 Luttrell, *Brief Historical Relation*, VI. 513.

192 2nd Earl of Portland to d'Alonne 25 November OS 1709, BL, Eg Mss 1705, f° 37.

193 *Biographia Brittanica*, I. 733. Portland was buried next to Schomberg. A vault stone with the names was inserted in 1868 but is now no longer visible, for the place is now a RAF chapel. I am thankful to the librarian of Westminster Abbey for the references.

194 Saunière to Heinsius 17 Dec. 1709, Veenendaal, *Briefwisseling*, IX. 515.

195 BL, Eg Mss 1708, f° 277–80. See page 97.

as the bulk of his fortune, across the North Sea. Portland had made several wills and codicils throughout the 1690s. The birth of a son, Willem, in 1704 was the reason he decided to divide his English and Dutch estates between his two surviving sons. An English will made in July 1704 allocated the estates in England to Henry, and one made in 1705 granted his Dutch estates to his son Willem. The will contained a deliberate clause that 'the goods we have there, have [no] community with our goods we have in these lands, which is why we have ensured, that the laws of these lands on the aforesaid English goods have no application'.[196] The daughters from his first and second marriages each inherited £10,000. His widow received a pension, the use of Sorgvliet and his town house in The Hague on the Lange Voorhout, as well as the silverware and furniture of Bulstrode and the Whitehall Palace apartment.[197]

The complications of the vastness of Portland's inheritance resulted in a prolonged dispute between his heirs, but the two branches in the United Provinces and England remained on good terms in the long run.[198] In a curious twist of fate, Portland's son Willem would become the main adviser of William's heir, Stadholder William IV. Willem Bentinck, Lord of Rhoon and Pendrecht (1704–1774), was like his father a member of the Holland *Ridderschap* and an active and dominant politician. Nicknamed 'the Grand Tribune', he became a leading spokesman of the Orangists and had a great influence on the weak stadholder.[199] During the stadholderate of William IV (1747–51) he was actively involved in strengthening the Orangist regime.

Willem was very different from his half-brother, Henry Woodstock, who had married a daughter of the Earl of Gainsborough in 1704.[200] Henry's career took off when he became MP for Southampton at 26 in 1708, and for Hampshire in 1709.[201] As 2nd Earl of Portland after his father's death in November 1709 his career took a very different spin. He did not display that tenacious desire for influence which had characterised his father, indeed he was an affected young man interested in the arts rather than in politics or military achievements. Portland had found his governor Paul Rapin de Thoyras knowledgeable in both modern and ancient languages, mathematics and particularly in music, which left their marks on Woodstock.[202] In 1719 the 2nd Earl was one of the founding directors of the Royal Academy of Music.[203]

The 2nd Earl had preserved the political pro-Whig inclinations of his father, and was frequently seen in the company of the Duke of Marlborough. In 1710

---

196   Ibid., f° 133, transl. from Dutch.

197   Ibid., f° 112–30.

198   BL, Eg Ms 1709; Egerton Charter 8305.

199   Quoted in J.A.F. de Jongste, 'De Republiek onder het Erfstadhouderschap 1747–1780' in: *Algemene Geschiedenis der Nederlanden, IX* (Bussum, 1980), 73–91, 84, transl. from French.

200   18 May 1704, 8 June 1704, Luttrell, *Brief Historical Relation* V. 425, 433.

201   Although in 1702 Portland had denied his son permission to join the army. On Henry's career, see D. Onnekink, 'Het Fortuin van Henry Bentinck (1682–1726), Eerste Hertog van Portland', *Virtus*, 2nd series, 2 (2004), 54–72.

202   P. Schazmann, *The Bentincks. The History of a European Family* (London, 1976), 102–3.

203   Onnekink, 'Het Fortuyn van Henry Bentinck', 62.

Portland magnificently fêted Prince Eugene on his famous visit to London. At this highly politicised event, Nassau-Ouwerkerk and the Whig lords in opposition – Marlborough, Townshend, Dorchester, Sunderland and Devonshire – assembled in his house.[204] In 1716 his career took a different twist when George I, recognising the services of his father for the Hanoverian succession – and undoubtedly on the wave of re-emerging Whiggism – bestowed on him the dukedom. The following year he was made a Lord of the Bedchamber. Gigantic losses incurred in the South Sea Bubble disaster of 1720 prompted him to take up office as Governor of Jamaica in 1721, where he died from a fever in July 1726.[205]

During the course of the eighteenth century the Portlands recovered from their misfortune. The 2nd Duke married Lady Margaret Cavendish Harley, a descendant of Robert Harley, through which connection the Portlands acquired the magnificent estate of Welbeck Abbey in Nottinghamshire – still one of the grandest in England. The 3rd Duke of Portland became prime minister in the 1780s, whereas his second son became the first Governor General of India of 1833.[206] Both the Portlands and the Bentincks continued to play an important role in the politics of England and the United Provinces. The comments of the Electress of Hanover about Woodstock– 'that English and Dutch blood mix well together' – is symbolic in this respect.[207]

VII

Portland was not eclipsed by his rival nor dismissed by a monarch tired of his favourite. Although animosity between Albemarle and Portland was certainly a factor in the latter's decision to retire, the deeper causes are much more important and illuminating. Several causes have been established. Firstly, Portland refused to take responsibility for William's policy when his influence was gradually eroding. Secondly, the years between 1697 and 1699 saw a complicated political transformation in which the Whig–Tory dichotomy temporarily made way for Court–Country struggles. The consequent decline of the Whig Junto weakened Portland, who failed to reconsider his position. Thirdly, he thus became highly vulnerable as a Court member when attacks by Country MPs (outbursts of xenophobia, protests against the Irish grants, threats of impeachment) remained unchallenged. Fourthly, the end of the Nine Years War had rendered one of his pivotal roles, as liaison between the Allies – in particular the Dutch – less important. Lastly, with the end of the war, the army was quickly disbanded. Portland's main role had been to mobilise resources for the war, and his influence was to a large extent based on his position as military manager. These combined factors gained strength between 1697 and 1699 and led to his resignation.

With the accession of Anne in 1702 neither favourite would be able to play a role of significance, but Portland still maintained important contacts and managed

---

204 NUL, PwB 79.
205 Onnekink, 'Het Fortuyn van Henry Bentinck', *passim*.
206 Most of this information is in Schazmann, *The Bentincks*.
207 Sophia of Hanover to Portland 13 January 1703, NUL, PwA 1193, transl. from French.

to gain the confidence of both the English and the Dutch. He assured John Somers that 'I flatter myself of not being partial and to be with you with the same zeal for the public good'.[208] After 1702 Portland thus remained an active proponent of Anglo-Dutch co-operation, consistently supporting the 'war parties' in both Holland and England. His knowledge of affairs, his experience and contacts made him suitable for such a task, and his ad-hoc advisory interventions helped to smooth out mutual misunderstandings and difficulties. In 1709 the Lord Treasurer Sidney Godolphin fittingly described the Anglo-Dutch earl as 'a great friend to both sides'.[209] His untimely death at a moment when the relations between the Dutch and English were optimal prevented him from playing a more challenging role when the pro-Dutch Whig government fell and a less-well-disposed regime came to power in 1710.

---

208 Portland to Somers 22 April 1709 (Bulstrode), SHC, Somers Mss 371/14/K/23, transl. from French.

209 Godolphin to Marlborough 4 February 1709, Snyder, *Correspondence*, III. 1220.

Conclusion

Descended from a regional Orangist baron's family in Overijssel, Portland rose to found one of the foremost noble lineages in the United Provinces and England. His career ran parallel to and was sustained by the fortunes of the Prince of Orange, whose page he became in 1664. His career gained momentum with the Prince's coming to power as Stadholder in 1672, after which he emerged as favourite at Court and dealt with military correspondence. He undertook several diplomatic missions to England between 1677 and 1685. Moreover, he was part of a select decision-making core group responsible for the formulation of (mainly foreign) policy, most notably in the period from 1685 leading up to the Glorious Revolution. In 1688 he joined the Dutch forces invading England and re-emerged as William's favourite after his coronation. Between 1689 and 1697, at the zenith of his political career, Portland was intimately involved in the formulation and implementation of the domestic and foreign policies of both Britain and the United Provinces. He retired from public life in 1699, but behind the scenes he remained active, most notably in negotiating the Partition Treaties with Louis XIV. The possibility of returning to active politics was abruptly removed by William's death in 1702, but the Earl was occasionally instrumental in the maintenance of Anglo-Dutch relations during the War of the Spanish Succession.

This book has tried to correct two views prevalent among historians, who have considered Portland either as a non-entity, as for instance Stephen Baxter supposed, or an all-powerful favourite, as for example Nicolaas Japikse asserted. The exact relationship between the King-Stadholder and his favourite must to some extent remain subject to conjecture. However, although Portland clearly owed his favoured position to the good-will of William, he gradually assumed more responsibilities in various fields and developed into a useful instrument of princely and royal policy. Thus, the favourite was neither insignificant nor omnipotent. Portland's influence can only be measured if analysed in different spheres of government, and must be understood as undergoing a dynamic process that extended over more than three decades.

Portland started off his career in both Holland and England dealing with military and diplomatic affairs and gradually acquired more power and influence in other spheres, such as parliamentary management and financial affairs. After 1688, his influence in matters not related to the war effort was marginal. There is, for instance, no evidence of his involvement in ecclesiastical appointments. At no point did he manage to monopolise any aspect of royal policy. The army was a field in which the King personally took control. Portland was outranked by such men as the Duke of Schomberg, but managed to encroach upon the responsibilities of the Secretary-at-War and the Secretaries of State. Parliamentary management was left to the Marquises of Halifax and Carmarthen, until Portland gained some control over it through the Earl of Sunderland. Ostensibly Portland was influential in ministerial management, although in practice he delegated most business to his aides, William Carstares and the Earl of Sunderland. In the United Provinces, William's provincial managers did most of the work, although Portland became a conduit for the Stadholder. It seems clear that Portland did not devise policy or strategy, but acted rather as an executive to whom the King delegated substantial power and room for manoeuvre. Thus Portland was deeply involved in most aspects of government, but hardly in the capacity of a 'favourite-minister'. Occasionally he managed to initiate a course of action or persuade the King to do so, but essentially he executed and implemented royal policy and gave it force and substance, rather than giving it direction or formulating it.

Portland's gradual accumulation of responsibilities contradicts the notion – prevalent in most literature – that his influence was on the wane after 1694. Portland significantly strengthened his position amongst William's confidants after the death of Gaspar Fagel in November 1688 and after the departure of Everard van Weede van Dijkveld after the summer of 1689. By the end of 1689, after Henry Sidney's dismissal, Portland was William's undisputed favourite. Although between 1694 and 1699 Portland and Albemarle achieved something of a balance of power, Portland maintained the upper hand over his rival until the end of his career. Indeed, despite Albemarle's ascendancy Portland's career reached a zenith between 1695 and 1697. During this period his responsibilities in the army and the diplomatic services were combined with ministerial and parliamentary management. From about 1695 he was nominally in control of powerful ministries in the three kingdoms.

The book has built on the presupposition that the nature of William's king-stadholdership was essentially supranational and must be understood within an international context. A perspective which pays more attention to the interconnectedness of the various parts of his realms has led to a reinterpretation of what seem solely domestic issues. Both the States of Holland and the English parliament tried to remove Portland from their assemblies on the grounds that he was a foreigner. The xenophobic attacks against Portland in England and Holland were utilised in order to criticise the King. They were also the expression of a genuine concern on both sides of the North Sea that the personal union would prove disadvantageous. Indicative for the connection between William's realms, Dutch domestic resistance died down after the Battle of the Boyne in 1690, although anti-Orangist pamphleteers still had their work translated and shipped to England.

Such an international perspective also exposes patterns in the nature and conduct of Portland's policy. He became involved in the 1690 Magistrates Affair in the United Provinces because the Irish campaign required the help of Amsterdam. Although a conciliatory policy was not his style, he was frequently obliged to compromise because circumstances elsewhere required his attention. Hence he tried to settle the controversy quickly and reached a compromise with the Amsterdammers. Portland's lenient stance towards the Scottish and Irish rebels was the result of William's desire to end domestic resistance and focus on the continent. In 1691 he supported the Earl of Breadalbane's mission to pacify the Scottish Highlands. He also encouraged General Godard van Reede van Ginckel to offer concessions in order to bring the Irish campaign to an end and make resources available for the continental war effort. Such a supranational perspective was also manifest in, for instance, William's refusal to repeal the Navigation Act when Amsterdam made such a request in 1689. Likewise, Portland opposed the Scottish Darien scheme. In both cases, the King-Stadholder's dual position would be compromised.

In this study an attempt has been made to study Portland's role on the British Isles as well as in the United Provinces and on the continent. Recent imposing specialist studies on Williamite policy have sometimes failed to take into account its wider international concerns, implicitly adopting a national perspective by focusing on only one part of his realms, or neglecting relevant source material.[1] This has sometimes resulted in a distorted image of Portland's career and position. Firstly, historians have too easily accepted contemporary anti-favourite rhetoric. Patrick Riley did so when he depicted Portland as an ignorant and lazy foreigner uninterested and uninformed about Scottish affairs. But such criticism cannot be sustained once the international scope of Portland's activities is surveyed; the favourite had to divide his time and energy between the various parts of William's realms. Secondly, historians have too easily presented Portland as a partisan politician. Patrick Riley saw Portland as a fervent Presbyterian, and Henry Horwitz depicted him as a Whig. Neither characterisation is satisfactory, as Portland was a court politician rather than a party leader. He was frequently criticised by Whigs and Presbyterians for supporting their political opponents. He supported Breadalbane's mission and Mackay's strategy in spite of opposition from the Presbyterian ministry under his tutelage. Portland was focused on the international war, to which partisan concerns were made subject. Thirdly, the image of William being surrounded by 'Dutch favourites' is distortive. William's entourage was formed by an international aristocratic circle, which not only held material interests in various countries but served a dynasty rather than a nation. This was certainly the case for Portland, but also for men like the Prince of Waldeck and the Dukes of Schomberg and Leinster. In Portland's view, they were concerned with 'the interest of the whole of Europe'.[2]

In this book the essence of Portland's role has been captured by the term 'Anglo-Dutch favourite', the closest confidant of the King-Stadholder and by implication involved with his realms on both sides of the North Sea. The favourite was a re-emerging phenomenon, not seen since the reign of Charles I (who relied on the Duke of Buckingham, the Earl Strafford and Archbishop Laud), as his sons had mainly depended on experienced parliamentary managers (such as the Earls of Clarendon and Danby). But in several respects, the Anglo-Dutch favourite was also a new phenomenon. This book has interpreted its rise against the background of three developments during the 1690s.

The first development was the emergence of a 'standing parliament' in England. Initially Portland's influence was particularly manifest at Court only. As Groom of the Stole he was able to control access to the King, but he also had a pretext to spend undisturbed time with the King during which policy was discussed. Portland also played a role in the Privy and Cabinet Councils. Increasingly his influence extended

---

1   For example, Simms studied the correspondence between Ginckel and Portland but (understandably) ignored all letters in Dutch.
2   Portland to William 22 March 1690 (Kensington Palace), Japikse, *Correspondentie*, XXIII. 153, transl. from French.

to other spheres. As from around 1692 he became actively involved in parliamentary affairs, although he usually did so in tandem with experienced managers, most notably the Earl of Sunderland. The court party endeavoured to strengthen or maintain royal prerogative and find funds to support the continental war. Thus the court-favourite increasingly developed into a ministerial and parliamentary manager.

The second development was the war. Portland obtained high military rank and became William's personal secretary for military affairs, dealing mainly with logistics, transferring royal instructions to the army commanders and overseeing troop movements. By dispensing royal patronage, he managed the King's expanding military clientele.[3] He was instrumental in co-ordinating the efforts of the Grand Alliance by maintaining a correspondence with the Allied commanders and leaders. Portland remained a tireless advocate of an anti-French alliance and a large standing army. He also had a fairly tight grip on diplomatic appointments, and advancement without his patronage was difficult, without his permission, impossible.

The last factor was the emergence of the Anglo-Dutch union, or more accurately, the conjunction of four separate states headed by the King-Stadholder. Portland played a co-ordinating role in the government of William's realms. William's favourites were Dutchmen who were naturalised Englishmen as well. In this way the Anglo-Dutch favourite could monitor William's affairs both in England and the United Provinces. Portland also supervised the King's ministers in Scotland and, to a far lesser extent, in Ireland. He formed an intermediary between the King and 'regional managers', such as William Carstares in Scotland, Henry Sidney in Ireland and Jacob van Zuylen van Nijvelt, Everard van Weede van Dijkveld and Willem Adriaan van Nassau-Odijk in the United Provinces and as such was situated at the apex of the international clientele of the King-Stadholder.[4]

Precisely because the Anglo-Dutch favourite personified the post-revolutionary developments, to the opposition he embodied the evils of the Williamite settlement. Hence the opposition targeted precisely those areas in which the favourite had become the instrument of royal policy: the continental strategy and the strengthening of the King-Stadholder's prerogatives. A supporter of the continental war, he clashed with the Court Tories over their blue water strategy in 1692. He was seen as encouraging the King to maintain a pro-Dutch policy in spite of the drawbacks for England. He became inextricably involved in a conflict with Country MPs who initiated a vehement anti-standing-army campaign after the war. In 1701 he quarrelled with Parliament over the Treaties of Partition. He was also seen as the evil genius behind the King's vetoing of the Place and Triennial Bills, designed to strengthen Parliament and weaken the King's prerogatives. Perceived as a 'Vice-Stadholder' in the United Provinces, a 'Dutch Prince of Wales' in England and a 'Superintendent' of Scottish affairs, Portland was accused of implementing a policy that trampled on liberties and privileges. His influence in Holland had been significant at Court, but not so much in politics or the army. The fact that in Holland critical pamphlets started to appear after 1689 indicates his growing influence there as well, although criticism was not so much directed at the Stadholder's foreign policy but rather at his increasing power.

---

3   E.g. *CSPD 1693*, 255; letters from Russell to Portland, NUL, PwA 1092–5.

4   Cf. P.W.J. Riley, *King William and the Scottish Politicians* (Edinburgh, 1979), 85.

The Anglo-Dutch favourite thus became the focal point of a political discourse during the 1690s in which the features of Williamite policy were being debated. Propagandists drew inspiration from two sources. Firstly, they employed traditional anti-favourite rhetoric as a vehicle for attack on the Court. Portland was accused of a standard repertoire of vices attributed to foreigners and favourites: pamphleteers accused him of sodomy, a parliamentary commission investigating the East India Company corruption scandal aimed at exposing him as corruptible, in parliamentary debates about the Welsh and Irish grants he was accused of excessive greed. As a foreigner, Portland was accused of taking a pre-eminent position within the 'Dutch councils' upon which the King relied when devising his continental policy. Secondly, as Portland became associated with the Whig Junto by the middle of the 1690s, it became increasingly difficult to avoid being caught up in party struggle. Country and Tory MPs attacked the favourite who had become the patron of the Court Whig establishment, and almost succeeded in impeaching him in 1701.

Williamite propaganda, contrariwise, aimed at defending the policies of the King-Stadholder. It presented William as a godly prince heading a virtuous court and fighting a righteous war abroad. The war with Catholic France ran parallel to the godly revolution in England itself. Portland became involved in the representation of Williamite ideology through his activities in garden architecture which had a distinct political flavour during these years, and patronised a number of court propagandists. He presented himself as Ganymede, the closest confidant of the King, an image, however, which was also employed by propagandists criticising him.

The aspects which were inextricably connected to the Portland's responsibilities and which explain the re-emergence of the favourite in 1689, also elucidate the reasons for his retirement as these elements lost significance precisely as a result of the end of the Nine Years War. Between 1697 and 1699 several of the pillars supporting Portland's position were torn down. Firstly, Albemarle encroached upon some of his responsibilities. Secondly, within two years the Whig Junto had crumbled and was replaced by a moderate Tory coalition, led by men with whom Portland had neglected to establish a relationship. Thirdly, mounting opposition to foreigners was fanned by a pamphlet war and targeted William's favourites during the Irish Resumption debates, which mobilised a powerful anti-court opposition. Fourthly, the end of the war had also triggered the demobilisation of the standing army. Portland had wielded substantial power in the vastly expanded army by extending his patronage to officers, supervising military commanders and preparing military campaigns. This dramatically changed after 1697 when the British army was reduced. Lastly, Portland's maintenance of diplomatic links with the Allies and communication with the Allied commanders now became redundant. Moreover, the liaison with the Dutch that had been important during the war was losing significance.

It is no coincidence that Portland expressed his wish to retire precisely at the end of the war in 1697 when the Ryswick negotiations had started, and ultimately did so as the challenge to his position became most vehement from various corners in 1699. Throughout 1698 and 1699 Portland's position with the King remained secure, but his effectiveness as a favourite diminished. His crumbling influence and the mounting parliamentary uproar combined with a genuine personal desire to attend to family affairs contributed to his unequivocal decision to retire in 1699. Nevertheless he never fell from power; Ganymede did not become Phaeton. He was still involved in the Partition Treaty negotiations. Drawing on his experience, Portland after his retirement occasionally acted as liaison between the Maritime Powers to smooth over frictions during the War of the Spanish Succession.

The central question posed in the introduction was how Portland's role as a key member of William's entourage within the context of the Dual Monarchy and during the Nine Years War should be interpreted. This book has shown how these elements were inextricably connected. Throughout the 1670s and 1680s Portland was the *primus inter pares* amongst William's favourites, but not necessarily the most influential in any single aspect of government. The Prince was well served by experienced parliamentary managers, diplomats and military commanders, though Portland remained a key favourite due to his intimacy with the Prince. However, after 1689 Portland managed to assemble more power and sidelined competitors for William's favour. As most Dutch confidants left London, Portland's influence became paramount. He was involved in all the key aspects of William's reign: diplomacy, warfare, parliamentary management and intelligence, defending and sustaining the Williamite settlement both domestically and abroad. Most importantly, he played a pivotal role in maintaining links with Scotland, Ireland and the United Provinces.

His career reached its zenith during the Nine Years' War. The Anglo-Dutch favourite was an anomalous, pivotal figure during the Anglo-Dutch war against France; he oversaw William's various realms and became involved in political processes on the British Isles. His influence declined after the end of the war. Portland's career can therefore be divided into three phases. Until 1688 he was William's adviser and confidant in the United Provinces. From 1689 he acted as the Anglo-Dutch favourite until he retired in 1699. Thereafter he was only occasionally involved in politics until his death in 1709.

It was precisely for this reason that the Earl of Albemarle's wings were clipped when he succeeded him during the interwar years as a favourite, and that the renewal of hostilities in 1702 saw the re-emergence of a favourite very much in the Portland mould. The Duke and Duchess of Marlborough and Sidney Godolphin, like Portland and Sunderland, again secured royal support for the growth of the standing army, parliamentary management, the continental war, the expanding diplomatic service and the maintenance of the Anglo-Dutch coalition. The similarity of the roles of Marlborough and Portland, both favourites involved in maintaining an alliance between the British Isles and the United Provinces during large-scale warfare, calls for a re-interpretation of the former's role as well. Portland was instrumental in mobilising resources in the three kingdoms and the republic to enable William to conduct the war. Understandably, then, his position quickly weakened at the end of the war as his role became redundant. Hence it can be concluded that Portland's role as Anglo-Dutch favourite of the King-Stadholder was epitomised by the waging of the war on the continent and the maintenance of the Anglo-Dutch alliance.

Bibliography

PRIMARY SOURCES: MANUSCRIPTS

England

Bodleian Library, Oxford

Carte Manuscripts
233

Norfolk Manuscripts
C2

Rawlinson Manuscripts
A241, A245, A326, D923, D924, D1079

British Library, London

Additional Manuscripts
4236, 4761, 15866, 15892, 15902, 17677, 18606, 20806, 21505, 24205, 28875, 28942, 29547, 29592, 30000, 32681, 32905, 33970, 34514, 34515, 34773, 35107, 36913, 37513, 38146, 38494–6, 38700, 38848, 40390, 40771–7, 41806–23, 46525, 46528, 46541, 47979b, 57861, 61118, 61153, 61159, 61419, 61471, 63629–30, 69955, 70022, 70945

Egerton Charters
103–5, 8305

Egerton Manuscripts
1704–09, 1717, 1754B, 2618, 2621, 2717, 3324

Harley Manuscripts
3516

Sloane Manuscripts
3962

Stowe Manuscripts
222–3, 226

Buckinghamshire County Archive,

D/RA1/60

House of Lords Record Office, London

Willcocks Collection, Hist. collection VI
Garter Rolls 29, 31

Lambeth Palace Library, London

Gibson Papers
Ms. 932.71–4

National Archive, London

Depositions
E133/100/21, E133/153/5, E133/153/6

State Papers
8/1–18, 80/17, 81/86–7, 84/188–233, 105/48–61, 105/82–9, 108/332

Nottingham University Library

Portland Manuscripts
PwA 1–2870, Pw2A 1–29, Pw2Hy 426, PwB 1–178, PwV49–68, PwV106

Surrey History Centre, Woking

Somers Manuscripts
371/14/E/11, 371/14/E/13, 371/14/J/23, 371/14/K/1–26

Scotland

National Archives of Scotland, Edinburgh

SP3, GD26, GD112, GD406

National Library of Scotland, Edinburgh

Manuscripts
1320, 3072, 3471, 7014, 7018–20, 7027–30, 14404, 14407–8

The Netherlands

Gemeentearchief, Amsterdam

5027/7, 5029/50, 5029/89

Nationaal Archief, The Hague

Gezantschapsarchief 1.02
01/83, 01/176, 04/7

Archief Gaspar Fagel 1.10.29
559

Archief Anthonie Heinsius 3.01.19
95, 402, 452, 517, 562, 611, 297, 623, 2189

Rijksarchief Utrecht, Utrecht

Huisarchief Amerongen, 1001
3128, 3134, 3183

France

Archives du Ministère des Affaires Etrangères, Paris

Cahiers Politiques Angleterre
123–4, 149–50, 166–7, 170–73, 180–86, 189–91, 203–4

Cahiers Politiques Hollande
141–56, 172–3

PRIMARY SOURCES: PRINTED

Correspondence

Het Archief van den Raadpensionaris Antonie Heinsius, ed. H.J. van der Heim (3 vols, The Hague, 1867).
Archives ou Correspondance Inédite de la Maison d'Orange-Nassau, ed. F.J.L. Krämer (3rd series, 3 vols, Leiden, 1907–09).
De Briefwisseling van Anthonie Heinsius 1702–1720, ed. A.J. Veenendaal (20 vols, The Hague, 1976–2001).
Calendar of State Papers, Domestic Series, in the Reign of William and Mary, ed. W.J. Hardy and E. Bateson (11 vols, London, 1913–69).

A Catalogue of Letters and other Historical Documents Exhibited in the Library at Welbeck, ed. S.A. Strong (London, 1903).
The Correspondence of H.H. Earl of Clarendon and of his Brother, Laurence Hyde, Earl of Rochester; with the Diary of Lord Clarendon from 1687 to 1690 ... and the Diary of Lord Rochester during his Embassy to Poland in 1676, ed. S.W. Singer (2 vols, London, 1828).
The Correspondence of John Churchill, First Duke of Marlborough, and Anthonie Heinsius, Grand Pensionary of Holland 1701–1711, ed. B. van 't Hoff (Utrecht, 1951).
Correspondence of the Family of Hatton, being chiefly Letters Addressed to Christopher, First Viscount Hatton. A.D. 1601–1704, ed. E.M. Thompson (2 vols, London 1878).
Correspondencia entre Dos Embajadores, Don Pedro Ronquillo y el Marques de Cogolludo 1689–1691, ed. Duque de Maura (2 vols, Madrid, 1951).
Correspondentie van Willem III en van Hans Willem Bentinck, Eersten Graaf van Portland, ed. N. Japikse (5 vols, Rijksgeschiedkundige Publicatiën 'Kleine Reeks', XXIII, XXIV, XXVI, XXVII, XXVIII, The Hague, 1927–37).
The Dispatches of Th. Plott (1681–1682) and Th. Chudleigh (1682–1685): English Envoys at The Hague, ed. F.A. Middlebush (Rijksgeschiedkundige Publicatiën 'Kleine Reeks', XXII, The Hague, 1926).
Letters Illustrative of the Reign of William III etc., ed. G.P.R. James (3 vols, London, 1841).
The Letters of Madame: the Correspondence of Elizabeth-Charlotte of Bavaria, Princess Palatine, Duchess of Orleans ... 1661–1708, ed. G.S. Stevenson (2 vols, London, 1924).
Letters of William III, and Louis XIV and of their Ministers etc. 1697–1700, ed. P. Grimblot (2 vols, London, 1848).
Leven and Melville Papers. Letters and State Papers chiefly Addressed to George Earl of Melville, Secretary of State for Scotland, 1689–1691, ed. W.L. Melville (Edinburgh, 1843).
The Marlborough–Godolphin Correspondence, ed. H.L. Snyder (3 vols, Oxford, 1975).
Private and Original Correspondence of Charles Talbot, Duke of Shrewsbury etc., ed. W. Coxe (London, 1821).
State Papers and Letters Addressed to William Carstares, ed. J. McCormick (Edinburgh, 1774).
Weensche Gezantschapsberichten van 1670–1720, ed. G. von Antal and J.C.H. de Pater (2 vols, The Hague, 1929–34).

Reports of the Historical Manuscripts Commission

Fourth Report (London, 1874).
Sixth Report (s.l., 1877).
Seventh Report (s.l., 1879).
Appendix to the Eighth Report, II (s.l. 1881).

Manuscripts of the House of Lords 1689–1702 (7 vols, London, 1887–1908).
Manuscripts of His Grace the Duke of Portland Preserved at Welbeck Abbey (10 vols, London, 1891–1931).
Manuscripts of Sir William Fitzherbert etc. (London, 1893).
Manuscripts of Lord Kenyon (London, 1894).
Manuscripts of the Duke of Roxburghe etc. (London, 1894).
Manuscripts of J.J. Hope Johnstone Esq. of Annandale (London, 1897).
Manuscripts of F.W. Leyborne-Popham Esq. (London, 1899).
Manuscripts of the Duke of Buccleugh and Queensberry (2 vols, London, 1903).
Manuscripts in Various Collections (8 vols, London, 1901–14).
Manuscripts of the Earl of Ancaster etc. (Dublin, 1907).
Manuscripts of the Marquis of Bath etc. (3 vols, Hereford, 1908).
Manuscripts of the late Allan George Finch, Esq., Of Burley-on-the-Hill Rutland (5 vols, London, 1913–2004).
Manuscripts of the Marquess of Downshire preserved at Easthampstead Park Berkshire, Papers of Sir William Trumbull (2 vols, London, 1924).
Manuscripts of the late Reginald Rawdon Hastings etc. (London, 1930).
Manuscripts of the ... Manor House, Ashby-de-la-Zouche (4 vols, London, 1930).
Supplementary Report on the Manuscripts of His Grace the Duke of Hamilton (London, 1932).
Manuscripts of the Rt. Hon. Viscount de L'Isle etc. (London, 1966).

Journals, Diaries and Miscellaneous Works

Acta der Particuliere Synoden van Zuid-Holland 1621–1700, ed. W.P.C. Knuttel (6 vols, The Hague, 1908–16).
The Acts of the Parliament of Scotland. A.D. M.C.XXIV–M.DCC.VII, ed. C. Innes and T. Thomson (12 vols, London, 1814–75).
Adamson, J., *The Reigns of King Edward II. And so far of King Edward III. As relates to the Lives and Actions of Piers Gaveston, Hugh de Spencer, and Roger, Lord Mortimer, etc.* (London, 1732).
Avelen, J. van den, *Sorgvliet* (Amsterdam, 1700?).
'B., Monsieur de', 'Mêmoires ... ou Anecdotes, tant de la Cour du Prince d'Orange Guillaume III, que des Principaux Seigneurs de la République de ce Temps', ed. F.J.L. Krämer, *Bijdragen en Mededelingen betreffende de Geschiedenis der Nederlanden*, 19 (1898), 62–124.
Banks, J., *The Unhappy Favourite: or, the Earl of Essex etc.* (London, 1682).
Bidloo, G., *Relation du Voyage de Sa Majesté Brittanique en Hollande etc.* (The Hague, 1692).
Bidloo, G., *Verhaal der Laaste Ziekte en het Overlijden van Willem de IIIde etc.* (Leiden, 1702).
Biographia Brittanica, or, the Lives of the Most Eminent Persons Who have Flourished in Great Britain and Ireland etc. (6 vols, London, 1747).
Boyer, A., *The History of King William the Third* (3 vols, London, 1702–03).
———, *The History of the Life & Reign of Queen Anne* (London, 1722).

Burnet, G., *History of his Own Time* (6 vols, London, 1725).
Calendar of Treasury Books 1689–1702, ed. William A. Shaw (7 vols, London, 1931–34).
Catalogue of the Pictures belonging to His Grace the Duke of Portland, at Welbeck Abbey, and in London, ed. C.F. Murray (London, 1894).
Catalogue of the Pictures belonging to His Grace the Duke of Portland, KG, at Welbeck etc., ed. R.W. Goulding (Cambridge, 1936).
Catalogue of Political and Personal Satires, ed. F.G. Stephens, M.D. George, and G.W. Reid (11 vols, London, 1870–1954).
The Character of an Ill-Court-Favourite: Representing the Mischiefs that flow from Ministers of State when they are more Great than Good, etc. (London, 1681).
Cobbets Parliamentary History of England etc. 1688–1702 (12 vols, London, 1806–12).
[Crouch, N.], *The Unfortunate Court-Favourites of England, Exemplified in some Remarks upon the Lives, Actions, and fatal Fall of divers Great Men, who have been Favourites to several English Kings and Queens etc.* (London, 1695).
Crowne, J., *The Ambitious Statesman, or, The loyal Favourite etc.* (London, 1679).
Dalrymple, J., (ed.), *Memoirs of Great Britain and Ireland etc.* (2 vols, London, 1790).
Davenant, C., 'An Essay upon the Balance of Power' in: *The Political and Commercial Works of ... Charles D'avenant*, ed. C. Whitworth (5 vols, London, 1771), III.
Diary of the Times of Charles the Second, by the Honourable Henry Sidney, afterwards Earl of Romney, ed. R.W. Blencowe (2 vols, London, 1843).
Droste, C., *Overblijfsels van Geheugchenis etc.* (The Hague, 1728).
English Historical Documents 1660–1714, VIII, ed. A. Browning (London, 1953).
Esdaile, K.A., Ilchester, Earl of, and Hake, H.M. (eds), *Vertue Note Books* (6 vols, Oxford, 1930–55).
Fox, C.J., *History of the Early Part of the Reign of James the Second etc.* (London, 1808).
'Gedenkschriften van Adriaan van Borssele van der Hooghe, Heer van Geldermalsen', ed. K. Heeringa, in: *Archief. Vroegere en latere Mededeelingen voornamelijk in Betrekking tot Zeeland* (Middelburg, 1916), 67–136.
Grey, A., *Debates of the House of Commons from the Year 1667 to the Year 1694* (10 vols, London, 1769).
Halifax, G.S., First Marquis of, 'The Spencer House Journals' in: *The Life and Letters of Sir George Savile, First Marquis of Halifax*, ed. H.C. Foxcroft (2 vols, London, 1898), II. 200–52.
The History of Prime Ministers and Favourites, in England; from the Conquest down to the Present Time: with Reflections on the Fatal Consequences of their Misconduct, etc. (London, 1763).
Hollandsche Mercurius, behelsende het Gedenckweerdigste in Christenrijck voorgevallen, binnen 't gansche Jaar 1664 (Haarlem, 1665).
Hollandsche Mercurius, behelsende het Gedenckweerdigste in Christenrijck voorgevallen, binnen 't gansche Jaar 1690 (Haarlem, 1691).

Hora Siccama, J.H., 'Mevrouw van Zoutelande en hare Gedenkschriften', *Bijdragen voor Vaderlandsche Geschiedenis en Oudheidkunde*, 4 (4th series, The Hague, 1903), 123–221.
House of Commons Journals.
House of Lords Journals.
Howard, R., *The Great Favourite, or, the Duke of Lerma. A Tragedy* (edn London, 1692).
Hyde, E., Earl of Clarendon, *The Characters of Robert Earl of Essex, Favourite to Queen Elizabeth and George D. of Buckingham, Favourite to K. James I and K. Ch. I with a Comparison* (London, 1706).
Journaal van Constantijn Huygens Gedurende de Veldtochten der Jaren 1673,1675, 1676, 1677 en 1678 (Utrecht, 1881).
Journaal van Constantijn Huygens van 21 Oct. 1688 tot 2 Sept. 1696 (2 vols, Utrecht, 1876).
Journal of the Extraordinary Embassy of His Excellence the Earl of Portland in France, ed. G.D.J. Schotel (The Hague, 1851).
Journalen van Constantijn Huygens, den Zoon (Utrecht, 1888).
Letters of Denization and Acts of Naturalisation for Aliens in England and Ireland, 1603–1700, ed. W.A. Shaw (Lymington, 1911).
Luttrell, N., *A Brief Historical Relation of State Affairs from September 1678 to April 1714* (Oxford, 1857).
Mackay, H., *Memoirs of the War Carried on in Scotland and Ireland 1689–1691* (Edinburgh, 1833).
Macky, J., 'Characters of the Court of Great Britain' in: *Memoirs of the Life of Sir John Clerk ... 1675–1755*, ed. J. M. Gray (London, 1895).
Manley, M. Delariviere., *Secret Memoirs and Manners of Several Persons of Quality of both Sexes from the New Atlantis, an Island in the Mediterranean* (London, 1709).
Mémoires d'Isaac Dumont de Bostaquet ... sur les Temps qui ont Précédé et Suivi la Révocation de l'Édit de Nantes (Paris, 1968).
Mémoires de Saint-Simon, ed. A. de Boislisle (21 vols, Paris, 1879–1930).
Memoirs of Sir John Reresby. The Complete Text and a Selection from his Letters, ed. W.H. Speck (London, 1991).
Memoirs of Thomas, Earl of Ailesbury, etc., ed. W.E. Buckley (2 vols, Westminster, 1890).
Négociations de Monsieur le Comte d'Avaux en Hollande depuis 1679 jusqu'en 1688 (6 vols, Paris, 1752–3).
Négociations de M. le Comte d'Avaux en Irlande, 1689–90 (Dublin, 1934).
Observations and Remarks upon the Lives and Reigns of King Henry VIII. King Edward VI, Queen Mary I, Queen Elizabeth and King James. With Particular Characters, after the Earl of Clarendon's Method, of all their Favourites etc. (edn London, 1712).
Oldmixon, J., *The History of England etc.* (London, 1735).
The Parliamentary Diary of Sir Richard Cocks, 1698–1702, ed. D.W. Hayton (Oxford, 1996).

The Perfect Picture of a Favourite:, or, Secret Memoirs of Robert Dudley, Earl of Leicester (edn London, 1708).
Poems of Affairs of State. Augustan Satirical Verse 1660–1714, V: 1688–1697, ed. W.J. Cameron (New Haven/London, 1971).
Poems of Affairs of State. Augustan Satirical Verse 1660–1714, VI: 1697–1704, ed. F.H. Ellis (New Haven/London, 1970).
The Political and Commercial Works of ... Charles D'avenant, ed. C. Whitworth (5 vols, London, 1771).
Political Ballads of the Seventeenth and Eighteenth Centuries, ed. W. Walker Wilkins (2 vols, London, 1860).
Political Tracts (s.l., 1688).
Prior, M., *Miscellaneous Works* (2 vols, London, 1740).
The Prose Works of Jonathan Swift, ed. T. Scott (12 vols, London, 1897–1908).
Pryme, A., *Diary of my Own Life etc.* (Durham, 1869).
Rapin de Thoyras, P., *The History of England etc.* (5 vols, London, 1789).
Refuge, E. de, *Arcana Aulica: or, Walshingam's Manual of Prudential Maxims, for the States-man and Courtier. To which is added Fragmenta Regalia: or, Observations on Queen Elizabeth, her Times and Favourites. By Sir Robert Naunton* (edn London, 1694).
The Register of the Privy Council of Scotland, XV, ed., E.W.M. Balfour-Melville (3rd series, Edinburgh, 1967).
Secreete Resolutien van de Ed. Groot Mog. Heeren Staaten van Hollandt. Beginnende met den Jaare 1679 en Eyndigende met den Jaare 1696 inclus (17 vols, The Hague, 1653–1795).
Seker ende Omstandigh Verhael van het Gepasseerde, sedert het Overgaen van Syne Hoogheydt naar Engeland etc. (The Hague, 1688).
Smith, A., *Court Intrigues: or, An Account of the Secret Amours of our British Nobility* (London, 1730).
A Supplement to Burnets History of my Own Time etc., ed. H.C. Foxcroft (Oxford, 1902).
Temple, W., 'Memoirs 1672–1679' in: *The Works of Sir William Temple etc.* (4 vols, Edinburgh, 1754). I.
Vassor, M. le, *Histoire du Regne de Louis XIII etc.* (10 vols., Amsterdam, 1700).
Verbaal van de Buitengewone Ambassade van Jacob van Wassenaar-Duivenvoorde, Arnout van Citters en Everard van Weede van Dijkveld naar Engeland in 1685 (Utrecht, 1863).
Wagenaar, J., *Vaderlandsche Historie, vervattende de Geschiedenissen der nu Vereenigde Nederlanden, Inzonderheid die van Holland, van de Vroegste Tyden af* (21 vols, Amsterdam, 1752).
Whittle, J., *An Exact Diary of the late Expedition of his Illustrious Highness the Prince of Orange into England etc.* (London, 1689).
Witsen, N., 'Verbaal' in: *Geschied- en Letterkundig Mengelwerk*, ed. J. Scheltema (6 vols, Utrecht, 1818–36). III.

Pamphlets

An Account of the Passages in the Assembly of the States of Holland and West-Friezeland concerning the Earl of Portlands Exclusion from, or Admission into that Assembly (London, 1690).
'Advice to a Painter' (1697), in: *Poems of Affairs of State. Augustan Satirical Verse 1660–1714*, VI: *1697–1704*, ed. Frank H. Ellis (New Haven/London, 1970), 12–25.
De Balliuw van Rotterdam in zijn Hemt (s.l., s.d.)
A Choice Collection of Papers relating to State Affairs during the late Revolution (London, 1703).
Defoe, D., *The True-born Englishman. A Satyr* (London, 1701).
——, *Legion's Memorial* (1701), in: *Political and Economic Writings of Daniel Defoe, II: Party Politics*, ed. J. A. Downie (London, 2000), 39–46.
A Dialogue between K.W. and Benting, Occasioned by his Going into Flanders after the Death of the Queen (London, 1695).
To the Earl of Portland on his Embassy to France in: *Poems on Affairs of State, from 1640 to this present Year 1704* (4 vols, 1703–07), III.
The Exorbitant Grants of William the III Examin'd and Questioned Shewing the Nature of Grants in Successive and Elective Monarchies, etc. (London, 1703), in: *A Collection of Scarce and Valuable Tracts etc.*, ed. J. Somers (4 vols, London, 1748), III.
The False Favourite's Downfall (1692), in: *Poems of Affairs of State. Augustan Satirical Verse 1660–1714, V: 1688–1697*, ed. W. J. Cameron (New Haven/London, 1971), 328–33.
Ferguson, R., *A Brief Account of some of the late Incroachments and Depredations of the Dutch upon the English etc.* (London?, 1695).
The French Favourites: or, the Seventh Discourse of Balzac's Politicks (London, 1709), in: *A Collection of Scarce and Valuable Tracts etc.*, ed. J. Somers (4 vols., London 1748), II.
De Gelukkige Aanstaande Gevolgen uit de Unie en Verbintenis tusschen Haar Majesteiten Willem III. en Maria II. ... en de Ho. Mo. Heeren Staten Generaal der Vereenigde Nederlanden (The Hague, 1689).
Gloria Cambriæ: Or, The Speech of a Bold Britain in Parliament, against a Dutch Prince of Wales, Mr Price (London, 1702), in: *A Collection of Scarce and Valuable Tracts etc.*, ed. J. Somers (4 vols, London, 1748), III.
Groot-Hans met de Privilegie-soeker (s.l., 1690).
His Majesty's most Gracious Speech to both Houses of Parliament etc. (1692).
De Hollandse Hollende Koe (s.l., 1690).
[Johnston, N.], *The Dear Bargain, or, A True Representation of the State of the English Nation under the Dutch. In a Letter to a Friend*, in: *A Third Collection of Scarce and Valuable tracts etc.*, ed. J. Somers (4 vols, London, 1751), III.
A Letter to a Member of the Committee of Grievances containing some Seasonable Reflections on the Present Administration of Affairs, since Managed by Dutch Councils, in: *A Second Collection of Scarce and Valuable Tracts etc.*, ed. J. Somers (4 vols, London, 1750), IV.

Letters to a Nobleman From a Gentleman Travelling thro' Holland, Flanders and France etc. (London, 1709).

Min Heer T. van C's Answer to Min Heer H. van L's Letter of the 15th of March 1689, Representing the True Interest of Holland, and what They have already Gained by our Losses, in: *A Third Collection of Scarce and Valuable Tracts etc.*, J. Somers (4 vols, London, 1751), IV.

A Modest Apology for the loyal Protestant Subjects of King James, in: *A Collection of Scarce and Valuable Tracts*, ed. W. Scott, (London, 1813), X.

The Names of the Lord of his Majesty's most Honourable Privy Council, in: *A Collection of Scarce and Valuable Tracts etc.*, ed. J. Somers (4 vols, London, 1748), II.

The Natives (London, 1700).

Oldmixon, J., *A Poem ... addressed to the ... Earl of Portland ... on his ... Return from his Embassy in France* (London, 1698).

The Marriage, Baptismal, and Burial Registers of the Collegiate Church or Abbey of St. Peter, Westminster, ed. J.L. Chester (London, 1876).

Pittis, W., *The True-born Englishman: a Satyr, Answer'd Paragraph by Paragraph* (London, 1701).

The Reverse: or, the Tables Turn'd (London, 1700).

Speach for Repealing Grants in Wales for Bentinck (1696), in: *A Choice Collection of Papers relating to State Affairs during the late Revolution* (London, 1703).

The Spirit of Jacobitism; or, Remarks upon a Dialogue between KW and Benting, in a Dialogue between Two Friends of the present Government (London, 1695).

A True and Impartial Narrative of the Dissenters' new Plot etc., in: *A Collection of Scarce and Valuable Tracts etc.*, ed. Walter Scott (London, 1813), IX.

Tutchin, J., *The Foreigners* (London, 1700).

Two Letters to a Friend, Concerning the Partition Treaty, Vindicating His Majesty, King William, From all Reflections; And Answering the Arguments of a late Designing Party, that were for Surrendring to the French King the Whole Spanish Monarchy (London, 1702).

A Very Remarkable Letter from King William III. To his Favourite Bentinck, Earl of Portland, in French and English, together with Reflections thereon, in: *A Collection of Scarce and Valuable Tracts etc.*, ed. J. Somers (4 vols, London, 1748), I.

Waarmont, L. van, *Missive van een Oprecht Patriot, Aen een Lidt van de Regeeringe, over de Geschillen wegens de Gepretendeerde Sessie van W. Benting, Grave van Portlandt* (s.l., 1690).

Walten, E., *Brief aan Sijn Excellentie, de Heer Graaf van Portland, etc.* (The Hague, 1692).

Whether the Preserving of the Protestant Religion was the Motive unto, or the End that was Designed in the late Revolution (1695), in: *A Third Collection of Scarce and Valuable Tracts etc.*, ed. J. Somers (4 vols, London, 1751), III.

LITERATURE

Aa, A.J. van der, *Biographisch Woordenboek der Nederlanden* (12 vols, Haarlem, 1852–78).
Aalbers, J., *De Republiek en de Vrede van Europa. De Buitenlandse Politiek van de Republiek der Verenigde Nederlanden na de Vrede van Utrecht (1713), voornamelijk gedurende de Jaren 1720–1733. I: Achtergronden en algemene Aspecten* (Groningen, 1980).
——, 'Holland's Financial Problems (1713–1733) and the Wars against Louis XIV' in: A.C. Duke and C.A. Tamse (eds), *Britain and the Netherlands VI: War and Society* (The Hague, 1977), 79–93.
——, 'Factieuze Tegenstellingen binnen het College van de Ridderschap van Holland na de Vrede van Utrecht', *Bijdragen en Mededelingen betreffende de Geschiedenis der Nederlanden*, 93 (1978), 412–45.
Agnew, D.C.A., *Protestant Exiles from France etc.* (2 vols, Edinburgh, 1886).
Alphen, G. van, *De Stemming van de Engelschen tegen de Hollanders in Engeland tijdens de Regeering van den Koning-Stadhouder Willem III 1688–1702* (Assen, 1938).
Ashley, M., *The Glorious Revolution of 1688* (London, 1966).
Bachrach, A.G.H., Sigmund, J.P. and Veenendaal, A.J. (eds), *Willem III, de Stadhouder-Koning en zijn Tijd* (Amsterdam, 1988).
Barclay, A., 'The Impact of King James II on the Departments of the Royal Household' (unpublished PhD thesis, Cambridge University, 1993).
——, 'William's Court as King' in: E. Mijers and D. Onnekink (eds), *Redefining William III. The Impact of the King-Stadholder in International Context* (Aldershot, 2007), 249–70.
Baxter, S.B., 'Recent Writings on William III', *Journal of Modern History*, 38 (1966), 256–67.
——, *William III* (London, 1966).
——, 'William III as Hercules: the Political Implications of Court Culture' in: L.G. Schwoerer (ed.), *The Revolution of 1688–1689, Changing Perspectives* (Cambridge, 1992), 95–106.
Beattie, J.M., *The English Court in the Reign of George I* (Cambridge, 1967).
Becket, J.V., *The Aristocracy in England 1660–1914* (Oxford, 1986).
Beddard, R. (ed.), *The Revolutions of 1688* (Oxford, 1991).
——, *A Kingdom without a King. The Journal of the Provisional Government in the Revolution of 1688* (Oxford, 1988).
Benze, J.F., *Anglo-Dutch Relations from the earliest Times to the Death of William the Third* (The Hague, 1925).
Berg, J. van den, 'Dutch Calvinism and the Church of England in the Period of the Glorious Revolution' in: S. Groenveld and M. Wintle (eds), *The Exchange of Ideas. Religion, Scholarship and Art in Anglo-Dutch Relations in the Seventeenth Century* (Zutphen, 1994), 84–99.
Bevan, B., *King William III, Prince of Orange, the First European* (London, 1997).

Bijl, M. van der, 'Willem III, Stadhouder-Koning, pro Religione et Libertate' in: W.F. de Gaay Fortman (ed.), *Achter den Tijd. Opstellen aangeboden aan dr. G. Puchinger* (Haarlem, 1986), 155–82.

Bots, J.A.H. and Posthumus Meyjes, G.H.M. (eds), *La Révocation de l'Édit de Nantes et les Provinces-Unies* (Amsterdam, 1986).

Boyden, J.M., 'Fortune has Stripped you of your Splendour; Favourites and their Fates in Fifteenth and Sixteenth Century Spain' in: L.W.B. Brockliss and J.H. Elliott (eds,), *The World of the Favourite* (New Haven/London, 1999), 26–37.

Brayley, E.W., *A Topographical History of Surrey* (5 vols, London, 1841–8).

Brewer, J., *The Sinews of Power. War, Money and the English State 1688–1783* (Cambridge MA, 1990).

Brockliss, L.W.B., and Elliott, J.H. (eds), *The World of the Favourite* (New Haven/London, 1999).

Broeyer, F.G.M. et al. (eds), *Een Richtingenstrijd in de Gereformeerde Kerk: Voetianen en Coccejanen 1650–1750* (Zoetermeer, 1994).

Brokken, H.M. and Koolen, A.W.M. (eds), *Inventaris van het Archief van de Ridderschap en Edelen van Holland en West-Friesland 1572–1795* (The Hague, 1992).

Browning, A.B., *Thomas Osborne, Earl of Danby and Duke of Leeds 1632–1712* (3 vols, Glasgow, 1951).

Bruin, G. de, *Geheimhouding en Verraad. De Geheimhouding van Staatszaken ten tijde van de Republiek (1600–1750)* (The Hague, 1991).

Bruijn, J.R., *Varend Verleden: de Nederlandse Oorlogsvloot in de Zeventiende en Achttiende Eeuw* (Amsterdam, 1998).

Bucholz, R.O., *The Augustan Court. Queen Anne and the Decline of Court Culture* (Stanford, 1993).

———, 'Going to Court in 1700: a Visitor's Guide', *The Court Historian*, 5/3 (2000), 181–221.

Carswell, J., *The Descent on England* (London, 1973).

Carter, J., 'Cabinet Records for the Reign of William III', *English Historical Review*, 88 (1963), 95–114.

Chapman, H.W., *Mary II, Queen of England* (London, 1953).

Childs, J., *The British Army of William III 1689–1702* (Manchester, 1987).

———, *The Nine Years War and the British Army 1688–1697: The Operations in the Low Countries* (Manchester, 1991).

Clark, G.N., *The Dutch Alliance and the War against French Trade 1688–1697* (New York, 1923).

———, 'The Dutch Missions to England in 1689', *English Historical Review*, 35 (1920), 529–57.

———, 'The Nine Years War 1688–1697' in: J. Bromley (ed.), *The New Cambridge Modern History VI* (Cambridge, 1970), 223–53.

Claydon, A.M, *William III and the Godly Revolution* (Cambridge, 1996).

———, *William III* (London, 2002).

Collin's Peerage of England ... Greatly Augmented, and Continued to the Present Time, ed. E. Brydges (9 vols, London, 1812).

Colvin, H.M. (ed.), *The History of the King's Works 1660–1782* (London, 1976).
Coombs, D., *The Conduct of the Dutch. British Opinion and the Dutch Alliance during the War of the Spanish Succession* (The Hague, 1958).
Corp, E. and Cruickshanks, E. (eds), *The Stuart Court in Exile and the Jacobites* (London/Rio Grande, 1995).
Corp, E. (ed.), *A Court in Exile. The Stuarts in France 1689–1718* (Cambridge, 2004).
Coward, B., *The Stuart Age* (London/New York, 1980).
Cruickshanks, E., Hayton D. and Jones C., 'Divisions in the House of Lords on the Transfer of the Crown and other Issues, 1689–1694, Ten new Lists' in: C. Jones and D.L. Jones (eds), *Peers, Politics and Power: The House of Lords, 1603–1911* (London, 1986).
Cruickshanks, E., Handley, S. and Hayton, D.W. (eds), *The History of Parliament. The House of Common 1690–1715* (5 vols, Cambridge, 2002).
Cruickshanks E. (ed.), *By Force or by Default: The Revolution of 1688/9* (Edinburgh, 1989).
———, *The Glorious Revolution* (Basingstoke, 2000).
Cuddy, N., 'The Revival of the Entourage: the Bedchamber of James I, 1603–1625' in: D. Starkey et al., *The English Court: from the Wars of the Roses to the Civil War* (London/New York, 1987), 173–225.
Deursen, A.Th. van, 'Wilhelm III von Oranien. Der Generalstatthalter der Niederlande (1672–1688)' in: H. Duchhardt (ed.), *Der Herrscher in der Doppelpflicht. Europäische Fürsten und Ihre beiden Throne* (Mainz, 1997), 141–64.
———, *Maurits van Nassau, 1567–1625: de Winnaar die Faalde* (Amsterdam, 2000).
Duindam, J., *Myths of Power. Norbert Elias and the Early Modern European Court* (Amsterdam, 1995).
Edwards, E., 'An Unknown Statesman: Gaspar Fagel in the Service of William III and the Dutch Republic', *History*, 87 (2002), 353–71.
Ehrman, J., *The Navy in the War of William III 1689–1697. Its State and Direction* (Cambridge, 1953).
Emerson, W.R., *Monmouth's Rebellion* (New Haven/London, 1951).
Feiling, K., *A History of the Tory Party 1640–1714* (Oxford, 1924).
Ferguson, W., *Scotland's Relations with England: a Survey to 1707* (Edinburgh, 1977).
Fouw, A. de, *Onbekende Raadpensionarissen* (The Hague, 1946).
Foxcroft, H.C. (ed.), *The Life and Letters of Sir George Savile, First Marquis of Halifax* (2 vols, London, 1898).
Francis, A.D., *The Methuens and Portugal, 1691–1708* (Cambridge, 1966).
Franken, M.A.M., *Coenraad van Beuningen's Politieke en Diplomatieke Activiteiten in de Jaren 1667–1684* (Groningen, 1966).
———, 'The General Tendencies and Structural Aspects of Foreign Policy and Diplomacy of the Dutch Republic in the latter Half of the Seventeenth Century', *Acta Historiae Neerlandica*, 3 (1968), 1–42.
Frey, L. and Frey, M. (eds), *The Treaties of the War of the Spanish Succession – An Historical and Critical Dictionary* (London, 1995).

Gabriëls, A.J.C.M., *De Heren als Dienaren en de Dienaar als Heer : het Stadhouderlijk Stelsel in de Tweede Helft van de Achttiende Eeuw* (The Hague, 1990).
Gardner, G., *The Scottish Exile Community in the Netherlands, 1660–1690* (East Linton, 2004).
Garrett, J., *The Triumphs of Providence: the Assassination Plot, 1696* (Cambridge, 1980).
Gebhard, J.F., *Het Leven van Mr. Nicolaas Cornelisz. Witsen (1641–1717)* (2 vols, Utrecht, 1882).
Geikie, R. and Montgomery, I.A., *The Dutch Barrier 1705–1719* (Cambridge, 1930).
Genderen, J. van, *Herman Witsius* (The Hague, 1953).
Gevers, A.J., and Mensema, A.J, *De Havezaten in Twente en hun Bewoners* (Zwolle, 1995).
Geyl, P., *Orange and Stuart 1641–1672* (London, 1969).
Gibbs, G.C., 'The Revolution in Foreign Policy' in: G. Holmes (ed.), *Britain after the Glorious Revolution 1689–1714* (London, 1969), 59–79.
Glozier, M., *The Huguenot Soldiers of William of Orange and the Glorious Revolution of 1688. The Lions of Judah.* (Brighton, 2002).
———, *Marshal Schomberg (1615–1690) – "The Ablest Soldier of His Age" International Soldiering and the Formation of State Armies in Seventeenth-Century Europe* (Brighton, 2005).
McGrath, C.I., 'English Ministers, Irish Politicians and the Making of a Parliamentary Settlement in Ireland, 1692–95', *English Historical Review*, 119 (2004), 585–613.
Gregg, E., 'France, Rome and the Exiled Stuarts, 1689–1713' in: E. Corp (ed.), *A Court in Exile. The Stuarts in France 1689–1718* (Cambridge, 2004), 11–75.
Grell, O.P., Tyacke, N., and Israel, J.I. (eds), *From Persecution to Toleration, the Glorious Revolution and Religion in England* (Oxford, 1991).
Grew, M.E., *William Bentinck and William III (Prince of Orange). The Life of Bentinck, Earl of Portland, from the Welbeck Correspondence* (London, 1924).
Grew, E., and Sharpe, M., *The Court of William III* (London, 1910).
Groenveld, S., *Evidente Factien in den Staet. Sociaal-Politieke Verhoudingen in de 17e eeuwse Republiek der Verenigde Nederlanden* (Hilversum, 1990).
———, ' "J'equippe une Flotte très Considerable": the Dutch Side of the Glorious revolution' in: R. Beddard (ed.), *The Revolutions of 1688* (Oxford, 1988), 213–46.
———, 'Willem II en de Stuarts 1647–1650', *Bijdragen en Mededelingen betreffende de Geschiedenis der Nederlanden*, 103 (1988), 157–81.
———, 'Frederick Henry and his Entourage: a Brief Political Biography' in: P. van der Ploeg and C. Vermeeren (eds), *Princely Patrons. The Collection of Frederick Henry of Orange and Amalia of Solms in The Hague* (The Hague/Zwolle, 1997), 18–33.
———, 'William III as Stadholder: Prince or Minister?' in: E. Mijers and D. Onnekink (eds), *Redefining William III. The Impact of the King-Stadholder in International Context* (Aldershot, 2007), 17–38.

Groenveld, S., and Wintle, M. (eds), *State and Trade. Government and the Economy in Britain and the Netherlands since the Middle Ages* (Zutphen, 1992).

——, *The Exchange of Ideas. Religion, Scholarship and Art in Anglo-Dutch Relations in the Seventeenth Century* (Zutphen, 1994).

Groenveld, S., et al. (eds), *Nassau uit de Schaduw van Oranje* (Franeker, 2000).

Haley, K.H.D., 'The Anglo-Dutch Rapprochement of 1677', *English Historical Review*, 73 (1958), 614–48.

——, 'The Dutch Invasion and the Alliance of 1689' in: L.G. Schwoerer (ed.), *The Revolution of 1688 – Changing Perspectives* (Cambridge, 1992), 21–35.

——, 'William III' in: A.G.H. Bachrach, J.P Sigmund and A.J. Veenendaal (eds), *Willem III, de Stadhouder-Koning en zijn Tijd* (Amsterdam, 1988), 31–5.

Hammer, P.J., 'Absolute and Sovereign Mistress of her Grace? Queen Elizabeth I and her Favourites 1581–1592' in: L.W.B. Brockliss and J.H. Elliott (eds), *The World of the Favourite* (New Haven/London, 1999), 38–53.

Harris, F., *A Passion for Government. The Life of Sarah, Duchess of Marlborough* (Oxford, 1991).

Harris, J., *William Talman, Maverick Architect* (London, 1982).

Harris, T., *Politics under the late Stuarts. Party Conflict in a Divided Society 1660–1715* (New York, 1993).

Hart, M. 't, 'The Devil or the Dutch: Holland's Impact on the Financial Revolution in England 1643–1694', *Parliaments, Estates and Representations*, 11 (1991), 39–52.

Hartog, M.W., 'Prins Willem III en de Hertogshoed van Gelderland 1673–1675', *Bijdragen en Mededelingen der Vereniging 'Gelre'*, 69 (1976–77), 125–55.

Hattendorf, J.B., *England in the War of the Spanish Succession. A Study of the English View and Conduct of Grand Strategy, 1702–1712* (New York, 1987).

Hatton, R., *Diplomatic Relations between Great Britain and the Dutch Republic* (London, 1950).

——, (ed.), *Louis XIV and Europe* (London, 1976).

——, *George I: Elector and King* (London, 1978).

——, 'Louis XIV and his Fellow Monarchs' in: R. Hatton, (ed.), *Louis XIV and Europe* (London, 1976), 16–59.

Hayton, D.W., 'The Country Interest and the Party System 1689–c.1720' in: C. Jones (ed.), *Party and Management in Parliament 1660–1784* (Leicester, 1984), 37–85.

Hayton, D.W., and O'Brien, G. (eds), *War and Politics in Ireland 1649–1730* (London, 1986).

Hill, B.W., *The Growth of Parliamentary Parties 1689–1742* (London, 1976).

Hoak, D., 'The Anglo-Dutch Revolution of 1688/89' in: D. Hoak and M. Feingold (eds), *The World of William and Mary: Anglo-Dutch Perspectives on the Revolution of 1688–1689* (Stanford, 1996), 1–26.

Hoak D., and Feingold, M (eds), *The World of William and Mary: Anglo-Dutch Perspectives on the Revolution of 1688–1689* (Stanford, 1996).

Holmes, G. *British Politics in the Age of Anne* (London, 1967).

——, (ed.), *Britain after the Glorious Revolution 1689–1714* (London, 1969).

——, *The Making of a Great Power. Late Stuart and early Georgian Britain (1660–1722)* (London/New York, 1993).

Hopkins, P., *Glencoe and the End of the Highland War* (Edinburgh, 1998).

——, 'Sir James Montgomerie of Skelmorlie' in: E. Corp and E. Cruickshanks (eds), *The Stuart Court in Exile and the Jacobites* (London/Rio Grande, 1995), 35–59.

Hoppit, J., *A Land of Liberty? England 1689–1727* (Oxford, 2000).

Horn, D.B., *The British Diplomatic Service 1689–1789* (Oxford, 1961).

Horwitz, H, *Revolution Politicks. The Career of Daniel Finch, Second Earl of Nottingham 1647–1730* (Cambridge, 1968).

——, *Parliament, Policy and Politics in the Reign of William III* (Manchester, 1977).

——, 'The Structure of Parliamentary Politics' in: G. Holmes (ed.), *Britain after the Glorious Revolution 1689–1714* (London, 1969), 96–114.

——, 'Historiographical Perspectives. The 1690s Revisited: Recent Work on Politics and Political Ideas in the Reign of William III', *Parliamentary History*, 15 (1996), 361–77.

Hughes, G.M., *A History of Windsor Forest, Sunninghill, and the Great Park* (London/Edinburgh, 1890).

Hunt, J.D., and De Jong, E. (eds), *The Anglo-Dutch Garden in the Age of William and Mary. De Gouden Eeuw van de Hollandse Tuinkunst* (Amsterdam/London, 1988).

Hunt, J.D., 'Anglo-Dutch Garden Art: Style and Idea' in: D. Hoak and M. Feingold (eds), *The World of William and Mary: Anglo-Dutch Perspectives on the Revolution of 1688–1689* (Stanford, 1996), 188–200.

Israel, J.I., *The Dutch Republic. Its Rise, Greatness and Fall 1477–1806* (Oxford, 1995).

——, (ed.), *The Anglo-Dutch Moment. Essays on the Glorious Revolution and its World Impact* (Cambridge, 1991).

——, *Monarchy, Orangism and Republicanism in the later Dutch Golden Age* (Amsterdam, 2004).

——, 'The Dutch Role in the Glorious Revolution' in: J.I. Israel (ed.), *The Anglo-Dutch Moment Essays on the Glorious Revolution and its World Impact* (Cambridge, 1991), 105–62.

——, 'William III and Toleration' in: O.P Grell, N. Tyacke and J.I. Israel (eds), *From Persecution to Toleration, the Glorious Revolution and Religion in England* (Oxford, 1991), 129–71.

——, 'Propaganda in the Making of the Glorious Revolution' in: S. Roach (ed.), *Across the Narrow Seas. Studies in the History and Bibliography of Britain and the Low Countries* (London, 1991), 167–78.

Israel, J.I., and Parker, G., 'Of Providence and Protestant Winds: The Spanish Armada of 1588 and the Dutch Armada of 1688' in: J.I. Israel (ed.), *The Anglo-Dutch Moment., Essays on the Glorious Revolution and its World Impact* (Cambridge, 1991), 335–63.

Jacques, D., et al. (eds), *The Gardens of William and Mary* (London, 1988).

Janssen, G.H., *Creaturen van de Macht: Patronage bij Willem Frederik van Nassau (1613–1664)* (Amsterdam, 2005).
Japikse, N., *Prins Willem III – De Stadhouder-Koning* (2 vols., Amsterdam, 1933).
——, 'De Stadhouder en zijn Alter-ego', *Handelingen van de Maatschappij der Nederlandse Letterkunde te Leiden en Levensberichten, 1927–1928* (1928), 20–36.
Jenkins, G.H., *The Foundations of Modern Wales 1642–1780* (Oxford, 1987).
Jones, C. (ed.), *Party and Management in Parliament 1660–1784* (Leicester, 1984).
Jones, D.W., 'Economic Policy, Trade and Managing the English War Economy, 1689–1712' in: S. Groenveld and M. Wintle (eds), *State and Trade. Government and the Economy in Britain and the Netherlands since the Middle Ages* (Zutphen, 1992).
Jones, J.R., *Country and Court: England, 1658–1714* (London, 1978).
——, *The Revolution of 1688 in England* (London, 1984).
——, (ed.), *Liberty Secured? Britain before and after 1688* (Stanford, 1992).
Jong, E. de, *Natuur en Kunst. Nederlandse Tuin- en Landschapsarchitectuur 1650–1740* (Amsterdam, 1993).
——, 'Netherlandish Hesperides. Garden Art in the Period of William and Mary 1650–1702' in: J.D. Hunt and E. de Jong (eds), *The Anglo-Dutch Garden in the Age of William and Mary. De Gouden Eeuw van de Hollandse Tuinkunst* (Amsterdam, 1998), 15–40.
Jongste, J.A.F. de, 'De Republiek onder het Erfstadhouderschap 1747–1780' in: *Algemene Geschiedenis der Nederlanden* (15 vols, Bussum, 1979–83), IX. 73–91.
——, 'The 1690's and After: The Local Perspective' in: J.A.F. de Jongste and A.J. Veenendaal (eds), *Anthonie Heinsius and the Dutch Republic 1688–1720. Politics, War and Finance* (The Hague, 2002), 65–88.
Kaiser, M., and Pečar, A. (eds), *Der Zweite Mann im Staat: Oberste Amtsträger und Favoriten im Umkreis der Reichsfürsten in der Frühen Neizeit* (Berlin, 2003).
Keeton, G.W., *Lord Chancellor Jeffreys and the Stuart Cause* (London, 1965).
Kenyon, J.P., *Robert Spencer, Earl of Sunderland 1621–1702* (London, 1958).
——, *Stuart England* (Harmondsworth, 1978).
——, 'The Earl of Sunderland and the King's Administration, 1693–1695', *English Historical Review*, 73 (1956), 576–602.
Kerkhof, M., 'De Carrière van Arnold Joost van Keppel na de Dood van Willem III', *Virtus*, 5 (1998), 13–19.
Kingsford, C.L., *The Early History of Picadilly, Leicester Square, Soho and their Neighbourhood* (Cambridge, 1925).
Kirby, C., 'The Four Lords and the Partition Treaty', *American Historical Review* 52 (1947), 477–90.
Kishlansky, M., *A Monarchy Transformed. Britain 1603–1714* (London, 1996).
Klopp, O., *Der Fall des Hauses Stuart und die Succession des Hauses Hannover in Grosz-Britannien und Irland im Zusammenhange der Europäischen Angelegenheiten von 1660–1714* (14 vols, Vienna, 1875–88).
Knetsch, F.R.J., *Pierre Jurieu, Theoloog en Politikus der Refuge* (Kampen, 1967).

Kooijmans, L., *Liefde in Opdracht: het Hofleven van Willem Frederik van Nassau* (Amsterdam, 2000).
Kuijl, A. van der, *De Glorieuze Overtocht. De Expeditie van Willem III naar Engeland in 1688* (Amsterdam, 1988).
Kurtz, G.H., *Willem III en Amsterdam 1683–1685* (Utrecht, 1928).
Lademacher, H., 'Wilhelm III. von Oranien und Anthonie Heinsius', *Rheinische Vierteljahrsblätter*, 34 (1970), 252–66.
Lane, M., 'The Diplomatic Service under William III', *Transactions of the Royal Historical Society*, 4th series, 10 (1927), 87–109.
Leeuw, K.M.M. de, *Cryptology and Statecraft in the Dutch Republic* (Amsterdam, 2000).
Legg, L.G.W., *Matthew Prior. A Study of his Public Career and Correspondence* (Cambridge, 1921).
Lenman, B., 'The Poverty of Political Theory in the Scottish Revolution of 1688–1690' in: L.G. Schwoerer (ed.), *The Revolution of 1688, Changing Perspectives* (Cambridge, 1992), 244–60.
Lipscomb, G., *The History and Antiquities of the County of Buckingham* (4 vols, London, 1847).
Lock, F.P., 'Swift and English Politics, 1701–1714' in: C. Rawson (ed.), *The Character of Swift's Satire* (London/Toronto, 1983), 127–50.
Lossky, A., 'Political Ideas of William III' in: H.H. Rowen and A. Lossky, *Political Ideas and Institutions in the Dutch Republic* (Los Angeles, 1985), 35–59.
Macaulay, T.B., *History of England from the Accession of James II* (6 vols, London, 1914).
MacFarlane, C., *The Sodomite in Fiction and Satire 1660–1750* (Columbia, 1997).
Manning, O., and Bray, W., *The History and Antiquities of the County of Surrey* (3 vols, London, 1804–14).
Marshall, A., *Intelligence and Espionage in the Reign of Charles II, 1660–1685* (Cambridge, 1994).
——, *The Age of Faction Court Politics, 1660–1702* (Manchester/New York, 1999).
Matthew, H.C.G, and Harrison, B. (eds), *Oxford Dictionary of National Biography* (61 vols, Oxford, 2004).
Maura, Duque de, *Vida y Reinado de Carlos II* (Madrid, 1990).
Mayer, R., 'Nathaniel Crouch, Bookseller and Historian: Popular Historiography and Cultural Power in late Seventeenth-Century England', *Eighteenth-Century Studies*, 27 (1994), 391–419.
McInnes, A., *Robert Harley, Puritan Politician* (London, 1970).
Mensema, A.J., Mooijweer, J., and Streng, J.C., *De Ridderschap van Overijssel. Le Metier du Noble* (Baarn, 2000).
Mijers, E., 'Scotland and the United Provinces c. 1680–1730. A Study in Intellectual and Educational Relations' (unpublished PhD thesis, University of St Andrews, 2002).
Mijers, E. and Onnekink, D. (eds), *Redefining William III. The Impact of the King-Stadholder in International Context* (Aldershot, 2007).
Miller, J., *James II – A Study in Kingship* (London, 1989).

Mörke, O., *Stadtholder oder Staetholder? Die Funktion des Hauses Oranien und seines Hofes in der Politischen Kultur der Republik der Vereinigten Niederlande im 17. Jahrhundert* (Munster, 1997).

———, 'William III's Stadholderly Court in the Dutch Republic' in: E. Mijers and D. Onnekink (eds), *Redefining William III. The Impact of the King-Stadholder in International Context* (Aldershot, 2007). 227–40.

Muilenberg, J., 'The Embassy of Everaard van Weede, Lord of Dykvelt, to England in 1687', *University Studies of University of Nebraska*, 20 (1920), 87–161.

Müller, P.L., *Wilhelm III. von Oranien und Georg Friedrich von Waldeck. Ein Beitrag zur Geschichte des Kampfes um das Europaischen Gleichgewicht* (2 vols, The Hague, 1873).

Murdoch, A., *The People Above. Politics and Administration in Mid-Eighteenth-Century Scotland* (Edinburgh, 1980).

Nicholson, T.C., and Turberville, A.S., *Charles Talbot, Duke of Shrewsbury* (Cambridge, 1930).

Nierop, H.F.K. van, *Van Ridders tot Regenten. De Hollandse Adel in de Zestiende en de Eerste Helft van de Zeventiende Eeuw* (s.l., 1984).

Nimwegen, O. van, *De Republiek der Verenigde Nederlanden als Grote Mogendheid. Buitenlandse Politiek en Oorlogvoering in de Eerste Helft van de Achttiende Eeuw en in het Bijzonder tijdens de Oostenrijkse Successieoorlog (1740–1748)* (Amsterdam, 2002).

———, *De Subsistentie van het Leger. Logistiek en Strategie van het Geallieerde en met name het Staatse Leger tijdens de Spaanse Successieoorlog in de Nederlanden en het Heilige Roomse Rijk 1701–1712* (Amsterdam, 1995).

Noordam, D.J., *Riskante Relaties. Vijf Eeuwen Homoseksualiteit in Nederland, 1233–1733* (Hilversum, 1995).

O'Connor, J.T., *Negotiator out of Season: the Career of Wilhelm Egon von Fürstenberg 1629 to 1704* (Athens, 1978).

Onnekink, D., '"Craignez Honte". Hans Willem Bentinck, Graaf van Portland, en diens Engelse Jaren', *Virtus*, 8/1–2 (2001), 20–34.

———, 'Het Fortuin van Henry Bentinck (1682–1726), Eerste Hertog van Portland', *Virtus*, 2nd series, 2 (2004), 54–72.

———, '"Dutch Councils": The Foreign Entourage of William III', Dutch Crossing, 29 (2005), 5–20.

Oudendijk, J.K., *Willem III, Stadhouder van Holland, Koning van Engeland* (Amsterdam, 1954).

Page, W. (ed.), *Victoria History of the Counties of England – Buckinghamshire* (5 vols, London, 1905–28).

Peck, L. Levy, *Court Patronage and Corruption in Early Stuart England* (London, 1991).

———, 'Monopolizing Favour; Structures of Power in the early Seventeenth-Century English Court' in: L.W.B. Brockliss and J.H. Elliott (eds), *The World of the Favourite* (London/New Haven, 1999), 54–70.

Pincus, S., 'From Butterboxes to Wooden Shoes: the Shift in English Popular Sentiment from Anti-Dutch to Anti-French in the 1670s', *Historical Journal*, 38/2 (1995), 333–61.

Ploeg, P. van der, and Vermeeren, C. (eds), *Princely Patrons. The Collection of Frederick Henry of Orange and Amalia of Solms in The Hague* (The Hague/Zwolle, 1997).

Plumb, J.H., *The Growth of Political Stability in England 1675–1725* (London, 1967).

Pocock, J.G.A., 'British History: A Plea for a New Subject', *Journal of Modern History*, 47 (1975), 601–21.

Preston, R.A., 'William Blathwayt and the Evolution of a Royal Personal Secretariat', *History*, February/June (1949), 28–43.

Rawson, C. (ed.), *The Character of Swift's Satire* (London/Newark, 1983).

Rand, B. (ed.), *The Life, Unpublished Letters and Philosophical Regimen of Anthony, Earl of Shaftesbury* (London, 1900, repr. 1995).

Richardt, A., *Louvois* (Paris, 1990).

Rietbergen, P.J.A.N. 'William of Orange (1650–1702) between European Politics and European Protestantism: the Case of the Huguenots' in: J.A.H. Bots and G.H.M. Posthumus Meyjes (eds), *La Révocation de l'Édit de Nantes et les Provinces-Unies* (Amsterdam, 1986), 35–51.

Riley, P.W.J., *King William and the Scottish Politicians* (Edinburgh, 1979).

Roach, S. (ed.), *Across the Narrow Seas; Studies in the History and Bibliography of Britain and the Low Countries* (London, 1991).

Rogers, J.E.T., *The First Nine Years of the Bank of England* (Oxford/New York, 1887).

Roorda, D.J., *Partij en Factie. De Oproeren van 1672 in de Steden van Holland en Zeeland, een Krachtmeting tussen Partijen en Facties* (Groningen, 1961).

——, 'William III and the Utrecht "Government-Regulation": Backgrounds, Events and Problems', *Acta Historiae Neerlandica*, 12 (1979), 85–109.

——, 'De Republiek in de Tijd van Stadhouder Willem III 1672–1702' in: D.P. Blok et al. (eds), *Algemene Geschiedenis der Nederlanden* (15 vols, Bussum, 1979–83), VIII. 282–96.

——, 'Le Secret du Prince. Monarchale Tendenties in de Republiek 1672–1702' in: S. Groenveld et al. (eds), *Rond Prins en Patriciaat: Verspreide Opstellen door D.J. Roorda* (Weesp, 1984), 172–92.

——, 'De Joodse Entourage van de Koning-Stadhouder' in: S. Groenveld et al. (eds), *Rond Prins en Patriciaat: Verspreide Opstellen door D.J. Roorda* (Weesp, 1984), 143–55.

——, 'Willem III, de Koning-Stadhouder' in: S. Groenveld et al. (eds), *Rond Prins en Patriciaat: Verspreide Opstellen door D.J. Roorda* (Weesp, 1984), 118–42.

——, 'Le Secret du Prince. Monarchale Tendenties in de Republiek 1672–1702' in: S. Groenveld et al. (eds), *Rond Prins en Patriciaat: Verspreide Opstellen door D.J. Roorda* (Weesp, 1984), 172–92.

Rose, C. *England in the 1690s: Revolution, Religion and War* (Oxford, 1999).

Rubini, D., *Court and Country 1688–1702* (London, 1967).

Rule, J.C., 'France Caught between Two Balances: the Dilemma of 1688' in: L.G. Schwoerer (ed.), *The Revolution of 1688–1689: Changing Perspectives* (Cambridge, 1992), 35–52.

———, 'The Partition Treaties, 1698–1700: A European View' in: E. Mijers and D. Onnekink (eds), *Redefining William III. The Impact of the King-Stadholder in International Context* (Aldershot, 2007), 95–109.
Sachse, W.L., *Lord Somers, a Political Portrait* (Manchester, 1975).
Sandars, M.F., *Princess and Queen of England, Life of Mary II* (London, 1913).
Schazmann, P., *The Bentincks. The History of a European Family* (London, 1976).
Schöffer, I., 'Het grote Waagstuk. De Overtocht van Prins Willem III naar Engeland in 1688' in: A.G.H. Bachrach, J.P. Sigmund, A.J. Veenendaal (eds), *Willem III, de Stadhouder-Koning en zijn Tijd* (Amsterdam, 1988), 9–31.
Schwennicke, D. (ed.), *Europäische Stammtafeln*, IV. *Standesherrliche Häuser*, (Marburg, 1981).
Schwoerer, L.G., *No Standing Armies! The Antiarmy Ideology in Seventeenth Century England* (Baltimore/London, 1974).
———, *The Declaration of Rights 1689* (Baltimore, 1981).
———, (ed.), *The Revolution of 1688–1689, Changing Perspectives* (Cambridge, 1992).
———, 'Propaganda in the Revolution of 1688–1689', *American Historical Review*, 132 (1977), 843–74.
Scott, J., *England's Troubles. Seventeenth-Century English Political Instability in European Context* (Cambridge, 2000).
Sharpe, K., 'The Image of Virtue: the Court and Household of Charles I, 1625–1642' in: D. Starkey et al. (eds), *The English Court: from the Wars of the Roses to the Civil War* (London/New York, 1987), 226–60.
Sharpe, K., and Zwicker, S.N., *Politics of Discourse. The Literature and History of Seventeenth-Century England* (Berkeley/Los Angeles/London, 1987).
Simms, J.G., *The Williamite Confiscation in Ireland, 1690–1703* (London, 1956).
———, *Jacobite Ireland 1685–1691* (London/Toronto, 1969).
———, 'Williamite Peace Tactics 1690–1691' in: D.W. Hayton and G. O'Brien (eds), *War and Politics in Ireland 1649–1730* (London, 1986), 181–201.
Somerville, D.H., *The King of Hearts. Charles Talbot, Duke of Shrewsbury* (London, 1962).
Speck, W.A., *Reluctant Revolutionaries, Englishmen and the Revolution of 1688* (Oxford, 1988).
Spens, S., *George Stepney, 1663–1707, Diplomat and Poet* (Cambridge, 1997).
Starkey, D., 'Intimacy and Innovation: the Rise of the Privy Chamber, 1485–1547' in: D. Starkey et al. (eds), *The English Court: from the Wars of the Roses to the Civil War* (London/New York, 1987), 71–118.
———, et al. (eds), *The English Court: from the Wars of the Roses to the Civil War* (London/New York, 1987).
Stephen, L., and Lee, S. (eds), *Dictionary of National Biography* (63 vols, London, 1885–).
Stork-Penning, J.G., 'The Ordeal of States: some Remarks on Dutch Politics during the War of Spanish Succession', *Acta Historiae Neerlandica*, 2 (1967), 107–40.
Storrs, C., 'Disaster at Darien (1698–1700)? The Persistence of Spanish Imperial Power on the Eve of the Demise of the Spanish Habsburgs', *European History Quarterly*, 29 (1999), 5–38.

Story, R.H., *William Carstares. A Character and Career of the Revolutionary Epoch 1649–1715* (Edinburgh, 1895).

Streng, J., 'Le Métier du Noble: De Overijsselse Ridderschap tussen 1622 en 1795' in: A.J. Mensema, J. Mooijweer and J.C. Streng (eds), *De Ridderschap van Overijssel. Le Metier du Noble* (Baarn, 2000), 49–109.

Strien, K., van, *Touring the Low Countries. Accounts of British Travellers, 1660–1720* (Amsterdam, 1998).

Swart, K.W., *William of Orange and the Revolt of the Netherlands, 1572–84*, eds A. Duke et al. (Aldershot, 2003).

Symcox, G., 'Louis XIV and the Outbreak of the Nine Years War' in: R. Hatton, (ed.), *Louis XIV and Europe* (London, 1976), 179–213.

Trevelyan, G.M., *England under the Stuarts* (London, 1997).

Troost, W., *William III, the Stadholder-King: A Political Biography* (Aldershot, 2005).

——, 'William III and the Treaty of Limerick 1691–1697' (unpublished PhD thesis, University of Leiden, 1983).

——, 'William III, Brandenburg, and the Construction of the anti-French Coalition, 1672–1688' in: J.I. Israel (ed.), *The Anglo-Dutch Moment. Essays on the Glorious Revolution and its World Impact* (Cambridge, 1991), 299–333.

——, 'Willem III en de "Exclusion Crisis" 1679–1681', *Bijdragen en Mededelingen betreffende de Geschiedenis der Nederlanden*, 107 (1992), 28–46.

——, 'Ireland's Role in the Foreign Policy of William III' in: E. Mijers and D. Onnekink (eds), *Redefining William III. The Impact of the King-Stadholder in International Context* (Aldershot, 2007), 53–68.

Turberville, A.S., *The House of Lords in the Reign of William* (Oxford, 1913).

——, *A History of Welbeck and its Owners* (2 vols, London, 1937–8).

Veenendaal, A.J. and Jongste, J.A.F. de (eds), *Anthonie Heinsius and the Dutch Republic 1688–1720. Politics, War and Finance* (The Hague, 2002).

Veenendaal, A.J., 'Who is in Charge here? Anthonie Heinsius and his Role in Dutch Politics' in: A.J. Veenendaal and J.A.F. de Jongste (eds), *Anthonie Heinsius and the Dutch Republic 1688–1720* (The Hague, 2002), 11–24.

Veenendaal Sr, A.J., *Het Engels-Nederlands Condominium in de Zuidelijke Nederlanden* (Utrecht, 1945).

Wijn, J.W., Raa, F.J.G. ten, and Bas, F. de (eds), *Het Staatsche Leger 1568–1795* (11 vols, The Hague, 1911–64).

Wijnands, D.O., 'Hortus Auriaci: de Tuinen van Oranje en hun Plaats in de Tuinbouw en Plantkunde van de late Zeventiende Eeuw' in: J.D. Hunt and E. de Jong (eds), *The Anglo-Dutch garden in the Age of William and Mary. De Gouden Eeuw van de Hollandse Tuinkunst* (Amsterdam, 1998), 61–86.

Wolf, J.B. *Louis XIV* (London, 1968).

Wood, C.W., 'A Study of Anglo-Dutch Relations in the Grand Alliance, 1701–1706' (unpublished PhD thesis, University of North Carolina, 1981).

Zandvliet, C.J. 'Het Hof van een Dienaar met Vorstelijke Allure' in: C.J. Zandvliet (ed.), *Maurits Prins van Oranje* (Amsterdam, 2000), 36–63.

Index

Hans Willem Bentinck is referred to as HWB in the index, except under his own main entry.

References to illustrated material are in **bold**.

Act of Settlement (1701) 207
Albemarle, Earl *see* Keppel, Arnold Joost van
Albeville, Marquis (Ignatius White), English Ambassador 41, 47
Almonde, Philips van, Admrl 52
Alonne, Abel Tassin d' 32, 40, 41, 42, 95, 208, 240, 241, 245, 250
Amsterdam, relations with William III 28, 29, 34–5, 71, 72, 73, 74, 75–6, 77–9, 223
Anglo-Dutch fleet 151, 158
Anglo-Dutch garden style 178
Anglo-Dutch grand strategy 155–61
Anglo-Dutch regiments 30, 31, 32, 33, 44, 68, 162
Anglo-Dutch War, Second (1665–67) 9, 10, 11
Anglo-French conflict 2, 197–201
Anjou, Duke 208, 214, 223, 226
Annandale, Earl 70, 114
Anne (Queen) 107, 207, 248
   accession 258
   sues HWB 248–9
anti-Dutch feeling *see* xenophobia, anti-Dutch
Argyle, Earl 30, 115, 141
Arlington, Earl 15
Arnhem, Johan van 19
art, propaganda value 177
Assassination Plot (1696) 104, 110, 168–9, 170, 189
Auersperg, Leopold, Count 145, 247
Augsburg, League (1686) 39
Avaux, Count d' 18, 29, 30, 31, 34, 38, 41, 45, 47, 48, 52, 118, 125

Baer, Frederik Johan van 252

Bagshot 91
Barclay, Andrew 95
Barillon, Paul, French Ambassador 27, 32, 33, 46
Barrier Treaty (1709) 254, 255, 256
Bastiaansen, Willem, Admrl 52, 119
Bavaria 39
Bavaria, Elector 176, 213, 214, 219, 222, 223
Baxter, Stephen 3, 103, 106, 173, 232, 261
Beachy Head, Battle (1690) 70, 80
Beauviller, Duke 209
Bentinck, Berend (HWB's father) 9
Bentinck, Eusebius (HWB's great-grandfather) 8
Bentinck family tree 8, 97
Bentinck, Hans Willem, First Earl of Portland
   accepts Earldom 68
   Ambassador Extraordinary, Paris 236, 237
   anti-Catholicism 125
   appearance 9
   archive sources on 5–6
   arrogance, perceived 106, 183, 233
   art collection 177
   biographies 2, 3
   birth 7, 9
   brothers 9
   character, perception of 17–18, 105, 183–4
   children 23, 96
   communication skills 104–5
   corruption, accusations of 184–5
   court, influence at 17–18, 22–3, 98–9
   death 256
   diplomatic missions
      France 207–9
      German principalities 38, 47–9

London 7, 24–6, 31–4, 36
diplomats, influence on 153–5
on Divine Providence 125
England
  first visit 12
  informer network 41–2
  invasion
    plan 52–3, **illus.5**
    preparations 51–6, 61
English language, command of 104–5
English society, integration into 95–6, 98
family
  background 8
  tree 97
favourite 4, 7, 23, 35–6, 85, 86, 100–101, 108, 121, 137, 175–6, 206, 233–4, 261, 263
  loss of influence 236–7, 240–41
'fixer' 107–8
France
  campaign 155–6
  peace negotiations 199–202
gardens 92–4, 176, 177–8
Ginckel, correspondence 81–3
Glorious Revolution, role 4, 36, 65, 84, 86, 149, 170, 261
grand strategy, involvement 155–7
greed, accusations of 185–7, 265
Heinsius, correspondence with 251
Huguenots, patronage 4, 124, 172–3
impeachment threat 224–5, 246
intellect 105–6
intelligence networks 169–73
Ireland
  campaign 80, 81–3
  influence 116–17, 142–5
Keeper of the Privy Purse 99–100
Keppel, rivalry 209, 217, 221, 229–32, 239–40, 258, 262
life
  early 9–11
  summary 261–2
Luxembourg campaign 29
Marlborough, contact 251–2
military service 13–14, 23, 36, 148–53, 197
military strategist/organiser 149–53
money raising 166–8, 173–4

News from the Army in Ireland 80, 149
Nine Years War, role 147, 197
pamphlet attacks on 22, 132, 182–3, 190–93, 206–7, 264
Parliamentary affairs, role 110–11
Partition Treaties, involvement 224–6, 248, 266
political
  power struggles 134–8
  preferences 127–31
portraits 177, **illus.4**
  with William III 176–7, **illus.1**
Prince of Orange (later William III)
  Chamberlain to 12–13, 17
  page to 7, 10–11, 261
  secretary to 14–15
  see also William III
property 16, 91–2
Protestantism 124
relatives, promotion of 22–3
religious affairs, influence on 126–7
remarriage 248
retirement 197, 221, 224, 227, 229, 231, 241–2, 247, 265
Ridderschap seat 16, 19, 36, 74–5, 107, 183
satirised in 'Hollands hollende koe' 193–4, **illus.6**
Scotland
  influence in 111–16, 139–42, 145, 244–5
  settlement, influence 69–71
significance 2–3
social inferiority 17–18
sodomy, accusations of 179, 187–9, 191
States Assembly, role 34, 35, 36
sued by Queen Ann 248–9
titles 68, 86, 95
United Provinces, influence 117–21, 249–50
War of Spanish Succession, negotiations 216–17, 243
wealth 88–90, 256–7
William III
  access to 100–103
  relationship 106–7
Bentinck, Hendrik (HWB's grandfather) 8
Bentinck, Henry (HWB's son) 7
Bentinck, Willem (HWB's son) 96, 257

Bernstorff, Andreas von 50, 151
Berry, Duke 208, 214
Beuningen, Coenraad van 24, 25, 27, 28, 35
Beverningk, Hieronymus van 76, 119
Blathwayt, William 151, 152, 153, 154, 159, 161, 163, 166, 178, 232
Blenheim, Battle (1704) 251
Bloemendaal, Anna van 9
Bonnet, Frederic 166, 187, 209, 217, 224, 231, 235, 240
Boreel, Jacob 10, 197, 199
Borgomañero, Marquis de 156, 157, 198
Borssele van der Hooghe, Adriaan van 23, 99, 229, 234, 245, 246
Bothmer, Johann 209
Boufflers, Duke 164–5, 199, 200, 201, 202, 208, 209, 210, 212, 223
Boyne, Battle (1690) 57, 79, 80, 116, 147
Breadalbane, Earl 70, 71, 113, 141, 262, 263
Breda 16, 71, 125, 171, 172
Bredehoff, Hoorn François van 22
Brederode, Wolfert van 19
Buckingham, Duke 107, 191, 208
    archetypal favourite 85, 108, 181, 187, 263
Bulstrode, HWB's English country estate 91, 177, 249, 257
Burgundy, Duchess 208
Burgundy, Duke 208
Burnet, Gilbert 9, 40, 43, 51, 53, 60, 65, 67, 86, 87, 124, 127, 206, 234
    on favourites 235
    History of My Own Time 38
    on HWB 17, 22, 112, 140, 142, 192–3

Callenburg, Gerard, Capt 51–2
Callières, François de 197, 198
Capel, Henry 64, 142, 143, 144, 145, 204
Capel family 96
Carlos II 213, 223, 225, 226
Carmarthen, Marquis (Earl of Danby) 109, 110, 111, 130, 133, 134, 135, 139, 149, 159, 160, 184, 191, 233, 261
Carmichael, John 242
Carstares, William 43, 60, 70, 106, 113, 114–15, 116, 121, 126, 139, 140, 141, 237, 256, 262, 264
Carswell, John 4
Catholicism, threat to Protestantism 39–40, 59–61
Cecil, Robert 91
Chambres des Reunions 27
Charles II 10, 12, 15, 23, 24, 27, 28, 85, 215
    death 39
    pro-Dutch foreign policy 25
    will 226
Chudleigh, Thomas 28
Churchill, John *see* Marlborough, Duke
Churchill, Sarah, royal favourite 107, 248
Citters, Arnout van, Dutch Ambassador 28, 31, 33, 42, 44, 45, 46, 54, 57, 132, 133, 154, 254
Clarendon, Earl 64, 66, 85, 86, 180, 263
Clarges, Thomas, Sir 130
Clark, George, Sir 81, 116, 132
Claydon, Tony 3, 65, 127, 190
Cologne crisis 37, 38, 46, 48, 49, 52, 55, 62
Condé, Prince 92, 209
Coningsby, Thomas 111, 116, 144, 204
Conti, Prince 209
Convention Parliament (1689) 63–4, 65, 66, 68
Court Tories 129, 130, 134, 135, 136, 139, 161, 164, 264
Court Whigs 110, 128, 129, 164, 238
Crawford, Earl 139
Crouch, Nathaniel
    A History of the House of Orange 181–2
    The Unfortunate Court–Favourites of England 179–80, 181, 182, 191

Dalrymple, James 43, 70, 112, 113, 140, 141
Danby, Earl 23, 24, 25, 26, 54, 85, 108, 179, 180, 263 *see also* Carmarthen, Marquis
Danckelmann, Eberhard von 47, 48, 49, 50, 153
Darien scheme 244, 263
Dauphin (son of Louis XIV) 177, 208, 213, 214, 215, 221–2, 223
Dear Bargain pamphlet 131, 132
Declaration of Indulgence (1687) 45
Declaration of Reasons (William III) 53, 61, 66
Defoe, Daniel
    Legion's Memorial 226
    The True-born Englishman 206–7
Desgotz, Claude 94

Desmarets, Daniel 60, 93
Desmarets, Samuel 127
Dijkveld *see* Weede van Dijkveld
Disbanding Act (1699) 240
Divine Providence, HWB on 125
Drimmelen 16, 183
Dual Monarchy, British Isles/United Provinces 3, 173, 266
Dubois, Simon, portraits
  HWB **illus.4**
  Jane Martha Temple **illus.3**
Dumont de Bostaquet, Isaac 43, 57
Duncombe, William 143, 237
Dundee, Viscount 68, 69
Dussen, Bruno van der 76, 118
Dussen, Gerard van der 118
'Dutch junto' 113, 131, 134
Dutch War, end (1678) 7
Dutch-French conflict 23–4, 28–9, 33, 55, 58

Emanuel, Max 49, 98, 151
Evertsen, Cornelis, Admrl 52
Exclusion Crisis (1679–81) 27

Fabricius, Willem 75, 118
Fagel, François Nicolaas, Baron 253
Fagel, Gaspar 11, 16, 18, 19, 26, 34, 43, 44, 45, 51, 53, 61, 62, 120, 178
  death 65, 71, 262
favourites
  archetypal, Duke of Buckingham 85, 108, 181, 187
  Burnet on 235
  disappearance/re-emergence 4, 263
  Dutch 2, 204, 264–5
  fear of 175
  HWB 4, 7, 23, 35–6, 85, 86, 100–101, 108, 121, 137, 175–6, 206, 233–4, 263
  Keppel 232–3, 234–6
  literary portrayal 179–95
  phenomenon 4, 85–6
  Sarah Churchill 107, 248
  William III's 22
Fenwick, John, Sir 237
Finale 223
Fontainebleau, Edict (1685) 39
Franco-Dutch conflict 23–4, 28–9, 33, 55, 58
Frederick I of the Palatinate 20

Frederick III, Elector of Brandenburg 48, 50, 107, 151, 176
Frederick Henry of Orange 10, 20, 21
Frederick William, Great Elector of Brandenburg 38
Fuchs, Paul 33, 48, 50, 60
Fürstenberg, Cardinal 47
Fürstenberg, Wilhelm von 37, 46, 49, 50

Gallican articles, Louis XIV/Pope dispute 37
Galway (city) 83
Galway, Earl 2, 151, 158, 159, 160, 161, 162, 203, 205, 253
gardens, Anglo-Dutch style 178–9
George I 99, 132, 254, 258
George III 180
Ginckel *see* Reede van Ginckel
Glencoe massacre (1692) 115, 140–41
Glorious Revolution 1
  Dutch influence on 37–8
  and England's greatness 215
  HWB's role 4, 36, 65, 84, 86, 149, 170, 261
Godolphin, Sidney 57, 94, 96, 136, 137, 138, 158, 166, 167, 185, 249, 251, 259, 266
Grady, John 82
Grand Alliance 156, 201, 213, 215, 264
Gravenmoer, Lord, 's- 13, 81, 116, 151

Halewijn, Cornelis van 72, 76
Halewijn, Simon van 118, 170
Haley, Kenneth 37
Halifax, Marquis 44, 57, 67, 101, 103, 108, 109, 111, 133, 134, 147, 233, 261
Ham, Johan 48, 49, 50, 59, 61, 154, 163
Hamilton, Duke 71, 112, 140
Hampton Court Palace 89, 91, 96, 98, 99, 100, 101, 103, 108, 120, 178, 238
Hanoverian Succession 255, 258
Harley, Margaret Cavendish, Lady 258
Harley, Robert 100, 130, 138, 186, 194, 202, 203, 237, 249, 258
Heemskerck, Coenraad van 33, 154, 157, 163, 201, 209
Heinsius, Anthonie 73, 74, 75, 76, 78, 117, 119, 120, 121, 133, 137, 150, 151, 155, 171, 199, 200, 201, 214, 215, 216, 217, 218, 232, 246, 252, 253

HWB, correspondence 219–20, 223, 249, 250, 251, 255
Hendrik, Casimir, 35, 118, 170, 171
Henning, Caspar Frederick (HWB's secretary) 94, 99, 172, 249
Herbert, Arthur 50, 52, 53, 56, 57, 67
Herbert, Edward, Sir 210
Hill, Richard 84, 109, 163, 168, 170, 198, 230
Holland, Anglo-French attack 12
Hollandsche Mercurius 38
Holy Roman Empire 37, 39
Honthorst, Gerard 20
Hooghe, Romeyn de 93, 177–8, 189
Horwitz, Henry 129, 263
Hove, Michiel ten 120, 147
Howard, Stuarta 190, 248
Hudde, Johannes 51, 55, 78
Huguenots 59
　expulsion from France 40
　HWB's patronage 4, 124, 172–3
Huls, Carel Willem van 246
Hume, Patrick 43, 115, 116, 141, 242
Humières, Duke d' 52
Hungary, recovery from Turks (1687) 39
Hutton, John (HWB's secretary) 42, 45
Huybert, Pieter de 12, 77
Huydecooper van Maarseveen, Johan 72
Huygens, Christiaan 92
Huygens, Constantijn 14, 15, 21, 22, 56, 65, 86–7, 92, 100, 102, 103, 104, 110, 117, 124, 133, 147, 173, 177, 189, 199, 230, 240
Hyde, Laurence 25

Ireland
　campaign 79–83
　French-Jacobite army 80
　HWB's influence 116–17, 142–5
　Jacobites 82, 83
　land grants 204–5
Israel, Jonathan 3, 21, 37, 59, 63

Jacobites
　at French court 210
　Ireland 82, 83
　opposition to William III 68–9, 168, 170
James II 29, 37, 58, 59
　in France 210–11
　leaves England 58–9
Louis XIV
　support from 199, 200, 201, 210–11
　understanding with 40, 44, 55, 60–61
　Prince of Wales birth, controversy 37, 45
　religious policies 37, 40
　seven bishops affair 37, 45, 46
　war preparedness 45
Jersey, Earl (Edward Villiers) 121, 219, 224, 239, 240, 244, 246
Johnston, James 42, 45, 46, 53, 54, 114, 115, 139, 140, 141, 145, 244
Johnston, Nathaniel, *The Dear Bargain* 122, 131, 132, 185
Jones, J.R. 46, 86, 197
Jong, Erik de 177
Jurieu, Pierre 60

Kenyon, John 4
Keppel, Arnold Joost van, Earl of Albemarle 2, 75, 95, 105, 133, 163, 180, 188, 189, 208
　garden 178
　military service 249
　rivalry with HWB 209, 217, 221, 229–32, 239–40, 258, 262
　royal favourite 232–3, 234–6
Killiecrankie, Battle (1689) 69
Kishlansky, Mark 2
Kneller, Godfrey, Sir 177

Lancashire Plot (1694) 169
Leeuwen, Jacob van (HWB's secretary) 54, 153, 172
Leinster, Duke 133, 149, 151, 158, 159, 160, 161, 263
Lenôtre, André 92, 94,
Lerma, Duke 85, 180
Lexington, Baron 111, 152, 154, 157, 163, 164, 168, 170, 184, 198, 201, 239
L'Hermitage, Rene Saunière de 173, 224, 230, 241, 250
Limerick, Treaty (1691) 82, 143
Lingen 16, 125
Livingstone, Thomas 70, 242–3, 245
London, George 94
Lorraine (region) 223
Lorraine, Duke 223

Louis XIII 124
Louis XIV 33, 46, 124, 162, 164, 177, 202,
    208, 209, 216, 217, 218, 221, 222
  Dutch, hostility to 55, 58
  foreign policy 2, 27, 28, 39
  Gallican articles, dispute with Pope 37
  gardens, Versailles 94
  James II
    support to 199, 200, 201, 210–11
    understanding with 40, 44, 55,
      60–61
  Partition Treaties 215, 219, 220, 223,
    227, 261
  Spanish succession, claim 212, 213, 214
Louis of Baden, Prince 151, 156
Lowther, John, Sir 238
Lumley, Richard 54, 98
Luxembourg (city) 199, 201, 214, 216
  fall 29
  siege 28
Luxembourg, Duke 135

Maas, Dirck 118, 147
Maastricht 165
Macaulay, T.B. 183
Mackay, Hugh 68, 69–70, 71, 113, 162, 263
Magistrates Affair (1690) 120, 262
Maritime Powers 197, 198, 213, 214, 215,
    216, 218, 220, 222, 243, 255, 266
Marlborough, Duke (John Churchill) 85,
    86, 94, 98, 105, 136, 152, 162, 229,
    237, 239, 249, 253, 255, 256, 257,
    258, 266
  Blenheim Palace 91
  HWB, rapprochement 251–2
  Jacobitism, suspected of 158, 170, 188
Marot, Daniel de 93
Mary II 23, 57, 67, 68
  death 137, 168, 232
  marriage to William 25–6
Mary of Modena 40, 41, 211
Maurice, John 92
Maurice, Prince 8, 10, 16, 20, 21
Mazarin, Cardinal 85, 182
Meinderts, Franz von 48
Melville, George 6, 43, 69–70, 71, 101, 104,
    112, 113, 114, 126, 139, 141, 142,
    171
Methuen, John 145, 153, 237

Meyercron, Henning, Danish Ambassador
    209
Milan 214, 216, 218, 221, 222, 223
Moerke, Olaf 14, 19, 20
Mollo, Francisco 154, 199
Monmouth, Duke of
  in Holland 29–31
  rebellion 31, 32–3, 56
Montagu, Charles 94, 104, 138, 144, 166,
    205, 218, 225, 238, 240, 253
Montgomery Plot (1690) 169
Mordaunt, Charles 41–2, 43, 45, 178
Moreau, Antoine, Polish Ambassador 47
Murray, John 115, 116, 141

Namur, Citadel 159, 160, 164, 165, 199
Naples 222, 223
Nassau-Beverweert, Maurits Lodewijk van
    19
Nassau-Odijk, Willem Adriaan van 12, 13,
    19, 22, 26, 34, 36, 77, 86, 87, 95,
    118, 121, 132, 209, 246, 264
Nassau-Ouwerkerk, Hendrik van 10, 12, 13,
    17, 18, 19, 30, 31, 32, 45, 87, 95, 99,
    162, 233, 240, 241, 249, 250, 258
Nassau-Zuylestein, Frederik van 10, 11, 12
Nassau-Zuylestein, Willem van (Earl of
    Rochfort) 18, 26, 36, 41, 45, 54, 58,
    59, 61, 62, 87, 95, 99, 133, 205, 230,
    233, 249
naturalisation, Dutch subjects 94–5
Naturalization Bill 132
Netscher, Gaspar 177
New Country Party 130, 203, 205
News from the Army in Ireland (HWB) 80,
    149
Nijmegen 52
  Peace (1678–79) 27
Nine Years War (1688–1697) 4, 147,
    151–68, 173, 197, 229, 266
Nottingham, Earl 57, 67, 70, 71, 81, 88,
    101, 103, 108, 109, 113, 126, 129,
    130, 133, 134, 135, 136, 151, 153,
    156, 158, 159–60, 161, 184, 189,
    249, 251

Ogilvy, James 113, 114, 115, 141, 236–7,
    242
Oije, Alexander Schimmelpennick van der

101, 132
Oije, Jacob Schimmelpennick van der 72, 76
Oldenbarnevelt, Johan van 16
Olivarez, Duke 85
Oldmixon, John 183, 217, 226
Orange family
    misfortunes 8, 10
    resurgence 11, 12
Orange, Prince of *see* William III
Orangism 11, 12, 65, 177
Orford, Lord *see* Russell, Edward
Orkney, Earl 232
Orkney, Lady *see* Villiers, Elizabeth
Orleans, Duchess 37, 208, 209, 248
Orleans, Duke 208, 209
Ormond, Duke of 26, 116

Palmquist, Johan, Swedish Ambassador 209
Parliament
    growing importance 123
    standing 4, 263
Partition, Treaties (1698/1700) 197, 217,
    224–6, 244, 246, 248, 266
    Louis XIV 215, 219, 220, 223, 227, 261
Peck, Linda Levy 85, 190
Pendrecht 17, 88, 90, 257
Perpetual Edict (1667) 11
Pfaltz-Neuburg, Philip Wilhelm 37
Place Bill 130, 145, 207, 225
Plukenet, Leonard 92
Pomponne, Marquis 212, 214
popery, fear of 40, 65
Portland, Earl *see* Bentinck, Hans Willem,
    First Earl of Portland
Portland family 258
Porter, Charles 116, 145
Price, Robert 186, 194
Prior, Matthew 106, 217, 220, 233, 239,
    242, 243
Protestant Succession 207, 254
Protestantism, threat from Catholicism
    39–40, 59–61
Putmans, Gerard 76, 118

Queensberry, Duke 114, 141, 142, 254
    administration 115, 145, 242, 244

Reede van Amerongen, Godard Adriaan van
    12, 48, 72, 73, 77

Reede van Ginckel, Godard van, Genrl, Earl
    of Athlone 23, 72, 95, 116, 133, 151,
    152, 162, 178,
    HWB, correspondence 29, 73–4, 81–3
    Irish campaign 81–3, 262
    peerage 143
    'religion and liberty' slogan 59, 60, 61
Reresby, Sir John 64, 65
Rheede, Frederik van 20
Rhoon 17, 88, 90, 171, 257
Richelieu, Cardinal 85
Rigaud, Hyacinthe 177
Rijn, Rembrandt van 20
Riley, Patrick 4, 113, 115, 126, 138, 142,
    263
Robéthon, Jean de 111, 173, 249, 250, 253,
    254
Rochester, Earl 30, 33, 40, 59, 130, 134,
    158, 159, 161, 249
Rochfort, Earl *see* Nassau-Zuylestein,
    Willem van
Ronquillo, Pedro, Spanish Ambassador 28,
    87, 101, 156
Russell, Edward (Lord Orford) 54, 158, 218,
    238, 225, 240
Ruyter, Michiel de 12, 14
Rye House Plot (1683) 27
Ryswick, Peace (1697) 197, 199–202, 211,
    213, 240

's-Gravenmoer, Lord *see* Gravenmoer, Lord,
    's-
Saint-Simon 209
Schomberg, Duke 2, 46, 48, 52, 60, 68, 81,
    95, 116, 133, 149, 151, 152, 161,
    261, 263
    in Ireland 80
Schonenberg, Francisco 51, 198
Schuylenburg, Willem van 79, 88, 101, 120,
    166, 172, 209, 241
Scotland
    campaign 69
    HWB's influence 111–16, 139–42, 145,
    244–5
    settlement 69–71
    William III's policy 138–9
Scottish Union (1707) 254
Seymour, Edward 134, 162, 248
Shaftesbury, Earl 128, 253

Sharpe, Kevin 106, 175
Shrewsbury, Earl (later Duke) 43, 101, 103, 104, 105, 107, 108, 113, 130, 133, 138, 143, 144, 145, 151, 156, 161, 164, 165, 166, 167, 169–70, 188, 199, 201, 202, 218, 230, 231, 237, 238, 240, 245
Sicily 223
Sidney, Henry 31, 32, 39, 40, 41, 42, 54, 67, 87, 88, 121, 143, 262
Simmern, Karl von, Elector Palatinate 37
Simms, John 4, 204, 205
Skelton, Bevil, English Ambassador 30–31, 32, 33, 40
Solms, Amalia van 10, 12, 20
Solms, Count, Lt–Genrl 13, 59, 81, 116, 149, 150, 151, 152, 162, 185
Somers, John 110, 136, 137, 166, 167, 169, 186, 218, 225, 238, 239, 253, 255–6, 259
Sorgvliet, HWB's Dutch country estate 17, 88, 90, 91–3, 176, 177, 178, 249, 257
South Sea Bubble (1720) 258
Spain 19, 28, 85, 155, 156, 157, 180, 198, 207, 212, 215, 223, 225–6
 and the Spanish Netherlands 214, 222
Spanheim, Ezechiel 48, 209
Spanheim, Fredericus 127
Spanish Netherlands 24, 52, 148, 149, 155, 214, 222, 223, 252, 255
 and Spain 214, 222
Spanish Succession
 claimants 213–16
 Louis XIV's claim 212, 213, 214
 negotiations 216–22, 243
 War of the (1702–13) 197
stadholderate
 abolition 10, 11, 21
 system 7
stadholders, power 19, 20–21
standing army
 establishment 138
 growth 161, 266
 opposition to 197, 229, 264
 reduction 202–4, 219–20, 265
 size 31
Stepney, George 153, 154, 156, 163, 239
Steward, James 43

Stuart, Elizabeth 20
Stuart, Mary 10, 20
Sunderland, Countess 41, 178
Sunderland, Earl 4, 5, 40, 41, 85, 106, 107, 108, 109, 110, 111, 121, 129, 130, 135, 136, 137, 138, 140, 142, 143, 144, 145, 167, 179, 199, 220, 221, 237, 238, 239, 240, 243, 248, 258, 261, 262, 264, 266
Swift, Jonathan 129
 on HWB 106, 226
Sylvius, Gabriel 15, 230
 on HWB 105–6

Tallard, Count, French Ambassador 128, 212, 214, 215, 216, 217, 218, 219, 220–21, 222–3, 224, 240, 244
 on William's favourites 234
Talman, William 91, 93
Temple, Jane Martha (HWB's second wife) 248
 portrait **illus.3**
Temple, William, Sir 15, 25, 129, 178, 248
Theobald's House, HWB's country house 89, 90, 91
Thoyras, Paul Rapin de 172, 217, 257
Torcy, Marquis 208, 212, 214, 250
Trenchard, John 136, 137, 138, 143, 151, 153, 161
Triennial Bill 123, 129, 130, 264
Tromer, Christoffel (HWB's secretary) 41, 42, 71, 96, 171–2
Troost, Wout 3, 4
Trumbull, William, Sir, English Ambassador, Paris/Secretary of State 33, 109, 134–5, 138, 161, 237
Turin, Treaty (1696) 198
Tutchin, John, *The Foreigners* 182, 185, 191, 206
Tweeddale, Earl 66, 115, 140, 141

United Provinces 1, 2, 3, 6, 7, 17
 HWB's influence 117–21
 invasions 47
 opposition to William III 71–9
 threat from England 37

Vaderlandsche Historie 38
Valckenier, Gilles 11

Vanbrugh, John 91
Vaudemont, Prince 151, 164, 198, 232
Vernon, James 104, 185, 217, 218, 225, 231, 234, 235, 237, 238, 242, 243, 245
Vienna 223
  Turks
    siege (1683) 28
    withdrawal 39
Villeroi, Duke 164
Villiers, Anne (HWB's wife) 23, 26, 95, 177
  death 9, 57, 96
  health 55
  portrait **illus.2**
Villiers, Edward *see* Jersey, Earl
Villiers, Edward, Sir 95
Villiers, Elizabeth (Lady Orkney) 23, 87–8, 188, 189, 205, 232, 238, 239
Villiers, George *see* Buckingham, Duke

Waayen, Johannes van der 35
Wagenaar, J. 38, 53
Waldeck, Prince of 13, 14, 18, 19, 48–9, 52, 72, 73, 76, 78, 118, 149, 150, 155, 263
War of Devolution 11
Waveren, Cornelis Bors van 72, 76
Wassenaar-Duyvenvoorde, Arend van 31, 33, 75, 96, 250, 255
Wassenaar-Obdam Jacob van, Admrl 75, 255
Waterlinie defences 12
Weede van Dijkveld, Everard van 2, 19, 26, 31, 33, 34, 41, 45, 51, 60, 62, 66, 67, 74, 86, 105, 118, 121, 197, 262
West Indies 45, 214, 216, 223, 251
Wharton, Thomas 138, 178, 186, 237, 238
White, Ignatius *see* Albeville, Marquis
White Mountain, Battle (1620) 20
Whitehall Palace 12, 69, 89, 94, 98, 101, 108, 109, 125, 158, 167, 168, 169, 257
Wildt, Job de 51, 52, 100, 101, 151
William II 8, 10, 20, 21
William III ('William of Orange') 2
  accepts English crown 68
  Amsterdam, relations with 28, 29, 34–5, 71–2, 73, 74, 75–6, 77–9, 223
  assassination plot 104, 110, 168–9, 170, 189
  biographies 3
  Declaration of Reasons 53, 61, 66, 171
  England
    concerns about 44
    court life 98
    invasion 56–60
    political circle 99
  favourites, reputation 22
  HWB, relationship 106–7
  Jacobite opposition to 68–9, 168, 170
  marriage to Mary 25–6
  network 19–20, 27
  painting of (with HWB) **illus.1**
  Parliamentary opposition 161–2
  Scotland, policy 138–9
  United Provinces, opposition 71–9
William IV 96, 257
William the Silent 20
Williamite Settlement (1689–91) 63–84, 86, 155, 157, 168, 170, 179, 190, 192, 195, 264, 266
Windischgrätz, Count 198
Windsor Castle 91
Witsen, Nicolaas 51, 65, 66, 67, 72, 78, 103, 118, 119, 131, 132, 184
Witt, Johann de 10, 11
  death 12, 141
Wittelsbach, Maximilian Henry, Archbishop of Cologne 37
  death 46
Woodstock, Henry (HWB's son) 89, 90, 96, 98, 124, 172, 195, 204, 208, 217, 257–8
  dukedom 99, 258
  Grand Tour 248, 254
Wotton, Lord 16
Wren, Christopher 91, 94
Wyche, Cyril 143

xenophobia, anti-Dutch 105, 162, 163, 183, 195, 206, 258, 262
  pamphlet literature 131–4

Yester, Lord 66, 112

Zuylen van Nijvelt, Jacob van 22, 118, 119, 120, 121, 264